# INC 2000
University of Plymouth, UK
3-6 July 2000

## Proceedings of the
## 2<sup>nd</sup> International Network Conference

Editor Dr Steven M Furnell

Department of Communication & Electronic Engineering,
University of Plymouth

**ISBN 1-84102-066-4**

# Preface

INC 2000 is the second in this series of international conferences. The first conference was held in Plymouth in 1998 and attracted an international audience and papers on a wide range of topics.

An important aim of this conference is to provide an opportunity for those involved in the design, development and use of network systems and applications to meet, share and exchange ideas. The conference brings together leading figures from both academia and industry to present and discuss the latest advances in networking technologies, from both research and commercial perspectives.

The conference proceedings contains 43 papers from 16 countries, organised into six thematic chapters. Each paper in the proceedings was accepted after a careful review by members of the International Programme Committee. The papers were subsequently revised and developed where appropriate, taking into account the comments of the reviewers.

The papers cover many aspects of network technologies and their applications, including Internet and World Wide Web technologies, network management, multimedia integration, distributed technologies, information systems security, and the social and cultural impacts of network technology.

We commend the authors for their hard work and for sharing their results, and the reviewers from the International Programme Committee for producing an excellent programme.

We are most grateful to Cliff Evans (Cisco Systems), John Lindsay (British Computer Society) and Gerry Mogg (Department of Trade and Industry) for accepting our invitation to share their expertise in keynote lectures. We are also indebted to Professor John Bull, the Vice Chancellor of the University of Plymouth, for his support for network research and his contribution to INC 2000.

We would like to extend our thanks to the Institution of Electrical Engineers, the British Computer Society, Internet Research, Orange Personal Communications Services and Netscient for their support as co-sponsors of the conference.

**Dr Steven Furnell**
**Conference Chairman, INC 2000**

**Plymouth, July 2000**

# INC 2000 Committee

## International Programme Committee

| | | |
|---|---|---|
| John Allen | Netscient Limited | UK |
| Udo Bleimann | University of Applied Sciences, Darmstadt | Germany |
| John Davey | HEIMDALL Limited | UK |
| David Finkel | Worcester Polytechnic Institute | USA |
| Steven Furnell (*chair*) | University of Plymouth | UK |
| Dimitris Gritzalis | Athens University of Economics and Business | Greece |
| Stephen Hope | Orange Personal Communication Services Limited | UK |
| Emmanuel Ifeachor | University of Plymouth | UK |
| Sokratis Katsikas | University of the Aegean | Greece |
| Dominique Le Foll | Wavetek Wandel Goltermann | UK |
| Benn Lines | University of Plymouth | UK |
| Joseph Morrissey | Morningstar | USA |
| Sead Muftic | SETECS AG | Sweden |
| Karl Posch | Graz University of Technology | Austria |
| Kimmo Raatikainen | University of Helsinki | Finland |
| Gavin Ray | Cisco Systems | UK |
| Paul Reynolds | Orange Personal Communication Services Limited | UK |
| Horst Röder | University of Applied Sciences, Darmstadt | Germany |
| Peter Sanders | University of Plymouth | UK |
| David Schwartz | Bar-Ilan University | Israel |
| Jeanne Stynes | Cork Institute of Technology | Ireland |
| Matthew Warren | Deakin University | Australia |
| Lars Wolf | University of Karlsruhe | Germany |

## Organising Committee

| | | |
|---|---|---|
| Paul Dowland | University of Plymouth | UK |
| Steven Furnell | University of Plymouth | UK |
| Bogdan Ghita | University of Plymouth | UK |
| Holger Hofmann | ABB Corporate Research Center | Germany |
| Denise Horne | University of Plymouth | UK |
| Benn Lines | University of Plymouth | UK |
| Andrew Phippen | University of Plymouth | UK |
| Phil Rodwell | University of Plymouth | UK |
| Harjit Singh | University of Plymouth | UK |
| Matthew Warren | Deakin University | Australia |

# Keynote Speakers and Session Chairs

## Introductory Addresses

*Dr Steven Furnell, University of Plymouth (Plymouth, UK)*
   Introduction and welcome to INC 2000

*Professor John Bull, University of Plymouth (Plymouth, UK)*
   Welcome to the University of Plymouth

## Main Keynote Lectures

*Cliff Evans, Cisco Systems*
   New World Internet Services

*John Lindsay, Internet Technical Committee, British Computer Society*
   The Internet: Ethical and social issues

*Gerry Mogg, Department of Trade and Industry*
   A DTI view of the Information Society

## Session Chairs

*Professor Udo Bleimann*, University of Applied Sciences (Darmstadt, Germany)

*Professor David Finkel*, Worcester Polytechnic Institute Worcester, USA)

*Dr Steven Furnell*, University of Plymouth (Plymouth, UK)

*Dr Holger D. Hofmann*, ABB Corporate Research Center (Heidelberg, Germany)

*Professor Emmanuel Ifeachor*, University of Plymouth (Plymouth, UK)

*Dominique Le Foll*, Wavetek Wandel Goltermann (Plymouth, UK)

*Dr Benn Lines*, University of Plymouth (Plymouth, UK)

*Professor Paul Reynolds*, Orange Personal Communications Services (Bristol, UK)

*Professor Peter Sanders*, University of Plymouth (Plymouth, UK)

*Dr Matthew Warren*, Deakin University (Geelong, Australia)

# Contents

# CHAPTER 5  Security and Privacy

# CHAPTER 6  Social and Cultural issues

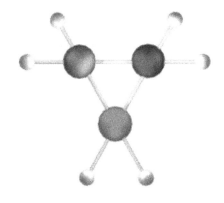

# Chapter 1

## Internet and WWW
## technologies and applications

# Performance Analysis of Dynamic Web Page Generation Technologies

Bhupesh Kothari and Mark Claypool

Department of Computer Science
Worcester Polytechnic Institute, Worcester, MA 01609, USA
{bhupesh|claypool}@cs.wpi.edu

## Abstract

The World-Wide Web has experienced phenomenal growth over the past few years, placing heavy load on Web servers. Today's Web servers also process an increasing number of requests for dynamic pages, making server load even more critical. The performance of Web servers delivering static pages is well-studied and well-understood. However, there has been little analytic or empirical study of the performance of Web servers delivering dynamic pages. This paper focuses on experimentally measuring and analyzing the performance of the three dynamic Web page generation technologies: CGI, FastCGI and Servlets. In this paper, we present experimental results for Web server performance under CGI, Fast CGI and Servlets. Then, we develop a multivariate linear regression model and predict Web server performance under some typical dynamic requests. We find that CGI and FastCGI perform effectively the same under most low-level benchmarks, while Servlets perform noticeably worse. Our regression model shows the same deficiency in Servlets' performance under typical dynamic Web page requests.

**Keywords**
World Wide Web, Web server, dynamic Web pages, benchmark, performance evaluation

## 1  Introduction

Dynamic Web pages are an important tool in the exchange of information in today's business community. Electronic commerce servers rely heavily on dynamic applications to access and present content to users distributed across the Internet. The need for dynamic Web pages is fueled by the requirements for interactive business transactions as well as Web sites that are personalized on an individual basis. The need for Web servers to create dynamic Web pages has resulted in the emergence of new dynamic page generation technologies. As a consequence of the increasing wide spread use dynamic Web page generation with the ever increasing growth of Web, Web servers are becoming more stressed then ever [8]. Performance of Web servers has become a critical issue.

The important movement away from static Web content to dynamic content is pushing the limits of the Common Gateway Interface (CGI), the de facto standard for dynamic Web page creation. CGI has benefits like ease of understanding, language independence and server architecture independence but with some significant drawbacks, including creation of a new process for each request. Two promising approaches to move beyond CGI are:

- *FastCGI:* FastCGI removes the inherent CGI performance problem by making the CGI processes persistent; after finishing a request, the FastCGI processes waits for a new request instead of exiting [19].
- *Servlets:* Servlets are Java objects that are invoked by the Web server and run in a resident Java Virtual Machine as threads [22]. They are loaded only once instead of being spawned at every request.

Web servers can easily be configured to deliver static pages to high numbers of concurrent users without substantial performance degradation [5] . Moreover, performance analysis of Web servers for static requests has been well studied [4] [23] [3] and modeled [23] [2]. However, to the best of our knowledge, Web server performance for dynamic documents has neither been experimentally measured nor thoroughly analyzed. Moreover, benchmark tools for measuring dynamic page generation technologies exist only for CGI.

This paper presents the performance of three dynamic Web page generation technologies: Servlets, CGI and FastCGI. We develop Web server benchmarks for measuring Servlets, FastCGI and CGI performance and present experimentally based results of the performance of each technology. Lastly, we develop a multivariate linear regression model based on our experimental results that predicts the performance of Web servers for different workloads. We show that, contrary to popular belief, performance of CGI is comparable or better when compared to other dynamic page generation technologies. Our analysis will help in comparing bottlenecks in the performance of dynamic page generation technologies to other bottlenecks in Web server performance.

The contributions of this work are:

- Experimentally based measurements of the fundamental parameters of three dynamic Web page generation technologies: CGI, FastCGI and Servlets.
- A flexible multivariate linear regression model for predicting dynamic Web page generation performance under varying request sizes.
- Performance predictions for typical requests as request size increases.
- A methodology for conducting future Web server performance measurements.

The remainder of this paper is organized as follows: Section 2 details our experiment design to measure the parameters of dynamic Web page requests and presents performance results obtained from running our experiments; Section 3 introduces our regression model for predicting dynamic Web page generation performance; and Section 4 summarizes our conclusions and lists possible future work.

## 2 Experiments

### 2.1 Design

In this section, we describe experiments designed to measure the parameters of dynamic Web page requests and present performance results obtained from running our experiments. In order to compare the performance of CGI, FastCGI and Servlets, we designed experiments to carefully measure the fundamental parameters of dynamic Web page generation technologies:

- *Input Size:* Amount of data the client sends to the server.
- *Output Size:* Amount of data that the server generates and sends back to the client.
- *Disk Write:* Amount of data the server writes to the disk on receiving a request from a client.
- *Disk Read:* Amount of data the server reads from the disk.
- *Computation:* The CPU load required by the server to service the client's request.

For the experiments, we measured the individual effects of each of these parameters on the performance of CGI, Servlets and FastCGI. The results presented in this paper represent the average of 10 experiment runs, where each run executes requests repeatedly for approximately 180 seconds.

We developed benchmarks to measure the above parameters and carried out a series of experiments to measure CGI, Servlets and FastCGI performance. The experiments consisted of running benchmarks on the client machine with specified request parameters and workload characteristics. Details on our benchmark are described in [13]. We performed the experiments on machines in single user mode on a dedicated network. In single user mode, the CPU runs a bare minimum of system processes and no other user processes.

Our server hardware platform was an Intel Pentium II 300 MHz system with 64 Megabytes of RAM. It had a standard 10 Megabits/second Ethernet card. The operating system was Linux version 2.0.35.

The server software was Apache, version 1.3.2, a public domain Web server. We ran the Apache Web server in stand-alone mode. There are pre-defined limits to the number of idle processes. The lower and upper bounds for our experiment were 5 and 10. The number of Keep Alive requests per connection was set to 0 (only one HTTP request was serviced per connection).

For adding Servlet support to Apache, we used JRun, version 2.2.1 [15]. For adding FastCGI support to Apache, we used the FastCGI Developer's Kit, version 2.0b2.

4

Our client hardware platform was an Intel Pentium 400 MHz system with 128 Megabytes of RAM. The operating system was Linux version 2.0.35. The workload was generated by our benchmark. The client was connected to the server by a dedicated 10 Mbps Ethernet network.

The CGI and FastCGI applications were written in C, compiled by gcc, version 2.7.2.1. All Servlets applications were written in Java and compiled with JDK version 1.1.6.

In the following sub-sections we present the results of each parameter on CGI, Servlet and FastCGI performance.

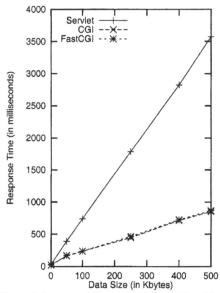

Figure 1: **Response Time vs Input Data Size. The horizontal axis is the size of the data sent from the client to the server. The vertical axis is the response time. The data points are the average time for a single request.**

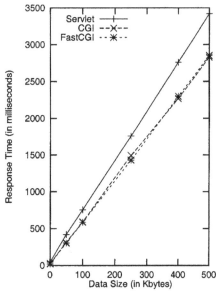

Figure 2: **Response Time vs Output Data Size. The horizontal axis is the size of the data sent back from the server to the client. The vertical axis is the response time. The data points are the average time for a single request**

## 2.2 Input Data Size

One of the main reasons for dynamic Web pages is to allow servers to process input data from a client. For example, a server application might be responsible for taking data filled in an HTML order entry form and applying business logic. We measured the affect of input data size on all the three technologies by having the client send POST requests to the server. Figure 1 depicts the performance of each of the server technologies obtained from the measurements for the input data size. The results show that CGI performs as well as FastCGI. For large data sizes, Servlets perform significantly worse than either CGI or FastCGI.

## 2.3 Output Data Size

No matter how much data the server application receives, it always has to send data back to the client. For example, typical search engines have server applications which dynamically generate Web pages and send these back to the client. We measured the affect of output data size by having the clients send GET requests to the Web server. The results in Figure 2 show that again FastCGI performance is the best, with CGI performing almost as good as FastCGI, even for small data sizes. The results clearly show that the cost of running Servlets is much more than the total cost of loading CGI programs into the memory of the server for each request and the cost to run the CGI programs.

5

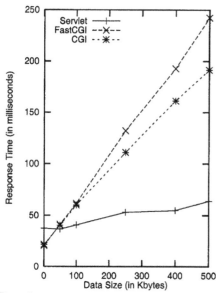

Figure 3: **Response Time vs Disk Read.** The horizontal axis is the size of the data read by the server. The vertical axis is the response time. The data points are the average time for a single request.

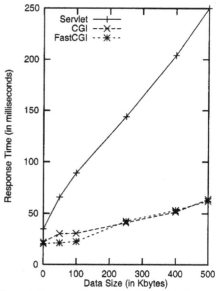

Figure 4: **Response Time vs Disk Write.** The horizontal axis is the size of the data written on disk by the server. The vertical axis is the response time. The data points are the average time for a single request.

## 2.4 Disk Read

The amount of data to be read from the disk depends on the role of the server application. For example, a server application might be responsible for retrieving chapters or sections of a book from the disk in response to a request on a typical virtual bookstore. Figure 3 shows the line equations for the performance of each of the server technologies obtained from the measurements for the data size read from the disk. Surprisingly, the results show that Servlets are able to do disk reads much more efficiently than CGI and FastCGI applications. For an increase of data size of 500 Kbytes, the increase in the response for Servlets is just around 40 milliseconds whereas for CGI, it is around 170 milliseconds. FastCGI in this test performs the worst out of the three.

## 2.5 Disk Write

It is quite common in business applications to record data to the disk. For example, a server application might be responsible for writing the data from a transaction entry form to the disk. In measuring the affect of disk-write, the clients sent GET requests to the Web server, with the amount of data to be written specified in the query parameters. Unlike the disk read results in subsection 2.4, Servlets take much longer time to do disk write than CGI and FastCGI application, as shown in Figure 4. Performance of FastCGI is better than CGI up to 250 Kbytes of data size and after that CGI does equally well as FastCGI.

## 2.6 Computation

The cost of computation is important to applications that do CPU intensive work. For example, on-line image processing servers might be required to run server applications to perform various graphic algorithms or different filtering techniques, which are CPU intensive. To measuring the affect of this parameter, the clients sent GET requests to the Web server, with the count for the computation specified in the query parameters. The server application incremented an int variable in a tight loop, counting up until the parameter specified. As soon as it completed the loop, the Web server is notified of the request completion and the Web server in turn, sends an acknowledgement back to the client. The Figure 5 shows the results obtained from the computation measurements. Servlets are much

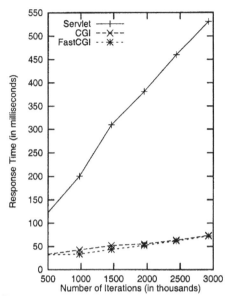

Figure 5: **Response Time vs Computation Time. The horizontal axis is the computation work by the server. The vertical axis is the response time. The data points are the average time for a single request.**

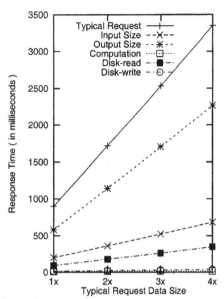

Figure 6: **Response Time vs Request Size. Weights, in terms of response time, as measured by our multivariate linear regression model for individual parameters for a typical large CGI request.**

slower than CGI and Fast CGI.

# 3  Performance Model

This section describes how we use the results obtained and analyzed in the previous section in developing a multivariate linear regression model with categorical predictors for dynamic Web page generation technologies. Our model is extremely flexible for predicting the performance of the Web server for different applications. For example, an electronic commerce Web server would have a traffic pattern different than from a Search Engine site. By studying the pattern of the traffic and formalizing the data sizes of each of the variables used in our model, our model can predict the performance. Moreover, by varying the size of the individual parameters we are able to predict the bottlenecks in dynamic Web page generation performance.

| Parameter | Size |
|---|---|
| Input Size | 500 bytes |
| Output Size | 2 Kbytes |
| Disk Read | 4 Kbytes |
| Disk Write | 1 Kbytes |
| Compute | 1000 increments |

Table 1: **A typical small request**

| Parameter | Size |
|---|---|
| Input Size | 50 Kbytes |
| Output Size | 50 Kbytes |
| Disk Read | 100 Kbytes |
| Disk Write | 100 Kbytes |
| Compute | 1 million increments |

Table 2: **A typical large request**

Our analysis consisted of modeling request sizes of two types: typical large requests and typical small requests, based on the study done in [1]. Table 1 shows a typical small request.

Server applications like database transaction modules or image processing filters performs massive processing at the server and return more data than the smaller dynamic requests. Table 2 shows a typical large request.

7

A multivariate regression model [9] allows one to predict a response variable y as a function of $k$ predictor variables $x_1, x_2, ..., x_k$ using a linear model of the following form: $y = b_0 + b_1x_1 + b_2x_2 + ... + b_kx_k + e$

Here $b_0, b_1x_1, b_2x_2, ..., b_kx_k$ are $k + 1$ fixed parameters and e is the error term. In vector notation, the model is represented as: $y = Xb + e$. Where: $y$ is a column of $n$ observed values of y; $X$ is an $n$ row by $k + 1$ column matrix whose $(i, j + 1)^{th}$ element $X_{i,j+1} = 1$ if $j = 0$ else $x_{ij}$; $b$ is a column vector with $k + 1$ elements; and $e$ is a column vector with $n$ error terms.

Our model is based on both quantitative and categorical predictors [9]. Our model has 8 predictor variables: input, output, disk read, disk write, computation time, operating system, Web server and dynamic page generation technology (ie- CGI, FastCGI and Servlets). The predictor variables: input, output, disk read, disk write and computation time are quantitative predictors, presented in Section 2.2 to 2.6. The three predictor variables: operating system, Web server and dynamic page generation technology are categorical variables. The categorical variable for dynamic page generation technology takes three values, CGI, Servlets and FastCGI. The categorical variable for operating system takes two values, Linux or Windows NT[1]. The categorical variable for Web server also takes two values, Apache or Netscape Enterprise.

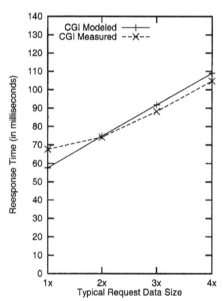

Figure 7: **Response Time vs Request Size.** Performance, as predicted by our multivariate linear regression model model for a small CGI request and as measured by our benchmark.

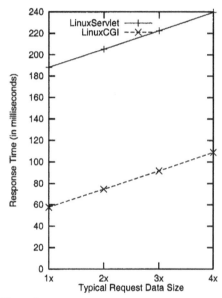

Figure 8: **Response Time vs Request Size.** Performance, as predicted by our multivariate linear regression model, for dynamic page generation technologies for a typical request. The horizontal axis is the data size for a typical request which the client sends to the server.

Based on the multivariate linear regression analysis in [9], we computed the multivariate linear regression coefficients for our model. The *coefficient of determination* for our model was 0.93. Thus the regression explains 93% of the variance of response time in our model.

In order to validate our performance model, we ran a typical small request. In doing so, we developed a CGI application which handles and service the typical requests the benchmark generates. The benchmark sends a POST request to this CGI application. The data sizes ranged from 1x to 4x, where 1x corresponds to the small request as described earlier in this section.

---

[1]The experiments for the impact of operating system and Web server on the performance of dynamic page generation technology are described in [13].

8

Figure 6 shows the individual weights of each of the parameters which amounts to the total weight of a typical large CGI request. A 1x on the x-axis for individual components corresponds to their data size in a typical large request size as described earlier. A 2x on the x-axis for individual components corresponds to twice the data sizes in the typical request size and so on. The result clearly shows that output parameter has a significant cost in terms of the response time for a CGI request.

Figure 7 shows the result of the evaluation of our model for typical request for CGI. The result shows that our model predicts the performance of CGI within 10% of measured values. We assume that differences of 10% in predictions made by our model are significant.

Figure 8 shows the total response time obtained on running our model for CGI and Servlets. CGI performs significantly better than Servlets. This clearly suggests that threads solely are not sufficient to achieve high performance. We attribute these results to the relatively small amount of time required for process creation in a CGI request. Our experiments in [12] show that the process creation time is of the order of 10 milliseconds whereas the response times here are of the order of 100 and 1000 milliseconds.

The results also show that Servlets are slower, having the drawback of being interpreted by a Java Virtual Machine. In the JDK interpreter, calling a synchronized method is typically 10 times slower than calling an unsynchronized method [16] [11]. With JIT compilers, this performance gap can decrease to as little as 5 times slower but the time to create an object does not improve at all. The time to create an object, 15 milliseconds, is high if the Java code creates many objects. Even with using Just In Time compilers and other optimization techniques, Java code is still anywhere from 10 to 30 times slower than compiled C or C++ code.

# 4   Conclusions

Dynamic Web page generation is becoming an increasingly critical component of Web server performance. Our goal was to empirically compare the performance of three dynamic Web page generation technologies: CGI, FastCGI and Servlets. We developed a benchmark tool for measuring the affect of the fundamental parameters of Web page generation technologies on the performance of the Web server. We also developed a model for predicting the performance of dynamic requests for a particular server technology.

Based on our analysis, CGI and FastCGI perform significantly better than Servlets. This results holds for all parameters but disk reads. Threads alone will not improve the performance of Servlets, since Servlets are inherently slower because of the dependency on a Java Virtual Machine. Even with the speed optimization techniques available, Servlets are still slower than compiled CGI (written in C) applications.

Future work includes studying other factors which may impact the performance of the dynamic Web page generation technologies. The concurrency strategy (single threaded, thread per request, thread pool, request pool, etc.) of the Web server [10], may influence the dispatch of the client request code, as well.

# References

[1] Almeida, V.A.F, Almeida, J.M, Analyzing the impact of dynamic pages on the performance of Web servers, *Computer Measurement Group Conference, 1998.*

[2] Almeida, V.A.F, Almeida, J.M, Murta, C.D., Oliveira, A.A, and Mendes, M.A.S., Performance Analysis and Modeling of a WWW Internet Server, *Fourth Telecommunication Conference, March 1996.*

[3] Aoki, P., Woodruf, A., Brewer, E., and Gautheir, L., An Investigation of Documents from WWW, *Proceedings of the Fifth International Conference on WWW, May 1996.*

[4] Arlitt, M. and Williamson, C., Web Server Workload Characterization, *Proceedings of the 1996 SIGMETRICS Conference on Measurement and Modeling of Computer Systems, 1996.*

[5] Arlitt, M. and Williamson, C., Internet Web Servers: Workload Characterization and Performance Implications, *IEEE/ACM Transactions on Networking, October 1997.*

[6] Banga, G., and Druschel, P., Measuring the Capacity of a Web Server, *USENIX Symposium on Internet Technologies and Systems ,USITS, 1997.*

[7] Douglas C. Schmidt, and James C. Hu, Developing Flexible and High-performance Web Servers with Frameworks and Patterns, *ACM Computing Surveys, May 1998.*

[8] Graphic, Visualization, & Usability Center's (GVU) 9th WWW User Survey, *http://www.gvu.gatech.edu/user_surveys/survey-1998-04/*

[9] Jain, R. (1991), *The Art of Computer Systems Performance Analysis*, John Wiley & Sons, Inc.

[10] James C. Hu, Sumedh M., and Douglas C. Schmidt, Techniques for Developing and Measuring High-Performance Web Servers over ATM Networks, *INFOCOM, 1998.*

[11] Java Microbenchmarks, *A report,* http://www.cs.cmu.edu/~jch/java/benchmarks.html

[12] Kothari, B., Claypool, M., PThreads Performance, *Worcester Polytechnic Technical Report, WPI-CS-TR-99-11, 1999.*

[13] Kothari, B., Claypool, M., Performance Analysis of Dynamic Web Page Generation Technologies.*Thesis Report, Worcester Polytechnic Institute, May 1998.*

[14] Krishnamurthy, D., Rolia, J., Predicting the QoS of an Electronic Commerce Server:Those Mean Percentiles, *Performance Evaluation Review, December 1998.*

[15] Live Software, Inc., JRun Servlet Engine, URL:http://www.livesoftware.com/products/jrun/jrun-manual/index.htm

[16] Make Java fast: Optimize, *An article, April 1997,* http://www.javaworld.com/javaworld/jw-04-1997/jw-04-optimize.html

[17] Manley, S., Seltzer, M., Courage, M., A Self-Scaling and Self-Configuring Benchmark for Web Servers, *Proceedings of the ACM SIGMETRICS '98 Conference, June 1998.*

[18] Mindcraft, Inc, WebStone 2.5, URL:http://www.mindcraft.com/benchmarks/webstone/

[19] Open Market, Inc., Fast CGI: A High-Performance Web Server Interface, *A Technical White Paper, April 1996.*

[20] Somin, Y., Agarwal, S. and Forsyth, M., Measurement and Analysis of Process and Workload CPU times in UNIX environments, *Proceedings of the CMG, 1996.*

[21] Standard Performance Evaluation Corporation, *A Technical White Paper, 1996,* SPECweb96, URL:http://www.specbench.org/osg/web96/webpaper.html

[22] Sun Microsystem, The JAVA Servlet API, *A Technical White Paper, 1998,* URL:http://www.javasoft.com/marketing/coll-ateral/servlets.html

[23] Wallace, R. and McCoy, T., Performance Monitoring and Capacity Planning for Web Servers, *Proceedings of CMG, 1996.*

# Defining the Mean Web Page Size and Improving the Latency in Web Page Transfer

P. Destounis, J. Garofalakis, P. Kappos, J. Tzimas

Department of Computer Engineering and Informatics, University of Patras, 26500 Patras, Greece
&
Computer Technology Institute, P.O. Box 1122, 26110 Patras, Greece
e-mail: {destoun, garofala, kappos, tzimas}@cti.gr

## Abstract

Internet bandwidth limitations increase the time needed to transfer data through the Internet. This paper presents a case study that calculates the reduction of the time needed for a web page to be fully downloaded. We present a way to calculate the reduction of data transfer, bandwidth resources and response time when the HTTP/1.1's compressing feature is enabled (either in plain hypertext files or the text output of CGI programs or dynamically generated pages). Also measurements are taken from five popular web sites to validate our statement for reduction in transfer time as well as the definition of the mean size of a web page that commercial web sites have.

## Keywords

Web Traffic, HTML Page Size, Web Performance, Download Time, HTTP

## 1. Introduction

The traffic provoked by the World Wide Web is the primary factor of the Internet traffic overload today. Although this traffic is due to the transmission of many types of information, such as text, sound and video, in the majority of cases the information is a hypertext document, a GIF or a JPEG image. In most cases, the image files cannot be further compressed without affecting the quality of the image. On the other hand, hypertext files can be compressed at a satisfying ratio due to the fact that they are text files.

More specifically, we present a way to calculate the reduction of data transfer, bandwidth resources and response time when the HTTP/1.1's compressing feature is enabled (either in plain hypertext files or the text output of CGI programs or dynamically generated pages). We made two tests. The first test was by using a web server that supported HTTP 1.1. Since not all web server or browser software implements all HTTP/1.1 features, the second test deployed we additionally developed a plug-in for the Netscape Communicator to request compressed hypertext documents from a web server (supporting any version of the hypertext protocol) and decompress them in the client's side after downloading.

The paper is structured as follows: Section 2 describes the characteristics of the hypertext transfer protocol and a comparison between the HTTP/1.1 and its predecessor is cited. Section 3 provides information on the development of the plug-in and the compression algorithm used. The results of our study deduced from measurements of the five popular sites are presented in section 4 and 5.

### 1.1 The Web and the HTTP

In order to understand the solution proposed in this paper, it is instructive to firstly explain several matters regarding the way that the HTTP (HyperText Transport Protocol) works, since the whole World Wide Web is based on the HTTP protocol. The HTTP is a client-server transaction oriented protocol. The user agent (web client) asks for a particular resource of a web server by contacting the server at a designated port number (by default, 80). Then it sends a document request by specifying an HTTP command called a method, followed by a document address, and an HTTP version number. For example:

**GET /index.html HTTP/1.0**

The requested document (in our example "index.html") is specified by the user directly or by clicking on a hyperlink inside a hypertext page. Next, the client sends optional header information to inform the server of its configuration and the document formats it will accept. Upon receiving the request, the server responds to the client's demand by sending the requested document, accompanied by a status line and a header, which usually contains information to assist the client in processing the file. The headers consist of cookies, expiration stamps or no cache indicators. After the header data, the actual Hypertext data (the requested documented or CGI response) are being sent to the client.

## 1.2 HTTP/1.1 versus HTTP/1.0

HTTP/1.1 is an upward compatible protocol to HTTP/1.0. Both HTTP/1.0 and HTTP/1.1 use the TCP protocol for data transport. However, the two versions of HTTP use TCP differently. HTTP/1.0 opens and closes a new TCP connection for each operation. Since most Web objects are small, this practice means a high fraction of packets are simply TCP control packets used to open and close a connection. Furthermore, when a TCP connection is first opened, TCP employs an algorithm known as slow start. Slow start uses the first several data packets to probe the network to determine the optimal transmission rate. Again, because Web objects are small, most objects are transferred before their TCP connection completes the slow start algorithm. In other words, most HTTP/1.0 operations use TCP at its least efficient. The results have been major problems due to resulting congestion and unnecessary overhead HTTP/1.1 leaves the TCP connection open between consecutive operations. This technique is called "persistent connections," which both avoid the costs of multiple opens and closes and reduce the impact of slow start. Persistent connections are more efficient than the current practice of running multiple short TCP connections in parallel.

By leaving the TCP connection open between requests, many packets can be avoided, while avoiding multiple RTTs due to TCP slow start. The first few packet exchanges of a new TCP connection are either too fast, or too slow for that path. If these exchanges are too fast for the route (common in today's Internet), they contribute to Internet congestion.

Conversely, since most connections are in slow start at any given time in HTTP/1.0 not using persistent connections, keeping a dialup PPP link busy has required running multiple TCP connections simultaneously (typical implementations have used 4 TCP connections). This can exacerbate the congestion problem further.

The "Keep-Alive" extension to HTTP/1.0 is a form of persistent connections. HTTP/1.1's design differs in minor details from Keep-Alive to overcome a problem discovered when Keep-Alive is used with more than one proxy between a client and a server.

Persistent connections allow multiple requests to be sent without waiting for a response; multiple requests and responses can be contained in a single TCP segment. This can be used to avoid many round trip delays, improving performance, and reducing the number of packets further. This technique is called "pipelining" in HTTP. HTTP/1.1 also enables transport compression of data types so those clients can retrieve HTML (or other) uncompressed documents using data compression; HTTP/1.0 does not have sufficient facilities for transport compression. Further work is continuing in this area.

The major HTTP/1.1 design goals therefore include:

> ➢ Lower HTTP's load on the Internet for the same amount of "real work", while solving the congestion caused by HTTP
> ➢ HTTP/1.0's caching is primitive and error prone; HTTP/1.1 enable applications to work reliably with caching
> ➢ End user performance must improve, or it is unlikely that HTTP/1.1 will be deployed

HTTP/1.1 provides significant improvements to HTTP/1.0 to allow applications to work reliably in the face of caching, and to allow applications to mark more content cacheable. Today, caching is often deliberately defeated in order to achieve reliability. This paper does not explore these effects. HTTP/1.1 does not attempt to solve some commonly seen problems, such as transient network overloads at popular web sites with topical news, but should at least help these problems.

### 1.3 HTTP Deficiencies

One can argue that bandwidth and latency of the Internet will improve dramatically over the next couple of years [4]. However, wireless PDA's, portable machines and satellite links will continue to impose severe practical limits on the available bandwidth, latency and on-line connectivity on parts of the Internet. We consider it likely that low bandwidths in the 9600-19200 bps range and latency in the >1/2 second range will be with us for a long time. It is important to note that latency and bandwidth are independent variables; for example satellite IP systems exist today which provide good bandwidth to remote locations, but poor latency. Most users of the Web are today at home using a dial-up connection with a 28.8 kbps. On the optimistic side, this provides a minimum of 160 ms from the closest part of the Internet. Cellular modems and many wireless systems have even higher latency and lower bandwidth. HTTP is a simple request/response protocol, not designed for the environment where it is now most heavily used. As described earlier persistent connections and pipelining in HTTP/1.1 will solve some, but not all of these problems. The reason is that HTTP/1.1 is designed to limit TCP overhead produced by HTTP/1.0 but not protocol overhead due to HTTP itself. As an example, HTTP/1.1 defines 5 different mechanisms for finding the length of a message, of which all but closing the TCP connection require significant parsing to determine which one is used.

Machine-readable messages are different from human readable messages even though they may both be encoded using ASCII strings. The choice of MIME based header encoding in HTTP has led to the general misconception that HTTP is intended as a human readable protocol. The result has been verbose messages and extremely complicated parsers. As an example, a typical HTTP request is about 250 bytes long. Due to the nature of typical Web usage, subsequent requests are often closely related leading to about 90% in redundancy between requests. This means slowing down information exchange over low bandwidth connections. If HTTP does not improve its performance dramatically on low bandwidth connections, it is likely that other more compact and lightweight protocols will be deployed with the risk of incompatibility between low bandwidth sensitive devices.

## 2. Defining Common Web Page Size

At the beginning of our measurements we grabbed the web contents of five popular web sites so as to define which is the distribution in the sizes of a common web page. When referring to a web page we have used either static or dynamically generated hypertext pages. We grabbed the pages of CNN.COM, DISNEY.COM, IBM.COM, NETSCAPE.COM, MICROSOFT.COM (Figure 3) from their main web sites. Figure 2 shows the analytic measurements for each site while Figure 1 summarises the results and shows the mean and median common web page size.

| Name of the Web Site | Mean HTML File Size (in Bytes) | Median HTML File Size(in Bytes) |
|---|---|---|
| CNN | 11.754 | 11.872 |
| DISNEY | 8.916 | 7.005 |
| IBM | 15.667 | 6.968 |
| NETSCAPE | 13.712 | 10.605 |
| MICROSOFT | 17.650 | 13.200 |
| TOTAL | 13.540 | 9.930 |

Figure 1: Measuring the Mean Web Page Size

## 3. Architecture and Implementation of the Method

Transferring web pages require a web server and at least a web client (web browser). Either they are static or dynamically generated pages, we can capture that data and interfere to the communication process of the server and its client(-s). Before the server sends the data to the client, we can compress them and then send them to the web browser. The web browser must be aware that the received data are compressed. Before parsing and displaying them, a plug-in decompresses the data and feeds the parser of the web browser with the plain Hypertext. Our intervention to the whole process of the browser to server communication and vice versa is the intervention of the plug-in application to help us determine the percentage gain in the delivery of hypertext as well as the benefits in terms of less bandwidth use.

### 3.1 Implementation

In the proposed solution, the client asks for a compressed version of the required file. It must be stressed out that a new file type has been defined for such compressed documents. We have given the name *.chf meaning compressed hypertext file.

The web browsers that are used today will prompt the user to save the file on the disk instead of displaying it, because they do not support the new file type, which is being identified by the MIME type application/x-chf-file. We have developed a plug-in for the Netscape Communicator. The plug-in enables Communicator to handle the new MIME type. Similarly, other also popular web clients, like MS Internet Explorer, can be equipped to recognise this new MIME type. **Plug-ins** [5], [6] are dynamic code modules, native to a specific platform on which Netscape Navigator runs. They extend Communicator's to include a wide range of interactive and multimedia capabilities, while blending seamlessly into the Communicator interface.

They can be designed and implemented using the plug-in API, provided by Netscape. The primary goal of this API is to allow existing platform dependent code to seamlessly integrate with and enhance Navigator's core functionality by providing support for new data types. The plug-in API is designed to provide the maximum degree of flexibility and be functionally equivalent across all platforms. In this case, when the browser encounters a file of type *.chf, it invokes the plug-in to decompresses (i.e. reproduce the original HTML code) and display the file.

Netscape Plug-ins communicate with Navigator via the Netscape Application Programming Interface (NS-API). Two types of functions make up the Plug-in API: plug-in methods and

Netscape methods. Plug-in methods are functions that you implement in your plug-in and are called by Netscape. Netscape methods are functions implemented by Netscape that your plug-in might call. For clarity, the names of all plug-in functions begin with "NPP_", while all Netscape functions begin with "NPN_". Creating a Navigator plug-in is a two-step process. First, you download and decompress the sample source code. Then, you make the necessary changes and write the required code in the files provided. Finally, you test your plug-in by creating an HTML document.

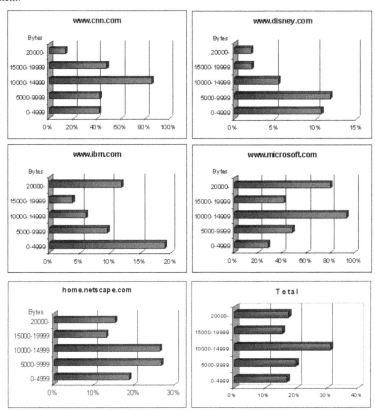

**Figure 2: Defining the Web Page Size**

In our plug-in, during the instance creation phase we initialise a stream with the server sending the requested compressed document. Streams are objects that represent URLs and the data they contain, or data sent by a plug-in without an associated URL. Although a single stream is associated with one specific instance of a plug-in, a plug-in can have more than one stream object per instance. Streams can be produced by Netscape Communicator and consumed by a plug-in instance, or produced by an instance and consumed by Communicator. Each stream has an associated MIME type identifying the format of the data in the stream. After the completion of the

15

download process, the stream's data are decompressed and a new stream is created to send the hypertext document (HTML file) to the Communicator.

## 3.2 Algorithms for compression/decompression

In this section, we present the algorithm used in our solution for the compression and decompression of the web pages. More specifically, our plug-in uses the zlib, a collection of procedures implementing a variation of the LZ77 algorithm.

## 3.3 Compression

The real question is, given a Huffman tree, how to decode fast. The most important realisation is that shorter codes are much more common than longer codes, so pay attention to decoding the short codes fast, and let the long codes take longer to decode. inflate() sets up a first level table that covers some number of bits of input less than the length of longest code. It gets that many bits from the stream, and looks it up in the table. The table will tell if the next code is that many bits or less and how many, and if it is, it will tell the value, else it will point to the next level table for which inflate() grabs more bits and tries to decode a longer code.

How many bits to make the first lookup is a trade-off between the time it takes to decode and the time it takes to build the table. If building the table took no time (and if you had infinite memory), then there would only be a first level table to cover all the way to the longest code. However, building the table ends up taking a lot longer for more bits since short codes are replicated many times in such a table. What inflate() does is simply to make the number of bits in the first table a variable, and set it for the maximum speed.

## 3.4 Decompression

The deflation algorithm used by zlib (also zip and gzip) is a variation of LZ77 [1]. It finds duplicated strings in the input stream. The second occurrence of a string is replaced by a pointer to the previous string, in the form of a pair (distance, length). Distances are limited to 32K bytes, and lengths are limited to 258 bytes. When a string does not occur anywhere in the previous 32K bytes, it is emitted as a sequence of literal bytes.

Literals or match lengths are compressed with one Huffman tree, and match distances are compressed with another tree. The trees are stored in a compact form at the start of each block. The blocks can have any size (except that the compressed data for one block must fit in available memory). A block is terminated when deflate () determines that it would be useful to start another block with fresh trees. Duplicated strings are found using a hash table. All input strings of length 3 are inserted in the hash table. A hash index is computed for the next 3 bytes. If the hash chain for this index is not empty, all strings in the chain are compared with the current input string, and the longest match is selected.

The hash chains are searched starting with the most recent strings, to favour small distances and thus take advantage of the Huffman encoding. The hash chains are singly linked. There are no deletions from the hash chains, the algorithm simply discards matches that are too old. To avoid a worst-case situation, very long hash chains are arbitrarily truncated at a certain length, determined by a runtime option (level parameter of deflateInit). So deflate() does not always find the longest possible match but generally finds a match which is long enough.

## 4. Reducing the Size of Web Data

As an example of our implementation, we present measurements produced by applying it on HTML files of five highly popular web sites that are listed in Fig. 3:

| Name of Company | URL |
|---|---|
| Cable News Network (CNN) | www.cnn.com |
| Disney Inc. | www.disney.com |
| IBM Corp. | www.ibm.com |
| Microsoft Corp. | www.microsoft.com |
| Netscape Communications Corp. | www.netscape.com |

**Figure 3: The Selected Web Sites for the Study**

## 4.1 Measurements in Web Page Sizes

During the measurements, we downloaded the whole web site of each of the five popular web sites (Figure 3) and the number of pages surveyed is shown in Figure 4. The mean compression gain by 75.2% shows that a web page size can be reduced to the one fourth by the proposed technique. Figure 5 shows the decrease in the time that a mean web page needs to be downloaded.

| Name Of the Web Site | Total number of HTML pages | Total size of html pages before compression (in Bytes) | Total size of html pages after Compression (in Bytes) | % compression of all HTML pages | % compression SUM(compress ion $_i$) |
|---|---|---|---|---|---|
| CNN | 3.047 | 35.697.972 | 10.710.039 | 70 | 67 |
| DISNEY | 423 | 3.771.650 | 1.050.447 | 72 | 66 |
| IBM | 659 | 10.324.668 | 1.771.300 | 83 | 71 |
| NETSCAPE | 1.325 | 18.169.655 | 4.592.147 | 75 | 69 |
| MICROSOFT | 3.827 | 67.549.106 | 16.004.609 | 76 | 72 |
| Mean Compression Gain: **75.2%** | | | | | |

**Figure 4: Compression Gain**

| Internet Connection Speed | Download time for a 30KB page without Compression | Download time For 30KB Page After compression |
|---|---|---|
| 33.600 | 7.14 sec | 1.77 sec |
| 57.600 | 4.17 sec | 1.03 sec |
| 128K | 1.88 sec | 0.47 sec |

**Figure 5: Gain in Download Time**

## 4.2 Charts

The charts of Figure 6 show the details in the compression range that has been achieved by the compression techniques stated above.

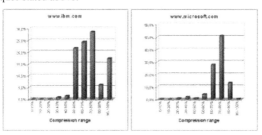

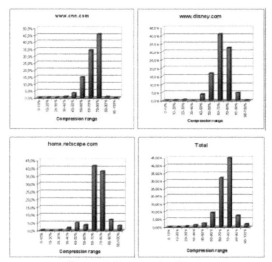

**Figure 6: Compression Range**

## 5. Conclusions

A large percentage of the Internet traffic comprises the downloading of hypertext pages (either static or dynamic). The transfer time of these pages can be reduced if these files are transferred in compressed form since hypertext pages are mere text files that can be compressed to a large extent. To calculate the gain in transfer time we have taken measurements of the five most popular web sites. The mean compression rate using LZ77 compression algorithm achieved in our case was 75,2% , meaning that a web page size can be reduced to the one fourth of its original size. The reduction of user's waiting time during for the downloading of the web pages, improves user's satisfaction during his Internet navigation.

## 6. References

[1]   Ziv J., Lempel A., "A Universal Algorithm for Sequential Data Compression," *IEEE Transactions on Information Theory*, Vol. 23, No. 3, pp. 337-343.

[2]   DEFLATE Compressed Data Format Specification', available at ftp://ds.internic.net/rfc/rfc1951.txt

[3]   Henrik Nielsen, Jim Gettys, Anselm Baird-Smith, Eric Prud'hommeaux, Håkon Wium Lie, Chris Lilley, Network Performance Effects of HTTP/1.1, CSS1, and PNG, http://www.w3.org/TR/NOTE-pipelining-970624

[4]   Henrik Nielsen, Mike Spreitzer, Bill Janssen, Jim Gettys, "HTTP-NG Overview Problem Statement, Requirements, and Solution Outline", W3C & Xerox PARC, http://www.w3.org/TR/draft-frystyk-httpng-overview-00.txt

[5]   Plug-in Software Development Kit:

http://home.netscape.com/comprod/development_partners/plugin_api/index.html

[6]   Plug-in Guide: http://developer.netscape.com/docs/manuals/communicator/plugin/index.htm

# Monitoring and Managing Users' Access to Internet

Huandong Sun, Dongsheng Zhao,Xueying Li,Minghu Wu

Network Information Center, 27 Taiping Road, Beijing 100850, P R China

## Abstract

This paper introduces a monitoring and managing system on a large campus network connected to Internet. Our goal is to provide Internet access and email service with MS Proxy2.0 and MS Exchange 5.5 respectively for the users on the network in a managable way. The system was developed in C/C++ Builder3 and MS Frontpage 98, and MS SQL6.5 was used to implement network databases, in which the information about users is stored. From the log files of MS Proxy2.0 and MS Exchange 5.5,the system implements accounting for web and email access and writes the data into SQL databases so as to complete network and users' management. This paper describes the designing consideration and implementing technologies of the system.

## Keywords

Internet access, automatic management, proxy access, email service, network accounting, dial-in service, access monitoring and controlling

## Introduction

AMMSNet is a large campus network we have built for years and provides Internet access for the users. In order to manage the network and its users, we had to develop an efficient management system which is able to account access bytes, log the websites and address to access Internet and safeguard the resource on interior LAN. On the network, we installed dual-firewall (or a two layers of firewalls[4]) on its exit routers, programmed a monitoring system to account bytes, control access authorization of the users and supervise the dial-in service. We focus on accounting bytes including access in browsers, email services and dial-in hours through PSTN(Public Services Telephone Network).We also developed the monitoring modules on Linux which can protect users' IP address from being stolen because some of our users access with IP address. A user has to pay the communication fee for those who occupy his IP address, which should be avoided. The management system includes mainly the following modules:

- Network information management modules based on MS Windows9x/NT clients[4].They consist of two modules, one of which runs on a client and is an information management system of network users in charge of inputting , modifying and outputting user information, the other on servers implements connection with SQL servers through MIDAS(Multi-tiered Distributed Application Service[2,3]) when the clients access the databases.
- Accounting and monitoring module based on LAN users. The module runs on MS WindowsNT4.0 server and is responsible for processing LAN users' accounting, access log and e-mail log.
- Accounting and monitoring module based on dial-in services. The module monitors dial-in users on MS Windows NT4.0 server and processes dial-in services such as accounting, access log and e-mail log.
- Web server modules based on MS Windows NT4.0 servers. One module lies in the LAN

server, and the other in the dial-in server. They support web browsing through ISAPI or ActiveX control components.

- Accounting and monitoring modules based on Linux which implement accounting bytes for a user to access with host IP and monitoring access to Internet so as to prevent illegal users.
- Browser module querying users based on web. This module administrates users' account name and queries access information through a browser.

The above modules cooperate with one another and work in client/server as following figure(figure 1).Thereby we make network management carry out automatization.

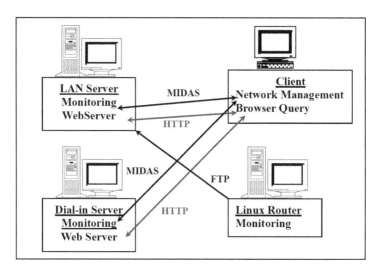

Figure 1 Connection among system modules

In the process of developing system, the key technologies we used are to program the modules of account dial-in time, account bytes of email service and safeguard the IP of users, which are mainly described in the following sections.

## Combining RADIUS[1] with C++ Builder application to implement authentication and account dial-in time

The dial-in services for users to access Internet through PSTN consist of three 3Com NetServer and a server on MS WindowsNT4.0. It is easy to implement dial-in service with these devices . To build valid dial-in services, we also had to implement account dial-in time when users access Internet, otherwise they could not hang up after they dial in, so they would hold dial-in wire for a longer time and other users can't dial in because dial-in wires only are limited.

In order to complete accounting time, we developed two program modules in C++ Builder 3, one of which is to account dial-in seconds for users to access our network, and the other is to control access authorization. We use Radius on MS Windows4.0 server to authenticate dial-in services, but we can't use it to account time directly, although Radius records the time for a user to dial in and disconnect. Radius writes session data of dial-in users into a log file or access database. Even though the data include users' account name, session id, IP address, start-time, end-time and persisting time to access network, it is difficult to use these data for accounting. When a user dials in the network once, Radius writes several records instead of one, so its data must be analyzed and processed so that they will be used to account time. In programming the module, we put the data of Radius authentication into an array, in which there is only a piece of information when a user connects once. According to account name, session id, IP address, start-time, end-time, processing time and other information, we pre-scan the data of Radius authentication and combine intelligently its several records into one record which is stored in SQL databases. Meanwhile, some unwanted data are deleted or modified. After such a processing, we get log data in SQL databases which are easily used to account connecting time. The module sums up the remaining time which equals the time that a user buys subtracting dial-in access time. Another module judges whether a user can dial in or not according to the remaining time. When the time is below 0 second, the module will stop the user's access authorization. Moreover, after a user pays for access time, the module opens the user's authorization automatically.

## Summing up access bytes from log files on MS Proxy2.0 and MS exchange5.5 server

When a user accesses Internet through MS Proxy2.0 server, the proxy writes access information into a log file or database, in which there are a lot of records whose bytes sent and received is 0 so these records must be removed. The log data on the proxy include the account name, log-in time, processing time, bytes sent, bytes received and other information, with which the system sums up access bytes of a user. However, When a user sends/receives a letter, MS Exchange5.5 server writes log data into log files, one of which is in the sub-directory "tacking.log" of Exchange home directory, and the email server writes one file of this kind every day and its content is not directly readable.

Analyzing the file, the system gets address sent/received, letter length and other control data of e-mail and writes the result into SQL databases. By the way, when a user sends a letter, a number of records are written in the file, so the system must discard redundant or faulty records. According the date, address and length sent/received, the system extracts the account name, bytes of letters and so on through matching key items intelligently.

In spite of the records made by analyzing Proxy or Exchange, the system puts them in SQL databases and these records are stored automatically into CD-ROM every three months in order to be ready for querying.

## Accounting and monitoring modules based on Linux[5]

On our LAN , a user also accesses Internet with IP address through the Linux router except MS proxy server. On the router, we developed accounting and monitoring modules whose functions are to account access bytes and monitor the IP of users so as to prevent users' IP from being stolen.
The modules were implemented under the support of the firewall on Linux. When the Linux system is installed on PC, it doesn't include the firewall. An administrator needs to recompile the Linux core and should choose the firewall. After having compiled it, the administrator moves file "/usr/src/linux/arch/i386/boot/zImage" into the root directory, modifies the file

"/etc/lilo.conf", into which a new line directing zImage is inserted, and then re-runs lilo module.

We know that Linux system outputs account log file, but its log file must be converted into the form we demand. This is the function of the accounting module we programmed. The module creates monthly a file summing up access bytes every host IP. When a new month starts, another module on MS Windows NT Server downloads automatically the file of last month into SQL database being used for the system of network information management.
Owing to account bytes with host IP ,we must safeguard host IP, otherwise account bytes lose their meaning. On a Linux system with a firewall, we use the following commands to open special ports and close other ports:

    # ipfwadm –I –a accept –P tcp –D 202.38.154.245 80  –V 203.93.66.81
    # ipfwadm –I –a deny –P tcp –D 0.0.0.0/0 80  –V 203.93.66.81

The above commands only allow users to access www service to host 203.93.66.81 on interior LAN from exterior, and not to other hosts. with the similar commands, other services such as ftp, mail and the like are also opened.

In principle, the monitoring module safeguards host IP. A host IP corresponds to only an Ethernet address. On Linux router, we construct a map table which describes host IP corresponding to its Ethernet address. The module checks the table every 5 minutes, and when a user modifies his host IP, it finds an incorrect map and uses the above command configuring firewall to stop the host accessing to Internet. After the user changes his IP to a legal one, the module finds correct IP and allows his access to Internet at the same time. With the technique, the module take a maximum of 5 minutes to find illegal IP and open/close users' access to Internet.

## Conclusion

On a LAN , it is necessary to implement automatic management of network users. To provide satisfactory services for users on Internet, we do our best to develop users' management systems. In further research of network management , we will study and develop some new technologies so as to support internet access more easily and securely.

## References

[1] Remote Authentication Dial In User Service (RADIUS), RFC2138, Apr. 1997

[2] Huandong Sun, Dongsheng Zhao and Lianzhong Dai: Network management systems on an enterprise network, Computer system application, Feb.1999

[3] Huandong Sun,Jun Huang, Hua Zhang and Weizhong Li: Designing of a Large Information Management System of Occupation Agency, Chinese Journal of Management Science, Vol.7,No.3,1999:P42-46.

[4] Huandong Sun,Dongsheng Zhao, Minghu Wu and Xueying Li:Monitoring and Managing the Access to Internet, Bullletin of the Academy of Military Medical Sciences, Vol.23, No.4, 1999,P286-288.

[5] Dongsheng Zhao and Huandong Sun, An Accounting and Network Secure Firewall Based on Linux, Medical Information, Dec.1999, P13-14

# Fenix - Personalized Information Filtering System for WWW Pages

Flávia Coimbra Delicato*, Luci Pirmez, Luiz F. Rust da Costa Carmo

Núcleo de Computação Eletrônica - Universidade Federal do Rio de janeiro  Tel: 21 5983159
Caixa Postal: 2324 Rio de Janeiro RJ  Brasil
e-mails: flavia@eng.uerj.br, luci, rust@nce.ufrj.br
* Master Student in Informatic at the Institute of  Mathematics of UFRJ

## Abstract

Nowadays Internet offers a large amount of information to a wide range of users, making it difficult to deal with. The present work suggests the use of intelligent agents for the personalized filtering of Web pages. A set of autonomous, non-mobile and adaptive agents was developed aiming to satisfy the user's need for information. The agents learn from the users' feedback and attempt to produce better results over time. This work presents the system description and the promising results of tests performed in a simulated environment. The proposed system has proven to be a useful tool in reducing the amount of information the user has to deal with.

## Keywords

Information Filtering, Web Pages, Agents.

## 1. Introduction

The exponential increase in the amount of information available on the Internet has been causing a significant impact on users. The World Wide Web (WWW) has made the Internet accessible to a wide range of users. Although the increase of the information available facilitates the spreading of knowledge and the acquisition of products and services, it also makes the search for relevant material a real challenge. Questions arise as how the users will be able to locate the information they need or how they will find the best offer for a service. The use of agents is a possible solution to this problem.

Agents can be defined as software with the aim of performing tasks for their users, usually with autonomy, playing the role of personal assistants.

The present work suggests the use of intelligent agents for personalized information filtering. The proposed system is composed of a set of autonomous, adaptive and non-mobile agents aiming to satisfy the user's need for information. The agents receive the user's feedback about the relevance of the retrieved information and improve their search, obtaining better results over time.

The set of agents is autonomous as it can perform its task without the user's presence, based on a previously built preference profile. The system is adaptive as it learns the user's preferences and adapts itself when these change over time. The agent's learning mechanisms are relevance feedback (Rocchio, 1971) and genetic algorithms (Goldberg, 1994). The information is represented by the vector space model (Salton, 1989), where queries and documents are represented as vectors in a vector space. This method was chosen for its efficiency, which has been proven in various works in the area of information retrieval (Sheth, 199?) (Balabanovic, 1997) and for its relatively easy implementation.

The results presented were obtained through a series of sessions with simulated users. The system's efficiency evaluation was made through the normalized distance performance measure (ndpm), suggested by Yao (1995).

This paper is organized as follows: In section 2 there is a comparison with related works. Section 3 describes the system, the development methodology and environment. The system architecture is detailed in section 4. The analysis of results is presented in section 5 and, finally, some conclusions are drawn in section 6.

## 2. Comparison with Previous Works

Feedback relevance techniques have been studied in the context of information filtering tasks, as described at the TREC Conferences (Harman, 1994). There are also many comparisons between these techniques and non-incremental Machine Learning techniques (Schutze *et al*, 1995) (Lang, 1995). One of the disadvantages of the non-incremental techniques is the great number of examples needed before the learning algorithms can be applied. In contrast, the present work adopts a model where the user is presented to pages that are gradually better, where influences on the pages from his feedback will be presented. The Newst system (Sheth, 199?) is a software agent which uses relevance feedback and genetic algorithms (GA) to provide personalized filtering of Usenets news. The approach differs from the present work mainly in the search space. When considering the filtering of WWW pages instead of news, there is a great impact on the information representation model and on the heuristics adopted in the GA. InfoScope (Fisher, 1991) learns by using systems based on rules that register interesting topics covered in the past. Recommendations of new topics are made based on how recent, frequent and spaced these past topics are. The disadvantage of such an approach is that it is restricted to recommendations of topics within the domain of the user's past interests. In contrast, in the proposed system, the agents search new domains for information that can be of potential interest to the user. He has probably never seen the presented topic before.

Balabanovic (1998) proposed a multiagent system which combines both content-based and collaborative techniques applied to the web pages recommendation. That work adopts the vector-space model (Salton, 1989), relevance feedback (Rocchio, 1971) as the learning method basis and he suggests the use of genetic algorithms (Goldberg, 1994) as a possible solution to some of the problems found in the content-based filtering.

## 3. Fenix System

The information filtering task involves repeated interactions over multiple sessions with the users having long-term goals. It differs from the information retrieval systems where the users typically have a short term information need that is satisfied in a single session. Information filtering systems assist users by filtering the data stream and delivering the relevant information to the user. Information preferences vary greatly from one user to another, therefore filtering systems must be highly personalized.

In the information filtering system proposed, an agent is modeled as a set population of individual profiles. As a whole, all the profiles in a set try to satisfy the user's interests and adapt themselves to these interests.

The agent is responsible for starting the execution of search and filtering tasks, one for each profile. As the tasks are autonomous, they are sub-agents in the Fenix system. Each sub-agent, using different search engines, goes through the web pages looking for documents containing the keywords provided by the user. The set of documents obtained undergoes the filtering process, according to the adopted model. The selected documents are the ones with the higher degree of similarity with the respective profile. The agent has to gather the results from all the sub-agents, classify them according to their potential relevance, and present them to the user. The user can provide positive or negative feedback for the documents. User feedback has the effect of modifying the profile used to retrieve that document.

### 3.1 Development Methodology and Environment

The Fenix system was developed according to the object oriented approach. The programming language adopted was Java, by Sun Microsystems Inc., and the development environment was Jbuilder Standard 1.0, by Borland Corporation, that uses JDK (Java Development Kit) version 1.1. Java language allows the implementation of two kinds of programs: applets and applications. The applications run on any platform with Java Virtual Machine (JVM), while applets are special programs designed to be executed from HTML pages. Fenix system was implemented as a Java application to be run locally.

## 4. Architecture

The Fenix system is composed of five functional modules (figure 1). The modules are implemented as groups of related classes. The description of each module is given below.

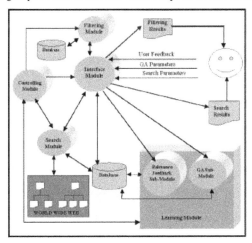

**Figure 1: System's architecture**

25

## 4.1 User Interface Module

This module presents a graphic interface to interact with the user. The user's interaction with Fenix system begins with his registration, where he must inform his personal data and choose a login and a password. After identification the user can choose from three options: to create a new agent, to load an existing one or to activate the autonomous mode.

When creating a new agent, the user must choose a name and a background color, and provide the following search parameters: maximum number of documents shown per session (default is 30); and the query expression. A query in the Fenix system is a combination of keywords (technically called terms), separated by blank spaces. The use of logical connectives is not allowed. The presence of the connective AND between the terms is automatically assumed.
As a result of the initial search, a series of retrieved documents is presented. After reading the chosen documents, the user can provide positive (+1) or negative (-1) feedback according to their relevance.

When saving a newly created agent, the references to the documents with positive feedback will be saved (their URLs) and the term vector and their weights will be created, building the initial profiles for that agent.

When loading an existing agent, the user can choose one of three actions: to read some retrieved document, to provide feedback about some document or to start a new search for documents.

The Fenix "Autonomous Mode" works performing search and filtering tasks based on the user's profiles without his interaction.

## 4.2 Search Module

This module is responsible for gathering information from web pages about the chosen subject and saving them in a local database. With the development of this work, there was a choice of using existing search engines, such as Altavista[1], Lycos[2] and others. Then, the search module became responsible for making the interface with these mechanisms.

The system keeps a list of search engines as part of its configuration parameters. The user's keywords are provided to those engines and the first page of results retrieved for each one of them are converted to the string form and processed by the search module. The processing includes going through the pages identifying all the significant links, extracting the textual content of the pages pointed by the links and delivering this content to the filtering module.

## 4.3 Filtering Module

The filtering process consists of translating the documents provided by the search module to their vector representations, calculating the similarity between documents and profiles, and selecting the top-scoring documents for presentation to the user.

---

[1] Available in: http://www.altavista.digital.com
[2] available in: http://www.lycos.com

### 4.3.1 Profiles and Documents Representation

The representation adopted in this work is based on the vector space model (VSM) (Salton, 1989). According to it, documents and queries are represented as vectors in a hyper-space. A metric distance, which measures the proximity between vectors, is defined over space. The filtering results are the documents with representation that have the highest degree of proximity to the query vector.

A standard method for indexing texts consist of removing punctuation marks, recognizing individual words, eliminating functional words (as "and", "that", etc) using a stop-list, and using the remaining words for content identification of the text. Since the terms are not equally important for content representation, weights are assigned to them, in proportion to their presumed importance to content identification purposes. A text is then represented as a vector of terms $T_i = \{W_{ij}\}$, where $W_{ij}$ represents the weight of term $t_j$ in text $T_i$.

In the representation adopted, the term weight is the product of the term frequency and the inverse document frequency. The term frequency (tf) is the occurrence frequency of the term in the text and it usually reflects the relevance of this term. The inverse document frequency (idf) is a factor that enhances the terms that appear in few documents, while it devaluates the terms occurring in many documents. As a result, the specific features of the documents are highlighted, while the ones spread through the set of documents have minor importance. The weight of the terms is then given as:

$$W_{ij} = tf_{ik} \; X \; idf_k , \qquad\qquad (1)$$

where $tf_{ik}$ is the number of occurrences of term $t_k$ in document i, and $idf_k$ is the inverse document frequency of term $t_k$ in the collection of documents. A commonly used measure for idf is $idf_k = \log (N/nk)$, where N is the total number of documents in the collection, from which nk contains a term $t_k$. In this work, a collection of documents is formed by all the documents retrieved by a profile.

A profile is a set of information about the retrieved documents as, for example, their location in the net (URL) and the user's feedback assigned to them. Besides this, it contains the vector representation of documents that got positive feedback. The representation consists of a vector of terms similar to the one previously described for documents:

$$P = \{W_{ij}^{\,p}\}, \q\qquad\qquad (2)$$

where "p" indicates a profile-field other than a document field.

### 4.3.2 Evaluation of Filtered Documents

A commonly used similarity measure in the vector space model is the cosine of the angle between vectors. In the proposed application, different formulae were tested, and the one proposed in (Salton, 1989) was adopted as follows:

$$S(F_i{}^d, F_i{}^p) = \frac{\sum_k w_{ik}{}^d \, w_{ik}{}^p}{\sqrt{\sum (w_{ik}{}^d)^2 \sum (w_{ik}{}^p)^2}} \qquad (3)$$

where "d" indicates that the field belongs to a document and "p" indicates that the field belongs to the profile.

### 4.3.3 Scoring and Selecting Documents

The documents retrieved through the search task started by the respective profile will have their similarities calculated in relation to that profile. The agents are responsible for gathering the documents generated by all the profiles, classifying them according to their similarity values, eliminating repetitions and presenting them to the user.

The similarity values are converted to a class scale to be presented to the user. A five points scale was adopted, with the adjectives:

- Terrible: for scores equal to 0.2
- Neutral: for scores between 0.3 and 0.5
- Excellent: for scores greater than 0.8
- Poor: for scores between 0.2 and 0.3
- Good: for scores between 0.5 and 0.8

The maximum score value is 1.0 and it only happens when the profile and the document representations are identical. In this work, the limit of 0.2 was adopted as the minimum score that a document should have in order to be presented to the user.

### 4.4  Learning Module

The learning methods adopted by the system are relevance feedback and genetic algorithms. Both methods were projected as independent sub-modules and only the relevance feedback has been implemented at the present stage. In the next stage, the genetic algorithm will be implemented as a complementary mechanism, introducing diversity to the search parameters used by the agents as a goal.

### 4.4.1 Relevance Feedback Sub-Module

The user's feedback for a document has the effect of modifying the respective profile. The profile has to incorporate the changes before new documents can be evaluated.

In the relevance feedback method, an original query vector (represented by the profiles) is modified based on the user's feedback for the documents retrieved by the profile.

For vector space representations, the method for query reformulation in response to user's feedback is vector adjustment. Since queries and documents are both vectors, the query vector is moved closer to the vector representing documents with positive feedback, and further from the vectors of the documents with negative feedback.

Take a profile P, which contributed to a document D for presentation to the user. The user provides feedback, which is a positive or negative integer. Each term in the profile is modified in proportion to the feedback received:

$$\forall i, k: \ W \, ik^P \ = \ W \, ik^P + \alpha * f * W \, ik^d \qquad\qquad (4)$$

that is, the weight of each term is changed proportionally to the learning rate ($\alpha$) and to the feedback. The learning rate $\alpha$ indicates the sensitivity of the profile to the user's feedback, and, in general, assumes values between 0.5 and 1 (Sheth, 199?).

This effects the weight of the terms already existing in the profile by modifying them in proportion to the feedback. The terms not existing in the profile must be added to it.

### 4.5 Other Modules

The Fenix system database is composed of all information from the user, his agents and respective profiles, as well as the documents retrieved in searches. This database is implemented through a group of classes existent in Java standard APIs. Users' and agents' data are stored in simple text files. Profiles and documents are stored in object files.

Besides all of these modules, Fenix has a controlling module (figure 1) responsible for controlling the global behavior of the system, the behavior of each user's set of agents and the specific behavior of each individual agent.

## 5. Analysis of Results

In this work, the performance measure proposed by Yao was adopted (Yao, 1995). The ndpm measure ("normalized distance-based performance measure") is a distance, normalized to range from 0 to 1, between the user's classification for a set of documents and the system's classification for the same documents. This will provide a relative measure, that will be more appropriate to the system's goal than recall and precision measures, commonly used in information retrieval.

An outline was adopted as suggested in (Balabanovic, 1997). A special list of documents is supplied to a simulated user who should classify it in agreement with his interests in a subject. That list is randomly selected from several documents retrieved from the web. The system also ranks the documents according to how well they match the profile previously built for that user.

The expected result is for the ndpm distance between the user and system classifications to decrease gradually over time, as the user's profile is adjusted.

Agents were created for twenty subjects of interest of a simulated user. For each agent, five simulated sessions of "user"-agent interaction were performed. After an initial search, the agent classified the retrieved documents according to the categories above, the "user" evaluated the documents, providing their feedback values and classification. With the feedback, the agent's profile was adjusted to later searches and, with the classification, the ndpm distance was calculated.

A progressive decrease of that distance in the course of the sessions (Figure 2) was observed, indicating that the agents were adapting themselves to the user's preferences, increasing, then, the probability of retrieving a larger number of relevant documents and discarding the irrelevant ones.

The obtained results are similar to the ones described in (Balabanovic, 1998), where a multiagent system was implemented for the WWW pages recommendation. Balabanovic proposed an architecture that combined content-based with collaborative filtering. His system performance was also evaluated with the ndpm measure and the obtained curve had a behavior quite similar to the one presented in the tests with Fenix (Figure 2). In his work 25 evaluation sessions were performed. The initial average ndpm values were 0.4 and the final values were 0.001.

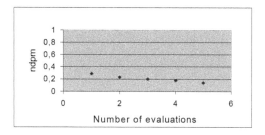

**Figure 2: Average ndpm distance between user and system rankings, over all agents at evaluation points.**

## 6. Conclusions

An information filtering system must be capable of becoming specialized according to user's interests, getting adapted to changes and exploring the domain of potentially relevant information.

The results of simulated tests using the ndpm distance in a controlled environment were quite satisfactory. The tests showed that the distance between the evaluation provided by the user and the one provided by the agents decreased in the course of the sessions, indicating the agents' adaptation to the user's interests. These results demonstrate that the relevance feedback technique alone is very efficient for the agent to become specialized in the user's specific interests.

The performance values obtained in simulated tests based on the ndpm measure were similar to the ones found in other works of information filtering. Balabanovic (1998) proposed an approach that combines content-based and collaborative techniques applied to the WWW pages recommendation. The results described in his work were quite similar to the obtained with Fenix, where a simpler architecture was adopted.

The impact of systems like Fenix on an enterprise may be quite significant. Several information search tasks could be automated, as the system is able to filter and classify different subjects of interest, therefore reducing the consumption of time and money spent on those activities.

Information filtering agents are a great promise to the management of extensive available information.

## 7. References

Balabanovic, M. (1997) "An Adaptive Web Page Recommendation Service". *Stanford Universal Digital Libraries Project Working Papers SIDL - WP.*

Balabanovic, M.(1998) "Learning to Surf: Multiagent Systems for Adaptive Web Page Recomendation Service". Dissertation submitted to the Department of Computer Science and the Committee on Graduate Studies of Stanford University. UMI Number: 9837173. UMI Company.

Fischer, G.and Stevens, C. (1991), "Information access in complex, poorly structured Information spaces". *Human Factors in Computing Systems CHI'91 Conference Proceedings,* New Orleans, LA, USA. April 27 - May 2, 1991, pp. 63-70.

Goldberg, D. E. (1994) "Genetic and Evolutionary Algorithms come of age". *Communications of the ACM,* 37(3):113-119, March 1994.

Harman, D. (1994). *Overview of the Third Text Retrieval Conference (TREC-3).* In Proceedings of the $3^{rd}$ Text Retrieval Conference. Gaithersburg, Maryland, USA. November, 2 - 4, 1994.

Lang, K. (1995). "NewsWeeder: Learning to filter netnews". In *Proceedings of the $12^{th}$ International Conference on Machine Learning.*

Rocchio, J.J. (1971) "Relevance feedback in information retrieval". In *The Smart Retrieval System - Experiments in automatic Document Processing,* p. 313-323, Englewood Cliffs: Prentice-Hall.

Salton, G.(1989), *Automatic Text Processing – The Transformation, Analysis and Retrieval of Information by Computer.* Addison-Wesley Publishing Company, Inc., Reading, MA.

Schutze, H.,Hull, D and Pedersen, J. O. (1995) "A comparison of classifiers and documents representations for the routing problem". In *Proceedings of the $18^{th}$ Annual International ACM SIGIR Conference on Research and Development in Information Retrieval.* Seattle, WA, USA. July 9 - 13.

Sheth, B. (199?) "NEWT: A learning approach to personalized information filtering".Thesis.[s.l.:199?]. Available in: http://agents.www.media.mit.edu/groups/agents/ papers/newt-thesis/ tableofcontents2_1.html.

Yao, Y. Y. (1995). "Measuring retrieval effectiveness based on user preference of documents". *Journal of the American Society for Information Science* 46(2):133-145.

# Combining Java Applet with CGI to Simulate a File System

Zheng Song and G N Toh

School of EEE, Nanyang Technological University, Singapore
email: p145692389@ntu.edu.sg

## Abstract

With the advent of Java applet technology in the recent years, it is very convenient to develop and deliver interactive teaching courseware on the World Wide Web (WWW). Java is designed to be "Write Once and Run Anywhere" owing to its platform-independence. Due to the security consideration, browser does not allow applets to save/read data to/from the local system. This paper suggests a method of building a communication between client side Java applet and server side Common Gateway Interface (CGI) script to simulate a file system and bypass these restrictions.

## Keywords

Java Applet, CGI, Server, Client

## 1. Introduction

There are two kinds of Java program, Java applet and Java application. Java applet can be included on a Web page using HTML tags in the same way images and other elements are included. When a Java-capable browser (such as Netscape Navigator and Microsoft Internet Explorer) loads a Web page that includes an applet, the browser downloads the applet from the Web server and runs it on the user's system. With the Java Plug-in technology of Sun Microsystems, browsers can fully support the latest Java version (Friesen, 1999). Compared to other Web components, applets can be more interactive by taking user input, responding to it, and presenting ever-changing content (Wie, 1996). It has been demonstrated that Java applet is most suitable for developing interactive distance learning courseware.

In order to protect Web users from a malicious applet storing a virus on local system, deleting hard disk files or retrieving private information from user's files, Java applets run under a "better safe than sorry" security model. As a general rule, an applet cannot read or write files on the users file system. It cannot communicate with an Internet site **other than** the one that served the Web page that included the applet. It cannot run any programs on the user's system (Lemay and Cadenhead, 1998). Browsers apply these security restrictions. There is no such restrictions for Java applications.

The CGI establishes a standard way of information exchange between Web server and clients. It allows the passing of information between a client and server to an external program (usually called CGI script) that performs some actions and then outputs its results back to the user's client.

CGI script is executed in real-time and it can output dynamic on-the-fly information (Kim 1996). Perl is the most powerful computer language for writing CGI programs.

There are two main methods (known as GET and POST) to invoke a CGI script. Methods define how the script receives the data sent from clients. They encode client data with Uniform Resource Locator (URL). By using a method, clients can make a request to the server and execute the CGI program. The GET method sends URL-encoded data appended to the URL string. With the limitation of a URL length (usually less than 1024 bytes), the GET method cannot send large amount of data to the CGI script. Different to the GET method, the POST method sends data after all the request headers have been sent to the server, and the Web server transmits the data to the CGI script through the stdin (standard input). The script uses the CONTENT_LENGTH environment variable to read the stdin correctly. The POST method should be chosen in sending arbitrary amount of information to the CGI program.

In Nanyang Technological University (NTU), Singapore, we are developing a new Java applet that can facilitate students in analyzing frequency response of analog circuits. It forms part of our research in methods for distance learning. By entering the Web page through a Web browser, students can edit a schematic and sweep the components' values. Due to the Java applet security restrictions, students cannot save the schematic in the local system. They have to reedit the schematic from the beginning whenever opening the page. So it is necessary to simulate a file system in this project.

One method to simulate a file system is to combine client Java applet with server side Java application and build a multithreaded socket communication between them (Zheng and Toh, 2000). But it requests the support of Java Virtual Machine (JVM) in the server side. It is also difficult for the Webmaster to scan if the Java application contains virus. In this paper, a file system is simulated for students to save the circuit schematics and reload them by building a communication between client side Java applet and server side CGI script. CGI is automatically supported by most servers and script language is difficult to contain virus.

## 2. Simulation of a file system

### 2.1 Software structure

To simulate a file system, it needs Java applet, Web server, CGI script and server hard disk to cooperate together, as shown in Figure 1. Java applet will send/receive circuit data to/from Web server according to HyperText Transfer Protocol (HTTP). Web server will communicate with CGI script using CGI standard. This CGI script, which is written with computer Perl language, should be installed in the same server as the Java applet, due to the Java applet security restriction. Under the request of Java applet, this CGI script can be launched and is able to receive data sent from the clients and save them in the server hard disk or vise verse. This script is named as communicate.pl here.

There is a Client.class in the client side Java applet, which is responsible for invoking the server side CGI script and sending/receiving circuit data to/from the server. Building a communication

34

between this Client.class and the server CGI script, a file system can be simulated to realize general file functions, as shown in Figure 2.

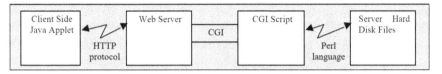

**Figure 1: A communication between applet and CGI script**

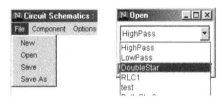

**Figure 2: A file system is simulated**

### 2.2 Client.class

In order to make Client.class simulate file functions, such as "Open", "Save" and "Save As", it is very important to predefine a protocol between the server and clients. In Figure 3 and 4, it can be seen that "1", "2" and "3" have been defined for different functions. A specified protocol code is put at the head of circuit data stream and encodes them as a string data, which will be sent to the server.

Then the encoded string data can be passed from Java applet to CGI script via the POST method. Part of Client.class code below illustrates the communication between clients and the server.

```
URL urlCGI = new URL("http://155.69.15.28/imee/cgi- bin/communicate.pl");
URLConnection connectionCGI = urlCGI.openConnection();
connectionCGI.setDoOutput(true);
BufferedWriter outCGI = new BufferedWriter(new
                        OutputStreamWriter(connectionCGI.getOutputStream()));
outCGI.write(data, 0, data.length());
outCGI.flush();
outCGI.close();
BufferedReader inCGI = new BufferedReader(new
                        InputStreamReader(connectionCGI.getInputStream()));
String input = inCGI.readLine();
```

The location of CGI script is specified as a URL instance first, which will be invoked by Java applet. With that URL, Java applet can create an appropriate URLConnection instance.

URLConnection represents a communications link between the Java applet and a URL. Instances of this class can be used both to read from and to write to the resource referenced by the URL. In order to write those POST data to the stream, setDoOutput() should be called with an argument of true. At the following step, Java applet can obtain an output stream from the connection, and write data to that stream. After closing the output stream, the Java applet can start reading data from the connection's input stream to obtain the output of the CGI script. Thus a complete communication is over.

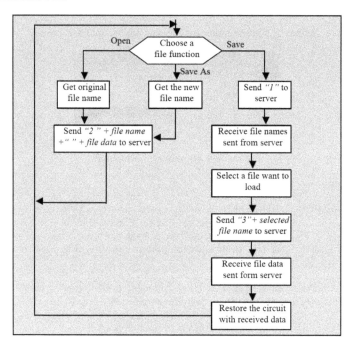

**Figure 3: Flow chart for Client.class**

### 2.3 Communicate.pl

Communicate.pl should be able to understand the requested file function by the clients. It decodes the receiving data stream, and makes response to them according to the predefined protocol.

Part of Communicate.pl code below illustrates how the server side CGI script receives Java applet data and processes them.

36

```
read (STDIN, $in, $ENV{'CONTENT_LENGTH'});
print "Content-type:text/plain\n\n";
$num=substr($in,0,1);
```

Because the POST method has been chosen to pass circuit data, server side CGI script must read data from stdin to a string $in first, with the length stored in environment variable CONTENT_LENGTH.

Then CGI script must print HTTP header to stdout (standard output), and the Web server will send it to the client and ask Java applet to prepare for receiving plain text type of content. It is mandatory to put two new line characters by the end of HTTP header, as shown in the second line of above script.

After getting the file function code from the first character of string $in by using substr() function, CGI script can process receiving data according to different requested functions. Part of its flow chart is shown in Figure 4.

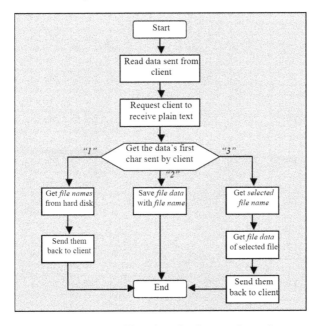

**Figure 4: Flow chart for Communicate.pl**

## 3. Conclusion and future work

By combining Java applet with CGI script together and building a communication between them, a file system can be simulated to realize general file functions. It is necessary to predefine a protocol for the communication. The file system can be enhanced further so that it can provide means to create and delete files/directories, print files. This CGI script will also open URLs and socket connections to hosts other than the ones where the applets come from.

## 4. References

Friesen G. (1999), "Plug into Java with Java Plug-in", *http://www.javaworld.com/javaworld/jw-06-1999/jw-06-plugin.html*

Wie C. R. (1996), "Application of Java Applet Technology", *http://jas2.eng.buffalo.edu/papers/mrs96_jme/paper.htm*

Lemay L. and Cadenhead R. (1998), *Teach Yourself Java1.2 in 21 days*, Sams Publishing, USA.

Kim E. E. (1996), *CGI Programming Unleashed*, Sams Publishing, USA.

Zheng S. and Toh G. N. (2000), "Combine Java Applet with Application to Bypass Security Restriction", *Journal of EEE Research of NTU*, January 2000.

# Trends in Building GUIs in Java:
# the Approach Used in an Advanced Course of Computer Science

Javier Diaz[*], Claudia Queiruga[*] and Laura Fava[*]

[*]Professors responsible for the 'Software Development Laboratory' course at the National University of La Plata, Buenos Aires, Argentina.
e-mail:jdiaz,claudiaq,lfava@info.unlp.edu.ar

## Abstract

This paper focuses on the experience on how to build a modern GUI[1] (Graphic User Interface) using the new features of the Java language (Gosling and Steele, 1996). In order to motivate advanced students of Computer Science to learn JAVA, we consider it would be useful to develop training applets to be used by students of basic courses as complementary material. The applets developed for the students illustrate concepts of data structures algorithms and network protocols by providing animations and interaction to a better understanding the key topics (Díaz, Queiruga, and Harari, 1996; Díaz, Queiruga and Schiavoni A, 1994; Díaz, and Fava , 1997). In this paper, a test of applicability of these applets and their results are depict.

Additionally, this paper illustrates the evolution from the primitive toolkit AWT[2] (Geary, 1998) to the modern approach using JFC[3] (URL1) and the use of both made by the students in their programs.

## Keywords

Java, AWT, Swing Component, GUI Event Models, educational applets

## Introduction

There was a need to include JAVA in an advanced course at the Computer Science career at our University due to the technological revolution brought by JAVA and the world trend to introduce this language in the Computer Science curricula (URL2;URL3). Unlike other courses in the world, 'Software Development Laboratory' focused on newer JAVA aspect such as portable graphic user interfaces, highly configurable, reusable, etc.

When we prepared the course in 1998, the develop of user´s interface in JAVA was based in AWT . As the news on JFC (URL4) benefits grew, it was decided to incorporate these concepts to the development of the final project. From the infrastructure provided by the JFC, the Swing package was basically used (Campione and Walrath, 1998).

The final projects assigned to the students consisted of educational applets for the purpose of illustrating data structure algorithms, making use of highly configurable interfaces, animations

---

[1] Graphic User Interface
[2] Abstract Window Toolkit
[3] Java Foundatin Classes

and a high degree of interaction in order to attract user's attention. The experience was quite interesting in terms of the generated codes and the applets observable features. In 1999, we repeated the experience choosing network protocols as applet subjects.

In the following, this paper presents an introduction to AWT, JFC, the results of the students experience and the conclusions.

# 1. The Original AWT

The first AWT, included in the JDK 1.0 version (URL₅), supplied programmers with a rudimentary library to build applets and applications with single GUIs[4]. The standard interaction components were buttons, text fields and lists. Its only visualisation being a text with a minimal set of font and lacking images. In spite of its limitations, it offered two important features for applets and applications:

> ✓ A 100% portability. A single source code could be used across any platform without previous modification.
> ✓ It assumed special look and feel for each platform.

The AWT 1.0 was the cornerstone for the development User Graphic Interfaces in Java, with good perspective of evolution.

As regards portability, we can say that Java proposed a first feasible solution. Before AWT, the proposals to build highly portable GUIs offered only propietary libraries. There were no proposals with open solutions such as Sun Microsystems with Java.

In addition, programs retained a look and feel, which complies with the platform across they was being run. However, this characteristic that at the very beginning was in agreement with a standard visualisation for each platform, afterwards became rigid and did not favour application customising.

## 1.1 AWT GUI Components

There are different alternatives to implement a GUI class library or environments to develop portable GUIs. One possibility is to locate a class library or API on the native toolkit[5]. This approach retains the platform look and feel, however it does not frequently work in a consistent way across all platforms. Another possibility is to have only one native toolkit and emulate the native look and feel across each platform. This method, although working consistently across all platforms, does not sometimes capture all the look and feel of the platforms.

The AWT 1.0 uses the first alternative, where each Java component creates a native component, called peer. The use of peer enables applets and applications using the AWT to retain the look and feel of native windowing system. This approach increases the complexity of the Java GUI components since these components store their own state; each GUI

---

[4] Graphic User Interface
[5] Platform native windowing system

component class encapsulates the native or peer implementation. This is why, the AWT 1.0 GUI components are called *heavyweights*.

Besides, another characteristic of the heavyweights components is that they are not transparent. Due to the fact that each component is drawn in a rectangular native window, as they overlap, the component laying below remains hidden by the one that is on top.

Since each native toolkit has its own event model and native component set, another problem arises at toolkit level.

All these problems can affect the end user during the designing and testing process for specific a platform. The UI[6] may have undesired effects on another platform, affecting the look and feel or even the behaviour.

## 1.2 Management of Event in the AWT 1.0. Inheritance Event Model

It is known that the AWT 1.0 uses the peer technology; in this way, the event management subsystem is native of each platform, where applets and Java applications are run. For example, if an Applet is run under Motif, it uses the event management subsystem of X-Windows. This approach may cause that certain GUI components, such as scrollbars, behave in an inconsistent way depending on the running platform.

The management of events generated by the GUI used by the AWT 1.0 is simple. When an event occurs inside a component, a method of that component is invoked. If you want to respond to an event, you simply override the appropriate method. For example, the setSize(int width, int height) method is invoked when the component changes size. If you wanted to take some action when a resize event occurs, you would override the setSize(int width, int height) method. Events of this type, occurring in and concerning only the component, are handled or ignored, but never propagated. There is another type of events called propagated events, occurring inside the components, which can be handled by the components or propagated into their containers. These events are handled by the handleEvent(java.awt.Event event) or action(java.awt.Event, Object anObject) methods of the component or container. The propagated event model is based on inheritance.

## 1.3 Shortcomings of the AWT 1.0 Architecture.

The AWT 1.0 architecture was appropriate for small applets or applications, with single user interfaces, both in its look and feel and in its event handling. However, this architecture is not scaleable by a number of issues that are detailed below:
- ✓ The AWT 1.0 components, both the standard and the customisable, are heavyweight; i.e. they require a native window in which to be rendered. These areas have a rectangular shape, and this fact does not allow locating overlapped objects, as they mutually cover one another.
- ✓ The components based on peers could not easily be extensible so as to overwrite their own look and feel. In order to implement customisable components, programmers

---

[6] User Interface

should create java.awt.Canvas subclasses, and to create special containers they should subclassify java.awt.Panel.

✓ It requires the GUI components to be subclassified, only for a minimum handle of events. It is desirable to extend a class to add new functionalities or visualisation aspects of the components (for instance, image support).

✓ It does not provide any kind of separation between application code and GUI code, since the application code is mixed up with that of the extended component.

✓ As all event types are processed by only two methods -handleEvent() and action()- their logic is quite complex and prone to errors. Long conditional statements are required to determine which object triggers an event and which event is produced.

✓ No events are filtered. The events are always sent to the components not taking into account whether the components respond to them. This becomes a performance problem, particularly due to the high frequency of occurrence of certain events (for instance the mouse movements).

Java multiplatform capability has been one of the fundamental reasons why Java has been adopted as development language. However, the Java GUIs multiplatform features -in versions earlier to 1.1- had problems that had to be enhanced in following versions.

## 2. The Java Foundation Classes

The JDK 1.2[7] [9] introduces the first deployment of the most significant cross-platform graphical user interface technology: the Java Foundation Classes.

The JFC is made up of several technologies: the AWT, Swing, Accessibility and Java 2D. These technologies are the core of Java's user interface support. Swing is the user interface component portion of JFC. Swing extends the original AWT by adding a comprehensive set of graphical interfaces class libraries that is completely portable and it is delivered as part of the Java Platform. Since the JFC is core to the Java Platform, it eliminated the need to download special classes at runtime and it is compatible with all AWT-based applications.

The JFC contains a powerful, mature delegation event model, printing clipboard support, a lightweight UI framework and it is 100% JavaBeans (Vanhelsuwé, 1997) compliant.

---

[7] Java Developer Kit

## 2.1 Swing Components

Swings are *lightweight* components. This means they do not need native or peer implementation. In this way, they are completely transparent because they do not require a native window.

The Swing components improve the GUI development providing high quality GUI components which are peerless or lightweight, look and feel pluggable, customizable (enabling to embed images, rounded shapes and organic in appearance) and transparent (allowing overlapp components). Additionally, applets and applications performance was greatly improved since the incorporation of lightweight components and the new event management model (based on delegation).

## 2.2 Management of Event in the AWT 1.1. Delegation Event Model

In order to solve the shortcomings of the AWT 1.0 event handling, the AWT 1.1 event model proposes a clear separation between objects generating events or *sources*, and those entities that need to act on them or *event listener*. In the AWT 1.1, the GUI components, are the sources that generate events and delegate their management to external entities.

Communication from the source object, generator of the event, to the listener object is rather simple: the events generated are passed from the source object to the listener object. The source object invokes a predefined method on the listener object, transferring the occurred event as parameter.

The communication from listener objects to source objects is more complex. On the one hand, source objects do not recognise in advance which listener objects will be interested in the events they generated. It is the listener object responsibility to adjust to a protocol defined by the source objects and not vice versa. This protocol allows an object (listener) interested in receiving notifications of the events generated by another object (source) to register. The two most important methods for this protocol are the following: add<EventType>Listener(<EventType>Listener listener) and remove<EventType> Listener(<EventType>Listener listener), where <EventType> represents the class of event produced, for example, MouseListener, KeyListener, etc.

In practical terms, source objects have "well-known" associate events (for example, buttons generate events: mouse down, mouse up, mouse released, etc.), that are the ones they can generate. The sets of events that a source object can emit are predefined. These events are accompanied by JAVA interfaces that are implemented by the listener objects interested in receiving notifications from the events produced.

## 2.3 Advancements of Swing Components

Swing components have several advancements over the AWT:

43

- ✓ Swing supports MVC. Each Swing components use *models* to separate the application's data from the data display and using *listeners* to receive messages about changes or events from other objects.
- ✓ As we explain bellow, many of the platform incompatibilities in Java were caused by the AWT components. Swing are entirely writing in Java and do not depend of native peers which allow them to be optimised and full compliant.
- ✓ Swing components are Java beans. The associated benefits are: easy of use in the Integrated Development Environment (IDE), serialisation support and full support for the 1.1 delegation model.
- ✓ Swing components support pluggable look and feel. This feature allows to retain the same appearance across different platform. The pluggable look and feel has a significant role in consumer electronic market.
- ✓ Swing allow easily create customised components setting adequate properties such as opaque, transparent, image, tooltips, etc. It's not require subclassing GUI components.
- ✓ Swing also improve the mechanism of painting components on the screen. They provide double buffered in order to avoid the onscreen erasing and flickering.

## 3. A teaching experience using JAVA Language

In the Computer Science curricula at the National University of La Plata, there is a course named 'Software Development Laboratory' belongs to fourth year of the curricula. During the years 1998 and 1999, in this course, several Java applets were developed to be used in interactive teaching for initial course on 'Data Structures' and 'Network Seminar'.

The course syllabus covered from basic concepts of JAVA language to its most attractive features, as for instance multithreading and advanced GUI. The final evaluation of the course was focused on the implementation of interactive applets with novel user interfaces that can be customised (settings colours, shapes, images, etc.). The most attractive feature was the animation of the typical data structure algorithms and network protocols.

Additionally another important features of the applets were:

- ✓ The data should be got from the tables stored in relational databases using JDBC.
- ✓ The GUI components should be edited (changing values, appearance, etc.).
- ✓ The objects of the GUI should be moved and placed using drag and drop feature.
- ✓ Different panels inside the applets show concurrent animations using multithreading.

The students taking this course have already approved 'Data Structures' and 'Seminar Network', a second and third year courses of the Computer Science curricula.

The final work developed by students of 'Software Development Laboratory' consisted on the construction of training applets:

**In 1998** the students were asked to develop applets on animating algorithm that manipulate classic data structures, making use of the new GUI components included in the AWT 1.1.

The methodology used by the chair was to assign different topics to each group of no more than two students. Each group selected one of the following algorithms: search for minimal paths using Dijsktra; insertion upon a 2-3 tree; retrieval of minimal path using the BFS (Breadth First Search) strategy; creation, insertion and elimination in a minheap; insertion upon AVL binary trees; topological ordering on a digraph representing the Computer Science curricula at the UNLP; heapsort and quicksort.

**In 1999** the students were asked to develop applets on animating algorithm on protocols network, making use of the new GUI components included in Java 2.

The methodology used by the chair was to assign different topics to each group of no more than two students. Each group selected one of the following algorithms: Address Resolution Protocol (ARP); Reverse Address Resolution Protocol (RARP); Routing Information Protocol (RIP); Traceroute program operation; Ping program operation; X.25 protocol (link and network layers).

We considered adequate to use the developed applets as complementary educational material in the 'Data Structures' and 'Network Seminar' courses. We made a test to evaluate the advantageous of the use of these applets.

The methodology of the test consist on:

  ✓ To take a population of volunteer students and split it in two groups: A and B.
  ✓ To fix a time deadline in 30 minutes.
  ✓ To request the modification of the following algorithms: AVL insertion considering duplicate values and became minheap into maxheap.
  ✓ The group A interacted with the training applets before the resolution of the test. The group B resolved the test without use the applets.

The outcomes of the test fulfil the expectations. The 83% of students of group A resolved the test in a correct way and in a shorter time. The 36% of the students of group B resolve the test in a correct way in the requested time.

Nowadays we are making a new test about network protocols. In this case the subjects are the resolution of errors occurring while an algorithm is running, such as link down in RIP and duplicate address in ARP. We hope finish this test soon and incorporate it in the final paper.

The applets can be accessed from the follow URLs:

  http://www.linti.unlp.edu.ar/catedras/Laboratorio/1998/applets.htm
  http://www.linti.unlp.edu.ar/catedras/Laboratorio/1999/applets.htm

## 4. Conclusions

The evolution of the approaches to develop GUI in Java has been positive regarding simplicity, easiness of use, portability, and efficiency. This paper illustrates the different alternatives of this evolution and its impact in educational applets development on the students of the Computer Science curricula at the National University of La Plata.

The experience of teaching how to develop GUI in JAVA was very positive in the following aspects:

- ✓ The course evolved from a theoretical course in JAVA (as given in 1997) to a hand on course with a final project.
- ✓ Semester course proved enough for teaching JAVA basics and also more advanced features (i.e.: threads and JFC).
- ✓ The final project of developing an educational applet fulfilled different needs: from a non trivial logic of the problem to a user friendly interface for a known problem.
- ✓ The students were highly motivated by the fact that the applet they developed will be use by other students of computer science career.

## References

Gosling J., Joy B. and Steele G. (1996), *"The Java Language Specification"*, Addison Wesley. ISBN: 0201634511.

Díaz J., Queiruga, C. and Harari, I. (1996), *"Testing the Usability of a Hypermedia Enclyclopedia in Data Networks"*, PANEL'96 (XXII Conferencia Latinoamericana de Informática), Universidad de los Andes, Bogotá, Colombia.

Díaz, J.; Queiruga C. and Schiavoni A. (1994), *"A proposed extension to the hypermedia model for training in networking technology"*, BIWIT'94 (Basque International Workshop on Information Technology), Biarritz, Francia.

Díaz, J. and Fava L. (1997), *"Un ambiente para el desarrollo de Interfaces de Usuario Adaptativas"*, III CACIC, Universidad Nacional de La Plata, Argentina.

Geary, D. (1998), *"Graphic Java 1.2: Mastering The JFC, Third Edition, Volume 1 AWT.* Prentice Hall, 1998. ISBN: 0130796662

$URL_1$, *"Java Foundation Classes: Now and Future"*, http://java.sun.com/marketing/collateral/foundation_classes.html.

$URL_2$, *"The JCampus Java Community"*, http://www.jcampus.org.

$URL_3$, *"Teaching at KOM"*, http://www.kom.e-technik.tu-darmstadt.de/Teaching/.

$URL_4$, *"The Java Foundation Classes. The New Standard for Java GUI Development"*, http://www.ibm.com/java/education/gui.html#toc9

Campione, M. and Walrath, K. (1998), *"The Java Tutorial Continued: The Rest of the JDK"*. Addison Wesley Publishing Company. ISBN: 0201485583.

$URL_5$, *"Overview of Java$^{tm}$ platform product family"*, http://java.sun.com/products/jdk/1.0.2/index.html.

Vanhelsuwé, L (1997), *"Mastering in JavaBeans"*. Sybex. ISBN: 0782120970.

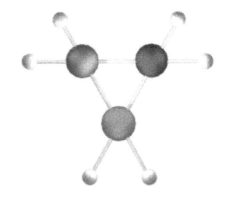

# Chapter 2

## Network Technologies and
## Management

# The Quality of Service as perceived by the Customer

Dominique Le Foll and Phil Bull

Wavetek Wandel Goltermann, Plymouth, United Kingdom
Dominique.le-foll@wwgsolutions.com, Phil.bull@wwgsolutions.com

## Abstract

This paper aims at presenting a possible implementation of the concept of Quality of Service (QoS) as it has been specified by the Tele-management Forum (TMF) in order to improve the relation between Telecom Operators and their customers.

A brief introduction of the market drivers, which force the Telecom operators to implement such solutions, is given as an introduction and then the basic foundation of the TMF principles are described.

At the end, an example of a real implementation (WG QMS) taken from a product under development at Wavetek Wandel Goltermann will show how these concepts can be implemented.

**Key Words** : TMF, QoS, Customer care, Network Management, NMS, OSS, QMS, WWG, Corba, SNMP, IP

## 1. Introduction

The recent changes of the European Telco environment from a monopoly situation to an open market has forced Telecom Operators to re-focus on their customers satisfaction. The general trend could be summarised easily by the slogan : "Get more for Less".

The management of the Quality of Service is one of the possible answer to the customer expectation for more care from the telecommunication provider, it is also the only way to implement a proactive fault management which is required to achieve the future availability commercial high class standards (no more unplanned unavailability of more than 10mn).

The implementation of a solution for such issues at WWG, has been carried out by the Remote Test System business unit located in Plymouth, Devon, UK. Wavetek Wandel Goltermann (WWG) is the European leader in Communication test Solutions which benefits from long established relation and close partnership with all the main World-Class Telcos.

## 2. Market needs

### a) The end of the monopoly

On January the $1^{st}$ of 1998, the European Union "fully" liberalised the Telecom Market. In practice, this deregulation will not be fully implemented in a single day, but already, in early 2000, the effect of this key change in the European market paradigm is very visible.

The bulk of the European Telcos, emanating mainly from the formal government owned PTTs, added to strong links with the local national governments has been (and is still in some countries of the Union) a strong brake for this real market opening.

Customers (private and business) are aware of competitive offers and the alternative providers have to prove their reliability as providers of the Telecom resource, which is today vital to most companies.

As usual, when a strong paradigm shift happens in a well-established market, the movement towards a new balanced position starts slowly, even if nothing can stop it. After a short period of hesitation the European customers will (and have already for some) start to shop for the best offers. For some of them the best will be the cheapest, for others it will be the most reliable. In this newly opened market many players are still looking for the best opportunities.

The first European experience of deregulation happened in the UK. If we look at it, we notice that the first newcomer's attempts have been to offer lower cost solutions. This strategy, due to the monopoly situation of the incumbent, has proved to be very risky and rarely viable in the long term. Furthermore the other major PTTs, who have been carefully watching the UK their competitiveness while they are still in a protected monopoly market.

Quickly the trend has shown that the competition will be world wide, the newcomers in a country are very often old, foreign PTTs (either directly or via a joined venture).

The price pressure is already quite high in Europe, (even if it is still far below the US). In order to keep the margins to a comfortable level, the Telecom operators have started to analyse clearly what could help them keep their customer base without having to constantly reduce their tariffs. The idea of using 'Quality of Service' as a marketing tool (QoS was already used as a deployment strategy) is now happening in the Telecom World.

### b)  From a PTT's administration to a Partner

Fairly quickly the major European Telecom Operators have understood that they will have to centre their strategy on providing a good service to their customers. This short statement which may seem obvious to any small shopkeeper, has forced the Telcos to run a major reorganisation of their operations. They must create real teams which work together (that idea is often very new for the old incumbents) to better serve their customers.

The first problem was to understand what was the major wish list of their business customers (they are the most profitable).

The main issues have been :

> ❖  Commit to greater availability (guaranteed repair time)

> ❖  Commit to a real business class service (the service that the customer wants, where they want, when they want)

> ❖  Offer a transparent access to the information (good performance is visible, as soon as the information is hidden the doubt starts).

The implementation of such concepts in a business environment, which is in a fast, permanent evolution is far from simple. Telecom operators must face new competitors every day, customers are asking for more bandwidth at a lower price and telcos need to offer a global world service which needs to rely on fairly volatile partners (e.g. Concert, Global One, Unisource, ...).

In case of failure the risks are to:

❖ Lose your existing customers (to gain a new customer cost as much as five times more than to keep an existing one),

❖ Fail to offer new services and keep the price as the only differentiator, forcing the trend towards lower profit and less investment (while they are mandatory to remain in the bandwidth race).

❖ Be down-classed and rejected by the biggest corporations which are the most profitable customers.

*c)* *Growing in the customer value chain.*

All these factors force the European Telecom operators to go up in their customer value chain. Offering tailored solutions, committing by contract not to provide only a phone plug but a real, well defined service. Delivering not only good technologies but also real help for their customers to be more efficient in their business.

Selling the quality forces the need to define and to measure it. Committing to limit repair times successfully requires operators to be pro-active in network fault management. Selling global QoS contracts implies a globalisation of the service management at the customer level independently of the technology or the regional location.

All these needs have driven the work done by the TMF for new Network Management principles.

## 3. ITU-T Telecommunications Management Network (TMN)

The ITU-T Telecommunications Management Network (TMN) is a set of recommendations which sets out a definition for an Open Systems management framework to allow various OSS (Operational Support Systems), NMS (Network Management Systems) and Element Managers to inter-work with each other.

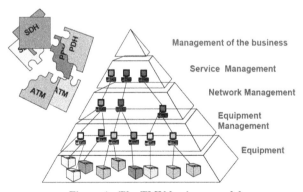

**Figure 1: The TMN business model**

The TMN business model describes a layered structure from the Business layer at the top, down through Service, Network and Element layers, each layer supporting the business and functional needs of the layer above it.

The X.700 series recommendations cover the Management Framework for Open Systems Interconnection (OSI) and definitions of interfaces and protocols to support Manager-Agent inter-working in a hierarchical topology. Physical interfaces such as Q3 allow for Manager-Agent interconnection whilst distributed object technology based on managed objects allows for communication between systems having different hardware and software operating systems.

Protocols such as CMIP[1] have been defined to provide inter-working at an abstracted level above that of the operating system where an object modelled MIB[2] is created between each Manager-Agent interface. A manager communicates with managed objects in the agents of other systems as through they were resident in the same operating environment.

TMN is structured around a vertical hierarchy rather than peer to peer systems and as such, is more suited for network element management.

As part of the TMN X.700 series of recommendations, X.745 describes the Test Management Function within TMN. This defines tests as packaged objects and a series of related tests are created in a container called a Test Session. X.745 can be usefully exploited in the Test-On-Demand, interactive testing which is required for network maintenance and service turn-up activities.

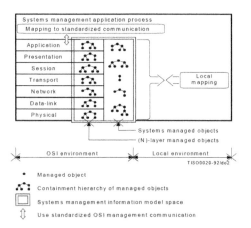

**Figure 2: Relationship between information and communication aspects of the systems management model**

---

[1] Common Management Interface Protocol
[2] Management Information Base

Although TMN has led to a considerable amount of work which has improved systems inter-working, the complex data modelling processes and protocols have made the development of such systems expensive and slow to implement. New open systems, object oriented standards such as CORBA have reduced the complexity and speeded up the development process for interconnecting and distributing systems.

## 4. Tele-Management Forum (TMF)

The Tele-management Forum (TMF) originally named Network Management Forum (NMF) is a non-profit consortium founded entirely by their members representing the world leading Operators and Manufacturers.

The TMF starts where standards Organisations leave off. They bring service providers and suppliers together to define highly specific, implementable approaches to service management.

The main issues addressed by the TMF are:

- ❖ Making partners out of customers
- ❖ Making multi-vendor environments work
- ❖ Simplifying alliances and joint provisioning agreements
- ❖ Delivering scaleable, cost effective distributed computing solutions
- ❖ Smoothly integrating legacy systems
- ❖ Offering a common business model for service level management
- ❖ Making TMN practical and cost effective

One of the main specifications issued by the TMF is the TMF-701 - Performance Reporting Definitions Document, which defines service management metrics in terms that can be used for service reporting to the end customer (for example, Service Level Agreement validation reporting).

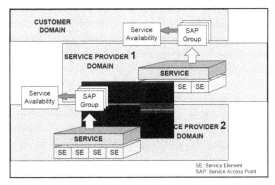

**Figure 3: Layered Service Concept**

In a layered service provision environment as illustrated in Figure 1, a Customer purchases a service from Service Provider 1, through a SLA or service contract which contains commitments on Quality of Service (QoS) and against which performance parameters such as

Service Availability is reported for a SAP Group. In order to provide this service, Service Provider 1 brings together a number of Service Elements (SEs) analogous to the construction of a Network from Network Elements, links and paths. Thus, a "service" can be considered as the combination of a set of SEs co-operating in an appropriate fashion to support the service.

Sharing of the same data by a group of people who have different interests presents some technical difficulties in the implementation of the access security or data validation. However it does provide an invaluable, seamless integration of the operations as soon as it works. It also forces the whole of the organisation to focus on the customer satisfaction instead of local optimisation.

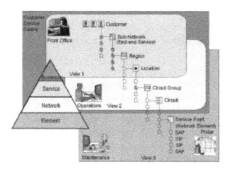

**Figure 4: A customer centric layered approach**

## 5. An example of a system implementation (WWG QMS)

### a)  End to End QoS cannot ignore the Local Loop

The RTS business unit of the Local Loop division of the Wavetek Wandel Goltermann group joined the TMF in 1998 in order to better understand the direction that would be taken by its customers.

The goal was to offer a facility to manage Service Level Agreements, which cover the end to end services including the local loop and the transport circuits provisioned over multiple carriers.

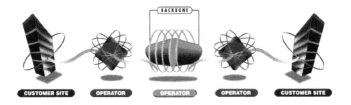

**Figure 5: The Service has a value only from end to end**

Traditionally the local loop portion of the telecom circuit, which links the customer to the first central office equipment, is not monitored because it requires an active element at the customer site with QoS measurement capability.

### b) Monitor the QoS at the customer site

The first challenge, to be able to offer an end to end vision, is to extract quality information from probes located at the customer sites. This must be done without creating an overlay network to collect this information. Solutions based on modem dial-up links to connect probes located at the customer site are only applicable to small sub-network configurations. A really global solution requires:

❖ Collection of the QoS data without significant extra cost in the installation and maintenance of equipment at the customer site

❖ Reporting the QoS data to the OSS/NMS utilising the bandwidth of the telecom service provided.

The demarcation point, which is located at the customer site (like a CSU/DSU), can be modified to extract the QoS data and some spare bits (depending of the technology used to link to the customer). These can be used as a communication channel with a QoS collection device located somewhere on the link.

WWG works in partnership with the company Celogic (Trappes, France - www.celogic.com) to provide the network and end customer equipment. The solution offers the collection of QoS data and fault localisation between a central office equipment (QT-100B) and an end customer demarcation equipment (QT-300B) on any type of 2mbps services including the 2048kbps clear channel mode (patent protected).

### c) Collect the QoS Data of thousand's of customers

Traditionally NMS have relied on dedicated networks to configure the equipment and to collect the QoS data. The reliability of the NMS collection process was based on the assumption that the control network was 100% reliable, so they were often quite slow. The deployment architecture of the NMS system was coping with this constraint by using a hierarchical organisation, which was mainly based on the geographic location of the equipment.

55

Implementing the TMF concept requires a complete focus toward the customers. These customers want to sign global service contracts, which are very difficult to provide with a hierarchical QoS information structure.

This constraint being understood, two obvious alternatives are:

❖ Increase the bandwidth of the control network while retaining its reliability (likely to be very expensive),

❖ Re-design the system to cope with the disadvantage of a quick but unreliable network (cheaper but more challenging).

At WWG we believe in the generalisation of the IP network and so we have decided to collaborate with our partner Celogic to design a new generation of equipment and probe manager which can provide a "carrier class" collection service while using a regular IP network as the control network. This proprietary technique (patents are pending) allows us to offer automatic mechanisms on top of a regular SNMP protocol. This can transparently recover from most of the control network transmission outages which are due to the IP best effort model and to the UDP connectionless protocol which is used to transport SNMP information over IP.Synchronisation and distribution of the Data

The difficulty of providing a good OSS comes from the different views required by the various users of the system.

❖ The equipment configuration teams want to be able to control their network element without having to be concerned about the specific services, which are passed on. Most of the time they expect a sophisticated but remote interface, which reflect the geographical implementation of the network elements themselves.

❖ The Network group will manage chunks of the network, but very often not the end to end views.

❖ The Customer (Business) group will face the customer and will have to manage the Service contracts generally independently of any geographical organisation.

This type of multi dimensional data representation is fairly easy to implement in a static model, but in our situation where we have decided to base the system on a "best effort" IP network for the control, it requires some attention in the design of the solution.

The WWG QMS is based on a non-blocking framework, which relies on Corba services to assure the transport of the information as well as the synchronisation. The Corba middleware is provided by the Irish company Iona (http://www.iona.com).

The Corba facilities, which have been used extensively, are:

❖ OMT for database synchronisation for the Manager and the equipment internal MIB.

❖ Naming services, which offer an easy solution to present an asynchronous view of typically synchronous services (e.g. SQL connection).

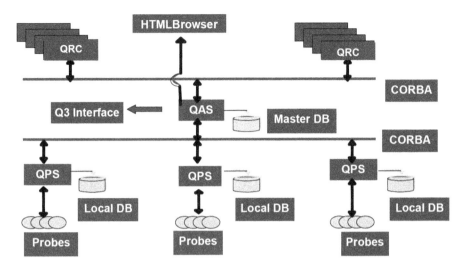

QRC : QMS Remote Client
QAS : QMS Application Server
QPS : QMS Probe Server

**Figure 6: The WWG Global architecture**

## 6. WWG QMS Services

*a) Typical configuration*

As it stands today the QMS offers a complete OSS solution for the management of 2Mbps digital leased lines. We work with our partner Celogic to offer equivalent solutions for E3, T3, E4 and STM-1 in the near future.

From an operators point of view the QMS serves four main functions:

1. Provisioning and configuration of the line.

2. Turn up of the service with end to end integration and G.826 qualification.

3. Quality of service monitoring related to customers.

4. Fault management with a customer oriented service view and a fault localisation function for the operation team.

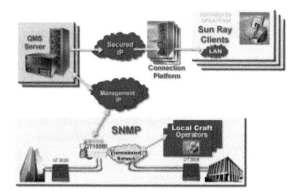

Figure 7: A typical QMS implementation

## 7. Conclusion

In a more competitive environment where the Operators must differentiate their commercial offers from their competitors, the Quality of Service becomes a very powerful marketing tool.

In the local loop portion of the network where the outages are frequent and not easy to pro-actively detect, this type of offering is even more valuable than in the core network.

An implementation in-line with the TMF vision is possible but requires the implementation quite innovative technology in order to achieve the goal without increasing the cost of a customer connection.

WWG with its partner Celogic have developed a solution which offer this type of service for 2mbits/s leased lines today but with a road map to cover all the other technologies used in the local loop in the near future.

# Towards QoS Management: An Improvement in OAM Performance Management

Zhao Yang and Wang GuangXing

Research Center for Network and Communication, Northeastern University, Shenyang, China
e-mail: zhaoyang@mail.neu.edu.cn

## Abstract

Monitoring the variability of network performance parameters is an important method to realize the QoS management in ATM networks. The OAM performance management function defined by ITU-T, however, simply monitors network performance and reports status information. It can not give QoS management an enough support. In terms of the relationship of QoS and network performance parameter, an ATM layered QoS management model is proposed and an improvement in OAM performance management functions is also made. Some new functions, which are necessary to QoS management, are defined in reserved field of activation and deactivation OAM cell and forward monitoring and backward reporting OAM cell.

## Keywords

QoS Management; Operations, Administration, and Maintenance; Network Performance Parameters

## 1. Introduction

ATM network guarantees many kinds of user's QoS requirement. When a connection is set up, the QoS parameters of user's application are mapped or translated into each layer's QoS parameters of protocol stacks. Meanwhile, they are translated into network performance (NP) parameters through call admission control (CAC) in switching system. These NP parameters include cell loss rate, cell delay, and cell delay variation, etc. Cell delay is induced by propagation delay, switching delay, and queuing delay; whereas, cell loss is caused by transmission error, lack of buffer space, and cell delay violation. The variations of the parameters reflect whether the ATM network fulfills its service contract for a given connection. Therefore, how to monitor and report NP parameters effectively is a key in ATM QoS management.

Recently, many works about QoS management [1,2,3,4] have been studied. The QoS framework, in which the QoS manager interacts with the network management framework and applications, has been proposed [1]. A similar research has been addressed as the QoS Broker [2]. The core function of the QoS Broker is QoS negotiation and translation. QoS-A as a structure that supports QoS management mechanism systematically is proposed in [4], and QoS management scenario in ATM layer is suggested in [3].

The OAM performance management function specified in ITU-T I.610, [5] periodically monitors the network performance along routing path in the boundary of end-to-end or segment. In addition, the OAM function could extract some control information according to the QoS parameters negotiated between users and networks at the connection establishment phase and then apply it to traffic control functions in user and control plane in order to prevent congestion within the networks. The OAM performance management function, however, simply monitors network performance and reports them by performance management OAM cell. So, the functions executing the OAM performance management function in the layer management of ATM protocol reference model should be extended for the purpose of supporting the requirements for QoS management.

Therefore, a new QoS management framework based on the extended OAM performance management function is proposed. We also integrate OAM functions with other QoS issues such as call admission control (CAC), usage parameter control (UPC), resource control, and congestion control to implement QoS management. In the extended OAM performance management, some new fields were defined to realize the scheme in the reserved field of OAM cells. In section 2, we discuss the QoS layered structure model admitted widely. The concepts of QoS and network performance parameters are also defined. The QoS management model was proposed for ATM layer. Section 3 gives the extended method for OAM performance management. At last, the conclusion is made.

## 2. QoS management framework

### 2.1 QoS layered structure model

From the ITU-T recommendations, it is generally admitted that the QoS is the user's view of a service as opposed to the network provider's view [6]. In order to plan, design and operate the network and its services such as voice, data, and video, future standards should refine the concept of QoS and propose an appropriate QoS framework. The framework must satisfy user's QoS requirements that not only change over time, but also depend on each application and user [7]. At present, a generally accepted concept of QoS architecture is layered QoS structure, in which each layer guarantees the requested QoS to its next-higher layer and demands a (possibly different) QoS from its next-lower layer [7,8,9]. The QoS layered structure we use is modeled after the concept and is illustrated in Fig. 1. The architecture consists of four horizontal protocol layers and three vertical control planes. The bottom three protocol layers are physical layer, ATM layer and adaptation (AAL) layer. The functions and features of these protocol layers are well defined in ATM UNI Specification. Application layer of QoS is defined for end-system.

The selection of QoS parameters in each layer depends on the requirements of its higher layer. Because each layer receives the SDUs(Service Data Units) from a higher layer and uses the corresponding PDUs(Protocol Data Units) to communicate with its peer layers. The QoS parameters are based on the SDU, and they can be accessed by SAP(Service Access Point) between the higher and lower layer. For example, from the SAP of AAL, we can obtain the AAL QoS parameter which is related to five kinds of traffic [10]; whereas, from the SAP of ATM layer, we get the ATM

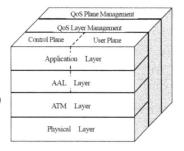

Fig.1 QoS layered structure model

QoS which reflect the end-to-end network feature, that is, namely network performance (NP). The network cannot understand the meaning of higher layer's QoS parameters. For instance, the definition of an image is described by the quantity of pels/frame, which is no sense for network. Only when it is translated into such as bandwidth parameter, can it be understood by network. Thus, it is necessary that application layer's QoS should be translated into ATM layer's QoS, and the QoS translation finally results in the NP parameters. The translation goes beyond this paper.

## 2.2 ATM layer's QoS parameter and NP

The QoS requirement is specified in terms of bounds on QoS parameter. These bounds can be either deterministic or statistical [7].

- Deterministic bound

QoS_Parameter $\leqslant$ Upper_bound

QoS_Parameter $\geqslant$ Lower_bound

- Statistical bound

Prob(QoS_Parameter $\leqslant$ Upper_bound) $\geqslant$ Prob_bound

Prob(QoS_Parameter $\geqslant$ Lower_bound) $\leqslant$ Prob_bound

For the sake of simplicity, we consider only deterministic bounds in this paper. For example, the ATM layer's QoS parameter and its bound are described as follow.

- Cell Loss Ratio(CLR) bound: $CLR_{max}$. It is an ATM specific parameter that results mainly from the buffer overflow in ATM switches due to congestion.

- Throughput bound: $W_{min}$. The throughput requirements at the ATM layer are given in terms of $W_{min}$ parameter. In the ATM layer, throughput bound describes the minimum bandwidth requested within a connection. This may correspond to the cell rate in traffic parameter when there is no use of the fast resource management in Available Bit Rate(ABR) and ATM Block Transfer(ABT) capabilities.

- Cell Delay and Cell Jitter bound: $D_{max}$ and $J_{max}$. The delay bound ($D_{max}$), and jitter bound($J_{max}$) in ATM the layer have the same definition as in the AAL with the understanding that these bounds are now concerned with ATM cells, not frames.

- Cell Misinsertion Rate(CMR) bound. The CMR is due to errors in ATM cell header. In our study we choose to neglect the CMR since the ATM switches detect and discard cells having an errored header, and the AAL function efficiently detects misinserted cells and therefore the CMR is negligible compared to the CLR.

The NP parameters are visible only to the network. They are under study in ITU-T [11] and are currently defined as follows:

- Bit Error Ratio(BER)
- Cell Error Ratio(CER)
- Cell Loss Ratio(CLR)
- Cell Misinsertion Rate(CMR)
- Cell Transfer Delay(CTD)
- Cell Delay Variation(CDV) or Jitter
- Severely Errored Cell Block Ratio(SECBR)

## 2.3 QoS management model for ATM layer

As being described above, the key QoS management depends on ATM layer's QoS management. QoS translation finally results in the NP parameters. These parameters determine whether the ATM network fulfills its service contract for a given connection. Thus, we emphasize the QoS management on OAM performance management. We consider the following two principles to define the QoS management model for ATM layer.

1. Protocol machines in user and control planes execute their own functions intelligently with autonomy [12].

2. The functions of upper planes should do more abstracts and integrated functions that lower planes can not control. The function of upper plane reacts to solve a request, when the function of lower plane issues it as an event.

This model is shown as Fig.2. Protocol plane consists of user and control planes, which include QoS translation function, QoS negotiation and maintain mechanism, call admission control (CAC), usage parameter control (UPC), congestion control, and resource control etc.

In layer management, there are extended OAM management function unit, performance OAM function unit, and fault OAM function unit, where, the functions of fault OAM function unit and performance OAM function unit are restricted to the functions specified in ITU-T recommendation I.610. The continuity check and loopback test

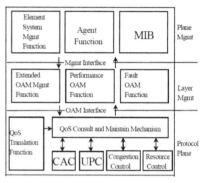

Fig.2   QoS management model for ATM Layer

functions also specified in the standard are executed as subfunction of fault and performance OAM functions. The extended OAM function unit act as an upper plane function of the protocol plane. He monitors the performance status of protocol machines and operates on them properly. The protocol machines adjust their action to guarantee the QoS for the existent connections according to the monitoring results. Meanwhile, the extended OAM function unit notifies the plane management the monitoring results. The OAM interface is defined between plane management and layer management. The management interface is also necessary between layer management and protocol plane.

Plane management consists of agent function unit, MIB unit and element system management unit. The element system management unit is responsible for the control in the level of whole switching system. MIB is a unit to store the managed objects, which are the abstraction of logical or physical resource. Agent function unit handles network management messages, it realizes the access to managed objects defined in MIB.

So, the process of QoS management can be concluded as following:

① QoS translation and classification. Translate users' QoS parameters to each layer's QoS parameters until NP parameters in ATM layer.

② QoS negotiation and setup. QoS consult and maintain mechanism demand the resource control through CAC. If there is enough resource, the connection meet the QoS requirement is set up, and then, the service begin with the actions of UPC and congestion control.

③ NP parameters monitoring, reporting, and storage. Once the connection is set up, the

OAM functions, periodically or depending on requirement, monitor and report NP parameter, reflect these parameters to plane management, and store it to MIB.

④ QoS notification. Plane management should notify the degraded QoS information to network manager.

## 3. The extended scheme for OAM performance management

In general, a connection has the route via several networks, which have heterogeneous configurations, topologies and protocol functions. But in ITU-T I.610, however, the method to select segment boundary is not defined. So, in this paper, we simply adopt the method that each ingress switching system node can be chosen as segment endpoints according to the purpose of performance management. As show in Fig.3, segment endpoints can be 1, 4, and 8. We hypothesize that the route of the VCC connection is (S, 1, 3, 4, 5, 7, 8, 10, D), then the definition of the end-to-end and segment of F5 and F4 flow is shown as Fig.3.

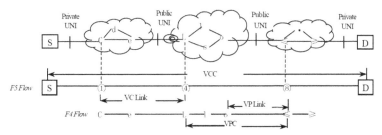

Fig.3   Illustration of definition of the end-to-end and segment of F5 and F4 flow

### 3.1 The extended mechanism

The extended scheme is to monitor more detail information about network performance, to provide it to traffic control functions, and to support QoS management mechanism. The scheme has two principles described as following.

1. Depending on the purpose of management function, monitoring boundary is switched between end-to-end range and segment range. End-to-end monitoring is used in the general management mode, while, segment monitoring is used to find out the switching system at which performance is degraded seriously, after detecting a degradation of performance in the general management mode.

2. Functions are discriminated between F4 and F5 flow. The functions of F4 flow support network-operating mechanism in view of network provider. Meanwhile, the functions of F5 flow should be capable of guaranteeing QoS required by users at the connection set up phase.

In the case of end-to-end performance management, forward monitoring OAM cells are inserted at the source endpoint, monitored at the destination endpoint and reported the monitored information to the source endpoint. Intermediate nodes are each ingress switching systems, and can be set to monitor forward monitoring OAM cells, apply some monitored results to traffic control functions, and check the status and performance of services in analyzing backward reporting OAM cells sent by the destination endpoint.

In the case of segment monitoring, the source endpoint selects some intermediate nodes and inform them of using a field in forward monitoring OAM cell and these selected nodes should sent a backward reporting OAM cell to the source endpoint immediately. The source endpoint receives backward reporting OAM cells from the selected nodes, extracts information about traffic congestion and the degree of QoS, and determines whether each switching systems have been degraded or not.

### 3.2 Activation

In the unused field of performance management activate/deactivation OAM cell, we define two fields, NC (Node Counter) and NTB (Node Tag Bit), as showing in Fig.4. NC field is used to count the number of nodes between the source and destination endpoints. The intermediate nodes and the destination endpoint increase this field by 1 and sent this information to the source endpoint by performance activation/deactivation confirm OAM cell. This field is finally applied to TNC (Total Node Counter) field of forward monitoring OAM cell. NTB field is used to distinguish the sequence of nodes by bit position. This field is applied to the NTB field of forward monitoring OAM cell to determine the boundary of segment in the case of segment monitoring mode.

### 3.3 Monitoring/Reporting function

Monitoring and reporting functions are defined differently according to monitoring range, end-to-end or segment mentioned in section 3.1. There, we define new fields in forward monitoring OAM cell and backward reporting OAM cell. Fig.5 shows these new fields.

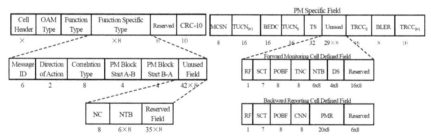

Fig.4 New definition fields of OAM activation/deactivation cell   Fig.5 New definition fields for performance management OAM cell

RF is a range field and it means whether monitoring scope is end-to-end or nor. SCT (Service Class Type) is to classify the service types. That is, this field allows a service provider to provide users with more flexible service. This field determines a set of monitoring and reporting parameters with relation to the next field, POBF (Parameter Optional Bit Field). Some bits set in POBF field means parameters monitored and reported by the destination endpoint. For an example, using SCT and POBF fields, the class may make use of parameters, minimum cell interval, cell error number, cell loss number etc.

As being described above, TNC (Total Node Counter) and NTB (Node Tag Bit) fields is obtained from the performance management activation confirm OAM cell that the destination endpoint sends in the phase of performance management activation. The source endpoint sets some bits in NTB field of the forward monitoring OAM cell to select nodes as segment boundary nodes in the case of segment performance management mode.

DS (Delay Stamp) field means the total delay time when the forward monitoring OAM cell pass through switching systems. Each switching system records the time of ingressive and egressive forward monitoring OAM cell, so the balance of the two data is the time which forward monitoring OAM cell pass through the switching system. This time include switching delay and queuing delay, whereas, the propagation delay is easy to get. Therefore, we can get the exact CTD, and then get CDV [13].

CNN (Current Node Number) field is used to notify which node sends backward reporting OAM cells. So, the value of this field is the same as the sequence number that each intermediate nodes and the destination endpoint has incremented by 1 in the phase of performance management activation. PMR (Parameter Monitoring Result) field is only used in backward reporting OAM cell and contains monitoring results.

We consider some scenarios applying new fields as followed. In the case of end-to-end performance management mode, the value of RF field is zero, where NTB field is ignored and monitoring and reporting functions are only performed in the destination endpoint. The destination endpoint processes monitoring and reporting functions based on the parameters set in POBF field. The information obtained by monitoring function is encoded to PMF field and sent to the source endpoint. The source endpoint and intermediate nodes can copy this backward reporting OAM cell to check the degree and the status of QoS parameters negotiated by connection admission control. In addition, they make use of the information to support traffic control functions. Of course, reporting information should be translated into analyzed information through a simple analyzing function defined in section 3.4.

In the case of segment performance management mode, RF bit is set to 1. The source endpoint makes use of NTB field to notify segment endpoint to intermediate nodes which are chosen as segment endpoint execute monitoring function and immediately send a backward reporting OAM cell to the source endpoint.

### 3.4 Analyzing reporting information

The source endpoint having received these backward reporting OAM cells analyzes reporting information and obtains useful information for QoS management. Through analyzing functions, switching system could extract information such as CLR (Cell Loss Ratio), CER (Cell Error Ratio), CTD (Cell Transfer Delay), ACR (Average Cell Rate), CDV (Cell Delay Variation) and so on. They are calculated by the following simple formula.

$$CLR = \frac{Cell\ Loss\ Number}{Total\ User\ cell} \quad (1) \qquad CER = \frac{Cell\ Error\ Number}{Total\ User\ cell} \quad (2)$$

$$CMR = \frac{Cell\ Misinsertion\ Number}{Total\ User\ cell} \quad (3) \qquad CTD = \sum_{i=1}^{n} T_i + Cell\ \Pr opagate\ Delay \quad (4)$$

$$ACR = \frac{Total\ User\ cell}{CTD} \quad (5)$$

## 4. Conclusions

With the discussion between QoS and networks performance parameter, an ATM layered QoS management scheme is proposed. The model's protocol machine, which supports intelligent and autonomic mechanism [12], is composed of user plane and control plane. With the machine's support, the QoS management is divided into layer management and plane management two levels. It also provides the interfaces among these layers and network management system. To realize the model, we extend the OAM functions defined in ITU-T I.610. According to this method, we can extract more detail information of the network performance information and the status of the given connection. This model emphasizes on the feedback mechanism of ATM network performance monitoring. Some new added fields defined in reserved field separate the boundaries of end-to-end monitoring and segment-to-segment monitoring in whole switch system. According to the difference of management goal, the former is called general management mode, and the latter is used for concrete segment problem monitoring when problem is detected in general management mode. Our study shows that the improvement is feasible and efficient in QoS management mechanism.

This method, however, might increase processing load of switching systems and let switching systems more complex. Therefore, studies about optimized architecture linking this method with related QoS management should be done continuously, and then encoding method of monitoring/reporting parameters will be required in the future.

## References

[1]. J.I Jung and D.Seret (1992), "Quality of Service in B-ISDN and relation with network management", *Proc. IEEE ICC'92*, Chicago.

[2]. K.Nahrstedt and J.Smith (1995), "The QOS broker", *IEEE Multimedia* 2(1).

[3]. J.I.Jung and A.Gravey (1993), "QoS Management and Performance Monitoring in ATM Network", *GLOBECOM'93* PP.708-712.

[4]. A.Cambell, G.Coulson, F.Garcia, D.Hutchison and h.Leopold (1993), "Integrated Quality of Service for Multimedia Communications", *INFOCOM'93*, 740-747.

[5]. *ITU-T Recommendation I-610* (1995), "B-ISDN Operation and Maintenance Principle and Functions", Geneva, Switzerland.

[6]. *ITU-T, Draft Recommendation* I-350 (1992), "General aspect of quality of Service and Network Performance in digital network, including ISDNs".

[7]. J.I.Jung (1996), "Translation of User's QOS requirements into ATM performance parameters in B-ISDN", *Computer Networks and ISDN System* 28(1996), 1754-1767.

[8]. L.Cheng (1997), "Quality of Service based on both call admission and cell scheduling", *Computer Networks and ISDN System* 29(1997) 555-562

[9]. C.Aurrecoechea, A.T.Campbell and L.Hauw (1996), "A Survey of QOS Architecture", *Multimedia System Journal, Special Issues on QOS Architecture*.

[10]. ATM Forum (1996), "Traffic Management Specification Version 4.0", *ATM Forum/af-tm-0056.000*.

[11]. *ITU-T, Draft Recommendation I-356 (1995)*, "B-ISDN ATM layer cell transfer performance".

[12]. D.Galti and G.Pujolle (1996), "Performance Management Issues in ATM Networks: Traffic and Congestion Control", *IEEE/ACM Trans. on Networking* Vol.4 No. 2, 247-257.

[13]. Thomas M.Chen, Steve S.Liu (1996), "David wang, Monitoring and Control of ATM Networks Using Special Cells", *IEEE Network September/October*, PP 28-38.

# Performance Evaluation of Local Recovery Retransmission in Reliable Multicast

Miki YAMAMOTO, Takashi HASHIMOTO, Hiromasa IKEDA
Department of Communications Engineering, Osaka University
2-1 Yamadaoka, Suita, Osaka 565-0871 JAPAN
e-mail: yamamoto@comm.eng.osaka-u.ac.jp

## Abstract

In reliable multicast communications, retransmission control plays an important role. Previous works show that implosion of control packets, e.g. ACKs or NAKs, degrades total performance of reliable multicast communications. Local recovery which enables receivers receiving a packet successfully to initiate recovery of a lost packet has a possibility to solve this scalability problem. This paper presents performance evaluation of local recovery in reliable multicast communication. There seems to be many features dominating performance of local recovery, the number of nodes in a group, shared loss occured simultaneously at multiple receivers and so on. When the number of receivers in a group increases, a geographical expansion of a group will degrade the delay performance of the receivers. With a configuration in which most nodes in local-recovery group suffer from a shared loss, failure of local recovery degrades total performance. Our simulation results under a hierarchical network topology like the real Internet show that a local-recovery group configration with two-adjacent MANs grouping performs well.

**Keywords**  Reliable Mulitcast, Local Recovery, Retransmission, IP Multicast

## 1  Introduction

Multicast communications can be classified into two categories; real-time and reliable, based on their quality requirement[1].  The former includes audio or video multicasting.  The latter includes wb(whiteboard)[2][3], stock information dissemination and DIS(Distributed Interactive Simulation)[4][5]. Multicast communication in the Internet can be supported by IP multicast[6][7]. IP multicast uses UDP as transport layer protocol, so it can only support best-effort reliability. In order to support reliability for IP multicast, retransmission control is necessary for transport layer. NAK-based retransmission scheme is more applicable to scalable reliable multicast communications due to ACK implosion[8].

Even when NAK-based retransmission scheme is applied, implosion of control packet (NAK packet) is also a technical problem for scalability in reliable multicast communications[8][9]. One sophisticated approach to resolve this problem is local recovery, in which a receiver receiving a packet correctly recovers loss of a corresponding packet. In local recovery, a recovery packet should be spreaded locally. To restrict a scope of recovery, a whole multicast group is divided into several subgroups and recovery packets cannot be expanded beyond its subgroup. RMTP[10], LGC[11] and TMTP[12] are examples of reliable multicast protocol adopting local recovery.

Subgroup configuration is an important technical issue for local recovery. With too large subgroup, control packet implosion cannot be avoided and delay performance also may be degraded with expansion of goegraphical distance among nodes inside a subgroup.  With too small subgroup, a probability of no receiver inside a subgroup receiving a corresponding packet correctly becomes large, which may degradade delay performance.  The paper evaluates local recovery performance in reliable multicast

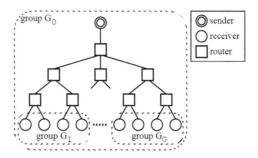

Figure 1: Subgroup Constructin for Local Recovery

communications under various conditions. The purpose of the paper is to indicate general guideline for subgroup configuration for local recovery in reliable multicast communications.

The remainder of this paper is structured as follows. Section 2 presents generic local recovery protocol which will be treated in the whole of the paper. Section 3 shows simulation results obtained with a network model reflecting the Internet structure and presents profound discussion about subgroup configuration in the Internet. Section 4 concludes this paper.

## 2 Local recovery protocol

In this section, we describe a generic local recovery protocol. The purpose of the paper is not to propose a new local recovery protocol but show a generic performance of local recovery protocol. So, protocol treated here is a generic one which includes general characteristics of local recovery protocol.

In the whole multicast group denoted $G_0$, a sender included in $G_0$ intends to multicast packets to all nodes in $G_0$. For local recovery, the whole multicast group $G_0$ is assumed to be divided exclusively into G subgroups, $G_g(g = 1, 2, \cdots, G)$, as shown in Fig.1.

We will mainly focus on a *generic* protocol which exhibits the following behavior rather than on a specific protocol:

- Whenever the sender transmits a packet, it multicasts it to all receivers in $G_0$.

- Whenever a receiver detects packet loss by gap of a sequence number of received packet, it schedules a pending NAK transmission at a randomly chosen point of time in the future. We call this randomly chosen timer interval "a NAK timer" for short.

- A receiver which schedules a pending NAK transmission,

  - cancels the transmission of its own pending NAK, if it receives a NAK (generated by another receiver) for this packet. This is called NAK supression. After NAK suppression, a receiver re-starts a NAK timer which will work for lost of NAK.

  - cancels the transmission of its own pending NAK, if it receives a corresponding packet.

  - multicasts a NAK, and re-starts a NAK timer, if, at the scheduled time for a pending NAK transmission, a NAK for this packet has not been received nor a corresponding packet has not been received since the pending NAK transmission was first scheduled. The first NAK since detecting a lost packet is transmitted only to a subgroup $G_i$ to which this receiver belongs. The second and following NAK transmission is multicasted to the whole group $G_0$ because the local recovery is failed.

- Whenever a receiver receives a NAK, if it has a corresponding packet, it starts a random timer. We call this randomly chosen timer interval "a recovery timer" for short. And if a recovery timer expires without receiving a corresponding packet transmitted by another receiver or a sender, it multicasts a corresponding packet. If a NAK is for a subgroup $G_i$, it multicasts a packet only to subgroup $G_i$. If a NAK is for a whole group $G_0$, it multicasts to $G_0$.

- Whenever the sender receives a NAK, it starts a recovery timer. And if a recovery timer expires without receiving a corresponding packet transmitted by a receiver, it multicasts a corresponding packet. If a NAK is for a subgroup $G_i$, it multicasts a packet only to subgroup $G_i$. If it is for a whole group $G_0$, it multicasts to $G_0$.

NAK timer started at a receiver when it detects a lost packet, enables NAK suppression mechanism. Recovery timer also enables recovery packet suppression, which suppresses redundant retransmission of a corresponding packet.

## 3 Subgroup configuration

In the real Internet, location of packet loss depends on network topology. In this section, adequate subgroup configuration for local recovery is investigated by using a sophisticated network model kreflecting real Internet hirearchical structure.

### 3.1 Packet Loss in Multicast Communication

In [13], packet loss behavior in the real Internet is measured by observing multicast packets at several geographically distributed points. It investigates local and time dependency of packet loss in the real Internet. In [13], the following observation is presented,

- Packet loss probability at Mbone is almost below 0.4%, i.e. little packet loss is observed in a backbone network.

- Between a Mbone node and a receiver, packet loss probability of a few percent is observed in some links.

- Between a Mbone node and the sender, i.e. at the source link, loss probability of about 5% is observed.

- All receivers belonging to the same LAN observe the same packet loss.

These characteristics of packet loss at the Internet has an effect on local recovery from the following viewpoints,

- Receivers in the same LAN suffers from the same packet loss, so local recovery always fails if a subgroup is constructed only with these receivers.

- When a cause of packet loss observed between a Mbone node and a receiver is mainly packet loss occured at a MAN gateway, receivers in the same MAN suffers from the same packet loss. This means that this kind of packet loss cannot be recovered by local recovery with a subgroup configuration of receivers in the same MAN.

- Packet loss at Mbone is especially low. So, subgroup configuration with different MANs connected through Mbone is a very promising way. However, geographical scope of a subgroup has a tendency to be extended because a subgroup configuration is through backbone network.

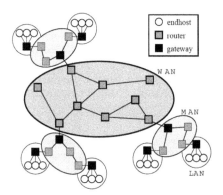

| | |
|---|---|
| ○ | endhost |
| ▣ | router |
| ■ | gateway |

Figure 2: Tiers Model

## 3.2 Performance Evaluation by Internet Model

In this section, a sophisticated network model, Tiers model[14] which reflects real Internet hierarchical structure is used in order to investigate how local dependency of packet losses in multicast communication affects to performance of local recovery. Figure 2 shows overview of a network model generated by Tiers model. As shown in Fig.2, Tiers model has three layer hierarchical structure with LAN, MAN and WAN. WAN is corresponding to Mbone in IP multicast communications. Assumptions used in this section are listed in Table 1. As shown in Table 1, time is normalized with average packet processing time of a receiver.

NAK timer interval is assumed to be as follows,

- For the first NAK : $[0, 10\tau_G]$

- For the second NAK : $13\tau_G + [0, 10\tau_S]$

- For the third and following NAK: $13\tau_s + [0, 10\tau_S]$

where $\tau_G$ is propagation delay to the farthest receiver in a subgroup and $\tau_S$ is propagation delay to the sender. Random timer interval is similarly set up as reference [8]. Recovery timer is also set up as $[0, 10\tau]$.

In this section, average delay of lost packet and total hop count of NAK/data packet per packet is used as performance measure. *Average delay of lost packet* is average time interval between generation time of a lost packet at the sender and successful reception time at a receiver. This performance metric can evaluate "how efficiently a lost packet is recovered". We call this performance metric average delay of lost packet in the paper. *Total hop count of NAK per packet* is computed as follows,

$$\frac{\sum_{k=1}^{N} \sum_{l=1}^{n_k} H_{k,l}^{NAK}}{N},$$

where $N$, $n_k$ and $H_{k,l}^{NAK}$ denotes total number of generated data packets, total number of generated NAKs for $k$-th generated data packet and the total number of hops of a $l$-th generated NAKs for $k$-th generated data packet, respectively. Total hop count of NAK indicates how many links in a network generated NAKs go through in total. Thus, it has proportional relationship with bandwidth used by NAK transmission. Total hop count of data packet is computed as follows,

Table 1: Assumptions for simulation

| Arrival Rate | $\lambda = 0.125$ |
|---|---|
| Packet Processing time | 1(normalized, exponentially distributed) |
| NAK Processing time | 0.2 (exponentially distributed) |
| number of receives | $R = 192$<br>Number of MAN: 8<br>Number of LAN per MAN: 8<br>Number of receivers in LAN: 3 |
| Average Propagation delay | WAN: $\tau_W = 10.0$    MAN: $\tau_M = 2.0$<br>LAN: $\tau_L = 1.0$ |

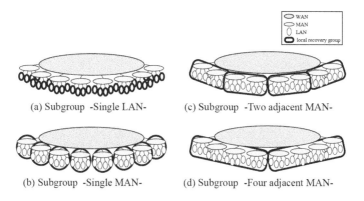

(a) Subgroup -Single LAN-        (c) Subgroup -Two adjacent MAN-

(b) Subgroup -Single MAN-        (d) Subgroup -Four adjacent MAN-

Figure 3: Subgroup configurations

$$\frac{\sum_{k=1}^{N} \sum_{m=1}^{d_k} H_{k,m}^{data}}{N},$$

where $d_k$ denotes the number of transmission of data packet. If data packet is only sent once i.e. no retransmission is necessary for successful reception of data packet to all receivers, $n_k = 1$. $H_{k,m}^{data}$ denotes total number of hops of $k$-th generated data packet in $m$-th transmission (original transmission is 1st transmission). Total hop count of data packet also indicates network bandwidth used by data packets in total.

There can be a lot of ways of subgroup configuration. To make discussion simple, we choose following four subgroup configurations(Fig.3).

**L: Subgroup of single LAN**
As shown in Fig.3 (a), each subgroup for local recovery is constructed with a single LAN, and local recovery is carried out inside this subgoup, i.e. a single LAN.

**M-1: Subgroup of single MAN**
Each subgroup is constructed with a single MAN and local recovery is carried out inside a single MAN(Fig.3 (b)).

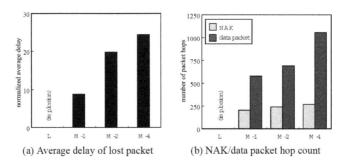

(a) Average delay of lost packet      (b) NAK/data packet hop count

Figure 4: Characteristics under shared loss at LAN gateway

**M-2: Subgroup of two adjacent MANs**
As depicted in Fig.3 (c), each subgroup is constructed with two adjacent MANs. Local recovery is carried out in these two MANs.

**M-4: Subgroup of four adjacent MANs**
Each subgroup is constructed with four adjacent MANs and local recovery is carried out in these four MANs(Fig.3 (d)).

We evaluate local recovery with these four type of subgroup configurations under two conditions, i.e. shared loss at LAN gateway and at MAN gateway. In the former case, shared loss tends to occur at a LAN gateway, so all receivers in the same LAN connected to a corresponding LAN gateway suffer from loss of the same packet. In the latter case, shared loss has a tendency to occur at a MAN gateway, i.e. all receivers in the same MAN suffer from loss of the same packet. How to implement these subgroup configuration is also an important technical issue for local recovery. There have been proposed several methods for local recovery implementation, e.g. using TTL field in IP header, preparing each multicast group for each subgroup and making use of adminisitrative scoping[3]. Some of them, e.g. preparing a multicast group for each subgroup and administrative scoping, can be applied for implementing the above subgroup configuration. Main purpose of the paper is to show a general guideline for subgroup configuration, so we would like to leave this implementation issue for further research.

**[Shared Loss at LAN Gateway]**
In this case, packet loss probability at a WAN router, a MAN gateway and a LAN gateway is assumed to be 0.002, 0.002 and 0.02, respectively. This means that shared loss at LAN gateway has larger probability to happen.

Figures 4(a) and 4(b) show average delay of lost packet and total hop count of NAK/data packet, respectively. In Fig.4(a), average delay is normalized with propagation delay averaged among all pairs of receivers. When subgroup configuration **L** is applied, data/NAK implosion is observed. This is because in subgroup configuration **L**, local recovery always fails due to shared loss in a LAN, which leads to increase of NAK packets. Increase of NAK packets causes overload inside a network and packet loss in a network, which causes much more NAK transmission and implosion of NAK and data packets. Among other three configurations, **M-1** has the minimum average delay. From total hop count characteristics in Fig.4(b), configuration **M-1** has the minimum hop count. With increase of subgroup scope, hop count necessary for reaching all receivers simply increases and probability of retransmission increases, which leads to increase of hop count and also delay performance.

**[Shared Loss at MAN Gateway]**

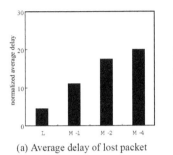 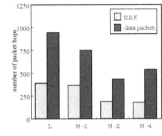

(a) Average delay of lost packet    (b) NAK/data packet hop count

Figure 5: Characteristics under shared loss at MAN gateway and $R = 192$

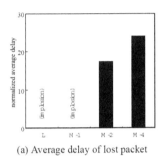 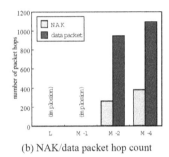

(a) Average delay of lost packet    (b) NAK/data packet hop count

Figure 6: Characteristics under shared loss at MAN gateway and $R = 384$

In this case, packet loss probability of a WAN router, a MAN gateway and a LAN gateway is assumed to be 0.002, 0.02 and 0.002, respectively, i.e. shared loss in a single MAN has larger probability to happen. Figures 5(a) and 5(b) show averege delay and NAK/data packet hop count characteristics. For delay characteristics, subgroup configuration **L** has the minimum average delay. With configuration **L**, local recovery cannot be expected because all receivers in a LAN suffer from loss of the same packet, so **L** would have had the worst characteristics. However, propagation delay inside a LAN is very small, so random timer interval has short interval as well. This leads to small delay even with failure of local recovery. However, as shown in Fig.5(b), retransmission overhead and NAK transmission overhead is maximum among four configurations. This is because failure of local recovery brings global NAK transmission and global re-multicast of data packet. Thus, from the viewpoint of consuming network bandwidth, **L** has the worst characteristics.

In addition, we also evaluate similar characteristics for larger number of receivers, $R = 384$. In this case, the number of MAN is 16 and othre parameters are the same as shown in Table 4. Figures 6(a) and 6(b) show average delay and NAK/data packet hop count characteristics under $R = 384$. For configuration **L** and **M-1**, divergence of delay performance due to implosion is observed. In other two cases where no implosion occurs, **M-2** has smaller average delay and hop count of NAK/data packet. In the case that $R = 192$, **M-2** also has better performance than **M4**.

From these simulation results, guideline for subgroup configuration can be descrived as follows,

- From the viewpoint of delay characteristics, subgroup of narrow geographical scope is preferable.

- From the viewpoint of overhead for retransmission of data packet and transmission of NAK, subgroup configuration in which all recievers in a subgroup suffer from shared loss is a bad choice.

As packet loss in the Internet has tendency to occur at a MAN and LAN gateway, shared loss at a single LAN and at a single MAN has larger probability to occur than ohter type of shared loss. Thus, subgroup configuration with two adjacent MAN (**M-2**) is the optimal one.

## 4  Conclusions

In the paper, we evaluate local recovery in reliable multicast communications. We use a sophisticated network model which reflects hirearchical structure of the Internet, Tiers model, to evaluate local recovery. Also, packet loss assumptions obtained from the real Internet observation are assumed in this evaluation. With this model, how local dependency of packet loss in the Internet affects to local recovery performance is evaluated. Simulation results obtained from this model show that subgroup configuration with two adjacent MAN is a good choice because it has appropriate delay characteristics with small overhead necessary for retransmission.

Further research includes the way to implement the obtained preferable subgroup configuration in reliable multicast communications.

## References

[1] Georg Carle and Ernst W. Biersack, "Survey of Error Recovery Techniques for IP-Based Audio-Visual Multicast Applications," *IEEE Network Magazine*, Vol.11, No.6, pp.24-36, December 1997.

[2] V.Jacobson and S.McCanne, "LBL Whiteboard: wb," Lawrence Berkley Laboratory, on-line software: ftp://ftp.ee.lbl.gov/conferencing/wb.

[3] Sally Floyd, Van Jacobson, Ching-Gung Liu and Steve McCanne, "A Reliable Multicast Framework for Light-Weight Sessions and Application Level Framing," *IEEE/ACM Transactions on Networking*, VOl.5, No.6, pp.784-803, December 1997.

[4] Institute for Simulation and Training, "Standard for Distributed Interactive Simulation - Application Protocols-," Technical Report IST-CR-94-50, University of Central Florida, Orlando, FL, 1994.

[5] H.Holbrook, S.Singal and D.Cheriton, "Log-Based Receiver- Reliable Multicast for Distributed Interactive Simulation," *Proc. ACM Sigcomm95*, pp.342-356, Boston, August 1995.

[6] S.Deering, "Host Extentions for IP Multicasting," *RFC-1112*, August 1989.

[7] S. Deering and D. Cheriton, "Host Groups: A Multicast Extension to the Internet Protocol," RFC-966, Dec. 1985.

[8] Miki Yamamoto, Jim Kurose, Don Towsley and Hiromasa Ikeda, " A Delay Analysis of Sender-Initiated and Receiver-Initiated Reliable Multicast Protocols," *IEEE INFOCOM'97*, 4C-4, Kobe, April 1997.

[9] M.Yamamoto, T.Hashimoto and H.Ikeda "Performance Evaluation of Reliable Multicast Communication Protocols under Heterogeneous Transmission Delay," *Proc. 11th ITC Specialist Seminor*, pp.9–16, Oct. 1998.

[10] J.C. Lin and S. Paul, "RMTP: A Reliable Multicast Transport Protocol," *IEEE INFOCOM'96*, pp.1414-1424, San Francisco, March 1996.

[11] M. Hoffmann, "Enabling Group Communication in Global Network," *Proc. Global Networking '97*, vol.II, pp.321–330, June 1997.

[12] R. Yavatkar, J. Griffioen and M. Sudan "A Reliable Dissemination Protocol for Interactive Collaborative Applications," *Proc. ACM Multimedia '95 conference*, pp.333–344, Nov. 1995.

[13] M. Yajnik, J. Kurose and D. Towsley "Packet Loss Correlation in the MBone Multicast Network," *Proc. 1996 IEEE GLOBECOM Global Internet*, pp.94–99, Nov. 1996.

[14] M.B. Doar, "A Better Model for Generating Test Network," *Proc. 1996 IEEE GLOBECOM Global Internet*, pp.86–93, Nov. 1996.

# Performance Analysis of Cut-Through Bridged Controller Area Networks

M. Tenruh, I. Erturk, E. Stipidis and M. J. English

University of Sussex
School of Engineering and Information Technology
Brighton, BN1 9QT, UK
e-mail: m.tenruh@sussex.ac.uk

## Abstract

The CAN protocol was initially specified for automotive applications, but rapidly it has also become a standard in industrial distributed real time control applications. Although CAN is an appropriate choice for real time control systems, it has a bus length limitation due to its medium access and error recovery mechanisms. Extending the CAN busses provides wider application choices, especially in industrial distributed control environments. This paper investigates possible solutions for extending CAN systems and introduces a novel approach, which provides extension beyond the present limitations. Simulation results show that the new design introduces much less delay than the conventional ones with no significant extra load introduced to the system.

## Keywords:

Controller Area Network (CAN), Bridges, Network Interconnection.

## 1. Introduction

A Controller Area Network (CAN) is an asynchronous real-time serial communication bus with high performance and a robust error recovery mechanism. CAN was first developed for combining all electrical controls on a serial data bus in automotive applications. Due to its small size, low cost and high speed, CAN technology has also become popular for industrial environments.

The CAN standard corresponds to Layers 1 (Physical layer), and 2 (Data link layer) of the OSI reference model. A scheme, known as non-destructive bit-wise arbitration, is used for medium access control. In this scheme, each station on the CAN bus has a unique identifier and this identifier is used for arbitration. While a station is competing for the bus, it also observes if its data is the same as the data on the bus. If different, the node assumes that a higher priority message is already on the bus and switches to receiving mode. In this way, the highest priority message is ensured to get the bus while lower priority messages are sent later. With this method, no time is wasted on collisions and valuable bandwidth is saved.

However, this arbitration mechanism limits the bus length, because all stations have to observe each other within a period of one bit time. Because of the propagation delay on a bus, CAN segments have to be short, only 40m at 1 Mbps. In industrial applications, to extend the network size provides more efficient use of large scale distributed control systems. Two solutions can be introduced to increase the useable distance. The first is to decrease the data rate, hence the time for one bit is increased. The second solution is to use additional interconnection devices, such as bridges.

Bridges can be used in CAN systems, because bridged subnets do not participate in the same medium access arbitration. Besides extending the network, bridges also introduce additional delay, which may impact on the performance of the real time networks. This paper provides performance analysis of a new design, which enables the use of CAN systems beyond their present distance limitations via cut-through bridges.

## 2. Cut-through Bridging and Controller Area Networks

Reducing the data rate to extend a CAN bus as a single segment is not a desirable solution for real-time control applications. Therefore, only the second solution, which is extending with interconnection devices, remains as an efficient option to extend CAN.

Bridges are intelligent devices and operate on the Data Link layer (Halsall, F. 1996). In a bridged CAN, each segment has independent medium access arbitration (Thomas, G. M. 1998). In this way, a CAN to CAN bridge doubles the network length. On the other hand, bridges also introduce an additional delay for storing and forwarding processes.

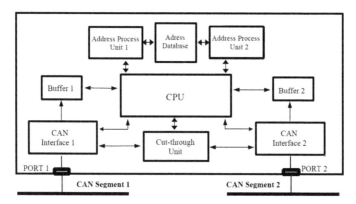

**Figure 1. The CAN to CAN cut-through bridge model.**

Cut-through bridges are used for interconnection of similar networks (Kwok and Mukherjee, 1990). Figure 1 shows the cut-through bridge model connecting CAN systems (Tenruh, Stipidis, and English, 1999). A Cut-through bridge reduces the delay caused by a normal bridge in the following way. In a normal bridge, each message received from one segment is stored and the address is compared with the forwarding database to decide whether the message should be discarded or forwarded. In the case of CAN, the arbitration field is used for the address database.

With a cut-through bridge, when a CAN message arrives from one segment, first, the other segment is checked to see whether it is free or busy. If the other CAN bus is free, the message is forwarded directly onto the other bus. In this process, the cut-through bridge operates like a repeater, reducing the delay to a minimum. While the forwarding is in progress, the bridge database is searched at the same time. If the CAN message is not to be forwarded, the forwarding operation is ceased. The number of CAN nodes on a single segment is generally low, for example, a maximum of 64 nodes in some applications (Lawrenz, 1997), and the arbitration field used for the forwarding database is just 11 bits for the standard CAN frame (CAN Specification, 1991). This results in a quite short forwarding database and fast address search operation.

If a message arrives on one port of the cut-through bridge while the other CAN bus is busy, the message is stored and the forwarding database is searched. In this case, the cut-through bridge operates like a normal store and forward bridge, introducing more delay.

Cut-through bridges provide some novel facilities for CAN to CAN interconnection. The new design decreases the message latency to the minimum possible, and more importantly, initiates a new arbitration session for the same message on the destination segment. As the main purpose of this work is to extend the capability of a single CAN bus, network topologies with multiple bridges and loops are beyond the scope of this paper.

The importance of the new design is that on the destination segment the re-arbitration for the same message is initiated as soon as the first bit is received from the source segment. This allows one message to be on both segments at the same time, this means that the distance limitation for the arbitration is exceeded. This is especially true at light to moderate loads and as long as immediate forwarding takes place. In this way, two CAN segments connected by cut-through bridges may get the same message almost at the same time. Hence, CAN frames can be sent beyond present distance limitations.

Beside these advantages, cut-through bridged CAN systems also have some disadvantages. Firstly, because of the immediate forwarding, extra traffic is generated on the destination segment. The amount of the extra traffic depends on the location of the arbitration field in the message and the time required searching the forwarding database. As the arbitration field in the CAN frame is located at the beginning of the message, no extra time is spent to receive this field. Secondly, immediate forwarding also does not permit the error handling at the bridge. Extra traffic is generally insignificant, because it occurs at light to moderate loads, and does not impact on the performance of the system. Error handling also does not cause a problem, as all stations have their own error handling mechanisms.

## 3. Modelling and Simulation

In order to explore these concepts network simulation was exploited. The models and simplified operations used for simulation are as described below:

The new design will perform immediate forwarding when the destination segment is idle and there are no frames in the queue of the bridge to forward. The forwarding operation will be terminated if a higher priority message is detected on the destination bus, or if the bridge determines that the message is not to be forwarded. With the acceptance filtering technique (Lawrenz, 1997), only those messages that have passed the acceptance filter hardware are forwarded by the bridge. In this case, the address search delay includes the time required to receive the identifier field of a CAN message, and the filter hardware delay, negligible compared to the total message delay. In the simulations, a CAN bus is extended with and without bridges:

A single 500 kbps segment represents the extended bus without bridging. In this model a single bus distance is doubled. While the original bus speed was 1 Mbps, in the extended bus this data rate was reduced to 500 kbps. A single 1 Mbps segment represents a CAN bus without extension. This is particularly useful to study the delay performance of the cut-through bridge. Figure 3 shows the model used for extended 500 kbps segment, and 1 Mbps segment. The only difference between the models is the speeds of the buses and consequently the lengths of the systems.

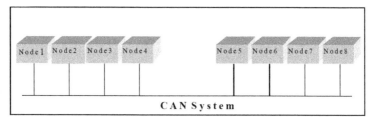

**Figure 3. The model for 1Mbps and 500 kbps CAN systems.**

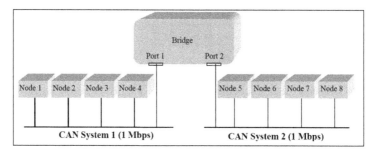

**Figure 4. The model for normal and cut-through bridged CAN systems.**

A normal bridge model interconnects two 1 Mbps CAN segments, the network distance is doubled and conventional store and forward operations are performed. When a bridge is used for extension, the original bus speed is preserved, while still doubling the bus distance. However, the normal bridge introduces additional delay for the storing and forwarding processes. A cut-through bridge model connects two 1 Mbps CAN buses, performs immediate forwarding and conventional forwarding as required. To reduce the additional delay, a CAN to CAN cut-through bridge is introduced and results are compared. Figure 4 illustrates the model to connect two CAN buses with a bridge. Both normal and cut-through bridge models have been used in the simulation. The lowest priority messages have been chosen to determine the worst case delays. 70% and 30% of the messages are assumed to be addressed to the local and remote segments respectively.

Message delay includes the bus access time and message travel time from the source to the destination nodes. For bridged models, message travel time also includes the bridge process delay in addition to the bus access and message travel time from the source node on one segment to the destination node on the other segment.

## 4. Performance Analysis

The operation and performance of the models were investigated under light, moderate and heavy loads. Although it is not feasible to describe certain limits for these load classifications, approximate values can be given based on the single segment 1 Mbps CAN segment for comparison purposes. System can be accepted as light loaded when the throughput is less than 30%. Up to the throughput less than 60%, the system load is moderate and over 60% throughput, the message delay rises quickly and the system is heavy-loaded (Tenruh, Stipidis, and English, 1999).

At light loads, immediate forwarding can be performed by the cut through bridge for almost all frames. The probability of the destination segment being idle is high and the delay is small. The load in the new design will be slightly higher because of the immediate forwarding, but it does not affect the throughput, because most of the bandwidth remains unused.

With moderate loads, the probability of finding the destination segment idle is less and only a fraction of the messages will be forwarded immediately. The remaining frames will be buffered and forwarded in a conventional bridging manner. The amount of extra traffic generated during immediate forwarding will be less as the total load increases. This is because a smaller portion of the frames can be forwarded under heavier loads, and the buffered frames whose destination and source are on the same segment will be discarded. The average delay is still less than the normal bridge delay, and throughput remains unaffected.

Under heavy loads, most of the frames will be buffered and only a small portion of them can be forwarded immediately, because the probability that the destination segment is busy will be high. Almost no extra traffic is generated because of the immediate forwarding. The average delay and throughput for both cut-through and normal bridges become closer. The performances of cut-through bridged, normal bridged and single segment CAN models are compared through simulation results. In Figure 5, the results for four different CAN models can be seen. In the figure, the single segment extended CAN model has 500 kbps bus speed. As all the nodes are on the same segment and the bus has half the normal speed with doubled length, the delay rises quickly compared to the others. Although the delay for the normal bridged system model is slightly higher than that of the single segment extended one at low throughputs, it has better delay characteristics at higher data rates, providing the same total system bus extension. In the figure, the results can also be seen for a single CAN bus with 1 Mbps bus speed and without extension. In this case, as the bus speed is 1 Mbps and the bus length is half of the extended one, the delay is the lowest of the all. This graph is important in terms of comparing the cut-through bridged model delay. It can be seen that at low to moderate data rates, the cut-through bridge has almost the same or only slightly higher delay than that of the single segment 1 Mbps model, while doubling the total system bus length. This is not possible with single segment extended or with normal bridged CAN systems. It is achieved by the immediate forwarding feature of the cut-through bridging. At high throughputs, the cut-through bridge operates like a normal bridge and shows similar characteristics since the possibility of immediate forwarding becomes less. Eventually, as almost all messages have to be stored and forwarded and no immediate forwarding is possible, both characteristics merge.

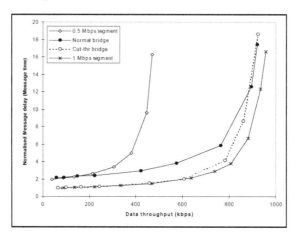

**Figure 5. Message delay versus data throughput.**

The performance of the cut-through bridge is also evaluated with different bus speeds. In order to compare the message delays, the SAE Benchmark values are used. The SAE Benchmark describes a set of signals with different latency requirements (Lawrenz, 1997). In Table 1, classification of the SAE Benchmark signal delays is given. Priority order is shown from high (P1) to low (P6). The table shows the message delay deadlines (D) with priorities and message transmission (T) periods. Benchmark contains 53 data types. Transformed benchmark signals combine all data types in 17 message types. At 125 kbps bus speed the bus has about 85 % utilisation (Lawrenz, 1997).

| 1 Mbps | T (ms) | D (ms) |
|--------|--------|--------|
| P1 | 50 | 5 |
| P2 | 5 | 5 |
| P3 | 10 | 10 |
| P4 | 50 | 20 |
| P5 | 100 | 100 |
| P6 | 1000 | 1000 |

**Table 1. Priority classification of SAE Benchmark message delays.**

| 1 Mbps | 25% | 75% | 85% | 95% | 99% |
|---|---|---|---|---|---|
| M1 | 0.111 | 0.215 | 0.263 | 0.335 | 0.373 |
| M2 | 0.111 | 0.215 | 0.263 | 0.332 | 0.387 |
| M3 | 0.113 | 0.226 | 0.289 | 0.378 | 0.490 |
| M4 | 0.113 | 0.233 | 0.296 | 0.386 | 0.492 |
| M5 | 0.110 | 0.260 | 0.342 | 0.545 | 1.249 |
| M6 | 0.114 | 0.266 | 0.365 | 0.552 | 3.997 |
| M7 | 0.111 | 0.336 | 0.585 | 2.771 | 113.343 |
| M8 | 0.111 | 0.342 | 0.616 | 3.985 | 124.041 |

Table 2. Message delays for 1Mbps cut-through bridged CAN segments.

| 500 Kbps | 24% | 73% | 84% | 95% | 99% |
|---|---|---|---|---|---|
| M1 | 0.210 | 0.366 | 0.462 | 0.510 | 0.578 |
| M2 | 0.203 | 0.386 | 0.450 | 0.533 | 0.637 |
| M3 | 0.208 | 0.401 | 0.499 | 0.629 | 0.942 |
| M4 | 0.206 | 0.412 | 0.518 | 0.672 | 1.044 |
| M5 | 0.202 | 0.457 | 0.659 | 1.008 | 18.091 |
| M6 | 0.208 | 0.480 | 0.673 | 1.129 | 21.571 |
| M7 | 0.220 | 0.673 | 1.455 | 5.374 | 98.122 |
| M8 | 0.211 | 0.720 | 1.701 | 7.106 | 114.002 |

Table 3. Message delays for 500 Kbps cut-through bridged segments.

| 250 Kbps | 25% | 64% | 80% | 92% | 99% |
|---|---|---|---|---|---|
| M1 | 0.417 | 0.657 | 0.815 | 0.893 | 1.219 |
| M2 | 0.432 | 0.718 | 0.770 | 0.988 | 1.259 |
| M3 | 0.402 | 0.728 | 0.876 | 1.166 | 2.100 |
| M4 | 0.398 | 0.695 | 0.972 | 1.250 | 1.835 |
| M5 | 0.434 | 0.771 | 1.054 | 1.958 | 37.543 |
| M6 | 0.419 | 0.876 | 1.079 | 2.113 | 58.951 |
| M7 | 0.426 | 0.932 | 1.820 | 5.652 | 233.158 |
| M8 | 0.428 | 1.055 | 2.060 | 8.914 | 345.509 |

Table 4. Message delays for 250 Kbps cut-through bridged segments.

| 125 Kbps | 25% | 65% | 85% | 92% | 99% |
|---|---|---|---|---|---|
| M1 | 0.848 | 1.299 | 1.629 | 1.781 | 2.759 |
| M2 | 0.834 | 1.279 | 1.819 | 2.003 | 2.965 |
| M3 | 0.824 | 1.406 | 1.888 | 2.218 | 5.031 |
| M4 | 0.835 | 1.361 | 1.999 | 2.237 | 5.105 |
| M5 | 0.818 | 1.545 | 2.770 | 4.034 | 78.226 |
| M6 | 0.854 | 1.700 | 2.847 | 4.180 | 102.635 |
| M7 | 0.806 | 1.729 | 6.632 | 14.466 | 336.644 |
| M8 | 0.798 | 2.159 | 8.618 | 22.150 | 467.075 |

Table 5. Message delays for 125 Kbps cut-through bridged segments.

In Tables 2, 3, 4, and 5, wide ranges of message delays of cut-through bridged CAN segments are evaluated. Message delays are shown according to message priorities and bus utilisation at different bus speeds.Message numbers (Mn) are given in priority order. Bus speeds were chosen according to the standard CAN specifications (CAN Specification, 1991). As can be seen from the tables, cut-through bridged CAN systems have message delays well below the benchmark deadline values.

As the benchmark values give 85% bus utilisation at 125 kbps bus speed, it can be said that not any benchmark deadline is exceeded by the cut-through bridged CAN systems. With 125 kbps bus speed and 85% utilisation only lowest two message delays are above 5 ms. However, these values are still well below the lowest two priority deadline values of the benchmark. The shaded areas in the tables show which benchmark deadline values are exceeded. It only occurs under extreme conditions, mostly over 90% bus utilisation.

## 5. Conclusion

In this study, the basic concepts in extending CAN systems have been investigated. After a brief explanation of CAN bus limitations, possible solutions for bus extension are reviewed and a new solution with cut-through bridging has been introduced.

In real-time applications, like CAN, the message delay is a critical issue, and reduced message delay improves the performance of the whole system. Four different model results have been compared and the advantages of the new approach have been explained. Simulation results showed that a cut-through bridge introduces less delay than a normal bridge with no significant extra load introduced to the system. Also, the comparison of the results with SEA Benchmark values showed that the new model provides acceptable delay performance. This study demonstrates how a cut-through bridge extends the CAN segments with better performance, combining features of both repeaters and normal bridges.

## References

CAN Specification (1991), Version 2.0, Robert Bosch GmbH, Germany.

Halsall, F. (1996), "Data Communications, Computer Networks and Open Systems," Fourth Edition, Addison Wesley Publishing Company Inc.

Kwok, C. K. and Mukherjee, B. (1990), "Cut Through Bridging for CSMA/CD Local Area Networks," IEEE Trans. Commun., vol. 38, no. 7, pp. 938-942.

Lawrenz, W. (1997), "CAN System Engineering From Theory to Practical Applications," Springer-Verlag Inc., New York.

Tenruh, M., Stipidis, E. and English, M. J. (1999), "Design and Software Implementation of a CAN/CAN Cut-through Bridge," Proceedings of the 6th ICC Conference, Torino, Italy,.

Thomas, G. M. (1998), "Real-Time Performance of Bridged CAN Networks," CAN Newsletter, pp. 50-52, Sept.

# A New Architecture for 3<sup>rd</sup> Generation Mobile Networks

Professor Paul Reynolds PhD, BSc(Eng), CEng, FIEE

Orange PCS, St James Court, Great Park Road, Bradley Stoke, Bristol, BS32 4QJ
Tel: +44 7973 746 050
e-mail: paul.reynolds@orange.co.uk

## 1. Introduction

The current mobile communications environment is in a significant state of entropy. Not only is technology enabling the rapid development of new services but also users are becoming more technically aware and demanding that service providers make available more innovative applications.

Computing and telecommunications are becoming more pervasive, and new classes of small, mobile, and, sometimes embedded, devices are becoming available. I estimate that, by the year 2002, more pervasive devices will be sold in Europe than personal computers. Such devices will release intrinsic value to users allowing a more convenient, mobile and productive life style.

The Internet is currently experiencing a metamorphosis by being rebranded as an eCommerce platform this will stimulate the demand to make the pervasive mobile device a commodity. By the end of 2000 I predict that in the UK nearly 5 million mobile users will have regular Internet access. The so-called "chips with everything and everywhere" will ensure that communication becomes only a marginal cost when developing devices that utilise the mobile telecommunications network. Users are finding new ways to fill time, on-net games, conducted over a protracted time period, are already popular, thus billing will no longer only be based upon elapsed time but additionally content, perceived value or gain. Work practices such as teleworking and virtual office are enabling a greater penetration of mobile devices.

The Internet has grown up and is now being used, if not understood, by technophobics. The Internet Protocol (IP) is no longer seen as a protocol but a product that almost every "soft" device comes with an IP plug. It is this ubiquitous nature of IP that makes the Internet a major driver to the form that transport technology takes. IP and pervasive devices will drive the need for IP to become wirefree. Indeed, 3<sup>rd</sup> generation is offering more capacity and when combined with techniques such as application transcodeing and wireless mark-up languages, wirefree IP based access is becoming more wire like but with the advantage of mobility.

The mobile world has a whole host of new technologies on its horizon. High Speed Circuit Switched Data (HSCSD) is available giving increments of 14kbit/s. This will allow either full duplex at 28kbit/s, or, asymmetric Internet access at 43kbit/s to 64kbit/s, six times current data speeds, and matching those offered by the majority of fixed-line modems. General Packet Radio Service (GPRS) and Enhanced Data rates for GSM

Evolution (EDGE) will push up the available data rate to 384kbit/s whilst Universal Mobile Telecommunication System (UMTS) will give 2Mbit/s.

For the core network, the exciting opportunity is the doors that are opened by software radio. The network being able to programme the terminal to support different codecs, applications or services. All these exciting technologies should be with us within the next four years!

Such technologies open up a whole new range of possibilities to the mobile user. Within the office segment, the wide area wireless is enabled. Mobile videophones will become reality – 3$^{rd}$ generation will enable mobile virtual reality and the mobile virtual shops. Even virtual terminals will one day come to existence. Most probably embedded within one at birth – the process of thinking of someone will set-up a call and thus mobile-network-enabled-telepathy becomes a reality.

## 2. Challenges for Mobile Operators

Demands for mobile services are ever increasing. Terminal penetration of over a 100% is expected. The EU has forecast that within the whole of the community there will be more mobile terminals than fixed by the year 2020. For example, Orange has seen over 1.1 million net customer growth in this first quarter, customer growth more than three times faster than 1999. Its current customer base is over 6 million

Also extended coverage and new services will generate greater demand. For example, Orange has become an Internet service provider – offering Internet access from their wirefree network as well as from fixed-line networks. Orange Internet Service Provider (ISP) customers will be able to access the full range of information on offer, including news, sports, travel, weather, entertainment and specially tailored information and entertainment services.

With services becoming more complex and bespoke, it has become necessary to support them overseas for our roamed customers. This requires the use of a virtual home environment, provided with a combination of terminal toolkits and service platforms.

So-called multimedia services are expected where multiple traffic streams converge onto a terminal in support of a single session. Terminals are required to be more generic, supporting the function of the time – one moment a voice terminal, the next a video, thence a browser. Time to market for new services needs to be reduced to a period of weeks rather than months and cost reduced to make service development for a small number of customers desirable. Thus services need to be built of reusable components rather than each being of new code.

Mobility will need to be provided seamlessly over a range of wireless access techniques including handovers between, for example, the public network and the private wireless LAN without service interruption. Additionally, terminals will need to support a range of access technologies like Wide Band Code Division Multiple Access (WB-CDMA), EDGE, Global System for Mobile Communications (GSM), GPRS, Satellite etc.

Intelligence is on the move! Being abstracted away from transport nodes and links to higher levels in the Network Architecture. Orange's network is already Intelligent Network (IN) compliant and we are currently migrating to Long Term IN compliancy. For example, Orange is introducing middleware to support database services; Intelligent User and Terminal agents are being designed that will support the user even whilst in disconnect mode; dumb transportation and switching allowing the use of commodity technology is being experimented with.

## 3. The current GSM architecture

The current mobile network consists of standard GSM network elements enhanced with IN platforms and service nodes. This combination enables Mobile operators to offer, not only an extensive set of popular GSM voice services, but also wire-free, value-added and IN services such as pre-paid and interactive voice messaging.

Only a small proportion of the current subscriber base makes use of the GSM data facilities. This is due to a number of factors, including poor data throughput. Imminent GSM enhancements such as HSCSD, GPRS, Subscriber Identity Module (SIM) toolkit and Mobile Ex-ecution Environment (MEXE) will go some way to improving this situation, providing data rates of up to 100kbit/s and user-friendly services and applications. However, further evolution will be constrained by the dated design and technology used in all parts of the system: terminals, radio, network and operations support.

Most of the hardware platforms used in the GSM infrastructure are of a "telecoms pedigree". Whereas no alternative existed 5 years ago, some of these "antiques" will be replaced by commercially-based IT platforms in the next two years. The business support and IT systems have been custom-made in-house to meet demanding customer and corporate needs. Although this has suited the operators purpose well to date, here too the constraints and limitations are becoming evident as they are being stretched beyond their original design objectives. Thus, as with the network, the time is approaching where a fundamental re-appraisal of the current technology and system design is needed to position operators better in the future.

Architecturally the GSM network can be represented as two concentric rings. The inner ring representing the transport layer that currently hosts call control, mobility management and network databases. Services such as prepaid and its associated data are not tied to the transport layer functions abstracted from the transport in the second ring. This architecture does not allow for the full separation of concerns. For example, the Visitor Location Register (VLR) databases are closely associated with switching matrix and if either becomes fully utilised it is necessary to change the whole irrespective of the status of the other, very inefficient and very costly.

## 4. Motivation for a New Architecture

In moving to UMTS, the operator has two implementation techniques - integration and overlay and two architectural approaches evolution and revolution. In deciding whether to use an integrated or overlay approach the issues of cost, risk and service offering need to be considered. The cost equation is dominated by start-up costs, the need to maximise current investment, operating costs and time to market. An overlay network is quick to provide and captures $3^{rd}$ generation customer first and hopefully holds them. An overlay network does provide challenges at the interworking layer for such functions as handover management. Alternatively, an Integration approach comes with risk. The current GSM network is very reliable and stable. Modifying its architecture and abstracting the intelligence from the transport layer is still an untried technique in a large scale venture and the last thing an operator wants is to upset its existing customer base.

In the integrated core network, buildings, transmission, Mobile Service Centres, Location Registers and Packet Nodes are reused. Traffic will then be routed over circuit switched low latency GSM network or the connectionless GPRS network. This allows one set of core intelligence and service platforms to serve both transport networks and support consistency of service offering. However, the disadvantages include the potential to de-stabilise the current GSM network with multimedia 3rd Generation traffic. Also the GSM service creation environment is not suited to the $3^{rd}$ generation requirements

The overlay approach makes the assumption that the existing GSM network is effectively encapsulated and allows either its use as a support of plain old voice and data services to UMTS customers or allows handover from a UMTS Base Station to a GSM base station when this is the only option and the Quality of Service (QoS) profile of the customer allows such a handover. Thus an overlay approach allows the operator to leave their existing voice and data users in a stable environment and provide a second route to the UMTS services. Dual mode phones will ensure that the user need not be aware of the overlay within the network. However, handover from a high capacity UMTS cell to GSM cell will require careful handling with the use of user agents to support some form of negotiation on whether to allow the handover or drop in the event that the GSM network capabilities prove unacceptable to the user's application.

An overlay network could still use the entire capital infrastructure within a GSM network and by careful arrangement of the protocol stack allowing reuse of transmission. Locating the UMTS functionality upon separate servers to GSM will isolate the performance of the two systems, thereby protecting millions of GSM customers from anticipated "running-in" problems of UMTS. The decision to merge the two systems can be deferred to a convenient, optimal point-in-time in the future, when UMTS is as stable and reliable as GSM now is.

UMTS servers and service nodes will be deployed alongside the GSM ones, thus mirroring the situation in the radio network. The requirements for the UMTS nodes are more demanding, with the need to support multi-media, advanced data services at widely varying bit rates. This separation also enables us to separately scale the GSM and UMTS servers/service nodes. Eventually, the GSM functions will be "folded into" the UMTS nodes, especially when the GSM equipment becomes obsolete.

Independent of whether an overlay or integrated approach is adopted for the core it is possible to take either a revolutionary or evolutionary approach. A revolutionary approach allows for a new open architecture. It is possible that such an architecture will support even a first generation radio access network, albeit not in a standardised way.

The drivers must be openness, distribution, cost and the market and not standards. Having understood that time to market and component constructed services are a pre-requisite to $3^{rd}$ Generation there is a need to reconsider network and service delivery architectures. Nothing should be ruled out at the conceptual stage.

Evolution from current 64kbit/s circuit based, MSC focused control to ATM and outboard server control is already being planned for the Orange GSM1800 network, to reduce operational costs, improve resilience and provide vastly improved flexibility in operation and service deployment.

The UMTS network functionality could be implemented using the same architecture. A common, fibre-based transport network (transmission and basic switching/routing) will need to be implemented to convey all traffic, UMTS, and GSM, based upon ATM technology. This will enable more efficient use of transmission facilities and at a lower cost. The transmission network is currently planned on the basis of microwave links - alternatives will need be evaluated (e.g. fibre, Local Multipoint Distribution Services - LMDS). At the switching/router nodes, the different types of traffic (Wide Area Network - WAN, GSM, and UMTS) will be separated and processed by different servers. These servers will handle session, mobility and call control for GSM and UMTS.

An evolution path thus ensures careful rollout of capital equipment at a pace that matches more correctly user demand.

A revolutionary architecture can be based upon the best of IT principle including the Open Distribution Processing methodology allowing concerns to be both separated and distributed so simplifying the matching of individual elements of the core in line with user and application demand.

## 5. A new $3^{rd}$ Generation Mobile Network Architectural Framework

The figure below presents the new architectural view of a third generation system. The Communication Manager receives a request for a call or session to be created. One or more of the database functions are used to confirm the authenticity of the customer, equipment and the call request. The Broker will then decide which technologies / networks will best meet the requirements of the call (which could be a simple speech call or a more complex multimedia call) and uses the Network Resource DataBase (NRDB) to confirm that the required resources are available. Using the NRDB the Broker can also determine the optimal end to end route before the network begins to route the call. The

Broker then compiles a list of commands that it issues to the Connection Performer which in turn instructs individual switches and routers to establish all the individual connections required to create the call. At anytime Service Control may modify instructions or data. Upon any successful creation, modification or termination of a call the NRDB is informed of the resources that have been used or released.

Points to note are:

- The Mobile Service switching Centres (MSC) and Serving GPRS Support Node (SGSN) no longer exists. They are now just a "dumb" switch or router respectively. Functions traditionally integrated in the MSC/SGSN like the VLR, mobility manager and call control are now separate;
- Databases are now distributed and mobile. i.e. data can now move around the network so as it is close to its user whether that be a customer or another part of the network;
- Processing could also be distributed. i.e. processes required to support a call would be run on the most convenient platform instead of a dedicated (possibly remote) platform.

The Intelligent Bus also deserves a special mention. It is a form of middleware and is a very powerful way of providing interoperability between different software modules or objects. In a client-server relationship, it allows a client to make use of objects on a server without having any knowledge of where the server is, what the server is, what operating system it uses or even what programming language was used to create the object. The client just issues a request to the Intelligent Bus that locates a suitable object and performs all necessary translation. It then delivers the result back to the client without the client knowing or caring where the work was done.

Doing away with the concept of an MSC/SGSN and splitting everything up ends an operator's dependence on the incumbent mobile network manufacturers. For instance, there are many more IP router manufacturers than there will be SGSN manufacturers. Increasing the competition in this way will improve the responsiveness of suppliers whilst at the same time drive down costs.

Today, IN systems are used to develop services independently of the MSC. Functions such as mobility management and call control can be thought of as just another service and separated from the MSC allowing development by suppliers other than the switch supplier. The Intelligent Bus will help realise this philosophy as it will allow service developers to choose the most appropriate operating systems, environments and programming languages for the job in hand whilst retaining interoperability with the rest of the network. Again this will reduce development times and costs.

Distributed data will make the network more resilient as failure of a node will only result in a small amount of data being lost. Data may also be able to move to be closer to its user, resulting in less resource being used to retrieve or update it.

Distributed processing will result in greater resiliency to faults and extraordinary traffic volumes. For instance, if there are no free local processing resources, processes will automatically be run on a remote processor.

New services such as multimedia are seen as key services for the future. An architecture such as described here with call control and mobility management functions being common to all technologies (e.g. GSM and GPRS) will help realise such services.

There are a number of benefits from separating the call control from the switch:

- The concept of an anchor MSC could be removed resulting in more efficient routing under handover conditions;
- The impact of switch failure could be reduced with the ability to re-route existing calls in the event of switch failure;
- Ability to change QoS in call;
- More sophisticated methods of dealing with congestion;
- Fixed mobile convergence will be supported by more generic switches;
- More efficient management.

Key: Circle = function, Octagon = agent
**Figure View of the overall UMTS**

# 6. Conclusions

The ability to forcast either technology changes or market condition over the coming years necessates an open and distributed architecture. This architecture will support the separation of concerns shuch that mobility amangement, databases, communications management and service control are independent modules each being able of development in incsolution without the need to be cognisant of the other modules that comprise the mobile network. No oondger will it be support the concept of utizing monolithic elements within the network rather each modul would be comprised of a set of objects distributed across anumber of hardware computor servers.

# Integrated network management system for access network

Bok-Kyu Hwang, Young-Wie Son, Hyun-Min Lim
Access Network Management Research Team
Telecommunications Network Laboratory, Korea Telecom
463-1 JeonMin-Dong, Yusung-Ku, Taejeon, Korea
TEL:+82-42-870-8664, FAX:+82-42-870-8649, E-Mail:bkhwang@kt.co.kr
TEL:+82-42-870-8666, FAX:+82-42-870-8649, E-Mail:ywson@kt.co.kr
TEL:+82-42-870-8666, FAX:+82-42-870-8649, E-Mail:hmlim@kt.co.kr

## Abstract

Coping with customer request for accessing Internet, as a network & service provider, KT(Korea Telecom) has support a various access networks which consists of copper line, LL(Leased Line), ADSL and FLC(Fiber Loop Carrier) systems. These systems support the telecommunication services such as PSTN, ISDN and ATM between a SNI and UNI. KT has designed ANSWERS in order to manage these access network elements integratedly from the point of the service maintenance view. This paper shows the system architecture and service maintenance framework of ANSWERS which has been developed using Java distributed environment with object-oriented methodology. The transport protocol used between the clients(applets) and server of ANSWERS is IIOP(Internet Inter-ORB Protocol) which is a CORBA transport protocol specified by OMG.

## 1. Introduction

With the introduction of the World Wide Web(WWW) over the Internet the need for network speed became a necessity. An inexpensive, easy-to-use Internet/WWW access service should be provided to the general public. The overwhelming majority of today's netisens use telephone lines via slow modems. The bottleneck is at the user end of the connection. This last-mile user connection is the connection from the Telephone Company's(TelCo) End-Office(EO) the user's home.

To give the general public Internet access service and the high-speed Internet access, KT supports the various access technologies including PSTN, ISDN, Hinet-P/F, LL, and ADSL. Figure1 shows the Internet access methods. AICPS allows people who do not subscribe to the ISP(Internet Service Provider) to access the Internet. KT has offered an existing but forgotten technology, ISDN(Integrated Services Digital Network) as a first step for large bandwidth. Always On/Dynamic ISDN(AO/DI) which have not to dial up to a packet service each time a connection is desired automatically adds circuit-switched B-channels of 64 Kbps each, for a total of 128 Kbps speed, when additional bandwidth is necessary. But ISDN will not be enough to compete with the 10-30Mbps bandwidth the other two industries including Cable TV networks and Satellite networks are preparing to offer. So KT supports ADSL(Asymmetric Digital Subscriber Line), to provide high band width on copper wire. Also KT has established the evolution plan of optical fiber access network since 1991. According to this plan KT has developed and deployed FLC(Fiber Loop Carrier)-A, -B systems for business applications(FTTO) and FLC-C, FLC-D systems for the densely populated areas(i.e. apartment complexes) and small business applications(FTTC).

KT has many OSS(Operation Support System)s that focus on the conventional copper access network. But there is no OSS that manages the broadband access network. In this circumstance, there is a strong demand for KT to manage these broadband access network elements integratedly from the point of the service maintenance view. Therefore KT has designed ANSWERS(Access Network Support and Warranty for End Resources). Service maintenance is responsible for monitoring the access network for alarms and/or performance management and testing the facilities and/or lines of broadband access network and copper access network. ANSWERS cooperates with DELMONS(Dedicated Line Maintenance & Operation System) and RIMS(Repair and Installation Management System) for Service maintenance and TIMS(Telephone Installation Management System) and ICIS for configuration information.

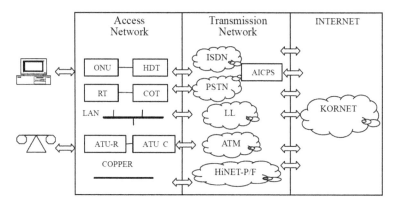

**Figure 1. Internet Access Method**

## 2. ANSWERS System Architecture

Figure2 depicts the ANSWERS system architecture. ANSWERS is located in the central office and plays a SML(Service Management Layer) and NML(Network Management Layer) role from the point of view of the TMN(Telecommunication Management Network). The NML gives a network level view to facilitate network planning and fault correlation. It consists of Fault, Performance functions for OAN(Optical Access Network), ADSL and copper wire. The SML of ANSWERS provides the service maintenance. It includes a customer complaint handling.

ANSWERS has communication services including CORBA and TCP/IP services. ANSWERS communicates with the FMS(FLC-C Management System), DMS(FLC-D Management System), RIMS and TS(Terminal Server) by TCP/IP, AWS(ADSL Work Station) by CORBA, the ICIS to get subscriber information by SQL/Net, the TIMS to get the configuration information by SQL/Net.

ANSWERS has a web-gateway for customer to be able to report the trouble to the system and retrieve the status of the subscriber line through Internet. Also customer can connect to the ANSWERS through the VRTS and test the subscriber line without the ANSWERS operators. ANSWERS operators can connect to the system through Intranet or directly and probe the subscriber line status by measuring the AC(Alternating Current), DC(Direct Current), CAP(Capacitance), RES(Resistance) and noise for analog service and BER(Bit Error Ratio) for digital and by retrieving the port status for V5.2 subscriber.

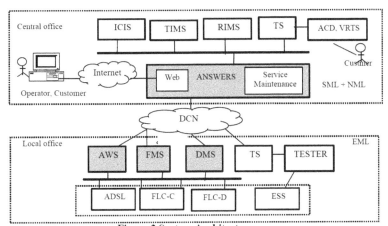

**Figure 2 System Architecture**

## 3. ANSWERS Software Architecture

Figure3 shows ANSWERS software architecture. The fault management modules are responsible for alarm handling and testing the network elements. ANSWERS operators can set the threshold of alarm and collect alarm information optionally. Alarms collected by ANSWERS are stored for analysis, diagnosis and displayed in a screen to the ANSWERS operators. When the ANSWERS operators find out the alarm status, They may start the testing procedure.

The performance management monitors the BER(Bit Error Rate), CRC checks and LOS(Loss of Signal). For error rates that exceed thresholds, alarms are generated and displayed. ANSWERS operators can change the performance thresholds.

TIMS provides the configuration management which maintains the configuration data used for provisioning the ADSL, the FLC systems and copper wire and managing subsequent changes. The configuration data includes NE equipment data and parameters, NE connectivity and subscriber data. The Interworking module of ANSWERS cooperate with TIMS to get configuration data which is stored in a TIMS's database. The data is stored in a database, which is available for the other modules to perform their functions. ANSWERS can communicate with another ANSWERS and RIMS through Interworking module.

The configuration specified by the ANSWERS operators must match the situation in the EMS(Element Management System)s. Because there can be a discrepancy between ANSWERS configuration data and EMSs in the field, ANSWERS and other OSSs. In order to solve the discrepancy ANSWERS has Audit module. Audit module operates on schedule or on demand.

ANSWERS has web module. Via web module the customer can inform the ANSWERS that his services(ISDN, Leased Line, Telephone, ADSL, Internet) provided by KT is out of order and can retrieve the status of the access line status which provide him with services.

To perform the service maintenance ANSWERS has to communicate with the other OSSs that have been already developed or is going to be developed. The existing OSSs supports only TCP/IP. The Interworking module allows ANSWERS to communicate with the existing OSSs. Also ANSWERS can cooperate with other ANSWERS that is located in another area through the Interworking module.

The broker module which identify the service type and facility type consists of Test Status management, Service Identification module, Facility Identification module and Test Procedure Management module.

The Driver Module consists of the SLMOS Driver and LCR Driver which manage the copper wire access network, FITL Driver which manage the OAN, and ADSL Driver which manage the ADSL access network.

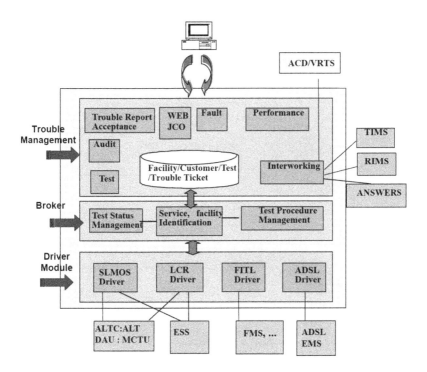

Figure3. Software Architecture

## 4. Service Maintenance

Service maintenance can be classified as three procedures. These are recognition of the problem of the access network, testing and repair. ANSWERS operators can recognize the problem of the access network from the alarm and/or performance data that is displayed in a screen. ANSWERS can receive the customer complaint through Internet or phone-call. If customer complaint received by ANSWERS is the complaint for the telephone, ISDN, ADSL, and Internet service using the copper, FLC, ADSL and LL, ANSWERS send the work-order for ADSL to ADSL EMS, for FLC to FMS or DMS and for copper wire to ESS and/or ALTC. ANSWERS may receive the trouble ticket from other OSSs and VRTS.

The equipments of the access network have testing units which are ATU(Analog Test Unit) and DTU(Digital Test Unit). ANSWERS uses these test units to test a facility and a subscriber line. ANSWERS operator is able to test individual network facilities such as channel cards or subscriber ports and subscriber line such as ISDN, telephone, leased lines, ADSL and FLC. ANSWERS operator is able to test a subscriber line after provisioning of the line, to measure its electric characteristics and to store the data of the testing results. ANSWERS operators compare the testing data performed at receiving the complaint to the testing data performed after service provisioning in order to verify and diagnose the problem or to verify whether repairs have corrected the fault.

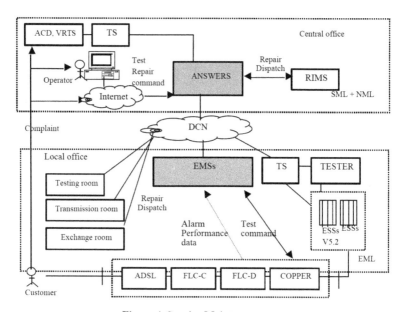

**Figure 4. Service Maintenance**

Also ANSWERS has the pre-testing features. The pre-testing features of ANSWERS allow the system to specify the subscriber lines or facilities to test and test the lines or facilities before the system receives the complaint.

ANSWERS operator first performs the process of alarm identification when he/she receives the customer complaints or trouble tickets from other OSS, as these problems can be correlated to existing equipment alarms. After that, ANSWERS operator starts the testing procedures. If he/she receives the test report that a line or facility is out of order ANSWERS dispatch a repair crew and the repair crew solve the trouble.

## 5. Client-Server communication path

Figure5 shows the communication path between an applet client and Server. If a browser requests an HTML page containing a java applet, the server downloads the page, applet class files, and JCORBA JAR file to the client. The applet runs and uses JNDI(Java Naming and Directory Interface) to acquire an object reference to a JCO(JCORBA object). The JCORBA runtime interacts with the ORB in the browser and the ORB in ther server to get an object reference. The applet uses the object reference to invoke methods on the object.

Web browsers impose security restrictions on Java applets. One of them is that applets can not accept any incoming connections from server. But alarms which are generated by NEs and collected by ANSWERS should be displayed in an applet. Also ANSWERS performs a variety of tests and measurements on a subscriber's line. As operator invokes AC-camp-on method on the JCO, ATU measures the AC on a subscriber's line continuously and returns the result of measurements to ANSWERS. The result of camp-on test should be displayed in an applet continuously.

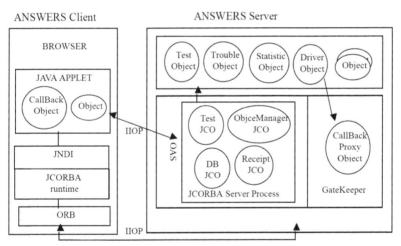

**Figure 5. Client-Server Communication path**

ANSWERS handles this security restriction using Gatekeeper. When a callback object is created in the applet, the ORB in the applet sets up a special connection with the GateKeeper. This special connection is an entirely separate connection and uses the callback port. The ORB exports the callback object to the Gatekeeper. This essentially creates a proxy object into the GateKeeper. The proxy object listens on the interior port on the interior IP address. All subsequent callback requests from the server object are sent to the proxy object which forwards the callback requests the applet and returns the result, if necessary

## 6. Summary and further work

KT has focused on the construction of optical fiber access networks in order to provide advanced services such as video or high bit-rate data and to enhance the conventional copper access networks since 1991. Also KT has focused on building the high-speed access networks based on ADSL technology on a parallel with optical fiber access networks. KT has designed ANSWERS for managing the NEs already installed and newly deployed in the access network, monitoring the network conditions and cooperating with other OSSs.

ANSWERS has main roles such as service maintenance. ANSWERS has communication services including TCP/IP, CORBA services, data base services, management functions services including Fault/Performance management. A customer sends ANSWERS a complaint and/or retrieve the line status through INTERNET. User authorization and authentication are more challenging in the ANSWERS because of the large number of potential users. ANSWERS needs more study on security to protect JCO.

## References

[1]   ANOSS requirements specification(draft), KT NMTL, May, 1998.
[2]   The Strategy for the operation and management of the broadband access network, Korea Telecom. May.1997
[3]   A Study on the Fiber Loop Carrier System, KTRC, Dec. 1994.
[4]   A Study on the Fiber Loop Carrier-C System, KTRC, Dec. 1995.
[5]   A System Overview of SLMOS, ETRI, Feb, 1986.
[6]   The Operation of SLMOS, KT, 1993.
[7]   FLC-B, KT TTRL, Mar. 1997.
[8]   A development for the DELMONS-PS(Performance monitoring System), KTRC, Dec. 1993
[9]   Development of the DCS management system, KTRC, Dec. 1994
[10]  A advanced development of telephone installation management system, KT, Dec.    1996
[11]  Development of the DCS management system. KTRC, Dec. 1994
[12]  Product description of MANOS(Modular Access Network Operations System), Lucent technologies, Jun. 1996.
[13]  http://ei.cs.vt.edu
[14]  Oracle Application Server
[15]  Visigenic gatekeeper guide

# Network Management of an $e$-Business Environment, Based on the New CCTA, ITIL Model

Colin Rudd

IT Enterprise Management Services Ltd. (*it*EMS Ltd.), Reading, England
e-mail: colinruddd@itemsltd.co.uk

## Abstract

This paper considers the challenges facing the managers of networks, providing today's e-business solutions. The requirement for these managers is to provide fully functional, high performance, secure, resilient services. However, these services also need to be capable of rapid expansion and rapid change. It is essential that the networks that deliver these solutions are built to a management architecture that supports these objectives. This papers advocates the use of the best practice architecture contained within the new Central Computer and Telecommunications Agency's (CCTA) IT Infrastructure Library (ITIL).

## Keywords

e-Business, Network Management, Service Management, IT Infrastructure Library, Network architectures

## 1. Introduction

This paper has been produced for presentation at the second International Network Conference to be held in Plymouth in July 2000. It attempts to develop a management architecture for the integration of all ICT management processes, tools and roles in the delivery of end-to-end service, in an e-business environment.

In recent years it has become increasingly recognised that information is the most important strategic resource that any organisation has to manage. Key to the collection, analysis, production and distribution of information within an organisation, is the quality of the Information Communications Technology (ICT) systems and services provided to the business. It is essential that we recognise that ICT systems are crucial, strategic, organisational resources. Organisations should therefore invest appropriate levels of resources into the design, planning and especially the management of these critical ICT systems. However, these aspects of ICT are often overlooked or only superficially addressed by many organisations.

Information technology has been widely utilised for the last forty years but it is only in the last five years or so that the Internet has had a real impact on the business community. That impact has been quite dramatic for some organisations, in fact in e-business organisations:

### "IT *is* the business"
and
### "The business *is* IT (or ICT)"

It is essential therefore to recognise the absolute dependence of most businesses upon the ICT infrastructure and the quantity, quality and the availability of the information that it provides. It is also important to recognise that many organisations have moved away from the scenario of providing online service from "9 til 5" and batch processing overnight, to the provision of online services in true "24 x 7" operation. In today's environment it is important to realise that for many organisations "ICT *is* the business". Without it there is no business! It is essential therefore that we plan and manage ICT systems and services appropriately for the business as a whole.

This is especially true of those businesses that are built and depend upon e-business processes and revenue. However, for all businesses the Internet has had a dramatic impact on the operation of both the business and ICT. The requirement then, is to provide business processes and ICT services that:

- *are flexible and adaptable*
- *can absorb an ever increasing demand in the volume and speed of change*
- *provide "24x7" operation*
- *are responsive with high availability*
- *are customer oriented, focussed and driven*

Therefore, the aim of Network Management or end-to-end, Enterprise Management should be to support these requirements and:

*" to provide a management architecture that maximises the business benefit and minimises the ICT investment in management tools and resources"*

It is essential, if this aim is to be achieved that an efficient, common business driven, architecture is used for the integration of business and ICT management, roles, tools and processes. The new CCTA's ITIL library provides guidelines in a best practice model, for the development of that architecture.

The ITIL library was initially developed in the late 80's and early 90's to provide "best practice" guidelines to government organisations on the management of IT infrastructure. Since than it has rapidly gained international acceptance, not only within public organisations but also in many private and global companies.

The ITIL library is now being updated and rewritten to incorporate the latest ideas and best practices in use by today's organisations. The author of this paper is actively involved in many aspects of this redevelopment process, acting as author and reviewer in many of the areas. This paper reflects the strategy and thinking used within the library and is based on this redevelopment work, including the experience and ideas of the author and many of the organisations and contributors involved in that process.

## 2. The development of Network Management

Network and IT Management has evolved from its early commercial beginnings in the sixties and seventies to what it is today. In the sixties and seventies the technology was more centralised and less complex. Today's network managers face much tougher challenges in the management of today's technology. The technology of today is much more powerful, more complex and even more distributed than ever before.

The key issues facing many of today's senior business managers, network managers and IT managers are:

- network, IT and business strategic planning
- aligning network, IT and business goals
- acquiring and retaining the right resources and skill sets
- measuring network organisation and efficiency
- reducing network costs and the Total Cost of Ownership (TCO)
- demonstrating the business value of networks and IT
- developing business and network partnerships
- improving network project delivery and success
- outsourcing
- using networking and IT to gain competitive advantage

The challenges for network managers are to co-ordinate and work in partnership with the business. This has to be achieved while reducing the overall Total Cost of Ownership (TCO). The main method of realising this goal is the reduction of the overall network management and support costs, while maintaining or even improving the quality of service delivered to the business. In order to do this the correct processes need to be developed and implemented. Network management and IT management are all about the efficient and effective use of the three P's, people, processes and products (tools and technology), as illustrated in Figure 1

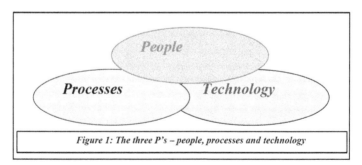

*Figure 1: The three P's – people, processes and technology*

Therefore these ICT Management functions should develop joint strategies and plans for all three areas within the above diagram. However, many organisations, in the past and still today, recognise these three P's but use them in the wrong way. Tools are bought to manage areas of technology and then the processes and people's roles are engineered to fit the tools and their limitations.

ICT management must recognise the importance of their role in underpinning the operation of the business. They must co-ordinate and work in partnership with the business, facilitating growth, rather than letting the technology and ICT dictate and drive the business. It is essential therefore that the issues and expectations of business managers are closely aligned with the objectives and deliverables of ICT management.

In facilitating business growth ICT has become more and more complex. The individual components deployed throughout the organisation have also become more complex and more powerful. More power and decision making is increasingly being distributed throughout today's business organisations. Today's desktop PCs and PC servers are more powerful than the mainframes of yesteryear and have necessitated a more powerful and complex infrastructure to support them. This complex and distributed ICT infrastructure has placed ever more stringent demands upon today's ICT management. The result is that today's ICT management processes have demanded more and more investment in resources.

All of these factors have contributed to an increase in the TCO of the ICT infrastructure. TCO can be defined as all of the resources and costs involved in the deployment and maintenance of the ICT infrastructure within an organisation. This includes not just the purchase cost of the hardware and software, but also the hidden costs of networks, installation, support, maintenance, upgrade etc., etc. The pressure is on today's ICT management to reduce all of these additional costs as well as to reduce the cost of the hardware and software. However, the real goal is:

> *"To reduce the overall Total Cost of Ownership (TCO) of ICT, while maintaining, or improving the overall quality of the ICT services provided."*

The specific goals of ICT are to maintain a management architecture for ICT that can:

- *meet the existing ICT requirements of the business*
- *be easily developed and enhanced to meet the future business needs of the organisation, within appropriate timescales and costs*
- *make effective and efficient use of all ICT resources*
- *contribute to the improvement of the overall quality of ICT service within the imposed cost constraints*

The only way of achieving these goals is to design, plan and implement ICT infrastructure and ICT management systems that deliver the information and solutions required by the business. The new ITIL modules provide best practice guidelines and architectures to ensure that ICT processes are closely aligned to business processes and that ICT delivers the correct and appropriate business solutions.

The effective IT and network organisations of today, design the people's roles and the processes first and then implement the tools to support and automate them. In the truly efficient organisations these roles and processes are aligned to the business, the business requirements and the business processes. This ensures that the business and ICT management process and information have similar targets and goals. This is the essence of the new CCTA's ITIL management architecture.

It is suggested that the architecture adopted for this co-ordination process is a development and refinement of the three P's. Rather than representing the management components as three inter-linked ellipses a more structured model is developed. To achieve this we need to recognise that these areas need to be further divided:

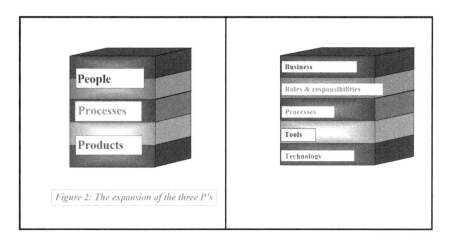

Figure 2: The expansion of the three P's

These five areas can be briefly defined as:

- **Business:** *the needs, requirements, processes, objectives and goals of the business units and managers within the organisation*
- **Roles and responsibilities:** *the scope, tasks and activities of the managers and staff involved in the support and delivery of IT and network services*
- **Processes:** *the processes and procedures used to support and deliver IT and network services to the business and its customers*
- **Tools**: *the management and support tools required to effectively manage the ICT infrastructure*
- **Technology**: *the ICT technology used to deliver the services and information to the right person, in right place at the right time.*

Once the architecture has been accepted it can be used to design and implement efficient, effective and integrated management solutions that are aligned to the business requirements of the organisation and its business managers. This architecture can be applied within an organisation to:

- **Design from the top down** *ensuring that the management processes, tools and information are aligned with the business needs and goals.*
- **Implement from the bottom up** *ensuring that efficient and effective management processes are fully integrated with the tools and technology in use within the organisation.*

103

## 3. The CCTA ITIL management architecture

The key to the development of a management architecture, is to ensure that it is driven by business needs and not developed for network and IT needs in isolation:

*"Business aligned NOT technology driven"*

This can be achieved using the overall IT Service Management approach contained within the ITIL library. This involves the identification of the essential processes required within a network or IT organisation to align it with the overall business needs. These processes are identified within ITIL as:

| Service Delivery: | Service Support: |
|---|---|
| Service Level Management<br>IT Financial Management<br>IT Service Continuity<br>Capacity Management<br>Availability Management<br>IT Customer Relationship Management | Configuration Management<br>Change Management<br>Release Management<br>Incident Management<br>Problem Management<br>Service Desk |

Within this overall structure, a management architecture is needed that can be applied to all areas of ICT management and not just to individual isolated areas. This can then be implemented in a co-ordinated program of inter-working, to provide overall end-to-end, enterprise management so essential to the effective management of today's ICT infrastructure. If only individual areas buy into the architecture, then individual "islands of excellence" will develop and it will be impossible to provide the complete end-to-end solutions, required to support today's e-business solutions.

As well as ensuring that all areas of the ICT are integrated it is key that the management architecture is developed from the business and service perspective (i.e. "Top down"). Therefore the key elements to agree and define before developing a management architecture are:

- *Management of the business processes: what are the business processes and how do they relate to network and IT services and components?*
- *Management of service quality: what is service quality, how is it going to be measured and where will it be measured?*

These are the key elements that need to be determined by Service Level Management. They provide crucial input to the development of business focussed management architectures. This architecture based on the 7-Layer model contained within the Network Services Management (NSM) module of the CCTA's ITIL library. This model was originally produced for the implementation of Network Services Management (NSM) but is equally applicable to all management disciplines. It is an extension of the three P's and the expansion of the three P's contained in figures 1 and 2:

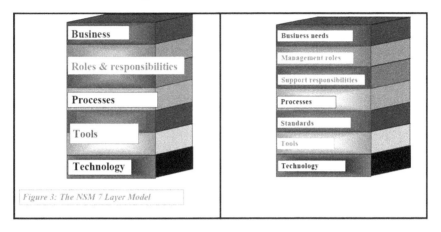

Figure 3: The NSM 7 Layer Model

This extension expands two of the areas into more detail:

- **Roles and responsibilities:** *the scope, tasks and activities of the managers and staff involved in the support and delivery of IT and network services:*
  - **Management roles:** *the definition of the scope, roles and ownership of the various ICT management functions. This will involve the definition, measurement, reporting and review of metrics and targets*
  - **Support responsibilities:** *the definition, scope and responsibility of the various areas involved within the delivery and support of ICT services, outlined earlier*
- **Tools:** *the management and support tools required to effectively manage the ICT infrastructure*
  - **Standards:** *the management standards required to ensure inter-operability of the management tools. This should include details of the protocols, interfaces and data formats for the exchange of information between management tools.*
  - **Tools:** *the actual management tools themselves, in terms of their facilities and functionality.*

## 4. Summary

The future of network management will be less focussed on network technology and become more integrated with the overall requirements of the business and ICT management. These new systems and processes are already starting to evolve and will continue to evolve of the next few years. This development will accelerate, as the management standards for the exchange of management information between tools become more fully defined, by organisations such as the Distributed Management Task Force (DMTF). In essence network management systems will become:

- *more focussed on business needs*
- *more closely aligned to business processes*
- *less dependent on specific technology and more "service centric"*
- *more integrated with other management tools and processes as the management standards evolve. This will involve the integration of Systems Management, Operational Management and Service Management tools and processes, with fewer "technology silos" and "island of excellence"*
- *part of "end-to-end" management systems and processes, more focussed on provision of quality, customer services*
- *less rigid and more flexible. There will be a move away from some of the more rigid, single supplier frameworks to a more open "best of breed" approach*

This will only happen if we adopt practices and architectures that are focussed on business needs and business processes. The CCTA's ITIL architecture gives a sound basis for achieving all of this, once management tools and interfaces become available.

Several organisations have used this approach to significantly improve the way network and IT services are delivered to the business. The benefits gained have included:

- *network and IT services are more closely aligned to business needs, processes and goals*
- *support staff are more aware of business processes and business impact*
- *a reduction in overall management and support costs leading to a reduced TCO*
- *improved service availability and performance, leading to increased business revenue*
- *improved service levels and quality of service*

## Colin Rudd
*IT Enterprise Management Services Ltd. (itEMS Ltd.)*
I have over 30 years experience in the IT and networking industries, working on and with, many national and international networks and network service providers. These activities included the design, installation, operation and management of LANs and regional, national and international WANs. These inter-working assignments involved the use of many different networking media and components together with the integration of a variety of networking technologies from many different equipment suppliers. During this time numerous training courses and programmes were developed and delivered to the majority of the organisations concerned.

More recently, since obtaining the BCS/ISEB Manager's Certificate in IT Service Management and the Diploma in Network Services Management, I have delivered extensive training and consultancy in all aspects of Service, Systems and Network Management, within the mainframe, distributed, PC and networking environments. These activities also included the development of many IT and networking, technology and management strategies.

As an internationally recognised expert within the Network and Service Management arena, the Central Computers and Telecommunications Agency (CCTA) asked me to write the Network Services Management module of the IT Infrastructure Library (ITIL). Subsequently I have worked with many of the leading industry bodies and associations, such as the itSMF, the TMA, the BCS and the NCC, in the development of network industry standard qualifications and accreditation programmes. I am now working with the CCTA and the itSMF on the re-writing of IT Infrastructure Library

# Evaluation of a Probabilistic Model for Tariffing in Multi-Service ATM Networks

P. McAtackney[1] and M.E. Woodward[2]

[1]School of Computing, University of Plymouth, Plymouth, Devon, PL4 8AA, United Kingdom, email: pmcatack@soc.plym.ac.uk
[2]Telecommunications Research Centre, University of Bradford, Bradford, W. Yorks., BD7 1DP, United Kingdom, email: M.E.Woodward@bradford.ac.uk

## Abstract

One major factor in determining 'quality of service' in a multi-service ATM network is 'cell delay variation', CDV. Significant CDV in delay-sensitive services such as voice and video traffic can reduce the perceived quality of such a service, whereas non-delay-sensitive traffic such as computer data is more tolerant of CDV. This paper evaluates the accuracy of a simple mechanism for providing a customer charging scheme which accounts for CDV in addition to traditional charging parameters of call distance and duration. This mechanism is based on cell delay variation in unrestricted discrete-time queueing networks following a geometric distribution.

The charging criterion within such an ATM network is based on the total number of cells transferred between a source and a destination and the distance over which the cells travel. The total number of cells, however, implies the total number of cells 'useful' to the receiver, i.e. only those which are not over-delayed. To accomplish this practically, only simple measurements should be taken from the live network and applied to a statistical model to produce cell delay distributions for the required virtual circuits.

The measurements taken from the live network are the mean delays through the nodes of a specific virtual circuit experienced by the cells traversing this virtual circuit. These delays are used by the model to form a truncated geometric distribution for the delay experienced by the cells of each active virtual circuit in the network. The resulting distributions are compared to those distributions generated by simulation for the following cases: networks in which only moderate virtual circuit interaction takes place; networks in which significant interaction between virtual circuits takes place; networks exhibiting increased queue lengths within the nodes of the virtual circuits; networks where varying levels of cell loss are observed.

The results of these experiments show that the statistical model used for the 'cell delay variation' is largely accurate where only moderate virtual circuit interaction at nodes is observed and very low levels of cell loss or no cell loss occurs. The statistical model however departs from the observed CDV when high levels of virtual circuit interaction or cell loss are present.

## Keywords

Queueing Networks, Discrete-time, Tariffing, ATM

## 1. Introduction

Asynchronous Transfer Mode, ATM, networks are multi-service networks capable of integrating diverse traffic types such as voice, video, and data services whilst minimising the complexity of the switching operation and the buffer management allowing for efficient operation within a high-speed transmission context. To aid in the efficiency required for such high-speed switching, data carried by ATM is transmitted in blocks called cells, which are relatively short in duration and of a fixed size. These fixed size, and therefore fixed duration, cells make it possible to model ATM networks as networks of discrete-time queues, therefore allowing discrete-time queueing theory to be used in their analysis as discussed in Henderson and Taylor [1]. In such an ATM network, these information carrying cells are multiplexed with other ATM traffic onto a transmission media and into an ATM network. At the switching points in this network, cells contending for the same output channel are queued at the output until they can be transmitted. Significant problems however inherently exist in such a system, namely 'cell packetisation delay' and 'cell delay variation'. Packetisation delay exists since a cell may not be transmitted until sufficient data exists at the source to allow full cells to be created. The level of such delay will depend upon the adaptation layer being used and the source bit-rate of the data. Delay variation, or 'jitter', occurs as a result of queueing delays experienced by cells of any given virtual circuit which must queue at a switch outlet as a result of output contention. The length of the queue encountered by contending cells will depend on the number of virtual circuits making use of the outlet and the 'squared coefficient of variation', SCV, of the traffic feeding those virtual circuits.

Such delay variation can be problematic for 'delay-sensitive' services such as speech where delayed cells may reduce the perceived quality of the service. Other services, however such as computer data or text transfers, are 'delay-tolerant' in that 'late cells' are still useful at the receiver and are therefore not classed as being 'over-delayed'. For this reason, a suitable customer charging scheme is required to account for such 'cell delay variation' in addition to the traditional charging parameters of call distance and duration. In ATM terms this equates to the total number of cells transferred between the ends of a virtual circuit and the distance between the source and destination of the circuit. The total number of cells however relate to the total number of cells that are useful to the receiver, i.e. those which have not been over-delayed.

The number of useful cells transmitted across a given virtual circuit could be determined simply by discriminating between those cells which are over-delayed and those which are not and counting the latter. Alternatively each cell could be marked with a 'birth' time on creation which could be subtracted from the arrival time at the receiver. Both solutions pose practical problems. The former would require that the delay encountered at the first node in the virtual circuit is determined and attached to the cell, with the amount of additional delay encountered by subsequent nodes determined and added to this value until the cell reaches its destination. This would require additional overhead thus reducing the effective bandwidth available for user data. In the latter case, it would be necessary for both sender and receiver to be synchronised. This paper will propose a more practical solution to this problem and attempt to evaluate its performance in practice. The basis of this solution is the provision of a mechanism whereby the delay encountered by a cell on a given virtual circuit may be predicted from simple measurements taken from the live network. The solution is feasible providing that both the route taken by a given cell through the network and the expected delays encountered by the cell through each node in this route are known. The probability of a cell having a particular delay can then be calculated and a cell delay distribution for the virtual circuit can be estimated. The number of cells which arrive at the receiver within specification, i.e. according to a previously agreed 'quality of service' contract, may then be charged to the customer according to a 'cell delay-based charging plan'. The development of a probabilistic model to evaluate delay distribution of cells in an ATM network is presented in this paper. The model is then evaluated against a network simulation model to assess its accuracy for use as a tariffing model for real-time services. To this end, a computer program incorporating both the simulation and statistical models has been developed. The model assumes a shared-buffer switching architecture at the ATM nodes with the program allowing for a variety of network topologies and switch buffer sizes to be modelled and evaluated. Multiple virtual circuits may be specified within the computer program in terms of both route taken and 'squared coefficient of variation'. The simulation model produces an accurate cell delay distribution for given virtual circuits by actually counting cells as they arrive at the receiver and classifying them according to their measured delay. In addition the simulator measures the expected delay encountered by cells through each individual node of each virtual circuit specified in the network. These expected delays are used within the statistical model to produce the predicted cell delay distributions for each virtual circuit.

## 2.    The Model

### 2.1    Overview

Both simulation model and statistical model reside within a single computer program. The simulation model is required for two reasons. First, the simulation model will calculate the expected delays of cells through each switching node. These measurements are then used by the statistical model to produce the estimated cell-delay distribution for the virtual circuits active in the network. Secondly, the actual cell-delay distribution will be calculated by the simulation model and used to assess the accuracy of the estimate produced by the mathematical model.

### 2.2    Traffic Modelling

Each virtual circuit in any given network is characterised by a traffic generator and a path through the network. The traffic generator produces cells according to an Interrupted Bernoulli Process, IBP. Such a process is required for modelling ATM traffic due to the bursty and correlated nature of such traffic. The parameters associated with this generator are the state-preserving probabilities, p, and q, and the arrival probability, $\alpha$. The state diagram below illustrates the basic operation of an IBP. The state-preserving probabilities, p, and q, allow the state of the generator to be switched between 'active' and 'inactive'. If the state is 'active', then the generator will produce arrivals with a probability of $\alpha$. When in the 'inactive' state, no arrivals are produced.

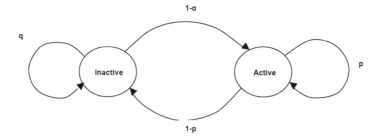

**Figure 1: State Diagram for an Interrupted Bernoulli Process.**

This generator model is used to produce the input traffic to each virtual circuit defined for the network.

## 2.3    Statistical Model Concepts

An estimation of the cell delay distribution for a given virtual circuit may be made based on simple measurements taken from the simulation model. In practice such measurements may be easily made from a live network. An objective of this study is to test the accuracy of a geometrically distributed delay as a tariffing model for ATM networks. Assume that an ATM network can be modelled as a discrete-time queueing network where each node in the network has release probabilities described by a binomial distribution. Since cells passing through such nodes are independent, then the binomial distribution provides a simple modelling method for such events thus reducing the complexity of the mathematics required for the analysis. The cells arriving at such nodes will therefore exhibit a geometrically distributed delay which is independent of other nodes in the network, since the release probabilities at the nodes are binomial. Then an end-to-end cell delay distribution for any given virtual circuit will simply be the sum of the products of the probabilities of delay through the nodes of that virtual circuit. Therefore since the mean cell delay through each node is known from the measurements taken by the simulation, then the reciprocals of these delays provide the parameters required to calculate the geometric distributions for the model.

For a geometric distribution, the probability of a cell being delayed by 'k' slots in a queue of infinite length is given as,

$$P(k) = \mu \cdot (1 - \mu)^{k-1} \qquad (2.3.1)$$

Therefore for an infinite geometric distribution, the following proof shows how the value, $\mu$, above is equivalent to the reciprocal of the mean delay through a queue of infinite length.

The expected delay, E[D], of a cell through a node is given as,

$$E[D] = \sum_{i=0}^{\infty} i \cdot P(D = i) \qquad (2.3.2)$$

$$= \mu \cdot \sum_{i=1}^{\infty} i \cdot (1-\mu)^{i-1}$$

$$= \mu \cdot \frac{1}{\left(1-(1-\mu)\right)^2}$$

$$= \frac{1}{\mu}$$

In practice, of course, these queues are not infinite. In this case it is necessary to consider a truncated geometric distribution as the basis for the model. In this case the mean delay through the queue is not equal to the reciprocal of $\mu$. It is equal instead to the following,

$$E[D] = \frac{\mu \cdot \sum_{k=N1}^{N2} (1-\mu)^{k-1} \cdot k}{\mu \cdot \sum_{i=N1}^{N2} (1-\mu)^{i-1}} \neq \frac{1}{\mu} \qquad (2.3.3)$$

Therefore by solving this equation, the roots give the value of $\mu$ for the truncated geometric distribution between the limits N1 and N2. This value of $\mu$ can then be used in the estimation of the cell delay distribution for the virtual circuit.

i.e.

$$\Phi[\mu] = E[D] - \frac{\sum_{k=N1}^{N2} (1-\mu)^{k-1} \cdot k}{\sum_{i=N1}^{N2} (1-\mu)^{i-1}} = 0 \qquad (2.3.4)$$

Therefore the value of $\mu$ that solves this equation is the required value of the parameter of the truncated geometric distribution.

The general form of the probability of a cell in any given virtual circuit being delayed by any number of slots is as given below,

$$P_{VCNum}(k) = \sum_{CombinationID=1}^{NumOfCombinations} \prod_{NodeID=1}^{NumOfNodes_j} P^{(n)}\left(Delay(CombinationID, NodeID)\right)$$

$$(2.3.5)$$

where 'VCNum' is the Virtual Circuit number,
       'k' is the number of slots delayed,

'NumOfCombinations' is the number of combinations for a delay of 'k',
'CombinationID' is the combination index variable,
'NumOfNodes' is the number of nodes in the virtual circuit,
'NodeID' is the node index variable
'n' is the position of the node, 'NodeID', in virtual circuit, VCNum,
'Delay' is the delay caused by node, 'NodeID' in the combination, 'CombinationID'.

The cell delay distribution for the statistical model is then simply given by this probability, $P_{VCNum}(k)$, for each virtual circuit, VCNum, for all values of 'k' required.

The following example illustrates this.

Assume a virtual circuit, $VC_1$ with a path consisting of four nodes, $1\rightarrow3\rightarrow4\rightarrow2$. To determine the probability of a cell being delayed by six slots through this virtual circuit, i.e. $P_1(6)$, then all combinations of four positive numbers greater than zero whose sum is equal to six must be determined. Four numbers are required since there are four nodes in the virtual circuit where each node will introduce a delay of at least one slot.

First determine all such combinations as listed.

1+1+1+3, 1+1+3+1, 1+3+1+1, 3+1+1+1, 1+1+2+2, 1+2+2+1, 2+2+1+1, 1+2+1+2, 2+1+2+1, 2+1+1+2.

Now if $P^{(i)}(k)$ is the probability that a cell is delayed by 'k' slots at node 'i', then the probability that a cell is delayed by six slots through this virtual circuit is given as,

$$
\begin{aligned}
P_1(6) = \quad & P^{(1)}(1).\,P^{(3)}(1).\,P^{(4)}(1).\,P^{(2)}(3) + \\
& P^{(1)}(1).\,P^{(3)}(1).\,P^{(4)}(3).\,P^{(2)}(1) + \\
& P^{(1)}(1).\,P^{(3)}(3).\,P^{(4)}(1).\,P^{(2)}(1) + \\
& P^{(1)}(3).\,P^{(3)}(1).\,P^{(4)}(1).\,P^{(2)}(1) + \\
& P^{(1)}(1).\,P^{(3)}(1).\,P^{(4)}(2).\,P^{(2)}(2) + \\
& P^{(1)}(1).\,P^{(3)}(2).\,P^{(4)}(2).\,P^{(2)}(1) + \\
& P^{(1)}(2).\,P^{(3)}(2).\,P^{(4)}(1).\,P^{(2)}(1) + \\
& P^{(1)}(1).\,P^{(3)}(2).\,P^{(4)}(1).\,P^{(2)}(2) + \\
& P^{(1)}(2).\,P^{(3)}(1).\,P^{(4)}(2).\,P^{(2)}(1) + \\
& P^{(1)}(2).\,P^{(3)}(1).\,P^{(4)}(1).\,P^{(2)}(2)
\end{aligned}
$$

The general form of this expression is as given in equation (2.3.5).

## 3.    Evaluation of the Accuracy of the Model

A number of experiments have been carried out to determine the validity of such a model as the basis for a simple tariffing mechanism for real-time services over ATM networks. The topologies and virtual circuit definitions specified for these experiments are as follows.

Shared Buffer Capacity at each Node = 5       Shared Buffer Capacity at each Node = 5

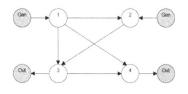       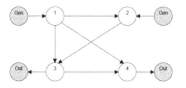

**Virtual Circuits:**
VC1: 1 =>2 =>3 =>4
VC2: 1 =>4
VC3: 1 =>3 =>4
VC4: 2 =>3

**Generator Specifications:**
VC1: p = q = 0.997, arrival prob. = 0.15
VC2: p = q = 0.997, arrival prob. = 0.09
VC3: p = q = 0.997, arrival prob. = 0.06
VC4: p = q = 0.997, arrival prob. = 0.15

**Virtual Circuits:**
VC1: 1 =>2 =>3 =>4
VC2: 1 =>4
VC3: 1 =>3 =>4
VC4: 2 =>3

**Generator Specifications:**
VC1: p = q = 0.997, arrival prob. = 0.4
VC2: p = q = 0.997, arrival prob. = 0.24
VC3: p = q = 0.997, arrival prob. = 0.16
VC4: p = q = 0.997, arrival prob. = 0.4

**Figure 2:** Network 1 with interaction between virtual circuits without cell loss

**Figure 3:** Network 2 with interaction between virtual circuits with light cell loss

Shared Buffer Capacity at each Node = 5       Shared Buffer Capacity at each Node = 7

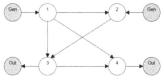       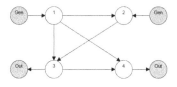

**Virtual Circuits:**
VC1: 1 =>2 =>3 =>4
VC2: 1 =>4
VC3: 1 =>3 =>4
VC4: 2 =>3

**Generator Specifications:**
VC1: p = q = 0.997, arrival prob. = 0.4
VC2: p = q = 0.997, arrival prob. = 0.24
VC3: p = q = 0.997, arrival prob. = 0.16
VC4: p = q = 0.997, arrival prob. = 0.8

**Virtual Circuits:**
VC1: 1 =>2 =>3 =>4
VC2: 1 =>4
VC3: 1 =>3 =>4
VC4: 2 =>3

**Generator Specifications:**
VC1: p = q = 0.997, arrival prob. = 0.4
VC2: p = q = 0.997, arrival prob. = 0.24
VC3: p = q = 0.997, arrival prob. = 0.16
VC4: p = q = 0.997, arrival prob. = 0.8

**Figure 4:** Network 3 with interaction between virtual circuits with heavy cell loss

**Figure 5:** Network 4 with interaction between virtual circuits with heavy cell loss

In each of the cases above, figures 2 to 5, a simulation was executed from which an actual cell delay distribution at each virtual circuit was obtained. In addition, the simulation made the simple measurement of mean cell delay through each node of each virtual circuit for use by the statistical model in estimating the cell delay variation for the virtual circuit. The comparison between the results produced in each case involves comparing the values of the absolute errors observed in each case between the probability of cell delays. The sum of these errors over the range of the cell delay distribution is therefore used to indicate the overall error and therefore provides an indication of model accuracy.

A sample of the results obtained for the experiments specified in figures 2 to 5 above showing the worst case deviations observed in each case are as below.

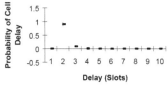

**Cell Delay Distribution for VC #4 in network 1**

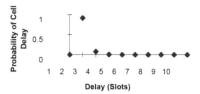

**Statistical Model: Cell Delay Distribution for VC #4 in network 1**

Sum of Abs. Err. for VC #4 = 0.01564

**Figure 6: Comparison of Cell Delay Distributions for Network 1**

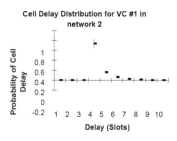

**Cell Delay Distribution for VC #1 in network 2**

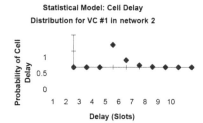

**Statistical Model: Cell Delay Distribution for VC #1 in network 2**

Sum of Abs. Err. for VC #1 = 0.12654

**Figure 7: Comparison of Cell Delay Distributions for Network 2**

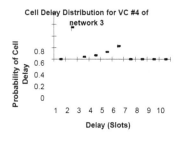

**Cell Delay Distribution for VC #4 of network 3**

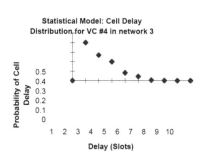

**Statistical Model: Cell Delay Distribution for VC #4 in network 3**

Sum of Abs. Err. for VC #4 = 0.75414

**Figure 8: Comparison of Cell Delay Distributions for Network 3**

114

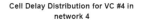

| Cell Delay Distribution for VC #4 in network 4 | Statistical Model: Cell Delay Distribution for VC #4 in network 4 |

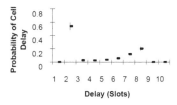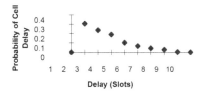

Sum of Abs. Err. for VC #4 = 0.98265

**Figure 9: Comparison of Cell Delay Distributions for Network 4**

It can be noted from these results that in the cases where virtual circuit interaction is relatively low and cell loss is light, accuracy of the statistical model is maintained to within 13%. However as virtual circuit interaction is increased resulting in longer queue lengths and increased arrival rates leading to higher cell loss then the model becomes extremely inaccurate.

## 4. Conclusions

The results presented in this paper show that in the case of low interaction between the cells of different virtual circuits in a given network, the statistical model provides a good model for predicting the cell delay distribution of all virtual circuits in the network. However as queue lengths increase indicated by the increasing average delay of cells through a node, the statistical model begins to depart from the simulation model but for low level cell loss, this is maintained below 13%. When the cell loss increases due to higher cell arrival rates within interacting virtual circuits, then the statistical model departs dramatically from the cell delay distribution produced by the simulation. Secondary peaks within the cell delay distribution are evident in these cases indicative of the effect of excessive queueing on the statistical model. These peaks are caused by the interactive queueing effects of different virtual channels. For example, in Figure 9 the delay distribution for VC4 shows a primary peak occurs at a delay of 2 slots and a secondary peak at 8 slots. There are two nodes in VC4 and this indicates that many of the arriving cells from VC4 find the node buffers empty and go through each of the nodes in a single slot. The secondary peak is caused by interacting cells from VC1 and/or VC3 filling the buffer at node 3. Then cells arriving at node 3 and belonging to VC4 that find buffer space available are delayed mostly by 7 slots at node 3 and 1 slot at node 2, giving the secondary peak in the distribution at 8 slots. The statistical model based on the truncated geometric distribution ignores these secondary peaks, thus accounting for the reduced accuracy of the model at heavy loads.

# 5.    References

[1]    Griffiths, J.M. and Cuthbert, L.G. *Real time renegotiation of ATM bandwidth*, Proc. of 6th IFIP Workshop on Performance Modelling and Evaluation of ATM Networks, Bradford UK, July 1998, pp 93/1-93/7, ISBN 0 9524027 8 5

[2]    Henderson, W. and Taylor, P.G. *Product-form in networks of queues with batch arrivals and batch departures*, Queueing Systems, 6, pp. 71-83, 1990

[3]    Kelly, F.P. *Charging and accounting for bursty connections*, Internet Economics, MIT press, 1997, pp.253-273, ISBN 0 262 13336 9

[4]    Law, A.M. and Kelton, D. (1982) *Simulation Modelling and Analysis*, New York, McGraw-Hill

[5]    Miah, B. and Cuthbert, L.G. *Charging and billing in ATM networks*, Proc. of 6th IFIP Workshop on Performance Modelling and Evaluation of ATM Networks, Bradford UK, July 1998, pp 92/1-92/10, ISBN 0 9524027 8 5

[6]    Miller, I. and Freund, J.E. (1985) *Probability and Statistics for Engineers*, Prentice-Hall International Press

[7]    Onvural, R.O. (1995) *Asynchronous Transfer Mode Networks - Performance Issues*, Boston, London, Artech House

[8]    Schwartz, M. (1987) *Telecommunications Networks: Protocols, Modelling and Analysis*, Reading, Addison-Wesley

[9]    Songhurst, D. *Charging schemes for multiservice networks*, Proc. of 13th UK Teletraffic Symposium, IEE, 1996, London

# Accounting management system enhancement supporting automated monitoring and storing facilities

C. Bouras S. Kastaniotis

[1]Computer Engineering and Informatics Department
University of Patras, Greece
[2]Computer Technology Institute, Greece
e-mails: bouras@cti.gr,kastansp@cti.gr,

## Abstract

In this work we present the design, development and implementation of a set of tools embedded in a network management system used in the University of Patras Network (UPatrasnet), providing advanced accounting management services. These tools help the critical network parameters monitoring and storing procedure in order to provide the information needed for efficient management. We defined which resources to be watched and what kind of information to be collected by the management system in order to deploy the specifications of the processing and analyzing tools. Finally, we used HP OpenView as a network manager.

## Keywords

Accounting management, MIB, SNMP, Network resources, Network administration

## 1. Introduction

All current management architectures have been developed after the design of network functions had been completed. Such approach indicates a specific conceptual view on the role of management functions and invites to apply different architectural concepts for the design of management functions.

Users obviously want the best possible network bandwidth / performance at the lowest possible price. On the other hand, it is unrealistic to expect that it will always be possible to find a good pricing and billing method for each network during the phase of designing the management functions.

In order additional experience to be obtained during the operational phase of a network there must be an enhanced subsystem supporting accounting management, e.g., the gathering and recording of data related to the network resources usage.

This work presents a set of applications that completes the accounting facilities offered by HP OpenView network platform. These applications help in monitoring the traffic for an administrative domain (UPatrasnet), as well as the storing of the formatted accounting information in a database.

Statistical (accounting) data is used for the right administrative decisions to be taken in order major network problems (congestions, drops, resource insuffiencies) to be avoided. Furthermore, the statistical data will be used as an input to a future charging and pricing policy, so that the appropriate network resources to be allocated with a fair and convenient way.

All the applications developed offer secure and easy administration.

This paper is organized as follows: in section 2 there is a short description of the applications context. The third section provides details of the applications architecture, specifically presenting analysis, design and implementation issues. In section 4 the functionality offered by the applications is outlined. The last section summarizes conclusions elicited from our work and presents future work issues.

## 2. Description of the applications

### 2.1 General Overview

The applications developed cover a wide range of accounting issues. The traffic information involves information about the flows that pass through a router, information about the selected routers, information about performance and congestion, information about the selected items (hosts) and information about all the events and traps (these that have been configured) generated during network operation.

We can distinguish the application in three categories. The first category provides traffic information from the network of UPatrasnet to Internet and vice versa, the second one for a specified node of UPatrasnet and the last one for a specified subnework of UPatrasnet (or a set of subnetworks of UPatrasnet).

### 2.2 Infrastucture

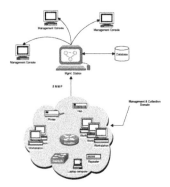

**Figure 1: The management model on which the applications are implemented**

The set of applications was designed, developed and implemented on a fully centralized network management model in which the entire network comprises a single management domain (UPatrasnet) and one powerful management station performs all monitoring and data collection for that domain (Figure 1).

## 3. Architecture

### 3.1 Applications Analysis

The design of the set of applications was based on a user needs analysis conducted, using interviews with the subnetworks administrators of UPatrasnet and questionnaires. This survey led to the following functional specifications:

- There should be a mechanism to access the routers without explicitly using telnet, so we used a simple-minded program to talk to the cisco console.

- There must be a Relational Database Management System (RDBMS) that works behind and provides the whole system with an efficient way of manipulation. The RDBMS will keep all the statistical data needed in order after their processing the appropriate decisions to be taken.

- All applications should provide a graphical user interface (GUI) to easily make anyone familiar with them. One way to achieve this is to access the applications through the OpenView Windows environment.

- Administrator must focus on managing the most critical elements and processes of the network, and build complete solutions for them.

- The menu items of the implemented applications should be displayed only on specific submaps, not on all maps of the OpenView Windows (OVW) environment.

- Due to the fact that UPatrasnet is a heterogenous network there are a lot of devices (entities) that does not support the SNMP protocol. There must be a way of distinguishing these *unmanaged* objects on the map.

There are, also, some non-functional specifications which ensure the quality of the accounting applications. They fall into the following categories.

*Performance*

- 24 hours availability of the applications.

*Safety*

- Any application must be able to recover from a failure within a reasonable period of time and without affecting other applications.

- Usage of backup mechanism in order to ensure the integrity of data.

*Security*

- The consistency of the data must be ensured.

*Maintenance*

- Small changes of enhancement, extension or adaptation can be performed without necessitating redevelopment of the applications.

- The applications architecture must be open in terms of smooth integration with new products or new services as additional experience is gained.

*Environment*

- The possible administrator must be able to use the applications' facilities within a short period of time.

**3.2 Applications design**

To determine which variables must be watched, administrators must understand the presice meaning of many management issues.

We have adopted the accounting framework used by OSI, which defines a generalized accounting management activity, that includes calculations, usage reporting and enforcing various limits on the use of resources.

The OSI accounting model defines three basic entities: 1) the *METER*, which performs measurements and aggregates the results of those measurements, 2) the *COLLECTOR*, which is responsible for the integrity and security of *METER* data in short-term storage and transit, and 3) the *APPLICATION*, which processes/formats/stores *METER* data. *APPLICATIONS* implicitly manage *METERS* [RFC 1272 (1991)].

The accounting model can be described as a complex client / server model that operates in two levels. In the first level the *METER* is the server, while the *COLLECTOR* is the client. In the second level, the *COLLECTOR* is the server, while the *APPLICATION* is the client. Obviously, the *COLLECTOR* plays a dual role in the model, that of a client and a server.

We recommend SNMP as the basic communication framework and more presicely a secure version of SNMP, such as SNMPv2.

What we did is the development of a set of applications (*Traffic Monitoring*) making use of an accounting MIB (*MyAccMIB*) writen in ASN.1 notation. The applications make use of the OVW NNM interface, under selected menu items.

The communication between an accounting agent and meters or between an accounting manager and accounting agents achieved through trap-directed polling. In each of these cases, administrator uses polling to periodically obtain an update of the accounting data from the routers.

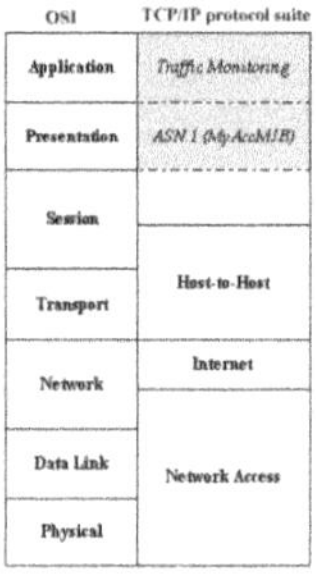

| OSI | TCP/IP protocol suite |
|---|---|
| Application | *Traffic Monitoring* |
| Presentation | *ASN.1 (MyAccMIB)* |
| Session | |
| Transport | Host-to-Host |
| Network | Internet |
| Data Link | Network Access |
| Physical | |

**Figure 2: The applications hierarchy in the TCP/IP protocol stack**

The information exchange with all the routers is done using globally the same community string "*public*". It is because we want to communicate with routers without using telnet and making use of the same mechanism for all of them.

Figure 2 illustrates the hierarchy view of our implementation as far as ASN.1 notation and 'Traffic Monitoring' concerns.

### 3.3 Implementation Issues

The use of *ANSI C* language is considered to be as an adequate choice for writing short and smart programs that can be easily modified in order to make several tests before the final implementation. Thereby, little work is needed for modifying the existed code so as new applications and services to be built.

*Awk* processing language has the unique capability of providing filters, entirely necessary for isolating the useful information. Using awk we managed to modulate the ip accounting table taken from several routers of UPatrasnet and finally obtain the desired information.

*ASN.1* is a language for describing structured information; typically, information intended to be conveyed across some interface or communication medium. It is widely used in the specification of communication protocols.

With ASN.1, the protocol designer can view and describe the relevant information and its structure at a high level and need not be unduly concerned with how it is represented while in transit. Compilers can provide run-time code to convert an instance of user or protocol information to bits on the line, using BERs (Basic Encoding Rules).

Finally, ASN.1 defines a set of simple types and specify them with a tag. We can refer to these types using this tag. Beyond the definition of types, ASN.1 provides a symbolism for the definition of the values of the above types. Subsequently, it defines mechanisms for constructing more complex types and tags for these types.

We have expanded an SNMP agent with the proposed Accounting MIB written in ASN.1.

*Symbol Registration Files (SRFs)*

HP OpenView NNM provides a whole range of Symbol classes and subclasses. The range of symbols can be enriched by means of SRFs.

Using the facility of SRFs we managed to assign custom symbols to specified nodes with a particular sysObjectID. Network Node Manager uses a file (oid_to_sym) to map an object's sysObjectID to the default ovw symbol type used to represent the node in the IP topology submaps it displays. Taking this fact into account we can cause all non-SNMP nodes to be marked unmanaged when automatically discovered. The special value that must be substituted for the SNMP object id (sysObjectID) for unmanaged nodes is DEFAULT_IP.

*Application Registration Files*

Application Registration Files (ARFs) have been used to integrate Network and System Management Applications with the OVW user interface. Many aspects of the application's interaction with OVW are defined using ARFs.

The Application Registration File contains fields that define the menu bar items, tool bar items and symbol pop-up items from which the application will be accessed, and fields that specify the command line, which invokes the application.

In more detail, applications are integrated into OVW by using structures in the ARFs called Application Blocks. Application Block defines many aspects of the interfaces between OVW and application and for a single application specifies the name of the application, the version of the application, the description of the application, the copyright information for the application, how the application is incorporated into the OVW Menu Bar, selection rules for the application and instructions for invoking the application command.

Application integration begins in the main menu bar. A MenuBar block is specifies the menu label on the menu bar under which the application will eventually appear. An optional mnemonic character can be specified to allow keyboard selection by typing a single character.

Additional menu items and the application invocation are defined through a Menu statement within the MenuBar block. The Menu statement specifies the menu label and its function.

```
MenuBar <100> "Misc" _i
    {
    <100> "Traffic Monitoring" _T f.menu "Traffic Monitoring";
    }

Menu "Traffic Monitoring"
        {
        <100> "General Traffic" _G CONTEXT "AllContexts || isIP"
              f.menu "General Traffic";
        <100> "Node Traffic" _N CONTEXT "AllContexts || isIP"
              f.menu "Node Traffic";
        <100> "Subnet Traffic" _S CONTEXT "AllContexts || isIP"
              f.menu "Subnet Traffic";
        }
Menu "General Traffic"
        {
        <100> "Internet->150.140.0.0" _I CONTEXT "AllContexts || isIP"
              f.action "General From Internet";
        <100> "150.140.0.0->Internet" _1 CONTEXT "AllContexts || isIP"
              f.action "General To Internet";
        }
Menu "Node Traffic"
        {
```

**Figure 3: A sample of the code generates the menu items of the applications**

*Facilities of HP OpenView Network Node Manager*

The administrative platform OVW provides a complete Graphical User Interface (GUI), which helps the creation of ARF files. For instance, using point-and-click, we could choose whether an application should display data in the form of a graph, table or form. The GUI also lets the developer key in the appropriate help text that should be linked with the application.

## 4. Functionality

All applications developed support point-and-click operations on the map of OVW NNM integrated environment. In proportion with the application used, the network administrator can select one active network device (e.g., a router) and several nodes from the map where the applications are active, and run the desired application. Obviously, multiple selections are allowed (multiple nodes can be selected each time by using *ctrl-click*).

If the network administrator wants to get information for a specific node on the map and cannot find it by the first look, he can use a dialog box to insert its ip address or alias name.

For the case a subnetwork is involved, only the dialog box can be used in order the specified subnetwork to be selected by the administrator.

The implemented applications capture only specific traffic information (specified by MyAccMIB variables) so that to indicate critical data and states of the whole network.

We made the assumption that there is a network administrator to whom Internet accounting is of interest. He "owns" and operates some subset of the Internet (one or more connected networks) that may be called his "administrative domain". This administrative domain has well defined boundaries. The network administrator is interested in 1) traffic within his boundaries and 2) traffic crossing his boundaries. Within his boundaries he may be interested in end-system to end-system accounting or accounting at coarser granularities (e.g., university department to university department).

The developed applications support three categories of traffic information. The first category provides traffic information from the network of University of Patras (UPatrasnet) to Internet and vice versa. This category includes the following modules:

- Traffic monitoring from Internet to UPatrasnet.

- Traffic monitoring from UPatrasnet to Internet.

The second category provides traffic information for a specified node of UPatrasnet. This category includes the following modules:

- Traffic monitoring from a node of UPatrasnet to UPatrasnet.

- Traffic monitoring from a node of UPatrasnet to Internet.

- Traffic monitoring from UPatrasnet to a node of UPatrasnet.

- Traffic monitoring from Internet to a node of UPatrasnet.

The third category provides traffic information for a specified subnework of UPatrasnet (or a set of subnetworks of UPatrasnet). This category includes the following modules:

- Traffic monitoring from a subnetwork of UPatrasnet to UPatrasnet.

- Traffic monitoring from a subnetwork of UPatrasnet to Internet.

- Traffic monitoring from UPatrasnet to a subnetwork of UPatrasnet.

- Traffic monitoring from Internet to a subnetwork of UPatrasnet.

*Accounting MIB*

The Accounting MIB developed is subdivided into six groups:

- **Flow**: information about the flows that pass through the selected router.

- **Meter**: information bout the selected router on the map and its interfaces gathered by meters.

- **Congestion**: information about subnetwork performance and congestion.

- **Host**: information about the selected host on the map.

- **Event**: a table of all events generated by the SNMP agent.

In all cases we managed to export accounting data from the selected router into text files, formating them similarly to the accounting MIB MyAccMIB.

All statistical (accounting) data are stored automatically (after monitoring) in an Oracle database and are kept there for a time period not longer than three months. Each saved file is been stamped by the date and time of creation and the selections made on the map, before using a specific application module.

## 5. Conclusions and furure work

Working for the UPatrasnet we implemented a set of applications enhancing the existing accounting facilities supported by HP OpenView platform. We defined an Accounting MIB (MyAccMIB) and used HP OpenView as an Accounting Manager. We recommend SNMP as the basic communication framework and more presicely a secure version of SNMP, such as SNMPv2. Our approach is completed by a storing mechanism for saving formated accounting data into a database.

We can expand the current accounting applications into an integrated accounting system included pricing policies. Pricing computer network traffic will be essential to manage network traffic and to control and provide different QoS required by different classes of applications and users.

For the time being, there are two pilot projects, MBS (Managed Bandwidth Services) and TrACe (Traffic Analysis and Charging Pilot Project), which involve traffic measurement, analysis, charging and bandwidth management. GUnet (Greek Universities Network, *www.gunet.gr*) funds both projects and the results of the completed work will be announced in the near future.

## 6. References

Stallings W. (1996), *SNMP, SNMPv2 and RMON, Practical Network Management*, Second Edition, Addison-Wesley.

Apostolopoulos T.K., Prokos I.G. (1998), "ACCOUNTING MANAGEMENT IN TCP/IP NETWORKS: CONCEPTS, ARCHITECTURE AND IMPLEMENTATION", *Proceedings of the Second IASTED International Conference PARALLEL AND DISTRIBUTED COMPUTING AND NETWORKS*, Brisbane, Australia.

RFC 1272 (1991), *Internet Accounting: Background*.

Fang K., Leinward A. (1993), *Network Management: A Practical Perspective*, Addison-Wesley.

Stevens W. R. (1991), *Unix Network Programming*, Prentice Hall.

Cisco Systems (1994), *Cisco MIB variables for version 10.0 of system software*.

Jander M. (1993), *Router Management Goes Beyond Pretty Pictures*, Data Communications.

HP OpenView Network Node Manager, *Fundamentals for Network Managers, Student Workbook*, Version C.01.

HP OpenView (1997), *Using Network Node Manager*, Edition 1.

Stevenson D. W. (1995), *Network Management: What it is and what it isn't*, Network Management White Paper.

# Flexible Multi-Service Telecommunications Accounting System

E. de Leastar and J. McGibney

Telecommunications Software Systems Group, Waterford Institute of Technology, Ireland
e-mail: edeleastar@wit.ie

## Abstract

Due to market deregulation and technological advances, a multi-service broadband environment is emerging, generating a requirement for a new approach to pricing systems. This paper presents such an approach and describes a working implementation of an innovative and flexible multi-service accounting system. The system is based on a mature understanding of the nature of charging algorithms, and is implemented as a set of interoperating distributed components. At the heart of the system is a rating engine built around a service portfolio, tying together spreadsheet specification of arbitrarily complex services, charging algorithms and tariff tables. The very wide range of service delivery technologies in existence motivates the design of a system that is independent of proprietary formats and based on a dynamic service portfolio structure and a generic service detail record definition.

## Keywords

Accounting, Charging, Rating, Multiservice

## 1. Introduction

Until fairly recently, communications services have generally been straightforward - a limited number of services on offer, limited scope for customer tailoring of such services, and limited complexity. Now, however, there is considerable growth in the quantity and diversity of services. New communication technologies are enabling the introduction of variable-bandwidth with quality of service guarantees. ATM (ATM Forum, 1999) and Frame Relay already support a mature set of such services, and work is emerging from the IETF on QoS-guaranteed IP[1]. Some services will be provided as standardised network services based on core technologies, and others as higher-level user services that are in effect an amalgamation of network services, information content, and other components.

A new kind of accounting system is needed to provide metering and pricing support for these complex services. It should be capable of supporting the creation new services, charging algorithms and tariffs without the need for frequent upgrades. It should provide support for near real-time online billing, where the customer can very quickly obtain information on the cost of the service just used. And it should hide as much of the complexity associated with charging algorithms as possible, delivering to service providers a mechanism for manipulating these algorithms in a familiar environment.

Recent work on the specification of charging schemes for ATM and emerging quality IP services has been carried out under the European *ACTS* (Advanced Communications Technologies and Services) programme, and forms the basis of the work reported on here.

This paper proposes an architecture for a flexible broadband pricing system and reports on a working implementation that has been used in European trials. An overview of accounting concepts is presented, identifying the major subsystems within broadband accounting. This is followed by analytical discussion of the structure of the charging algorithms. A Service Portfolio is introduced encapsulating the proposed charging approach, and the outline of an implementation is presented, in CORBA IDL.

## 1.1. Accounting Concepts and Subsystems

The overall accounting process can be divided into *metering*, *rating* (or pricing), and *billing* systems, as shown in Figure 1. The role of the metering system is to measure, collect and forward information that identifies and describes the usage of network services. This information can then be used for charging purposes. The metering system retrieves this information from specific measuring points, distributed throughout the network. The measuring points are dependent on the network. For ATM these are switches, for IP these are routers and so on. This service usage information is organised in the form of *Service Detail Records* (SDRs). The SDR is a generalization of the Call Detail Record (CDR) provided by most conventional telephony switches.

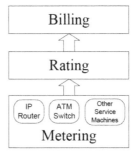

**Figure 1 Accounting Systems**

The main role of rating, the focus of this paper, is to provide support for the billing system so that it can invoice customers for telecommunications services. The rating system *computes the charges* from which the billing system composes the customer bills.

## 2. Multi-service Charging Algorithms

Charging in a multi-service environment is complex. Many different services can be delivered on the same equipment, and a wide variety of charging schemes and tariffs are possible. The charging approach proposed here stipulates that all the necessary and sufficient information for charging be encapsulated in four entities – a charging algorithm, a tariff table, an SDR type specification, and set of service determination rules. Particular reference is made to an implementation of charging for ATM and Quality IP services. However, the architecture is sufficiently flexible for wider applicability to as yet unforeseen technologies.

## 2.1. Charging Algorithms

The central task of rating is to evaluate the charge for a given service usage so that the user can be billed appropriately. This involves the application of a charging regime to SDR data to yield a monetary charge. Charging for a service can be considered as containing elements relating to *subscription* and usage *sessions* (CANCAN, 1997). Of most interest to us is the session charge. This is the variable component of charging that is normally highly dependent on the contents of the relevant SDR(s). Generally, the session charge can be expressed as:

$$C = a_1X_1 + a_2X_2 + ... + a_nX_n \qquad \text{(Equation 1)}$$

where $X_1, ..., X_n$ are charging parameters or functions of charging parameters that do not depend on numeric tariffs,

$a_1, ..., a_n$ are charging scheme numeric coefficients, known as tariffs, and,

$C$ is the charge for the session.

Thus $X_1, ..., X_n$ represent the commodities that are being charged - e.g., duration, packet counts, bit rates, etc., and it must be possible to express them in terms of SDR field parameters. The tariff coefficients $a_1, ..., a_n$ are then the price factors that are applied to the chargeable commodities. For example, a proposed charging scheme (SUSIE, 1999) for MPLS real time service looks like this:

$$C = a_1*P*T, \qquad \text{(Equation 2)}$$

where $T$ is the duration of the connection, $P$ is the peak data rate (i.e. the guaranteed bandwidth) and $a_1$ and $C$ are as above

Table 1 gives an analysis of this charging scheme and how its terms derive from SDR fields

| Parameter | Parameter Type | SDR field(s) | Units |
|---|---|---|---|
| $C$ | | | [$] |
| $a_1$ | Tariff | | [$/kbit] |
| $P$ | Charging | *ContractedPeakDataRate* | [kbits/sec] |
| $T$ | Charging | *(CollectionTime + CollectionTimeOffset) - (CallStartTime + CallStartTimeOffset) - DisruptionDuration* | [sec] |

**Table 1: Example charging scheme expressed in terms of SDR Parameters**

## 2.2. Tariff Tables

Tariffs are the coefficients of a charging scheme; they are the price component of each term. Consider again the charging schemes above (equation 2). Here $P$ and $T$ are charging parameters as they relate directly to values that can be retrieved from the SDR. $a_1$ is viewed as the tariff as it is effectively the price that can be altered as the market demands. This tariff is not necessarily a fixed value however but may depend, for example, on time of day or geographical location of called party. Such variable tariffs are traditionally organised in tariff tables, examples of which are the rate cards available from most telephone companies and published in telephone directories.

## 2.3. Service Determination Rules

The third, and perhaps most significant, key to charging in a multi-service environment is to have a means of specifying service determination rules. The purpose of such rules is to allow us to take an SDR and unambiguously identify the service that was used to produce this SDR. Then the correct charges and tariffs can be applied. For maximum flexibility it is allowed to use any combination of SDR parameters to identify the service. An example service determination rule is as follows:

| Service: | "ConstantBitRate, local, night, no quality guarantees" |
|---|---|
| Condition: | if ServiceCategory is "CBR" <br> and CallingNumber and CalledNumber have the same first 3 digits <br> and CallCreationTime is between 00:00 and 08:00 <br> and CollectionTime is between 00:00 and 08:00 on the same day |

It is important that the service identification rules unambiguously identify a single service from an SDR. It would be too much of a burden on the user to expect all service rules entered to be mutually exclusive, and to cover the entire "SDR space", ensuring that any SDR causes one and only one identification rule to be satisfied. Thus the user is allowed to assign a priority level to each service rule, and rules of higher priority are tested first.

## 2.4. Representing the Schemes

The challenge for the implementation of the accounting system to support these schemes is to define a representation that is flexible and user-friendly, but sufficiently powerful to permit the most complex of charging regimes to be captured. Specifically, the representation format must:
- be easy to manage.
- permit arbitrarily complex formulae.
- allow multiple SDR types to be manipulated.
- be consistent with the world of accounting and billing.

Flexible representation of charging algorithms, satisfying the above requirements, is achieved by providing the user with a spreadsheet-like user interface. Usage data is specified for selection *a priori* to be placed into cells in the worksheet, and other cells can be used by the user to enter formulae or conditions. Sample usage data can be entered for testing purposes, but actual usage data is taken from the SDRs and placed into the specified positions at runtime, and the calculations are performed automatically.

# 3. Service Portfolio

A service provider will typically offer a range of services, some at the bearer communications level and others that are termed "value-added". The term service portfolio is used to represent this service offering. A present day public fixed line network provider might have the following service portfolio:

- PSTN residential
- PSTN business
- Virtual Private Network (VPN)
- Freephone

- Call Answering
- Telephone equipment rental
- Directory assistance
- ISDN

Some of these services are entirely different from one another (e.g. Directory Assistance vs. ISDN) while others have little technical difference and only differ in how they are charged (PSTN business vs. PSTN residential).

For the purposes of accounting, the service portfolio can be defined as the collection of service information that is necessary to support the rating process. Formally, we define service portfolio as a set of *service templates* that are offered by a service provider, where each template contains the following:

- SDR type - format of usage data from the service machine
- Service Determination Rule - logic to identify the service
- Tariff Table - algorithm to generate coefficients of the charging scheme; i.e, the *prices*
- Charging Scheme - algorithm to generate charge for billing

There is no restriction on reuse of any of these elements across multiple service templates. For example, the same charging algorithm could be applied to different services, but the tariffs tables could be different.

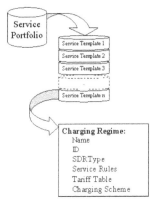

**Figure 2: Service Portfolio**

The Service Portfolio is modelled as a set of CORBA IDL types. This facilitates the centralised management of the service portfolio, with remote access across a CORBA infrastructure. Client applications include Graphical User Interface (GUI) applications to create, edit, modify and delete service portfolio entries (the *service templates*), generalised report generators, and of course the rating process itself, which will need to match service templates against incoming SDRs and compute charges accordingly.

The Service Portfolio IDL is divided into three categories, defined as separate modules. The first category, *SDRTypes*, specifies a comprehensive generalised representation for usage data gathered by the metering system. The second category, *Schemes*, defines the structure of the algorithms maintained within the service portfolio, specifically the service rules, tariff tables and charging algorithms. The third category, *ServiceTemplate*, models individual entries within the service portfolio in terms of the *SDRTypes* and *Schemes* modules.

### 3.1. SDR Types

The structure of the SDR is at the root of the accounting model, as SDRs are ultimately the origin of the charges generated by the system. The model developed in IDL is completely generic, catering for current and future metering technology and service types. Struct *t_ChargeParameter* defines a meta-type, describing the name, type, default value, and unit denomination of one element within an SDR.

```
struct t_ChargeParameter {
    string    name;
    any       defaultValue;
    string    units;
};
typedef sequence<t_ChargeParameter> t_SDRType;
typedef string                      t_SDRId;
```

**Figure 3: SDRType Structure**

The default value and type are represented as a single *any* value, which by definition has a *typecode* field. For instance a charge parameter for an MPLS-SDR might consist of:

*"ContractedPeakCellCount", 0 (long long), "kbits"*

An SDRType is simply a collection of these structures; i.e. a sequence of *t_ChargePatameter* objects. SDRType is thus regarded as a meta-type, describing a category of SDRs. This allows us to define an MPLS-SDR for MPLS traffic, or an IP-SDR for IP based transport, or we may define an SDR for content delivered. Defining different SDRType representations for each of these types of service technology is critically important to the composition of charging algorithms. Essentially the SDRType for a particular category of service defines a vocabulary in which the charging algorithms can be expressed. This vocabulary permits the composition of these algorithms in an intuitive manner; with charging formulae manipulating named charging parameters derived from the SDRType associated with the service.

The actual usage data itself, as measured during the delivery of a service, is represented as a collection of *t_MeterParameter* structs. Each meter parameter consists of an identity, locating a descriptive *t_ChargeParameter* in a corresponding SDRType sequence, and the actual data itself, encoded as a CORBA *any*.

```
struct t_MeterParameter {
    octet identity; //attribute identifier
    any   value;    //Value
};
typedef sequence<t_MeterParameter> t_UsageData;

struct t_SDR {
    t_SDRId          type; // Type + version information
    t_UsageData      data;
};
typedef sequence<t_SDR> t_SDRList;
```

**Figure 4: SDRs**

Thus for an MPLS-SDR, a meter parameter might simply be:

*12333314, 5*

The first number is some parameter gathered from a service machine, and the second

130

associates this measurement with some *t_ChargeParameter* meta-type within an SDRType sequence (say *ContractedPeakDataRate* from the example above). A *t_SDR* is defined as a sequence of these charge parameters, along with an id of the *t_SDRType* of which this SDR is an instance.

## 3.2. Schemes

Each of the three algorithms that compose a service template: the service determination rules, the tariff table and the charging algorithm, are modelled in IDL as a struct *t_Scheme*. Using structs, as opposed to interfaces, is a strategic decision, as client applications will be capable of preloading the full service portfolio without having to continually invoke remote functions to access scheme attributes (Mowbray et al, 1997). This reduction in remote invocations is an important consideration for GUI applications manipulating the portfolio, but absolutely crucial for the rating process, which will be unable to tolerate network latency implied by remote invocations during charge computation.

```
typedef unsigned long    t_SchemeId;
typedef string           t_Name;
typedef sequence<octet>  t_SchemeFormulae;
struct t_Scheme
{
    t_SchemeId        ID;
    t_Name            Name;
    t_SDRId           SDRtype;
    t_SchemeFormulae  Algorithm;
};
typedef sequence<t_Scheme> t_SchemeList;
```

**Figure 5: Scheme IDL**

Each Scheme consists of an ID, a Name, an SDRType and an Algorithm. The SDRType identifier maps to an SDRType structure defined above, defining the vocabulary of the algorithm.

Modelling the algorithm itself in IDL poses a dilemma. Spreadsheet technology has been introduced as the appropriate mechanism for defining and manipulating charging algorithms. In this scenario, the SDRType entities are mapped to specific cells within a spreadsheet, and a set of interrelated algorithm formulae can be assembled using these cell references to compose a "result", or set of results for the algorithm. A spreadsheet is a complex structure, with multiple internal dependencies between cell contents, and sophisticated formulae of arbitrary length and structure. Modelling this in IDL would be counter-productive, pushing a degree of complexity into a domain fundamentally unsuitable for it.

The dilemma was resolved by completely abstracting the entire algorithm within the *t_Scheme* structure as a sequence of octets – essentially a binary stream. Within the database management system hosting the Service Portfolio, the stream is stored as a Binary Large Object (BLOB) and placed in a relational table. Within the concrete classes that manipulate schemes, this binary stream is serialized into its native format. For the GUI applications this native representation is attached to a visual component rendering it as a traditional spreadsheet. During the rating process, they are similarly serialised into native worksheet format, but no GUI is attached. Here the calculating engine is employed to recalculate all cells, and generate results employed in the rating process.

### 3.3. Service Templates

The Service Template can now be defined as a structure encapsulating naming information + IDs of the Charging Scheme, Tariff Table and Service Rules objects as defined above.

```
typedef unsigned long   t_ServiceTemplateId;
typedef string          t_Brand;
typedef string          t_Description;
struct t_ServiceTemplate {
  t_ServiceTemplateId ID;
  t_Name                Name;
  t_Brand               Brand;
  t_Description         Description;
  t_SchemeId            ChargingScheme;
  t_SchemeId            TariffScheme;
  t_SchemeId            RulesScheme;
};
typedef sequence<t_ServiceTemplate> t_ServiceTemplateList;
```

**Figure 1: Serviceportfolio Servicetemplate IDL**

A Service Template embodies a *charging regime,* i.e. a complete set of algorithms which, when applied to some usage data gathered from a service machine (an SDR), will compute a charge for that service. The Service Portfolio is thus modelled as a sequence of *t_ServiceTemplate* objects – a collection of charging regimes that can be used to compute charges for all the offerings a service provider may choose to make available.

## 4. Rating

In order to realize the charging approach embodied in the Service Portfolio, a software component must be designed to compute the charges based on usage data gathered from network elements. This is termed a *rate engine.* This component must be supported by other components: database and GUI applications to store, retrieve and edit the service portfolio itself; agents to gather the usage information (SDRs) from the service machines; gateway components to route these SDRs to rate engine(s), and to route generated charges to database and/or interested client applications (web browsers for online accounting, for instance).

The components are completely decoupled, with minimal dependencies on shared IDL specified interfaces. This is achieved through widespread deployment of the OMG Event Service (Wang et al, 1999), facilitating the asynchronous transmission of the key data structures (SDRs and Charge Records). While the Event Service does not provide Quality-of-Service (QoS) guarantees, is serves as a stepping-stone to next generation event service implementations, specifically those taking advantage of the CORBA 2.3 (OMG, 1998) messaging and notification services (OMG, 1998). These have a range of QoS parameters, which can be tuned to meet the demands of the accounting system.

The rate engine is the most computationally intensive of these components, and its structure is the key to a flexible, performant accounting system. Rate engine components are instantiated within a multithreaded rating server, each engine listening to one or more event channel for SDRs, and pushing charge records to an output channel. The SDR channel is fed by metering agents, typically interfacing with Service Machines (switches & routers) through SNMP. Attached to the Charge Record channel are listeners pumping the records to a DBMS, or distributing them to online client applications.

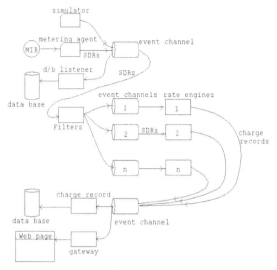

**Figure 2: Rating Components**

## 4.1. The Rate Engine

Within the engine, the actual charges themselves are computed. Essentially the engine, preloaded with the service portfolio using interfaces defined above, applies the appropriate charging regimes to the incoming SDRs, generating the charge records accordingly. This is carried out in five stages (Figure 3):

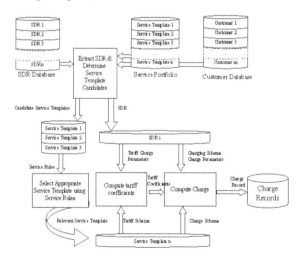

**Figure 3: Rating Process**

1. Identify candidate service templates from the service portfolio
2. Step through these service templates and apply the service determination rules until a rule is satisfied. This is the unique service template applicable to the SDR.
3. Using the tariff worksheet for this service template, compute tariff coefficients based on the received SDR field values
4. Compute the charge by applying the appropriate charging scheme worksheet
5. Write the resultant charge with other relevant information to a Charge Record.

Stages two, three and four involve replacing terms within formulae, and re-evaluating the formulae to yield results. It is analogous to a recalculation that takes place within a spreadsheet, with usage data placed on spreadsheet cells, and cell references within the formulae ensuring that this data percolates through the entire charging algorithm during recalculation.

### 4.2. Spreadsheet Component

Having determined not to publish the format of this algorithm/spreadsheet in the IDL, the issue of structure of the sheet itself can no longer be postponed - or perhaps it can? Spreadsheets are one of the most widely used application categories, and programmable spreadsheet software components are among the most common items on commercial component catalogues[2]. Classical component reuse technology can be deployed here to significantly cut the cost of development, and reduce the complexity of the implementation.

## 5. Conclusion

The accounting system described here has been realised as a set of interoperating components delivering a flexible multi-service accounting system. The system has been trialled primarily over ATM broadband networks, utilising in-house development testbeds, and that of the SUSIE project at Basel in Switzerland. The system has proved robust and performant, delivering a flexible and innovative "laboratory" for devising new types of charging algorithms appropriate for broadband services. Work is ongoing in deploying the system for Voice over IP services, implementing charging algorithms appropriate to this technology.

## 6. Acknowledgements

The authors wish to thank the *SUSIE, Bandwidth 2000* and *FlowThru* consortia for several helpful discussions. The work of these projects is part-funded by the European Commission.

## 7. References

ATM Forum, (1999), *Traffic Management Specification, Version 4.1.*
CANCAN Consortium, (1997), *Final Report on Static Charging Schemes and their Performance, Deliverable 9a.*
SUSIE consortium (1999) *Trials: Accounting* Results, Deliverable 6.
Mowbray,T, et.al. (1997), *CORBA Design Patterns*, Wiley.
Wang,R, et.al. (1999), "Event Bridges Across CORBA Event Service and Programming Language Event Models", *Journal of Object Oriented Programming*, Vol.12, No.4.
Object Management Group (1998), *The Common Object Request Broker Architecture, Revision 2.3.*
Object Management Group (1998), *CORBA Messaging*, Revised Submission.

---

[1] http://www.ietf.org
[2] http://www.componentsource.com

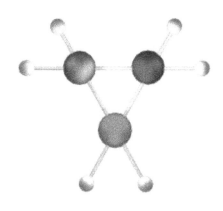

# Chapter 3

## Multimedia integration

# QoS support for real-time applications in IP over ATM networks

I. Erturk, M. Tenruh, E. Stipidis

A. Kutlu

The University of Sussex
School of Engineering and
Information Technology
BN1 9QT, Brighton, UK

Suleyman Demirel University
Technical Education Faculty
Isparta, Turkey

i.erturk@sussex.ac.uk

## Abstract

Several approaches have been proposed for IP and ATM integration so far; however, a key problem (i.e., QoS support) in future networking applications remains as a challenging task. This paper describes an extension to CLIP protocol, providing ATM service classes to the IP end users. It defines that different service classes are mapped to the associated IP addresses, enabling different IP end user applications to obtain their own dedicated VCs. The simulation results show that using this approach, real-time applications in IP over ATM environments are well achievable, and restrictions of the IP's only BE service are easily overcome.

## Keywords

IP over ATM, Real-time Applications, Quality of Service

## 1. Introduction

In recent years IP (Internet Protocol) has dominated other protocols deployed in global networks. Considering its use in data communications, IP was initially a significant success in networking technologies. However, its inadequacy for Quality of Service (QoS) support has resulted in failing to provide emerging real-time multimedia applications to the desktop satisfactorily. Several approaches since 1990 have been proposed for IP and Asynchronous Transfer Mode (ATM) interoperability so that QoS can also be achieved. Classical IP and ARP (Address Resolution Protocol) over ATM (CLIP) is one of the most promising integration methods, utilising the connection-oriented nature of ATM to carry IP traffic. This technique has been driven into the reality since IP is already widespread from an access point of view, and after the increasing use of ATM in Local/Wide Area Networks (LANs/WANs). ATM has universal support for both present and future applications.

The Internet Engineering Task Force (IETF) has introduced a complex DiffServ model to provide QoS support at the IP level. With this approach, user flows are only controlled at the edge of the network and then aggregated into a small set of traffic classes (Nichlos *et al.,* 1998, and Eichler *et al.,* 2000). Aiming to achieve similar objectives, this paper describes an extension to CLIP protocol in order to provide ATM service classes to the IP end users and to bring real-time multimedia applications to desktops.

## 2. Internet Protocol and Asynchronous Transfer Mode

Having considered the multi-service nature of the information technologies in present applications, neither a pure IP network nor a pure ATM network is adequate to fully cover all requirements. Therefore an IP network adapted to an ATM core is essential, taking advantage of the utter power of ATM for its performance and QoS. Both ATM Forum and IETF encourage this concept. The IETF has named IP as the common glue for interconnecting heterogeneous networks into a single, large internetwork (Gupta, 1999 and Hankins, 1999).

One of the strengths of IP is that a significant variety of user applications are available with IP. With its connectionless datagram delivery service, IP has been designed to handle bursty traffic and network congestion conditions. Its easy scalability and applications in very large networks with less central management are particularly valuable for network designers. On the contrary its datagram-based packets are unsuited to real-time traffic, and since they are routed independently, out of order delivery is also probable. Furthermore, the number of fields of an IP header and its variable length cause slow processing of packets (Fan, 1999, and Decina *et al*, 1997). In contrast to IP, ATM networks are inherently connection-oriented (though more complex) and allow QoS guarantees. It has superior features including flexibility, scalability, fast switching, and use of statistical multiplexing, utilising network resources efficiently. Different traffic characteristics are supported in a scalable manner. Like IP, there are also several problems with ATM. First and the most important of all, it must allow interoperability with existing network infrastructure using specially designed signalling protocols. An adaptation layer has to be used to provide necessary services (e.g., segmentation /reassembly) in order to transport variable size data frames over fixed size ATM cells (Fan, 1999, and Erturk *et al*, 1999).

## 3. ATM Integration with Existing Networks

The ATM Forum and IETF have been carrying out most of the work on ATM and IP interoperability. The former has emerged with two solutions evolving since 1995, namely LAN Emulation (LANE) and Multi Protocol Over ATM (MPOA) (The ATM Forum, February 1999, and The ATM Forum, May 1999). The latter has proposed a different approach in its work, called CLIP, where an ATM network environment is configured as a Logical IP Subnetwork (LIS) (Laubach *et al*, 1998). In addition to these specifications, (Barnett, 1997) also suggested a method based on a hardware scheme to provide special support for connectionless traffic in ATM networks in his individual attempt, called Connectionless ATM. The potential size of the hardware routing tables required for each link or group of links is its main limit to scalability.

LANE is a service provided over an ATM network, which operates at the Layer 2 of Open Systems Interconnection (OSI) reference model and emulates the services of existing Ethernet and Token Ring applications. It hides the features of ATM from applications. Therefore, applications with QoS are unable to exploit the unique capabilities of ATM although they can work over ATM through LANE without modification. However, the newly completed LANE Version 2.0 provides some locally administered QoS for communication between ATM-attached end systems (Sun *et al*, 1998). Later, MPOA has been created to improve LANE by allowing inter Emulated LAN (ELAN) traffic to go through shortcut connections rather than routers. As a result, it precludes slowing packet throughput at intermediate routers significantly. However, MPOA does not support multicast traffic over ATM shortcut connections and its complexity is a major practical obstacle in the industry.

The CLIP approach (Figure 1) preserves the IP characteristic at the Layer 3 for the existing applications while switching Layer 2 from Ethernet/Token Ring to ATM. IP packets are carried in ATM AAL-5 Payload Data Units. The behavioural characteristics of ATM LISs are identical to the well-known IP subnets. CLIP can run over both Permanent and Switched Virtual Circuits, and is based on the notion of logically independent LISs. Similar to an IP subnet, a LIS consists of a group of IP hosts directly connected to a single ATM network and belonging to the same IP subnet. Like in LANE, the traffic between the hosts on different LISs has to travel over a router that is also a member of both subnets. Every IP address is resolved to its corresponding ATM address, and vice versa, using ATMARP mechanisms and ATM connections are consequently set up. As a result of this basic mapping definition described in RFC1577 and RFC2225 (Laubach *et al*, 1998), all the traffic with different characteristics is transmitted through only one VC providing only a Best-Effort (BE) service and set up between two communicating hosts at a given time. In this paper, the IP over ATM protocol is modified so that different traffic types (e.g., real-time) can benefit from the QoS guarantees provided by the underlying ATM network (Figure 2).

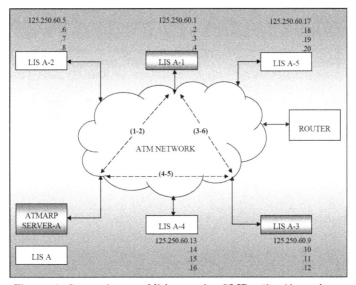

**Figure 1 Connection establishment in CLIP:** *(1) A1 sends an ATMARP request to the server-A on the LIS A and (2) the server returns ATM address of the A3. (3) A1 establishes an ATM link using this address. (4) When A3 receives the first packet, it also sends an ATMARP request to the server-A to find out the ATM address of the A1 (sender). (5) Once the server returns the appropriate address, (6) A1 and A3 can communicate directly without any further server involvement.*

## 4. Real-time Applications

Real-time multimedia is a class of technologies and applications that span two or more media (data, audio and video). It can operate with delivery from 56 Kbps to 155 Mbps of information to a user. The 1.5-6 Mbps data rate per user is a basic range designed to support multimedia technology developers (Minoli *et al*, 1996). Real-time digital audio and video applications require Constant Bit Rate (CBR) and Variable Bit Rate Real-Time (VBR-RT) service categories respectively. For CBR services, the Peak Cell Rate (PCR) descriptor must be provided to the ATM network whilst for VBR services, Minimum and Sustained Cell Rates (MCR and SCR) are also mandatory. Interactive traffic and LAN interconnect traffic are carried over Available Bit Rate (ABR) service. Applications using this service specify the MCR descriptor and can also add PCR and MCR. Applications where packet delivery is not guaranteed (e.g., e-mail) are provided over Unspecified Bit Rate (UBR) service. This is the ATM counterpart of the Internet BE service category.

## 5. Support for ABR, VBR, CBR and UBR Service Classes in IP over ATM Networks

Our goal is to extend the CLIP protocol so that all ATM Service Classes can be utilised in IP over ATM environments (Figure 2). This approach is designed to provide IP end users with ATM CBR, VBR and ABR service classes in addition to the UBR (i.e., BE). This scheme improves the only classical support of IP BE service, enabling each IP host pair to have 4 dedicated VCs with different QoS. The idea behind this approach is that each service category is carried using a different IP address. Thus, this technique providing all ATM service classes requires 3 more IP addresses for every CLIP end user that demands real-time multimedia applications. Same types of service classes are mapped to the associated IP addresses at the source IP user. This processe is realised using a locally configured entity to switch VBR, CBR, ABR and UBR traffic to the IP1, IP2, IP3 and IP4 addresses respectively, and vice versa at the destination IP user.

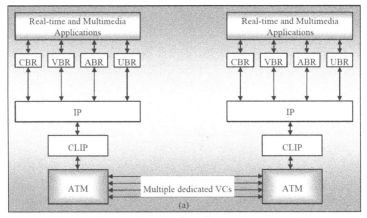

**Figure 2 CLIP with multiple dedicated VC connections**

140

## 5.1 Simulation Models

The simulation environment is comprised of two models. The first model, representing the new proposed approach, is used to evaluate the effect of the different service classes offered by the underlying ATM network to the IP users running real-time multimedia applications whilst the second one represents the classical CLIP approach (Figure 3). The latter provides only a BE (i.e., UBR) service to the IP end users whilst the former enables the IP end users to use also CBR, VBR and ABR service classes. In both models each IP end user (i.e., $A_1$-$A_n$) is connected to an ATM Network (155.520 Mbps), and has 4 applications with different traffic characteristics to be presented on the network, namely, an e-mail transfer (ET) requiring a UBR service, a file transfer (FT) requiring an ABR service, a real-time compressed video transfer (CVT) requiring a VBR service and finally a real-time voice transfer (VT) requiring a CBR service. Although one-way traffic would produce similar results, for more realistic and accurate results the data traffic is chosen to be two-way, from source to destination, both of which are on the same LIS, and vice versa. The service parameters of the ATM network are given in Table 1.

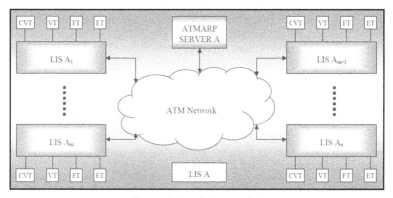

**Figure 3 Simulation model**

Both the ABR and the UBR traffic management are accomplished using Resource Management (RM) cells employed to determine network congestion. To obtain network feedback, the ABR and UBR traffic sources send RM cells (53 bytes) after every Nrm-1[1]. Destinations simply return these RM cells containing the Congestion Indication (CI) flag back to the sources. If upon return of the RM cell no congestion is indicated, the transmission rate is increased by the Additive Increase Rate (AIR). Otherwise, transmission rate is decreased by the Rate Decrease Factor (RDF) (i.e., the current transmission rate is divided by the RDF).

Throughout the simulation time (i.e., 300 seconds), ET, FT, CVT, and VT are created and introduced to the network every IAT[2] seconds (i.e., 1 second) with an exponential distribution by every IP user on the LIS. Since this traffic is far higher than the one the ATMARP mechanisms introduce, resulting delays by the latter are considered insignificant.

---

[1] The default value for Nrm is 32.
[2] Inter Arrival Time.

| Service Class (ATM Adaptation Layer) | Data + Header (Bytes) | PCR (Mbps) | MCR (Mbps) | SBR (Mbps) | ICR* (Mbps) | AIR (Mbps) | RDF |
|---|---|---|---|---|---|---|---|
| CBR (AAL1) | 47 + 6 | 6 | - | - | - | - | - |
| VBR (AAL2) | 47 + 6 | 6 | 1 | 2 | - | - | - |
| ABR (AAL3/4) | 44 + 9 | 6 | 0.5 | - | 0.5 | 0.5 | 2 |
| UBR (AAL5) | 48 + 5 | 6 | 0.01 | - | 0.1 | 0.2 | 4 |

ICR*: Initial Cell Rate

**Table 1: ATM network service parameters**

### 5.3 Simulation Results

The following paragraphs explain the simulation results (i.e., end-to-end message delays as a function of both the message sizes of the ET, FT, CVT and VT, and the simulation time).

Initially all of the traffic introduced to the network by each application is chosen to be equal so that the evaluation of the ATM services can be easily justified (Figures 4). Having considered that the maximum agreeable buffer size is 1000 ATM cells for real-time services (Key, 1995), all of the results are provided for 53,000 byte buffer size used in the models (indicating the congestion threshold). Figure 4 clearly shows the improvement in the average end-to-end delay with our approach enabling IP end users to have ATM services. Although all of the multimedia applications experience an enormous and almost equal amount of delays over the BE service, they are well below the acceptable limits (especially the real-time voice, i.e. VT, and compressed video applications, i.e. CVT) over the ATM services.

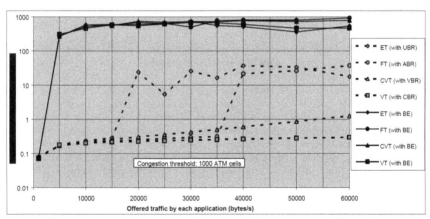

**Figure 4 Average end-to-end delay with ATM services and BE service**

Figure 5 illustrates the maximum and average end-to-end message delays of the each multimedia traffic for the proposed model as a function of simulation time. The modelled traffic is chosen to be similar to the real multimedia (i.e., ET = Exp[3] (80) Kbps, FT = Exp (800) Kbps, CVT = Nor[4] (320, 320) Kbps (Lauderdale, 1996), and VT = 80 Kbps). The average VT and CVT end-to-end delay graphs are of particular interest. They are almost constant and predictable (around milliseconds level) although the maximum CVT end-to-end delay is 4 times more than its average value.

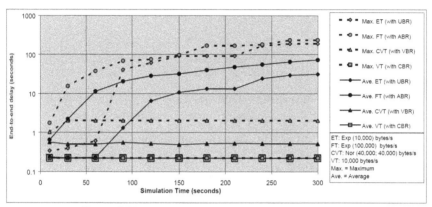

**Figure 5 Message delay as a function of simulation time**

## 6. Conclusion

QoS support in IP over ATM networks is a hot topic. First implementations of LANE, MPOA and CLIP do not provide real-time multimedia support. The proposed scheme offers a simple approach allowing IP end users with real-time multimedia applications to run over ATM networks with QoS support. It can be realised between the ATM and the TCP/IP stack as a mapping layer.

Compared to the classical approach, the new scheme not only supports CBR, VBR and ABR service classes in addition to the BE (i.e., UBR) but also provides over 100 times better end-to-end message delay results for real-time voice and compressed video traffic.

Simulation studies and performance analysis of the proposed approach together with the classical one, providing real-time applications to the IP end user desktops, have shown that different multimedia applications can be satisfactorily supported in IP over ATM networks.

---

[3] Exponential Distribution Function takes one positive number (mean) and returns a positive real number.
[4] Normal Distribution Function takes two positive numbers (mean, standard deviation) and returns a positive real number.

## 7. References

Nichols, N., Blake, S., Baker, F. and Black, D. (1998), *Definition of the Differentiated Services Field (DS Field) in the IP4 and IP6 Headers,* IETF, RFC 2474.

Eichler, G., Hussmann, H., Mamais, G., Venieris, I., Prehofer, C. and Salsane, S., (2000), "Implementing Integrated and Differentiated Services for the Internet with ATM Networks: A Practical Approach", *IEEE Communications Magazine,* Vol. 38, No. 1, pp. 132-141.

Gupta, R. (1999), "The glue of networks: Looking at IP over ATM", *53 Bytes,* Vol. 7, No. 1, pp. 4-5.

Hankins, M. L. (1999), "Protocol spawns debate over future of voice, data, video communications", *Signal Magazine (May'99),* pp. 5.

Fan, Z. (1999), "New trends in ATM networks: a research view", *Computer Communications,* Vol. 22, pp. 499-515.

Decina, M. and Trecordi, V. (1997), "Convergence of telecommunications and computing to networking models for integrated services and applications", *Proceedings of the IEEE (December 1997),* pp. 1887-1914.

Erturk, I., Tenruh, M., Stipidis, E. and Kutlu, A. (1999), "Interconnection of ATM LANs with legacy LANs across an ATM backbone using LAN Emulation Service", *Proceedings of 14th ISCIS,* pp. 703-710.

The ATM Forum (February 1999), *LAN Emulation over ATM, Version 2,* The ATM Forum.

The ATM Forum (May 1999), *MPOA Baseline, Version 1.1,* The ATM Forum.

Laubach, M. and Halpern, J. (1998), *Classical IP and ARP over ATM,* IETF, RFC 2225.

Barnett, R. (1997), "Connectionless ATM", *Electronics Communication Engineering Journal,* Vol. 9, No. 5, pp. 221-230.

Sun, H., Huang, K. and Li, L. (1998), "Supporting IP on the ATM networks: an overview", *Computer Communications,* Vol. 21, No. 11, pp. 1020-1029.

Minoli, D. and Alles, A. (1996), *LAN, ATM, and LAN Emulation Technologies,* Artech House.

Key, P.B. (1995), "Connection Admission Control in ATM Networks", *BT Technology Journal,* Vol. 13, No. 13, pg. 52-65.

Lauderdale, J. (1996), *Variable Bit Rate Video Transmission over ATM Networks (pg. 61),* The Hong Kong University of Science and Technology.

# IP network performance monitoring of voice flows for IP telephony

B.V.Ghita[1], S.M.Furnell[1], B.M.Lines[1], D.Le-Foll[2], E.C.Ifeachor[3]

[1] Network Research Group, School of Electronic, Communication & Electrical Engineering, University of Plymouth, Plymouth, United Kingdom
[2] Wavetek Wandel Goltermann, Plymouth, United Kingdom
[3] SMART Systems Research Group, School of Electronic, Communication & Electrical Engineering, University of Plymouth, Plymouth, United Kingdom

## Abstract

This paper presents a non-intrusive method of determining network performance parameters for voice packet flows within a VoIP (Voice over IP, or Internet Telephony) call. An advantage of the method is that it allows not only end-to-end performance monitoring of flows, but also makes it possible to inspect the transport parameters a specific network or link when delay sensitive traffic transits through it. The results of a preliminary test, to check the validity of the method, are also included.

## Keywords

Voice over IP, Quality of Service parameters, non-intrusive monitoring.


## 1   Introduction

Over the last two decades, the Internet has evolved from a few interconnected networks that linked research laboratories, universities, or military infrastructure, to an everyday tool which is easy to access and use by many people. The dramatic evolution can be assessed in terms of growth in the number of hosts and Internet applications. The initial use of the Internet was different to that of today.  Contrasting two studies of Internet activity, from 1991 (Caceres et al, 1991) and 1997 (Thompson et al, 1997), it can be seen that the nature of activity has changed from applications such as telnet or file transfer to become dominated by web browsing (75%).  The increased computational power of end-user stations has allowed new types of applications to be implemented.  In addition, the speed and reliability of the Internet itself has been substantially enhanced due to the new technologies used. These advances have allowed application content to move from text to multimedia and real-time.

A major challenge in Internet development is how to support real-time applications, typified by Internet Telephony, within the existing structure. Internet Telephony aims to replace the traditional concept in telecommunications from data over voice to voice over data. The method for achieving this is to use the Internet as a transport carrier for voice, instead of the PSTN (Public Switched Telephone Network). The most obvious advantage is the low cost for long-distance phone calls.

An important barrier in the development of VoIP is the Internet Protocol (IP). IP works as a best-effort connectionless protocol. It was designed for data files that can tolerate delays, dropped packets and retransmissions; there are no guarantees about the delivery time or the reliability of a packet being transferred over the Internet. The most important aspects, when considering an audio conference are exactly those that Internet cannot guarantee: time and bandwidth. The quality of the resulting conference depends upon the satisfaction of these requirements. Within this context, the concept of Quality of Service (QoS) was introduced. Although the Internet represents an environment in which the QoS cannot be guaranteed, there are measurable parameters for a specific service, as presented in a QoS overview study (Stiller, 1995).

This paper presents an offline method of determining network performance parameters for voice packet flows within a VoIP call. An advantage of the method is that it allows not only end-to-end performance monitoring of the flows, but also makes it possible to inspect the behaviour of the network when faced with delay sensitive traffic.

## 2  QoS concept for VoIP and current state of monitoring

The QoS is the overall rating for a service. Measurement of QoS essentially includes measuring a number of application dependent parameters and then gathering them in a weighted sum. If we consider QoS for VoIP, the object of the analysis is the voice at the receiving end, with its two main characteristics, sound and interactivity. There are two main sources of impairments for the voice heard by the receiver.  The first is the codec, which compresses the speech flow in order to send it over the network at a lower bandwidth than original.  Aside from the positive result in terms of bandwidth utilisation, this process degrades the quality of the speech.  The second source of impairment is the transport.  After encoding, the audio flow is packetised and sent over the Internet. However, because of the Internet's structure, the arrival of the packets at destination cannot be guaranteed. The paper is focused upon a consideration of this latter impairment.

Building a list of performance parameters for a service should start by identifying the application that requires that specific service. For example, if the targeted application is a file transfer then the delay or jitter parameters are almost irrelevant when compared to throughput or packet loss. In a similar manner, for a real-time application, delay is far more important than the other parameters. The paper does not intend to prescribe a specific weighting here, but it is good to bear in mind their priorities when assessing the overall performance.

When considering QoS for VoIP applications, a network-related view of the performance should include the following parameters:

-   delay - the time elapsed between the sending of a packet and its arrival at the destination;
-   jitter - the variance of the delay value;
-   packet loss - the number of lost packets, reported in the time elapsed;
-   throughput - the amount of data transferred from one place to another or processed in a specified amount of time.

There are several suggested methods that can improve or guarantee the QoS for transport, such as DiffServ (Differentiated Services) (Nichols et al, 1998), Tenet (Ferrari et al, 1994), or QoS Routing combined with RSVP (Reservation Protocol) (Crawley et al, 1998).

Unfortunately, none of them are applied on global basis because of the scale and complexity of the Internet. Therefore, it is vital to determine in such an environment whether or not a specific connection meets the requirements of a VoIP call.

Transport QoS has two main areas: end-to-end measurements and, in case there are changes in the level of parameters, fault localisation. An example is given in Figure 1 which shows, for an arbitrary division of the entire route of the packets, the end-to-end parameters, and two sets of parameters, 'East' and 'West'. The latter can be used to localise a fault in either 'East' or 'West' sub-network, by comparison with the end-to-end parameters.

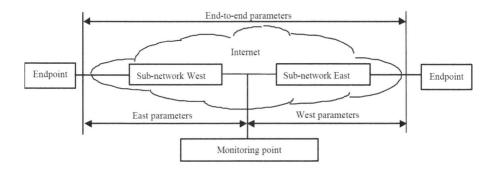

**Figure 1: The Performance parameters for a general example of monitoring**

In a traditional approach, the two aims would require a 3-tool configuration. For end-to-end measurements, testing clients should be put at both ends and, for fault location, a testing server should be placed at the monitoring point. After that, traffic should be collected by the end stations, then sent to the server, in order to be analysed and compared with the data collected by it. There are two main disadvantages with this approach:

- it is intrusive; in the best case, even if the endpoint clients are just monitoring, they have to send the data to the server in order to be analysed,
- it requires placement of monitoring devices at both ends.

The QoS for transport can be determined from the audio flows within a call (which run on RTP, Real Time Protocol). Current tools (e.g. Hammer VoIP Analysis System, HP Internet Advisor, rtpmon (Bacher and Swan, 1996)) base their calculations upon parsing both the RTP and/or the accompanying control flows (running on RTCP, Real Time Control Protocol) and displaying the available data. The main disadvantage is that none of these tools can establish fault location without using the traditional approach mentioned above. More than that, they do not build any relation between the end-to-end parameters, obtained from the RTCP flows, and the end-to-monitoring-point parameters, obtained from the RTP monitoring.

Considering these limitations, we aim to obtain a better view of the network performance, without using several devices and without injecting additional traffic into the network. This paper presents a non-intrusive method of determining the transport performance parameters for the real-time traffic within a VoIP call, using a single point of monitoring. The proposed method can reveal both the end-to-end performance and the fault localisation, if the monitored parameters change their value along the route, and also avoids both of the disadvantages identified.

## 3  Description of H.323 calls

VoIP is a relative new concept and, therefore, most of the work performed in this area is still at a developmental stage. From the large range of standards for VoIP, the H.323 protocol stack (ITU, 1998), developed by ITU, was selected as the basis for the work presented in this paper.

The focus of the QoS for transport is, as mentioned, on the audio flows. Because of the H.323 call structure, which will be detailed below, these flows cannot be identified unless the entire call is monitored. The information exchanged in a H.323 conference is classified in streams, as follows: audio (coded speech), video (coded motion video), data (computer files), communication control (control data), and call control (signalling data).

We will consider the simplest case - a direct connection between two computer terminals, similar to a classic phone call. The call begins with a call signalling phase – signalling messages (Q.931 using H.225 specification) are exchanged, on specific ports. At the end of this phase, the call is established and a call control channel is opened, on ports dynamically allocated. The control channel then provides for various functions: capabilities exchange, logical channel signalling, mode preferences, master – slave determination. After the terminals decide which of them will act as a master for the call (in order to easily resolve conflicts), they exchange their capabilities and open an audio channel, using logical channel signalling. The logical channel is also opened on a dynamically allocated port, decided within the control messages. The audio flows run on the opened logical channel. When one of the users wants to terminate the call, the logical channel is closed, using call control, then specific call signalling messages are exchanged, and the call is closed.

The audio (as well as video) flows within an H.323 conference are transported using RTP, as it provides end-to-end network transport functions suitable for applications transmitting real-time data over multicast or unicast network services (Schulzrinne et al, 1996). It does not address resource reservation and does not guarantee quality-of-service for real-time services. In fact, the whole protocol is conceived not as a separate layer, but as a framework, to be integrated within other applications. RTP is usually run on top of UDP (User Datagram Protocol), an unreliable transport protocol. TCP (Transport Control Protocol), although reliable, brings additional delay problems, by delivering the packets in order and recovering the lost packets, and, therefore, is not recommended for carrying real-time flows.

RTCP is the control protocol for RTP. One of its functions is to provide information about the packets loss and inter-arrival jitter for the accompanying RTP flow. The information is provided periodically by all the senders / receivers within a conference using specific packets, and is based on the RTP flow measurements. The RTCP flow also runs on UDP.

# 4   Experimental method and implementation

## 4.1   Monitoring procedure

The monitoring procedure comprises three steps. First, the voice flows (RTP) are identified and then captured using one of the capture programs. In the monitoring phase, the RTP header fields and the RTCP packets are used to determine the performance parameters. Then correlation of RTP and RTCP is used to establish the location of the problem area. The stages are described in more detail in the following paragraphs.

### 4.1.1   Identification of the audio flows

The analysis is targeted on the audio streams. The ports on which the audio streams run can be determined only by capturing the connection establishment phase, then parsing the setup and control messages, which contain the audio stream ports as parameters. The parsing process is not straightforward, as the content of the setup and control messages is not header-like (using fields), but encoded using ASN.1 syntax.

### 4.1.2   Parameter measurement using RTP monitoring and RTCP parsing

The header fields of RTP packets are used as input to the analysis, together with the timestamp of the packet arrival, given by the capture program. The structure of the RTP header is described in (RTP 1889, 1996).

The following types of parameters can be determined using the RTP header fields and the arrival timestamp of each packet, taken from the packet capture program:

a. delay-related parameters:
- inter-arrival delay – by subtracting the capture timestamps of successive packets
- inter-arrival jitter – by comparing the previous delay with the actual one
- one-way delay jitter – by comparing the inter-arrival delay with the sender delay (the interval between sending two sequential packets).

b. packet-accounting parameters
- lost packets and out of order packets – by comparing the expected sequence number with the sequence number of the incoming packet. The lost packets variable is increased, but the presumed lost packets sequence numbers are memorised, in case the packets were not lost, but only misordered.

c. flow speed parameters
- throughput – determined by dividing the actual received number of bytes by the time of the connection

The RTCP packets can be used as an instrument for end-to-end measurements. Their fields provide the values for inter-arrival jitter and lost packets.  The following observations can be made in relation to using RTCP to analyse the flows:

- it runs on UDP (User Datagram Protocol) and, therefore, it is possible that a number of packets will not arrive, so no data will be available for that period of time.
- it has scalability problems (Rosenberg and Schulzrinne, 1998). The RTCP messages are limited to 5% of the whole traffic. In the case of a many-to-many conference, on normal behaviour, there would be a low number of RTP messages per-terminal (in order to maintain the 5% limit) (Schulzrinne et al, 1996).
- it returns only end-to-end parameters and, therefore, cannot locate the cause of parameter changes (this problem exists regardless of the conference characteristics)

Note: the analysis is performed on a 'per-flow' basis. Prior to performing the analysis, the incoming packets (from several audio channels) are split into flows (each flow representing a channel). When saying successive packets, we refer to packets belonging to the same flow.

### 4.1.3   Correlating RTP  analysis with RTCP content

By correlating the two sets of parameters, obtained from RTP and RTCP, it is possible to determine whether or not a specific problem (e.g. a high number of lost packets) is caused by a problem which exists in the East sub-network or the West sub-network. Figure 2 presents the captured flows.

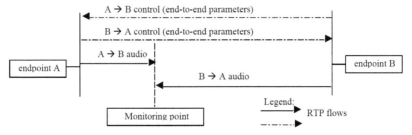

**Figure 2: RTP and RTCP flows monitoring**

The RTP streams, as captured on the monitoring point, are: A → B (after passing through the West sub-network) and B → A (after passing through the East sub-network). Therefore, by measuring the parameters of these flows, we can determine the performance of the West sub-network (from the A → B flow) and the East sub-network (from the B → A flow).

We have to bear in mind that the A → B direction does not fully characterise the behaviour of the network, as it can be very good for one direction and bad for the other (it does not have to be symmetrical in terms of performance).  Meanwhile, as mentioned, RTCP provides the end-to-end parameters, i.e. the performance of the entire A → B and B → A routes, but it has no indication about how these parameters change on the route (i.e. cannot establish where a faulty behaviour of the network determined a change in the values of the parameters).

Putting together the two sets, we obtain parameters for the following segments:

- A → B and B → A, end-to-end – from the RTCP flows
- A → monitoring point and B → monitoring point – from the RTP flows

-   monitoring point → B and monitoring point → A – by subtracting the RTP obtained values from RTCP end-to-end parameters.

Therefore, by using both RTP and RTCP, we obtain both the end-to-end and the end-to-monitoring point parameters for the monitored flows.

## 4.2   Implementation

The monitoring module was first built within the tcptrace program (Ostermann, 2000). Tcptrace is an offline analysis program, that uses tcpdump traces as input. Although the program had limited support for UDP (it was able to separate the UDP flows), and no support for RTP, it was considered a useful tool because of its per-flow analysis capabilities. The module was subsequently migrated to ipgrab (Borella, 2000) to reduce the complexity of the program (tcptrace includes a lot of functions, spread over various modules, most of them related with TCP analysis). Most of the analysis (e.g. the distributions), as described in the following section, was performed offline, under Microsoft Excel. As no equipment to simulate several calls was available, the analysis was performed for only a single VoIP call. The module will work for more than one call, but a proper filtration of the output should be added. In addition, the refresh period of the analysis (i.e. each packet) could create computational problems for a high number of flows. A proper solution would be to display the parameters at certain intervals (e.g. every second).

Special attention is given to the marker, payload type and timestamp fields within the RTP header. During a VoIP call, if there is no speech from the user, an endpoint does not send RTP packets. Therefore, when calculating the flow speed and the delay parameters, the silence periods should be ignored. The silence periods can be identified using the marker field: an RTP packet with the marker field set signals the end of a silence period. Also, if the payload characteristics are known (e.g. each RTP packet contains a 30ms frame), the delay between successive packets at the sender can be determined. Thus, by subtracting this value from the inter-arrival delay, we obtain the one-way delay jitter.

# 5   Validation

## 5.1   Experimental testbed configuration

A network testbed was constructed in order to validate the proposed method. Figure 3 presents the testbed configuration, which included two networks, connected through a faulty link. The monitoring point is placed on the route, at the exit point (after the router) of one of the networks.

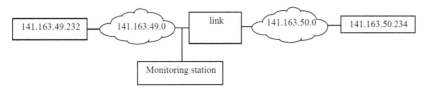

**Figure 3: Network testbed configuration**

The link is emulated using the NISTNet program (NISTNet, 2000). NISTNet emulates various network problems by forwarding packets, under specific parameters like packet loss, delay or jitter, between two network interface cards, on a Linux station. For our test, we used the following parameters (symmetric for the two directions): 5% packet loss, 300 ms delay, 25 ms jitter, unlimited bandwidth, normal distribution. The measurements were based on a capture session; number of packets captured: ~20000 (some of them were removed in order to eliminate the transitional behaviour);

The software tools used for generating, capturing and monitoring the VoIP flows were:

- NetMeeting (WinNT) – to establish and run a H.323 VoIP call;
- codec: Microsoft G.723.1, 6400 bits/second, continuous speech;
- tcpdump, ipgrab (Linux) – to capture packets transmitted over the network (between the two VoIP endpoints);
- the analysis module (Linux) – first developed within tcptrace, then transferred to ipgrab, to allow online capturing.

The measurements aim to locate the jitter and the packet loss by dividing the route of the packets, as presented in Figure 2 into sub-network East (network 141.163.49.0), and sub-network West (emulated link and network 141.163.50.0). After obtaining the various parameters, we will try to identify the fault location on the 141.163.50.0 network and link side of the route. In the following paragraphs, we will refer at 141.163.49.232 station as A and at 141.163.50.234 as B.

## 5.2  Results and value comparison

A. Throughput and packet loss
Table 1 presents the following information:

- normal – the normal behaviour, on a network without any loss;
- RTP results – the values determined from the RTP monitoring;
- RTCP results – the values determined from the RTCP parsing.

| Parameter | normal | RTP results | | RTCP results | |
|---|---|---|---|---|---|
| | | A → B | B → A | A → B | B → A |
| throughput [bytes/sec] | 800 | 800 | 760 | 760 | 760 |
| packet loss [%] | 0 | 0 | 5 | 5 | 5 |

**Table 1: Throughput and packet loss statistics**

The RTCP throughput is determined from the RTCP sender reports, using the 'sender octet count' which indicates how many octets were transmitted since the beginning of the call. The RTCP reports also include report blocks, which give the performance parameters of the senders 'heard' by the emitter of the report. The RTCP packet loss is determined from these report blocks, using the 'cumulative number of packets lost' field.

It can be noticed that the B → A values differs, which indicates a 5% packet loss on that direction, located in the right side of the route. Also, the A → B values indicate that there is no alteration, in term of packet loss, in the left side of the route (the 141.163.49.0 network).

B. Jitter

From the RTP monitoring the jitter was determined by subtracting the average interarrival delay from the interarrival delay for the actual packet. The results are presented in Figure 4.

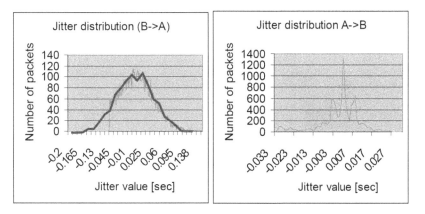

Legend for B → A jitter distribution:

▬▬▬▬▬   the injected jitter (approximate shape)

──────   the measured jitter

**Figure 4: RTP jitter distribution (from RTP monitoring)**

Note: In the left graph, the thick line indicates the shape of the average distribution (based on separate measurements on same environment). It can be seen that the measurements are valid.

In the RTCP parsing the values were extracted from the RTCP report blocks (the 'interarrival jitter' value).

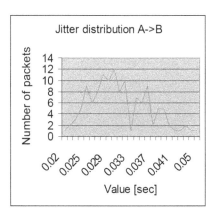
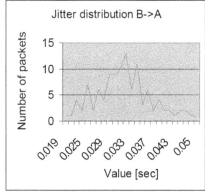

**Figure 5: RTP jitter distribution (from RTCP parsing)**

As can be seen from Figure 4, the distribution for the B → A flow can be approximated with a Normal (Gaussian) one (the interval (-inf;-0.6) could not be reproduced because of some measurement limitations), while the A → B flow shows no distribution of the jitter. For both of the flows, the is an additional 3 ms jitter, caused by Netmeeting behaviour: although the packets interarrival delay should be constant (60 ms), from time to time, the program transmits a voice packet after 30 ms.

If we consider the absolute values for the jitter, it results an average value of 28 ms, which, if we extract the 3 ms caused by NetMeeting behaviour, it results the value of the emulated link: 25 ms. As a conclusion, the tool, together with the results analysis identified the 5% loss and 25 ms jitter generated by the right side of the monitored route.

Although the monitoring tool was built, and these preliminary tests were performed, a full assessment requires further analysis in a real or simulated VoIP environment. Such an environment would include several simultaneous conferences, running between endpoints situated at different locations, over various routes.

## 6   Conclusions and further work

This paper has described an off-line method to measure the QoS transport parameters for a H.323 VoIP call from a single point, by non-intrusive monitoring, and we presented a test performed in order to validate our method. The jitter and packet loss analysis seems promising, but further work is required to determine, monitor and analyse the other parameters. Also, a specific change in the performance parameters group can be related with a specific network event (e.g. a congested router). Therefore, analysis of the dynamics of the calculated parameters is required.

There are also other parameters still to be measured. In measurement systems for POTS (Plain Old Telephone Systems), a useful parameter for the call performance is the round trip time (RTT) delay (i.e. the time needed by a signal to go from one end to the other and then back). There is no possibility to determine such a parameter for H.323 calls because the standard is built for multicast conferences (multi-to-multi conferences), and so it does not include mechanisms for single end-to-end connection; the flows between the endpoints do not run in pairs, there is no correlation between them (they run independently). There are several methods to determine RTT for VoIP calls:

- Using the setup and control messages; they run on TCP, and the values obtained might differ from the (theoretical) ones for UDP
- Using RTCPs' 'delay since last source report(SR)' field.
- Correlating the RTP and RTCP flows. The RTCP packets include a 'extended highest sequence number received' field. If the value of this field is correlated with the sequence number of the sender, together with its timestamp, the RTT can be measured.

Another useful parameter would be the one-way delay of the packets (i.e. the time between when the packet is sent and when it arrives at the destination). This measurement also cannot be performed, as this would imply synchronisation between the clocks of the endpoints, and there are no procedures for this. All the timing information from the packets is either synchronised with the sender clock, or is dynamic (significant only for the time subtractions; the initial value is random).

# References

Bacher D. and Swan A. (1996), 'rtpmon: A Third-Party RTCP Monitor', *ACM Multimedia '96*.

Borella M. (2000), 'ipgrab homepage', http://home.xnet.com/~cathmike/MSB/Software/index.html.

Caceres R., Danzig P.B., Jamin S., and Mitzel D.J. (1991), 'Characteristics of Wide-Area TCP/IP Conversations', *Proceedings of ACM SIGCOMM '91*.

Ferrari D., Banerjea A., and Zhang H. (1994), 'Network Support for Multimedia – A Discussion of the Tenet Approach', *Computer Networks and ISDN Systems*, December 1994.

ITU. (1998), 'Packet based multimedia communication systems', *H.323 ITU Recommendation*, February 1998.

Nistnet. (2000), 'The NIST Net home page', *http://snad.ncsl.nist.gov/itg/nistnet/index.html*

Ostermann S. (2000), 'tcptrace homepage', http://jarok.cs.ohiou.edu/software/tcptrace/tcptrace.html.

Schulzrinne H., Casner S., Frederick R., and Jacobson V. (1996), RFC 1889 - 'RTP – A Transport Protocol for Real-Time Applications', *RFC depository*, January 1996.

Crawley E., Nair R., Rajagopalan B., and Sandick H. (1998), RFC 2386 - 'A Framework for QoS-based Routing', *RFC depository*, August 1998.

Nichols K., Blake S., Baker F., and Black D. (1998), RFC 2474 - 'Differentiated Services Field', *RFC depository*, December 1998.

Rosenberg J. and Schulzrinne H. (1998), 'Timer Reconsideration for Enhanced RTP Scalability', *Proceedings of IEEE Infocom 1998*, March 29 - April 2 1998.

Stiller B. (1997), 'Quality of Service Issues in Networking Environments', internal report, *http://www.cl.cam.ac.uk/ftp/papers/reports/TR380-bs201-qos_isues.ps.gz*, September 1995.

Thompson K., Miller G.J., and Wilder R. (1997), 'Wide-Area Internet Traffic Patterns and Characteristics', *IEEE network*, November-December 1997.

# VoIP Speech Quality Simulation and Evaluation

L. F. Sun[1], G. Wade[1], B. M. Lines[1], D. Le Foll[2], E. C. Ifeachor[1]

[1]School of Electronic, Communication & Electrical Engineering,
University of Plymouth, United Kingdom
[2]Wavetek Wandel Goltermann, Plymouth, United Kingdom

## Abstract

The paper first presents briefly the current ITU P.861 PSQM objective speech quality measurement algorithm. Then the influence of packet loss and packet size on objective speech quality are simulated and analysed on a VoIP simulation platform. The limitations and possible improvements of the PSQM algorithm for use in VoIP applications are also given, together with future work.

## Keywords

Voice over IP, QoS, Objective Speech Quality, Speech Quality Assessment

## 1. Introduction

Common VoIP network connections normally include the connection from phone to phone, phone to PC (VoIP Terminal or H.323 Terminal) or PC to PC. The end-to-end speech transmission quality will depend on the quality of the gateway (G/W) or VoIP/H.323 terminal and IP network performance.

Current research, worldwide, is concentrating on how to guarantee IP Network performance in order to achieve the required Quality of Service (QoS). Also, the impact of network parameters such as packet loss and jitter on speech quality have been broadly analysed (ETSI TR, 1999) (Yamamoto and Beerends, 1997). On the other hand, research is underway to improve the speech quality for "best effort" IP networks, and different compensation strategies for packet loss (Rosenberg, 1997) and jitter (Rosenberg and Qiu et al, 2000) have been proposed to improve speech quality even under poor network conditions.

Regardless of the strategy that is used to improve IP network performance or gateway/terminal performance, the purpose is to achieve a satisfactory speech transmission quality. The final judgement of speech quality still depends on the end user's perception. Subjective speech quality MOS (Mean Opinion Score) scores are considered the most powerful and recognised measure of speech quality, although the exact MOS value depends upon the measurement conditions. Since subjective measurement is time-consuming and expensive, objective speech quality measurement has been proposed to estimate the subjective quality of a network. Typical objective measurement methods include PSQM (Perceptual Speech Quality Measurement) (ITU, 1998) and PAMS (Perceptual Analysis/Measurement System) (ETSI EG, 1999). PSQM has been chosen as the ITU standard (P.861, 2/98) for objective speech quality measurement. Since these objective measures were originally developed for the assessment of speech quality for low bit rate codecs, the impact of packet loss or variable delay (two important impairments in VoIP) were not considered in their first versions. Current work in ITU Study Group 12 therefore focuses on new objective speech quality assessment methods for VoIP, GSM and other networks. Modified PSQM or PAMS (e.g. PSQM+ (ITU, 1997), PSQM99, PAMS release 2.0 and 3.0) and other new algorithms have been proposed for the competition of the new ITU standard, which is expected to be available at the end of this year (ITU, 2000).

In this paper, we will first introduce briefly the ITU P.861 objective speech quality measurement algorithm in section 2. Then the structure, basic function and main parameters of a VoIP simulation platform are presented in section 3, preliminary test results about the influence of packet loss and packet size on objective speech quality are also given. In section 4, the limitations and possible improvements for PSQM while used in VoIP applications are presented, together with future work.

## 2. Objective Speech Quality Measurement

Objective perceptual speech quality measurement systems normally use two input signals, namely a reference signal and the degraded signal measured at the output of the network or system under test. Due to non-linearity arising from the codec, the signals should be speech recordings or artificial speech-like test signals. Typical measurement methods are PSQM and PAMS. Signal processing normally includes pre-processing, psycho-acoustic modelling, and a speech quality estimation model. The differences between these algorithms lie in differences between models. For example, the ITU P.861 PSQM algorithm consists of a perceptual model and a cognitive model (Figure 1), whilst PAMS includes an auditory transform (psychoacoustic model) and perceptual layer processing.

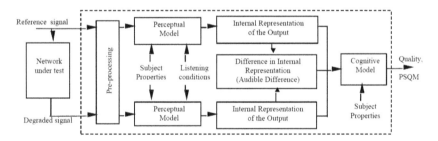

**Figure 1. Structure of PSQM**

As an example, we summarise the processing of PSQM as follows:
- Pre-processing
In order to compare the two signals, a pre-processing unit is used to perform delay adjustment (time alignment), loudness adjustment (equates loudness) and duration adjustment.

- Transformation
Each signal is passed through a "perceptual model". This transforms the signal into a psychophysical representation that approximates human perception. These internal

representations make use of the psychophysical equivalents of frequency (critical band rates) and intensity (compressed sone).

- Calculation of perceptual difference distance, Noise Disturbance N or PSQM value
The perceptual difference distance is calculated between the two model output signals. This perceptual distance is expressed as a noise disturbance $N_i$ for frame i (frame length 32ms), or N (PSQM value) by averaging for the whole speech segment. PSQM value indicated the degree of subjective quality degradation caused by the whole system under test. The PSQM value has a range from 0 to 6.5. 0 means no degradation (perfect quality), whereas 6.5 indicates the highest degradation.

- Mapping to objective MOS
The PSQM value is useful in itself for expressing speech quality degradation. In order to estimate subjective quality, mapping from the PSQM value to MOS score is necessary. The mapping part is not included in the ITU P.861 documents (ITU, 1998) and is also not taken into account in our current test.

## 3. VoIP Simulation Platform and Speech Quality Evaluation

### 3.1 VoIP Simulation Platform
An experimental VoIP speech quality evaluation system is set up as shown is Figure 2. Sender (A) and receiver (B) are two PC running a VoIP terminal simulation program under Linux. The third PC (C) works as a router running NIST NetDisturber (NIST, 2000), which can emulate various network problems by forwarding packets under specific parameters like packet loss, delay or jitter, between two network interface cards under a Linux system.

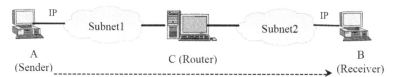

**Figure 2. VoIP simulation platform**

The sender process includes coder, packetizer and socket interface as shown in Figure 3. The receiver process covers socket interface, depacketizer, decoder, playout buffer, and sound driver interface as shown in Figure 4. It also includes an objective speech quality evaluation block, which completes ITU P.861 PSQM objective speech quality measurement algorithm.

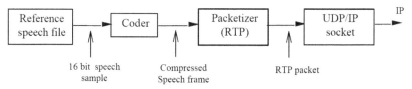

**Figure 3. Sender process**

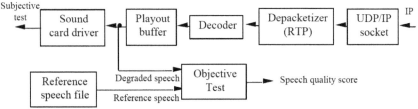

**Figure 4. Receiver process**

### 3.2 Test Conditions and Parameters

RTP/RTCP (Real-time Transport Protocol/ Real-time control Protocol) are chosen as the transport protocol for VoIP's real-time speech transmission. No signalling is considered in the experiment platform and only RTCP is used for setting up the connection between the sender and receiver.

ITU G.729A (8Kbps, low complexity version), G.723.1 Dual-rate (6.3/5.3Kbps) and ETSI GSM-FR (13Kbps) speech codecs are simulated in VoIP simulation platform. The type and frame size for each codec are shown in Table 1. VAD (Voice Activity Detection) is not included in the simulation. All the frames (for active or silent speech frame) are with the same length and have the same packet loss probability under simulation. For G.723.1, the high-pass filter and post-filter are enabled.

| Codec | Type | Bit rate (Kb/s) | Frame Size (ms) | Frame length (bytes) | Lookahead (ms) | Encode Algorithmic Delay (ms) |
|---|---|---|---|---|---|---|
| GSM-FR | RPE-LTP | 13 | 20 | 33 | 0 | 20 |
| G.729 | CS-ACELP | 8 | 10 | 10 | 5 | 15 |
| G.723.1 | MP-MLQ | 6.3 | 30 | 24 | 7.5 | 37.5 |
| | ACELP | 5.3 | 30 | 20 | 7.5 | 37.5 |

**Table 1. Codec type and frame information**

The RTP payload may include one to several speech frames according to the packet size. For example, if choosing three frames per packet, then the payload size is 24 bytes for G.729 as shown in Figure 5. The overhead of RTP/UDP/IP is 40bytes. Clearly, the more frames in one packet, the higher efficiency of transmission bandwidth and the longer delay for packetizing.

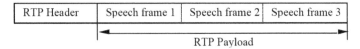

**Figure 5. RTP packet structure (e.g. 3 speech frames per packet)**

For P.861 PSQM, the frame length is 256 samples for 8000 Hz sampling rate (32ms) and adjacent frames overlap each other by 50%. The default global calibration factors ($S_p$ and $S_l$) for long test sentence are used in the experiment, no other calibration work is done.

Two speech files in the ITU corpus are used in the experiment. Sentence 1 is female speaker and sentence 2 is male speaker. Both are about 5 to 6 seconds in duration and contain 16 bit signed linear PCM speech samples at 8kHz.

As PSQM is not suitable for variable delay happened during silence period or talkspurt, we do not consider the jitter adjustment in the experiment. Only a fixed size of jitter buffer (playout buffer) is considered in order to compensate some late packets at the cost of a buffer delay.

Time-alignment at the beginning of test sequence is considered. Except the codec's internal loss concealment, no other external concealment algorithms are taken into account in the simulation. The combination impact of packed loss, packet size and codec type on objective speech quality is the main purpose of the experiment in the paper.

### 3.3 Preliminary test results and analysis

We first test the PSQM values (both $N_i$ and N) for G.723.1, G.729 and GSM-FR without any frame/packet loss. Then for G.729, we choose the 5% random frame loss for one frame per packet (independent or single frame loss) and 5% frame loss for 5 frames per packet (burst frame loss). The PSQM $N_i$ vs frame $i$ and corresponding speech waveform for the first 1.3 seconds of sentence 1 are shown in Figure 6 and 7. The PSQM value (N) for sentences 1 and 2 are shown in Table 1.

It is clear that all $N_i$ values for codecs without packet loss are relatively stable within a limited range (no obvious peak). The reference and degraded speech waveform are similar (no gap) as shown in Figure 7 (A) and (B) for G.729. The PSQM values reflect well the subjective test results (MOS) for 3 codecs (The MOS scores from (Rudkin and Grace et al, 1997) are also listed in Table 2, MOS score for G.723.1 (5.3Kbps) is not available). However when a packet loss occurs, especially burst frame loss, there is an obvious peak in $N_i$ curve for the lost period. It is also clear from comparing two waveforms of Figure 7 (A) for reference speech and (C) for degraded speech with burst loss that one frame is concealed by G.729's built-in one frame loss concealment algorithm. Four silent frames in the case of 5 consecutive frame loss follow this concealment frame. As the G.729 (G.723.1 is similar) decoder is highly dependent on the past state, the burst loss packets cause a divergence of encoder and decoder state. Even if subsequent packets after the burst loss sequence are received, they will not be decoded correctly. We can see this phenomena from the waveform after the burst frame loss in Figure 7 (C) and from the wider peak of $N_i$ curve for G.729 (C) in Figure 6. If a random single frame is lost as shown in Figure 7 (D), the lost frame is concealed by the codec's concealment scheme. There is no gap in the waveform of the degraded signal while compared with the reference signal and also a narrower $N_i$ peak for G.729 (D) in Figure 6.

From the test results and our analysis, we classify the influence of a packet loss on an active speech frame (the frame for a talkspurt, not for a silence period) into the following 3 categories.

- concealment frame (for a lost frame concealed by codec's built-in concealment algorithm or by external concealment algorithms)

- real-lost frame (for a lost frame filled by silence or comfort noise)
- inferred frame (for a normal received frame, which can not be decoded correctly due to lack of the parameters of the previous frames.)

Except the above 3 frames related with packet loss, the others are normal frames, which only suffer the normal codec impairment.

The PSQM $N_i$ value and its variation (e.g. peak and its width) can also be used for analysis and estimate the end-to-end packet loss and the influence of packet loss on objective speech quality.

In addition, we deliberately erase 1/2/3/4/5/6 consecutive frames for every 100 frames and get the PSQM values as shown in Table 3. It is clear that the longer the burst frame loss size, the more serious the objective speech quality degradation. Burst frame loss (corresponding to the larger packet size) has much more influence on perceived speech quality.

**PSQM(Ni) vs speech frame i**

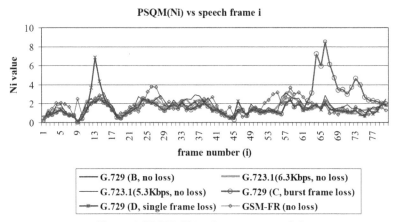

Figure 6. PSQM ($N_i$) value versus speech frame

| Codec type packet loss | G.723.1 (5.3Kbps) no loss | G.723.1 (6.3Kbps) no loss | GSM-FR (13Kbps) no loss | G.729 (B) (8Kbps) no loss | G.729 (C) 5% random frame loss (for 1 frame per packet) | G.729 (D) 5% burst frame loss (for 5 frames per packet) |
|---|---|---|---|---|---|---|
| PSQM (N) Sentence 1 | 1.74 | 1.51 | 1.64 | 1.35 | 1.64 | 2.17 |
| PSQM (N) Sentence 2 | 1.81 | 1.71 | 1.77 | 1.60 | 1.85 | 2.04 |
| MOS | - | 3.8 | 3.7 | 4.0 | - | - |

Table 2.  PSQM value for different codec and packet loss

| Burst size | 1 | 2 | 3 | 4 | 5 | 6 |
|---|---|---|---|---|---|---|
| PSQM | 1.38 | 1.53 | 1.96 | 2.05 | 2.17 | 2.30 |

**Table 3. PSQM value for different burst frame loss size**

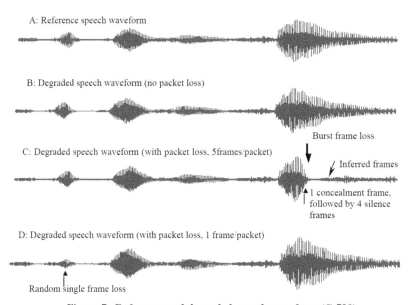

**Figure 7. Reference and degraded speech waveform (G.729)**

## 4. Future work

Simulation and analysis of VoIP speech quality under different codecs, packet size and network performances are ongoing.

As PSQM treats all frames (three types of loss influencing frames and normal frames) with the same processing method or the same weighting factors. PSQM+ was proposed by introducing an additional scaling factor especially for the lost (silence) frames, thereby compensating for the lost frame effect. While for the concealment and implicated frames, their impact on objective speech quality should also be taken into account with other additional scaling factors. The whole impact of packet loss on objective speech quality needs further research.

Another major problem for PSQM in VoIP applications, is the end-to-end jitter (not network jitter) (Sun and Wade et al, 2000), which is caused by the adjustment of jitter buffer. As we have mentioned in the paper, the PSQM algorithm only works well under strict time-alignment for two comparing signals and will give a very high PSQM value if two signals are not time-aligned (the PSQM value is almost meaningless if severe end-to-end jitter exists).

For an adjustment happening in a silent period, it is only necessary to perform realignment before the next talkspurt. For an adjustment happening in mid-talkspurt, time-alignment strategies e.g. cross-correlation could be used to find the matching signal frames for the calculation of the Noise Disturbance for each frame after the adjustment.

Obviously if buffer adjustment is very small, the effect could be imperceptible by the end user. In this situation, only delay jitter needs to be removed to keep the two signals aligned and the corresponding subjective impairment does not need to be considered. If the end-to-end delay jitter is greater than a subjective threshold, the playout impairment itself should be considered as one factor to weight the speech quality measurement algorithm.

## 5. References

ETSI, TR 101 329 V 2.2.2 (1999), "Telecommunication and Internet Protocol Harmonization Over Networks (TIPHON); General aspects of Quality of Service (QoS)", *European Telecommunications Standards Institute.*

ETSI, EG 201 377-1 V1.1.1 (1999), "Specification and measurement of speech transmission quality; Part 1: Introduction to objective comparison measurement methods for one-way speech quality across networks", *European Telecommunications Standards Institute.*

ITU-T COM 12-20-E (1997), "Improvement of the P.861 Perceptual Speech Quality Measure", KPN Research, Netherlands, *International Telecommunication Union.*

ITU-T, P.861 (1998), "Objective quality measurement of telephone-band (300-3400 Hz) speech codecs", *International Telecommunication Union.*

ITU-T COM 12-117-E (2000), "Report of the question 13/12 rapporteur's meeting", Germany, *International Telecommunication Union.*

NIST Net home page (2000), *http://snad.ncsl.nist.gov/itg/nistnet/index.html.*

Rosenberg, J. (1997), "G.729 Error Recovery for Internet Telephony", Project Report, Columbia University, *http://www.cs.columbia.edu/~jdrosen/e6880/index.html.*

Rosenberg, J., Qiu, L. and Schulzrinne, H., (2000), "Integrating Packet FEC into Adaptive Voice Playout Buffer Algorithms on the Internet", *Proceedings of IEEE Infocom 2000*, Tel Aviv, Israel.

Rudkin, S., Grace, A. and Whybray, M.W., (1997), "Real-time applications on the Internet", *BT Technology J*, Vol. 15, No.2, pp. 209 – 224.

Sun, L., Wade, G., Lines, B., Ifeachor, E. and Foll, D.Le, (2000) "End-to-end speech quality analysis for VoIP", *IEE 16$^{th}$ UK Teletraffic Symposium*, Harlow, U.K.

Yamamoto, L.A.R. and Beerends, J.G. (1997), "Impact of network performance parameters on the end-to-end perceived speech quality", *Expert ATM Traffic Symposium*, Greece.

# Improving Real-time Voice Transmission Quality over Internet

Ke Zhang  Zhong-cheng Xie  Jiu_bin Ju

Department of Computer Science, Jilin University, ChangChun, P.R.China

Email: kezhang@public.cc.jl.cn, jjb@mail.jlu.edu.cn

## Abstract

With the development of computer multimedia and network technology, a new network technique - Internet Telephony is in the ascendant. Compared with the PSTN, its most attractive advantage is saving cost greatly in long distance calls. And the cost of the IP phone call is the price of local telephone calls plus the Internet connectivity charges. But due to the present characteristic of IP network, the voice quality of IP phone is not as good as that of the PSTN, and can not satisfy the demands of customers. In this paper, the main factors impairing the voice quality of transmitting are analyzed and some loss repair schemes are introduced briefly. Then a new scheme for repairing packet loss – splitting is proposed and its validity is testified in our simulating environment.

## Keywords

IP Telephony, packets lost, delay jitter, delay

## 1. Introduction

Owing to the phenomenal growth of the Internet, and the declining cost of computer hardware, real-time voice communication over Internet is emerging--Internet telephony. This technology is developing very fast. Internet utilizes the standard TCP/IP protocol for communication, so we also call it IP phone. It has the huge potential cost saving by making long distance call at the prices of local telephone calls plus the nominal Internet connectivity charges.

Continuous media like audio are time-sensitive and have vast quantity. It requires the network provide enough bandwidth, transmission speed and small delay jitter. Over Internet, all voice packets are treated like data, under peak loads and congestion, their packets loss rates are same. A characteristic of network, the special concern in this paper, is the dropping of packets. A number of studies conducted on the loss characteristics of the Internet, show that the majority of loss is of single packet whereas the burst losses of two and more packets are less frequent. Therefore the primary focus of a repair scheme must be to correct single packet loss, since this is by far the most frequent occurrence. In this paper, we propose a simple splitting-scheme for handling packet loss. One of the key advantages of this scheme is that it is not based on redundancy, and hence requires no extra bandwidth. Furthermore perceptual studies have shown that it is suitable for practical application.

The rest of this paper is organized as follows. Section 2 presents some factors that impair IP phone transmitting quality and introduces some related loss repair work. Section 3 proposes a new method for recovering lost packet. Section 4 evaluates this scheme in a simulating test environment developed by us. Finally, section 5 presents some conclusions and discussions on the future work.

## 2. Background and related work

### 2.1 Factors that impair IP phone transmitting quality

Speech quality of IP phone correlates to both the performance of employed Codec and the network conditions. Factors impairing QoS of voice transmission over Internet are described as follows:

1.  Delay: On transmission, all voice packets will be subjected to unpredictable delay, which causes echo, talker overlap and packets loss. The delay in an end-to-end communication is composed of accumulation delay, process delay and network delay. The network delay can be a main part of the overall delay.
2.  Jitter: The jitter is variable inter-packet timing caused by the network a packet traverses. It impairs the speech playback quality.
3.  Packet Lost: Packet lost is an even more severe problem. Lost voice packets cannot be corrected though the process retransmission like data.

Disregarding the influence of those factors will lead to poor adaptive abilities over Internet and such system can not meet customers' demands well.

### 2.2 Related work

In Internet, both congestion and delay jitter will cause packet lost. So, the repair of packet loss is a must in improving speech quality. There exists a number of loss mitigation schemes (Perkins and Hodson, 1998) which have been found to be of use in a number of scenarios.

Retransmission-based schemes have been proposed and shown effective under some condition (Dempsey and Liebeherr el al, 1996), but it is not applicable over Internet. Redundancy (Hardman and Sasse, 1995) scheme has the advantage of low-latency, with only a single-packet delay being added, at the expense of additional CPU and the bandwidth requirements, and approximate repair (LPC is better than silence anyway). Parity-based FEC based techniques have a significant advantage in that they are media independent, and provide exact repair for lost packets. Its processing requirements are relatively light. The disadvantage of it is that the encoding has higher latency in comparison with the redundancy schemes and it increases bandwidth requirements. Interleaving(Perkins and Hodson, 1998) and Error Spreading(Ngo and Varadarajan, et al, 1999) scheme disperses the effect of packet losses. They do not increase the bandwidth requirements of a stream. But large latency is introduced at source and destination, which limits their use for interactive applications. A comparison of the relative overheads of the schemes discussed is provided in the first four lines in table 1. It can be seen that redundancy scheme is preferable for interactive use.

## 3. Loss Repair Scheme: Split

We propose a new mechanism splitting for loss recovery. The key idea of it is that we do not try to recover overall loss packets, but mitigate the effect of loss. For example, in the following case, when audio is sent encoded by PCM. Speech data to be compressed into one RTP packet will be split into two blocks by selecting samples every other one. The operation is depicted as following.

**Source:**

Samples of original unit: $S1$ $S2$ $S3$ $S4$ $S5$ $S6$ $S7$ $S8$ $S9$ $S10$ … …;
Samples of split block 1: $S1$ $S3$ $S5$ $S7$ $S9$ … …;
Samples of split block 2: $S2$ $S4$ $S6$ $S8$ $S10$ … …;
Block 1 and 2 are compressed by one Codec, and transmitted in two separate RTP packets marked with same timestamp.

**Destination:**

Samples of uncompressed block 1: $S'1$ $S'3$ $S'5$ $S'7$ $S'9$ … …;
Samples of uncompressed block 2: $S'2$ $S'4$ $S'6$ $S'8$ $S'10$… …;
Let combination function is $f(x1,x2)$, then samples of combined block: $S'1$ , $f(S'1, S'2)$ , $f(S'2,S'3)$ , $f(S'3,S'4)$ , $f(S'4,S'5)$… …

The receiver conducts the reverse procedure, combines the uncompressed samples into one block data and playback. It can be seen that the loss of a single packet from a split stream results in multiple one-sample gaps in the reconstructed stream. When a packet lost, receiver could use any half speech data received to restore most of the original information by using interpolating method, as depicted above. Thus all the isolated loss could be repaired.

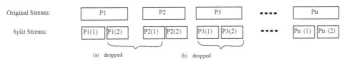

**Figure 1: Two consecutive losses scenario**

Moreover, splitting scheme has approximately repair capability for consecutive losses. Consider the example discussed above. The original stream was split as illustrated in Fig.1. If two consecutive loss packets are across the boundary of two original packets, like scenario(a), such loss effect is the same as that of the two single loss, P1 and P2 can be repaired respectively well. When the two packets are from the same original packet like scenario(b), the loss effect is degraded, for the loss effect is the same as that of one single loss P3 in original stream. If three consecutive losses happen like scenario(c) in Fig.2, it can be seen that the loss effect is the combination of one single lost P2 in the original stream and one single loss P1(1) that can be repaired. The rest may be deduced by analogy, consecutive losses can be regarded as the combination of fewer single losses that can be repaired and those can not be repaired in the original stream. We can see in all these scenarios, consecutive loss effect was lowered than un-split. After splitting, packets number will be doubled, hence the RTP header overhead. We can use packet header compress scheme to reduce bandwidth requirement. Considering the recovering function of splitting packets, together with the fact that large packet usually has higher loss probability than smaller one (Hardman and Sasse, 1995), we can come to the conclusion that the method of splitting can bring higher quality.

**Figure 2: Three consecutive losses scenario**

This scheme can be flexibly utilized. When network is congested, an application can positively discard some split packets to lower the bit rate, hence loss rate. It is obtained that the repaired audio quality as measured by intelligibility can also meet users' requirement. As an alternative, the repair capability of multi-transmitting one copy of split packet is much better than that of transmitting one time at the expense of medium bandwidth overhead, no extra latency or CPU overhead is required.

|  | Delay | Bandwidth Overhead | Processing Overhead |
|---|---|---|---|
| Retransmission | Medium | Variable | High |
| Interleaving | High | None | Low |
| Media-independent FEC | High | High | Low |
| Redundancy | Small | Variable | Variable, may be large |
| Split | Small | None | Low |

**Table 1: Overheads of different lost repair schemes**

Splitting disperses the effect of loss, which is the analogous to interleaving, but they are different in nature: in interleaving, some units must be buffered to interleave at source, which increase the packet's appended delay; While splitting can be committed to a single unit without buffering more units. Although accumulating more packets to split is permissible (that can reduced the number of splitting packets as well as the overhead of packet header), it is not indispensable. Although the two split units are sent out simultaneously, receiver should buffer one split unit coming first to wait for combination, for split packet will also be subject to delay jitter. The overhead of destination buffering is related to the network transmitting condition. In practice, whether speech data is split or not, destination should setup a certain long buffer to remove effect of delay jitter. Split units are also restored in this buffer to remove jitter, the buffering delay of removing jitter and that of waiting for combination are concurrent. Moreover, no redundant data and extra bandwidth requirement are needed, so this method is suitable for interactive application. It hardly increases bandwidth requirements, only slightly adds additional CPU computational overhead and small latency. A comparison of this method with other schemes is provided in table 2.

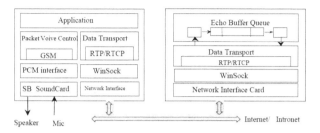

IP phone client architecture       Transporting simulation server architecture

**Figure 3: Architecture of simulation test environment**

## 4. Simulating test environment and evaluating results

Because of the unpredictable performance of Internet, we can not easily test the affect under all possible circumstances Thus we develop a simulating test environment. Basing on the simulation method, we reproduce the effect of packet lost and delay, then by rating the received voice quality, we quantified the impact of these factors to the speech quality. The testing environment consists of IP phone clients and a server for simulating transport (Fig.3). IP phone clients can communicate with the server.

Voice data must be compressed at the source and decompressed at the destination. Fig.4 depicts the data flow transferring over IP network. Real-time Transmission Protocol (Schulzrinne and Casner, et al, 1996) was selected to be the transmitting protocol. Audio data is carried in RTP data packets, and the receivers to restore packets sequence and reconstruct media data use the timestamp and sequence number in the RTP headers. RTP also offers a control protocol called RTCP that supports the protocol control functionality, such as network QoS monitoring and congestion control, etc. Furthermore, RTP data packet size also affects end-to-end delay and bandwidth requirement. The relationship between them is analyzed as follows. First, definitions of a Codec are provided as follows:

| | |
|---|---|
| *frame* | : a group of speech samples that it can process once a time. |
| *f* | : number of samples in each frame. For example, GSM f = 160. |
| *F* | : speech data sample rate. |
| $N_f$ | : number of frames it can process per second, $N_f = F/f$. |

Each RTP data packet contains some frames of compressed voice frames. We have RTP operate over UDP/IP protocol, thus UDP and IP header envelops each RTP packet. We know that the size of RTP header $R_L$ = 12 bytes, UDP header $U_L$ = 8 bytes, IP header $I_L$ = 20 bytes. If each data frame compresses to **B** bytes, and one RTP data packet contains **n** frames, the bandwidth requirement is calculated as: **Band = (F / (f * n)) * ((R_L+U_L+I_L)+B\*n) = 40 N_f \*(1/n) + B \* N_f** . A certain Codec determines $N_f$ and B, thus Band is an inverse function about n. The larger the **n** is, the lower the bandwidth is required. However, with the augment of **n**, the accumulation delay will increase. Over Internet, delay is usually far more than 50ms. In practical applications, we must make trade off between network bandwidth requirement and accumulation delay. So, the value **n** should be confined in a proper range. In our environment, **n** is 4. Thus the bandwidth requirement is approximately 17.3Kbps, and the accumulation delay is 80ms. We implemented the test environment over Windows'98 platform with a SoundBlaster16 card.

| Rating | Impairment | Quality |
|--------|------------|---------|
| 5 | Imperceptible | Excellent |
| 4 | Perceptible, not annoying | Good |
| 3 | Slightly annoying | Fair |
| 2 | Annoying | Poor |
| 1 | Very annoying | Bad |

**Table 2: Quality rating on a one to five scale**

**Figure 4: Real-time Voice transmission over packet-switched network**

The server for simulating transport saves all voice packets received from remote client in a buffer queue. After transmission is over, the simulating server fetches packets from the buffer queue and sends back to the remote client. At the queue exit, there is a transporting simulator. During the course of packets returning, the simulator randomly selects and discards packets at a certain rate to simulate packets loss phenomenon. The loss rate depends on the experimental instance. Then we can evaluate the quality of transmitting service according the speech quality of the client's playback.

We use a five-level scale(Grusec, et al, 1998), subjective testing standard (reported in Table 2) to evaluate speech quality. Many studies in the literature dealing with quality estimation of audio sequence(Daumer, 1982) also use this method for quality rating. Unlike the method described in Ref. (Grusec, et al, 1998), no strict testing material or trained tester is required in our experiment. During the test period, the nolost speech is deemed to be excellent quality (5 point), and the other cases are rated on the base of this standard. We choose a piece of utterance that is about 21 seconds long and have ten persons to evaluate the quality.

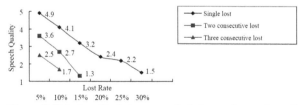

**Figure 5: Relationship between packets lost and speech quality**

170

Over unloaded LAN in our lab, we design this group testing.

Packet loss without repairing: A certain number of speech packets are discarded from the buffer queue according to the chosen loss rate and loss mode (single, two consecutive or three consecutive packets lost). And then "white noise" is padded into the empty element in case of speech "shrink". The probability of more than three consecutive packets loss is small in reality, so we do not simulate this case in the experiment. Test results depict in Fig.5. From this figure it can be seen that when single loss rate exceeds 15%, as well as the two and three consecutive lost rate are more than 6-8% and 2-3% respectively. Speech quality cannot meet users' requirement.

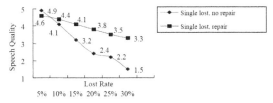

**Figure 6: The relation of single lost rate and speech quality repaired with split scheme**

After starting the split scheme, we gained the results in Fig.6 and Fig.7. It can be seen that even when single loss rate exceeds 30% and two consecutive loss rates exceeds 10%, speech quality still satisfied our requirement, although it drops down slowly. When loss rate is lower than 5% speech quality is worse than that of not split. This is because Codec usually demands that input data have certain sample rate. When there isn't packet loss, quality of split data manipulated by Codec will drop a little bit. In our experiment, we choose GSM (sample rate 8000Hz). At destination, the speech quality is worse than that of not split somewhat, but is much better than that of LPC. When loss rate is higher than 5%, the quality will be better than that in no recovery scheme, although it drops down slowly. So we consider this method is feasible for repairing audio stream when loss rate exceeds 5%,. Overhead of splitting is close to that of interleaving. In IP phone system design, RTCP is usually employed to monitor current network condition (Ingo Busse, Bernd Deffiner, 1996), and when loss rate and delay augment to a certain extent, some media repair methods should be utilized to ensure speech quality not to drop too low.

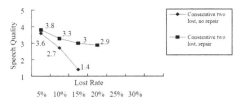

**Figure 7: The relation of consecutive two lost rate and speech quality paired with split scheme**

# 5. Conclusion

In this paper, we deliberately describe a new scheme for repair packet loss – splitting, and compare it with some exiting ones, then prove the validity of this mechanism by evaluation. We first analyze factors affecting QoS over IP network, and introduce some related loss repair scheme. Then, describe the new splitting scheme, and finally testify its validity by a simulating test environment developed by us. Through test, It can be seen that when loss rate exceed normal range, repaired speech quality can still satisfy users well. Our testing was conducted over non-loaded LAN, and the situation over Internet is more complicated in that congestion usually accompanies loss and delay jitter. And loss rate usually increases with packet size increasing. So, there exists a trade-off between the requirements of the network and real-time voice connections as described in Ref.(Hardman and Sasse, 1995).

# References

Ingo Busse, Bernd Deffiner, Henning Schulzrinne (1996), "Dynamic QoS Control of Multimedia Applications Based on RTP", *Computer Communication*, Vol.19, pp49-58

W.R. Daumer (1982), "Subjective evaluation of several efficient speech coders", *IEEE Trans. On Communications*, pp655-662

Bert J.Dempsey, Jorg Liebeherr, Alfred C. Weaver(1996). "On retransmission-based error control for continuous media traffic in packet-switching networks", *Computer Networks and ISDN System*, Vol.28, pp719-736.

Thedore Grusec, etc (1998). "Subjective Evaluation of High Quality Audio Coding Systems: Methods and Results in the Two-Channel Case", *<URL : http://www.drb.crc.doc.ca/list.html>*

V. Hardman, M. A. Sasse, M. Handley, and A. Watson (1995), "Reliable audio for use over the Internet", In *Proceedings of INET'95*

Hung Q.Ngo, Sriviatsan Varadarajan, and Jaideep Srivastava(1998). "On Archiving Lower Consecutive Losses for Continuous Media Streams", University of Minnesota - Computer Science and Engineering Technical Report. *<URL : http:// www.umn.edu/tr1999/99-005.ps>*

Colin Perkins, Orion Hodson (1998), "Options for Repair of Streaming Media". *Internet Draft(work-in-progress) draft-ietf-avt-info-repair-03*

H. Schulzrinne, S. Casner, R. Frederick, and V. Jacobson (1996), "RTP: A transport protocol for real-time applications", *IETF Audio/Video Transport Working Group*, January 1996. RFC1889.

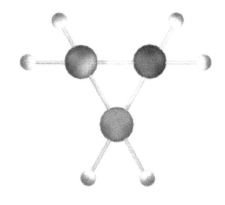

# Chapter 4

## Distributed technologies

# An Applet-Based Approach to Large-Scale Distributed Computing

David Finkel, Craig E. Wills,
Kevin Amorin, Adam Covati, and Michael Lee

Department of Computer Science
Worcester Polytechnic Institute
Worcester, MA 01609 USA
e-mail: dfinkel@cs.wpi.edu

## Abstract

This paper describes a continuation of a project to develop a system for large-scale distributed computing on the Internet. A user wishing to participate in a computation connects to a Distribution Server which provides information about available computations, and then connects to a Computation Server with a computation to distribute. A Java class is downloaded which communicates with the Computation Server to obtain data, performs the computation, and returns the result. Since any computer on the Internet can participate in these computations, potentially a large number of computers can participate in a single computation.

## Keywords

Distributed Computing, WWW, Java Applets

## 1. Introduction

The goal of this project is to develop methods for distributing computational workload to available machines on the Internet. The system is implemented in Java, and provides a framework for an application programmer to develop a Java applet to permit multiple machines to download and execute portions of a computation. Using this system, programmers could potentially have a large number of machines executing their computations.

The current project uses Java to provide a parallel programming environment suitable for coarse-grain parallel computations. A Java applet is downloaded from a server to a machine on the Web. The applet then downloads from the server a set of parameters that define a portion of the computation. When the computations are completed, the applet returns the results to the server. This approach is a further development of the system described in [2], [3], and [5].

The remainder of the paper describes the architecture and implementation of the distributed computation system, how it differs from previous work, and our experience in using it. Finally, the paper presents some ideas for extension of this work in future implementations.

## 2. Design and Implementation

### 2.1 The Distriblet Framework

In this section, we describe the three components of the distributed computation: the Helper Computer, Distribution Server, and the Computation Server. The Helper Computer can be any computer on the Internet with a Java-enabled Web browser. When a user wishes to participate in a distributed computation, the user makes a Web connection to the Distribution Server to locate a computation to be performed. The Helper Computer then connects to a Computation Server with work to distribute, downloads a Java class to execute (a distriblet), executes it, and returns the result to the Computation Server.

The Distribution Server, the Computation Server, and the distriblet class have all been implemented as part of this project. An application programmer who wishes to prepare an computation for distribution must prepare a Java class, called a distriblet, to perform the computation. This class must extend a class we have written, distributable. The class distributable includes some pre-written methods that perform handle the communications between the Helper Computer and the Computation Server. Other methods, directly related to the computation the programmer wishes to distribute, must be implemented by the programmer. The Computation Server registers the computation with the Distribution Server, so that Helper Computer can locate the Computation Server.

The distriblet is a Java applet. Java applets are designed to be downloaded by Web browsers and execute within the browser. Java applets have security restrictions so that they cannot damage the computer on which they are running. For example, Java applets cannot access local files on the machine on which they are running, and cannot make network connections to sites other than the one from which they have been downloaded. By implementing the distriblet as a an applet, the user of the Helper Computer can be assured that the distriblet cannot do damage to their computer.

On the other hand, the current version of Java allows a Java applet to ask the user to violate any of the applet security restrictions [6]. So, for example, if the programmer of the applet needs to make third-party network connections, the distriblet can ask the user of the Helper Computer for permission. If the user denies permission, then the distriblet terminates. When the user selects a computation to participate in, the user is given an opportunity to indicate whether or not they are willing to allow applet security violations.

### 2.2 Comparison with Previous Work

There have been two earlier versions of the Distriblet system, described in [2], [3], and [5]. In the first version, the Helper Computer could be configured to automatically download a computation whenever it was idle. This automatic participation required that the user install a Java application, instead of an applet, on the Helper Computer. This requirement was a barrier to participation, and also did not provide the user with the same level of protection against malicious code as that provided by an applet.

In the second version of the Distriblet system, the Helper Application was replaced by an applet, which provided increased security. The Helper Applet had two functions: presenting an interface to allow the user to communicate with the Distribution Server to select a computation to participate in, and downloading the necessary Java code and parameters from the Computation Server. Since the Helper Applet had to communicate with both the Distribution Server and the Computation Server, it violated the applet security model. To work around this restriction, the Helper Applet always had to ask the user for permission to violate the applet security model, another barrier to participation.

In the current version, the functions of the Helper Applet have been separated. The user selects a computation to participate in by using an HTML form downloaded from the Distribution Server. The communications with the Computation Server is initiated by the Distribution Server. This causes the distriblet to be downloaded to the Helper Computer from the Computation Server, and then the distriblet itself handles further communications with the Computation Server. Any request to violate an aspect of applet security is made by the distriblet itself, instead of the Helper Applet as in the second version.

Other research groups have also implemented systems for large-scale distributed computation [1, 4, 7, 8, 9]. The best-known of these is the SETI@home project [8], in which users download radio telescope logs to search for evidence of extra-terrestrial intelligent life. This system requires the user to download and install a screen-saver. Since their application runs as a screen-saver, it only operates when the system is idle.

The Charlotte project [1] provides a processing environment based on the World Wide Web. Charlotte implements a shared memory and inter-process communication paradigm currently used in multiple processor machines. Charlotte gave Java applets the ability to access variables on the host computer as if they were their own. Thus Charlotte uses the medium of the World Wide Web to create a parallel programming environment.

### 2.3 Details of the Implementation

We now describe the operation of our system, from the point of view of the Helper Computer:

1. Connect to the Distribution Server
   When the user of the Helper Application wishes to participate in a computation, the user makes a Web connection to the Distribution Server. It is expected that there will only be one, or a small number of, Distribution Servers, so the user will know the URL of the Distribution Server, or have it saved as a Favorite / Bookmark. Alternatively, there can be a link to the Distribution Server from well-known Web portals.
2. Select a Computation to Assist
   The Distribution Server will provide the user with a Web page indicating available computations, called the Chooser page. The user can either select a specific computation, or select Continuous Execution, in which case the Helper Computer will participate in multiple computations, one after another, until the user manually terminates participation in these computations.
3. Download Work
   Based on the user's selections on the Chooser page, the Distribution Server selects a computation for the user to participate in. The Distribution Server then provides another Web page to the user, called the Distriblet Runner page; one section of this Web page includes a reference to the distriblet applet on the appropriate

Computation Server. When the Distriblet Runner page is loaded into the user's Web browser, it downloads the distriblet applet from the Computation Server.

4. Retrieve Data

   When the distriblet begins running, it calls its *getArgs* method, which retrieves whatever data is needed to execute this particular portion of the distributed application.

5. Execute

   The distriblet's computation is performed by calling the distriblet *execute* method. The programmer's *execute* method can operate on the data in any way permitted by the applet security model. Since Java allows the programmer to ask the user for permission to violate some aspect of the applet security model, the programmer can ask for such permission in the *execute* method.

6. Transmit Results

   After the *execute* method completes, the distriblet calls its *sendResults* method, which transmits any necessary results to the Computation Server.

7. Get More Work

   The distriblet then calls its *getArgs* method again to retrieve more data from the Computation Server and continues to run the *execute* method on that data. If the Computation Server has no more data to distribute, it send a *NoMoreData* message to the distriblet. When this occurs, if the user has not selected Continuous Execution, the user's participation in the distributed computation ends. If the user has selected Continuous Execution, then the distriblet causes the Distriblet Runner Web page to reload, which allows the Distribution Server to provide a reference to a new distributed computation for the user to participate in.

8. Terminate Participation

   If the user wishes to stop participating in a distributed computation, the user presses the "Stop" button provided on the Distriblet Runner Web page.

### 2.4 The Distribution Server

The job of the Distribution Server is to keep track of what computations are available, and to provide Chooser Web pages and Distriblet Runner Web pages to Helper Computers. Our design envisions having only a single Distribution Server, so that users would have only one place to contact to gain access to many different distributed computations. Having a single point of contact is justified by the fact that the Distribution Server's job is just to put the Helper Computer and Computation Server in contact, and then the Distribution Server is no longer involved in the communications. Furthermore, the design on the Distribution Server would make it relatively easy to have multiple machines serving the Distribution Server's URL if the load on the Distribution Server increased..

### 2.5 The Computation Server

When the Computation Server starts, it registers with the Distribution Server, so that the Distribution Server can direct Helper Computers to this Computation Server. On request from the Helper Computer, the Computation Server downloads the distriblet to the Helper Computer. It also provides parameters in response to a *getArgs* request and receives results when the Helper executes *sendResults*. When the Computation Server downloads a set of parameters, it starts a timer; if the timer expires before the corresponding results are received, the Computation Server considers this set of parameters lost, and will send them to another Helper Computer for execution.

Since the Helper Computer downloads the distriblet applet via a Web connection, the Computation Server must be running a Web server. In order to minimize the software requirements for running a Computation Server, we have implemented a light-weight Web server for use on a Computation Server that does not otherwise need a Web server. The light-weight Web server only responds to requests for the distriblet, and doesn't implement the other services normally provided by a Web server.

### 2.6 Off-Line Computation

The earlier versions of the distriblet system assumed that the Helper Computer was connected to the Internet throughout its participation in the distributed computation. In this version, we have allowed for the possibility of off-line participation in a distributed computation.

If a Helper Computer connects to the Internet through a dial-up connection, off-line computation allows the user to connect to the Internet, connect to the Distribution Server and the Computation Server and download several sets of parameters, and then disconnect from the Internet. When all of the computations are done, typically overnight, the user re-connects to the Internet and uploads the results of the computations. The Computation Server needs to set an appropriate timeout for off-line computations.

## 3. Results

In order to test the functionality and performance of our distriblet system, we wrote distriblets for several applications. We report on one of those applications here.

We wrote a distributed application to check for primality of Mersenne numbers. In 1644, Mersenne conjectured that numbers of the form $2^p-1$ were prime for certain prime numbers $p$. Even though Mersenne's conjecture was incorrect, number of the form $2^p-1$ are called Mersenne numbers, and those that are prime are called Mersenne primes [10].

There has been significant mathematical research devoted to the discovery of Mersenne primes. A large-scale Internet-based search for Mersenne primes called the Great Internet Mersenne Prime Search (GIMPS) has been running since 1996, and has led to the discovery of four new Mersenne primes [10].

Like the GIMPS software, we have used the Lucas-Lehmer primality test to search for Mersenne primes [10]. We implemented this test in the distriblet framework, and each chunk of the computation included several primes $p$ which would be used to create candidate Mersenne numbers $2^p-1$ to test for primality. Since the goal of this application was to test the functionality and performance of the distriblet system and not to discover new Mersenne primes, we did not uses values of $p$ which could have led to the discovery of new primes; instead, we used values of $p$ for the primality of $2^p-1$ is already known. This allowed us to create chunks that could be computed in times on the order of minutes;

values of $p$ for the which the primality of $2^p$-$1$ is unknown would require on the order of years to complete.

We performed two tests using this Mersenne prime distributed application. The first test used a fixed number of identical helper computers to run chunks of the distributed application; all were Pentium-class personal computers. We compared the use of one helper computer to the use of ten helper computers. In each case, we ran five hundred chunks. The results showed total elapsed time of 37.77 minutes with one computer vs. 5.35 minutes, a speed up by a factor of 7.06 with 10 computers.

In the second test, we invited a large number of users to access the system. We used this experience to test the ability of the servers to serve a moderate number of simultaneous users. We collected data for nine days of system usage. The results are shown in Figures 1 and 2. In Figure 1, we show the number of unique hosts participating as helper computers for each hour of the test period. We saw an average of 4.7 hosts per hour, with a maximum of 15 hosts and a minimum of 1.

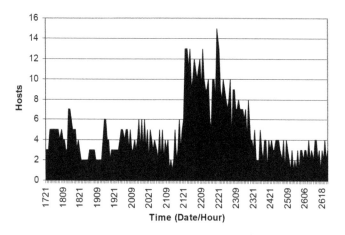

**Figure 1: Unique Hosts Per Hour**

Figure 2 shows the number of chunks per hours served by the Computation Server. On average 9.6 chunks were served per hour during the test period, with a maximum of 120 and a minimum of 1. We note that the largest number of chunks per hour were served at the beginning of the test period, but the largest number of hosts per hour occurred in the middle of the test period. The reason for this mismatch is that the chunks served at the beginning of the test period were for smaller values of $p$, for which the chunk computation time was smaller. The chunks served later in the test period required longer computation times, so more helpers were able to complete fewer chunks per hour.

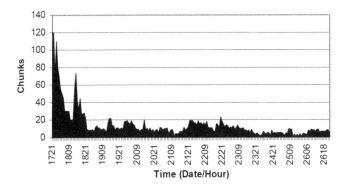

**Figure 2: Number of Chunks Per Hour**

Overall, the test shows the ability of our system to handle a moderate number of simultaneous users over a long period of time, and to serve distriblets to helper computers not under our administrative control. The test system is available at http://distriblets.wpi.edu.

## 4. Conclusions and Future Work

We have described a project to design and implement a distributed computation system written in Java to run over the World Wide Web. We implemented the framework of the system: the distriblet applet, the Distribution Server, and the Computation Server. A programmer wishing to prepare an application for execution using our system needs to create a Java class, following our specifications, to carry out the computation. A user willing to help by executing part of the computation needs only to connect to the Distribution Server on the Web and then download the distriblet applet. The distriblet downloads the arguments to use, executes the computation, and returns the results.

In the course of our work on this project, we have identified some opportunities for extensions or improvements which could make the system more useful in the future. One set of improvements focus on security and authentication, so that a Computation Server could authenticate the identity of a host returning results to it, and that the results being returned were correct.

To provide an incentive to users to participate, a micropayment system could be used. Micropayment systems have been proposed as a way of collecting small payments for access to Web resources. These same micropayment systems could be used to pay users a small amount for allowing their system to be used to download and execute distributed computations. Thus users could use the time when their systems would otherwise be idle to earn credits to be used later for access to Web resources. This could provide sufficient incentive for large numbers of users to make their systems available for distributed computations. We have implemented hooks in our system to allow a micropayment system to be added in the future.

# References

1. A, Baratloo, M. Karaul, Z. Kadem, and P. Wyckoff. "Charlotte: Metacomputing on the Web", *Proceedings of the International Conference on Parallel and Distributed Systems*, Dijon, France. September, 1996.

2. Brian Brennan, Chris Brennan, David Finkel and Craig E. Wills, "Java-Based Load Distribution on the World Wide Web", *Proceedings of the International Network Conference 1998* (July, 1998), pp. 9 – 14

3. James F. Carlson, David V. Esposito, Nathaniel J. Springer, David Finkel and Craig E. Wills, "Applet-Based Distributed Computing on the Web," *Proceedings of the Workshop on Distributed Computing on the Web* (June, 1999), pp. 69 – 76.

4. Distributed.net, "Distributed.net Node Zero", http://www.distributed.net/, 1999.

5. David Finkel, Craig E. Wills, Brian Brennan, and Chris Brennan, "Distriblets: Java-Based Distributed Computing on the Web," *Internet Research* Vol. 9 No. 1, pp. 35 – 40, 1999.

6. JavaSoft. "The JavaSoft Homepage". World Wide Web, http://www.javasoft.com. 1999.

7. "The POPCORN Project", http://www.cs.huji.ac.il/~popcorn/index.html, 1999.

8. "SETI@home: Search for Extraterrestrial Intelligence at Home", http://setiathome.ssl.berkeley.edu/, 1999.

9. Woltman, George, "The Great Internet Mersenne Prime Search," http://www.mersenne.org/, 1999.

# Mobile Agent Applications

Rosane Maria Martins, Magali Ribeiro Chaves, Luci Pirmez and Luiz F. Rust

NCE/UFRJ - Núcleo de Computação Eletrônica
Universidade Federal do Rio de Janeiro
Tel.: +55 21 598-3159 - Caixa Postal: 2324 - Rio de Janeiro  RJ  Brasil
{rosanemartins, magalichaves}@uol.com.br, {luci,rust}@nce.ufrj.br

## Abstract

Automatic, autonomous browsing has an increasingly important task in information discovery and assisted browsing on the Internet. Where users could once keep up to date with information of interest on the Internet, the recursive growth of the network has made this process increasingly time consuming and less rewarding. We present two possible solutions to this problem: Data Agents and CollaborAgents which were developed with IBM's Aglet Workbench – a particular implementation of mobile agents. This paper also surveys the agent technology and discusses the agent building package used to develop both mentioned applications. Finally, it concludes that the future of local interaction, reduced network loading, server flexibility and application autonomy which are supported by mobile agent technology all help to provide a level agility above distributed problem solving.

## Keywords

Mobile Agents, Distributing Computing, Aglets

## 1. Introduction

Internet based electronic commerce of today has not made shopping that much easier for the consumer. In fact, it has maybe even made it worse. We have more information  about products than ever, more stores to visit. The difference between the electronic marketplace and the real-world marketplace is that you visit the store electronically instead of physically.

So, finding and combining the relevant information/service is becoming a critical task. There is a need for facilities that perform these integrating tasks and thus overcome problems such as distribution and heterogeneity. These facilities are often referred to as integrated systems. In an integrated system, the user is not exactly aware of which and how many information sources that are used, neither does he know how they are used. The user is provided with the vision that only one information source exists.

To address this problem, several exciting new technologies have been developed. Several groups of Artificial Intelligence (AI) researchers are already actively involved in trying to design Internet assistants that will make easier the filtering or retrieving information from the network and the virtual purchases.

Each intelligent assistant is composed by autonomous agents and is based on AI and Distributed Artificial Intelligence (DAI) concepts.

DAI is concerned with all forms of social activity in systems composed of multiple computational agents [1]. An important form of interaction in such systems is cooperative problem solving, which occurs when a group of logically decentralized agents choose to work together to achieve a common goal.

The "agent" term is largely used in different areas, such as Distributed Systems or Software Engineering, for this reason, there are almost many definitions for it. However, agent systems present key characteristics which differ them from other softwares.

Agents are autonomous, persistent (software) components that perceive, reason, communicate and act in someone's favour, influencing its environment. This environment presents many agents which will interact. This interaction is the Multiagent Systems' principal element .

This paper contributes with two applications that emphasize the mobile agents technology as an significant and revolutionary paradigm for distributed problem solving: *Data Agents* and *CollaborAgents*. Both were implemented using IBM's mobile agent framework known as Aglets Software Development Kit (ASDK).

Data Agents is a mobile and intelligent multiagent auxiliary prototype for the retrieval of distributed structured information in a scenario of several "on-line" bookstores. The proposed system is based on a group of agents trying, simultaneously, to find products of users interest in several virtual places known by them, presenting the results in an homogeneous way.

CollaborAgents is a prototype where users create autonomous agents to buy and sell goods in a context of the automobile components distribution problem. A car assembler looks for suitable supplies to attend the subsidiaries' orders. This commercial transaction is done through the Internet.

This paper is organized as follows. An overview of agent concept and detailed descriptions of a mobile agent environment known as Aglets WorkBench are given in section 2. Section 3 describes the overall architecture of two applications: Data Agents and Logistic Agents. Finally, section 4 presents the conclusion and future work.

## 2. Mobile Agents

Mobile Agents are processes dispatched from a source computer to accomplish a specified task [ 3,4 ]. Each mobile agent is a computation along its own data and execution state. In this way, the mobile agent paradigm extends the RCP communication mechanism according to which a message sent by a client is just a procedure call. After its submission, the mobile agent proceeds autonomously and independently of the sending client. When the agent reaches a server, it is delivered to an agent execution environment. Then, if the agent possesses necessary authentication credentials, its executable parts are started. To accomplish its task, the mobile agent can transport itself to another server, spawn new agents, and interact with other agents. Upon completion, the mobile agent delivers the results to the sending client or to another server.

In order for these agents to exist within a system or to themselves form a system they require a framework for implementation and execution. This is known as the agent environment.

## 2.1 Agent Environments

There are a large number of agent building packages on the market that allow users to attempt to build and manage their own agents and agent systems. First, and probably foremost is the Tabriz AgentWare package from General Magic [6], which executes and manages agent-based applications on servers, and Tabriz Agent Tools for creating agent applications deployable on Web sites.

General Magic Inc. invented the mobile agent and created Telescript, the first commercial mobile agent system. Based on a proprietary language and network architecture, Telescript had a short life. In response to the popularity of the Internet and later the steamroller success of the Java language, General Magic decided to reimplement the mobile agent paradigm in its Java-based-Odyssey. This system effectively implements the Telescript concepts in the shape of Java classes. The result is a Java class library that enables developers to create their own mobile agent applications.

ObjectSpace's Voyager is a platform for agent-enhanced distributed computing in Java. While Voyager provides an extensive set of object messaging capabilities, it also allows objects to move as agents in the network. You can say that Voyager combines the properties of a Java-based object request broker with those of a mobile agent system. In this way, Voyager allows Java programmers to create network applications using both traditional and agent-enhanced distributed programming techniques.

Developed by the IBM Japan research group, this package is a framework for programming mobile network agents in Java. We can use a few expressions to describe an Aglet [5]: written in pure Java, light-weight object migration , built with persistent support, event-driven. It is easy to understand why JAVA is necessary for WAN application's existence in today's heterogeneous networking environment. Besides providing platform independence, JAVA also provides sandbox security to protect host against malicious attacks from alien applications.

Unlike an applet´s short and boring period of execution, an aglet can exist and execute tasks forever. One of the main differences between an aglet and the simple mobile code of Java applets, is the itinerary that is carried along with the aglet. By having a travel plan, aglets are capable of roaming the Internet collecting information from many places. The itinerary can change dynamically giving the aglet the sense of self-governing and the look of an intelligent agent (that of course is in the hands of the programmer).

An aglet can be dispatched to any remote host that supports the Java Virtual Machine. This requires from the remote host to have preinstalled Tahiti, a tiny aglet server program implemented in Java and provided by the Aglet Framework. A running Tahiti server listens to the host´s ports for incoming aglets, captures them, and provides them with an aglet context (i.e., an agent execution environment) in which they can run their code from the state that it was halted before they were dispatched. Within its context, an aglet can communicate with other aglets, collect local information and when convenient halt its execution and be dispatched to another host. An aglet can also be cloned or disposed. The both applications discussed later has been achieved through use of the Aglets Workbench.

## 3. Applications

Two applications based on agent technologies were implemented in this paper: Data Agents and CollaborAgents.

### 3.1 Data Agents – A Group of Mobile Agents for E-Commerce

The agents for electronic commerce considered in this context are those that somehow help the users to shop over the Internet. This type of agent, called shopping agent, may carry out several tasks, such as: to help the user decide what product should be purchased; to make suggestions based on its knowledge of its owner; to find out new things, discounts and special prices; to find stores that sell the desired product or service, among other things.

In order to show the feasibility of the search process for structured and distributed information through the mobile agents technology, this paper proposes the development of a multiagent, mobile and intelligent system called "*Data Agents*" in the context of several "on line" bookstores. The goal is to accelerate the retrieval of distributed structured information. This is achieved by improving the phase of the process of data selection, in which the agents run parallel among the servers related to them and at the end returning with all the information requested by the user, without the need to make a call to each one of the servers separately. The information obtained is then presented in a uniform and organized way. Using the information thus presented by the system, it is much easier for the user to choose a product with the most satisfactory characteristics.

Among the possible functions described above, the Data Agents Agent is intended to help find the stores that sell the desired product and to list the prices of the products found.

The operation of the prototype to achieve this objective is the following:

- user selects the specific product and the desired characteristics of that product (these characteristics will be the restrictions for the search);
- the purchase agent searches for products with the desired characteristics among products of that type;
- as a result of the search, Data Agents sends an e-mail or shows a screen to the user with a list of products, their respective prices and where they can be found.

### 3.1.1  Proposed Architecture

The following architecture is proposed to enable the Data Agents system to have the functionality mentioned above and, in the future, to be applied to many products and stores.

The system presented comprises the following components: Interface Module, Control Module and Purchase Agents. What follows is a detailed list of the system components:

**Interface Module**: this is the component through which the user contacts the system and places his order. This module is also responsible for presenting the result obtained by the group of agents to the user.

"Title", "author" ,"price range" and "type of itinerary" are the information that the user must provide to the Interface Module so that it may request the Control Module to create and dispatch the purchase agents according to the restrictions imposed by the user.

There are three possibilities of choices for itineraries:

a. *one agent for each server:* According to the quantity of servers registered in the system, one agent is created for each server and dispatched to do its task. When each agent arrives at its destiny, it does its search, send the result as a message to Control Module and "dies".

b. *only one agent that visits all the servers:* It is created only one agent that has in its travel plan the addresses of all servers. It will go to all servers, one by one, do the search, send the result as message to Control Module and "dies" at last visited server.

c. *one agent that goes through the servers until to find the first occurrence*: It is created only one agent that contains in its travel plan the addresses of all servers. But it will travel to next server only if doesn't find any book at former server, that is, the agent travels until to find the first occurrence that satisfies the order user.

As soon as the result manager (a component of the control module)  compiles all answers received, it sends these answers to the interface module so that they are delivered to the user: on the screen  or via e-mail.

**Control Module**: This module is responsible for the creation and release of purchase agents to begin the search requested by the buyer. This module also aggregates the results found by the different agents. There is a control module for each type of product available in the system, e.g. a control module for books and a different one for CDs.

After receiving the user's requirements from the interface module, the Control Module creates the agents according to such requirements and sends them to the addresses available at a Storage Structure.

Storage Structure is a hash structure that contains the addresses of the various stores associated with the system. There is a storage structure for each type of product researched by the system.

When the Control Module receives a request to send an agent, the latter is created on the "aglet"  layer according to user's requirements and travels through the runtime layer, which converts the agent into an array of bytes and such array, on its turn, passes on to the ATP layer – Agent Transfer Protocol, to be sent to its destination. This protocol, then, builds a "bit stream" that contains both general information, such as the system name, and its identification, such as the "byte array" resulting from the runtime layer.

Upon returning to the server with the information from its search, each purchase agent sends its contents to the Result Manager (Control Module), so that the Results Manager may aggregate all answers obtained and send them to the interface module.

**Purchase Agents :** Make contact with the stores by accessing their databases, place the order and interpret the answers generated, converting them into a format that is understood by the control module. Before proceeding to their destination, the agents are coded in bit stream: the first segments are general information, such as the agent's identification, and the last segment is the byte array, the agent per se: code and state. The goal of the agents is to check the information found at their destination address, selecting only the information considered relevant and recommended according to the pre-determined rules. Such information shall represent the basis of rules to be used by the agent to make appropriate decisions in the process of evaluation of the items found.

With this architecture, the extension of this system to deal with new products and new stores is simple, although it is necessary to build a control module for each new product.

### 3.2 CollaborAgents – Solution for a Logistic Problem Applying Multiagent Systems

The Internet has been extensively explored as an environment which brings great ease to integrate clients and suppliers willing to negotiate products and services. Under that light, an area that deserves special attention is the automatic negotiation between clients and suppliers.

The negotiation model presented consists of a system of agents that acts in the process of integration among clients, represented by the subsidiaries of an automaker, and a network of suppliers. This system contributes to the mastering of electronic commerce, since some client agents interact with supplier agents trying to find products and buy products that meet their needs.

The subsidiary which wishes to purchase a product may ask the client agent to initiate the negotiation with a network of supplier agents remotely distributed on the Internet. After a number of interactions with other agents the client agent returns to its original computer and shows the result of its negotiations, i.e. a list of suppliers that best fit its needs in terms of price, freight cost and quantity of product.

As supplier/client agents are created, they are sent from their original computer to an agency, where they will communicate to achieve their overall goal. The Agency, or Meeting Place, is a host computer, where the agents do business. Each agency represents a certain region. In that respect, the client agent will run the network searching for possible suppliers to its demand, and will prioritize agencies located in regions closest to the location of the subsidiary represented by the agent , in order to reduce freight costs.

This section of the paper will try to describe the components forming the model developed and analyze its operation.

### 3.2.1 Architecture of Model

The architecture of the model is characterized by the exchange of messages among three categories of agents: facilitator agent, supplier agent and client agent.

**Facilitator Agent:** It is responsible for managing the negotiation between client agents and agency suppliers. The facilitator agent works as an intermediary for such agents. The facilitator records all suppliers with their respective offers and indicates to the client agent the best supplier to establish the negotiation process with. The facilitator agent has an optimization module to carry out that job. That optimization module inquires each supplier able to meet the subsidiary's demand through the "SearchOffer" message and decides which is the most favorable candidate based on which supplier made the best offer (lowest cost).

**Supplier Agent:** It represents the interests of the supplier. Interests of the supplier means the offer of parts and their respective costs (unit price and freight).

A List of Offer of Material Form is opened when the supplier agent is created. The description of the part, the quantity available for sale and unit price will be typed into the List of Offer of Material.

After confirmation of the information typed in the list of offer of material, the supplier agent will be sent to an agency. At the host computer the agent will make the first contact with the facilitator agent, subsequently requesting to be listed in the database by using the "Register" message.

The supplier agent is responsible for calculating the total cost of the material requested by a subsidiary (price of merchandise, including freight). It is noteworthy that the freight legislation is too wide and this paper is not intended to study all rules and effectiveness in each State. Suppliers hire the service of a shipper, which calculates that cost. This information will be sent to the supplier and will become part of the context of its agent. This case highlights the main advantage of the object-oriented programming: polymorphism. Each class of supplier has a different internal policy to carry out the same method (calculation of freight) and the facilitator agent is not responsible for knowing the procedures of all suppliers. When the facilitator agent inquires the supplier agent in relation to the cost of the material requested by the subsidiary, that agent is not interested in the internal details of that calculation, only in the result. The example shown in Table 1 shows the table of costs used by a supplier agent. Notice that the cost of freight varies according to the distance. Transportation of a unit of part 0260118 from Manhumirim, MG (supplier's location) to Vila Velha, ES costs R$116,00 (for conventional shipping) or R$200 (express shipping). If the same part is shipped to Fortaleza, CE, freight would cost R$150,00 or R$256,00, depending on the type of shipping selected.

| CD_PC | DEST | CST_PC (R$) | CFC (R$) | CFE (R$) | CFUC (R$) | CFUE (R$) | INSURANCE (%) |
|-------|------|-------------|----------|----------|-----------|-----------|---------------|
| 0260118 | ES | 500, | 116, | 200, | 11,66 | 22,00 | 0,17 |
| 0260118 | CE | 500, | 150, | 256, | 15,00 | 25,60 | 0,22 |

**Table 1.** Table of costs used by a supplier agent

Where :

**CD_PC** = material code;
**DEST** = Destination. The client's city;
**CST_PC** = unit price of the part;
**CFC** = conventional shipping cost ( for a unit of part);
**CFUC** = conventional shipping cost (when there is more than one unit of part to be shipped);
**CFE** = express shipping cost ( for a unit of part);
**CFUE** = express shipping cost (when there is more than one unit of part to be shipped);
**INSURANCE** = cargo insurance;
**QTDE_REQ** = unit quantity required by the client (subsidiary)

The calculation of freight at both categories is represented by formulae (1) or (3). The cargo insurance is also included in that calculation. This variable is determined according to distance and value of cargo. The Total Cost, represented by formula (4), is found with the result of the calculations of the Cost of Material (1) and the Cost of Conventional (2) or Express Freight (3).

$$\text{MATERIAL COST} = \text{QTDE\_REQ} * \text{CST\_PC} \qquad (1)$$

$$\text{CONVENTIONAL SHIPPING COST} = \text{CFC} + (\text{QTDE\_REQ} - 1) * \text{CFUC} + (\text{INSURANCE} * \text{MATERIAL COST}) \qquad (2)$$

$$\text{EXPRESS SHIPPING COST} = \text{CFE} + (\text{QTDE\_REQ} - 1) * \text{CFUE} + (\text{INSURANCE} * \text{MATERIAL COST}) \qquad (3)$$

$$\text{TOTAL COST} = \text{MATERIAL COST} + \text{SHIPPING COST} \qquad (4)$$

When the entire inventory of the supplier agent has been negotiated, the agent will send a "Unregister" message, requesting to leave the list kept by the facilitator agent. After its exclusion from the database, the supplier will return to its original computer and will show to the user the result of its negotiation with the different client agents that contacted the supplier agent.

**Client Agent:** It represents the interests of a subsidiary. This means the demand for parts that a subsidiary is willing to buy.

A List of Request of Material form is opened when the subsidiary agent is created. That form will contain the subsidiary's identification, description and location entered by the user, as well as the description and quantity of the material requested, later on confirming the information.

After that information is confirmed, the client agent will migrate to an agency searching for the best supplier to meet its demand. After arriving at the agency, the agent will communicate with the facilitator, which will indicate the context of the best suitable supplier. Upon obtaining the answer, the client agent will initiate the negotiation process through the "Negotiate" message. If the client agent does not find the desired supplier, it will go to other agencies searching for new proposals to meet its demand. After making all negotiations, the client agent will return to its original computer and show the result of its interaction with other agents.

## 4. Discussions and Future Work

We have built two simple prototypes to test the basic concepts and feasibility and conducted some simple experiments.

Nowadays, the Data Agents system presents a simplified configuration, allowing just one kind of product to be investigated. The selected product to this stage was "book". The purchaser agent is created at the user machine and migrates to the target server. This target server is an aglet server where it may be found the offered service by the supplier.

The results obtained in this initial phase were considered acceptable, due to the information filtering be executed on the server where the resources are located. This circumstance leads to a significant reduced network loading.

The possibility of existence of more than one kind of product to be investigated is a task to be implemented in another phase of this project. Another improvement is an implementation of an intelligent module that permits the Data Agents system, besides of the conventional search, makes suggestions to the user.

Concerning the CollaborAgents system, a logistic model was implemented to solve the issue of automotive parts distribution. In this case, each subsidiary and supplier creates an agent which shares information seeking for a global solution.

From this experimentation, it was obtained good results, once the implementation of mobile agents avoided the overload on the web. In a next stage, it will be developed a sophisticate negotiation scheme for buyers and sellers. We are studying two models : first, involving "price-raise" and decay functions similar to Kasbah's technique [2] and the second, based on computational intelligence, where the agents will be able to make proposals through the experience that they acquired a long their life cycle.

Future works is focused on making smarter agents which are directable at a more natural level for users. Though we have only just scratched the surface in terms of making a truly useful system, we are excited about these works and think they have the chance to essentially change the way people acquire goods and services in the not-too-distant future.

# References

1. Bond, A.H.; Gasser , Les.(Eds) Readings in Distributed Artificial Intelligence. San Mateo, California: Morgan Kaufmann, 1988.
2. Chavez, A. and Maes, P.: An Agent Marketplace for Buying and Selling Goods, Proceedings of the First International Conference on the Practical Application of Intelligent Agents and Multi-Agent Technology, London, UK, April 1996.
3. Chess, D.; et al. Itinerant Agents for Mobile Computing. Journal IEEE Personal Communications, Vol.2, N° 5, October, 1993.
4. General Magic Inc. Mobile Agents. http://www.genmagic.com
5. IBM Japan Research Group. Aglets Workbench. http://aglets.trl.ibm.co.jp

# Risks in Anonymous Distributed Computing Systems

Michael J. Ciaraldi, David Finkel, and Craig E. Wills
Department of Computer Science
Worcester Polytechnic Institute
Worcester MA, USA 01609 USA
e-mail: ciaraldi@wpi.edu

## Abstract

Anonymous distributed systems consist of potentially millions of heterogeneous processing nodes connected by the global Internet. These nodes can be administered by thousands of organizations and individuals, with no direct knowledge of each other. Several approaches have been proposed to handle the technical aspects of such systems; this paper addresses some social, ethical, and legal aspects, particularly the potential risks, to nodes both within and outside such systems.

We describe the structure of anonymous distributed systems, then identify potential risks and where they occur within the structure. We then examine which risks can be addressed through existing techniques and technologies, and which require further study.

## Keywords

Distributed computing, Risks, Security

## 1. Anonymous Distributed Computing Systems

A number of approaches have traditionally been used in research and practice to build distributed computing environments using a set of networked machines. These approaches include:

- Autonomous systems where machines run standalone, but users can explicitly access services on other machines, such as remote login or file transfer.
- Distributed operating systems which hide the details of the network and the existence of multiple machines from the user, providing the abstraction of a single virtual computer system. All of the machines in the system are under the control of a single administrative domain.
- Network file systems, the most common distributed computing environment, in which mostly autonomous machines share file systems located on remote file servers. Here, too, the machines are controlled by a single administrative domain.

Against the backdrop of these traditional approaches has arisen a new approach that seeks to solve distributed computing problems on a scale not possible with previous approaches. We refer to this approach as anonymous distributed computing (ADC) and these systems as anonymous distributed computing systems (ADCSs).

An ADCS consists of three types of nodes: distributor nodes for distributing pieces of a distributed computation, client nodes for executing these pieces and reporting results back to a distributor node, and portal nodes for serving as central sites where client nodes can be directed to distributor nodes. In general, these three types of nodes are not under the same administrative control.

ADCSs have several distinguishing characteristics:

- They consist of potentially millions of client nodes, each anonymously providing a piece of a distributed computation.
- The client nodes can vary widely in processing speed, memory capacity, and architecture.
- Each client node may be under the control of a different administrative domain.
- Client nodes may be unaware of each other.
- Client nodes may not always be available in the ADCS.
- Communication between client and distributor nodes is through the global Internet. This communication may be unreliable, intermittent, and at varying bandwidth.
- Client nodes may crash or unexpectedly withdraw from the ACDS at any time.
- A client node might participate in several ADCSs.
- Client nodes in an ADCS may participate voluntarily or they might receive payment, perhaps dependent on the quantity or quality of their computations.

Two general approaches are currently being used for anonymous distributed computing systems. In the first approach a client node first downloads an executable program from a portal node. When the client node wishes to actively participate in the distributed computation, it contacts a distributor node for specific data to use for processing and reports its results back to the distributor. At this point, the client node may request additional data from the distributor for execution of another computation piece. This approach is used by two ADCSs – The SETI@home project [10] and distributed.net [4]. The SETI@home project uses a distributor node to coordinate the work of client nodes to download radio telescope logs to search for evidence of extra-terrestrial intelligent life. Client nodes execute the program as a screen-saver so it is run when each node is otherwise idle. The distributed.net project is focused on solving DES encryption problems by using client nodes to test possible encryption keys. Client nodes execute the program as a low-priority background process. Owners of client nodes are not paid for participation, but part of a prize for solution of the distributed.net problem is given to the owner of the client node which solves the problem.

The second approach used by ADCSs is to execute Java applets on the client node. This approach is used by the POPCORN [9], Charlotte [1] and distriblets [2, 5] projects. In contrast to the first approach, these client nodes in these ADCSs do not download any executable code prior to active participation in the ADCS, but rather join an ADCS through a Web browser. Client nodes find distributors using portal nodes and then download a Java applet along with data from the distributor at the time of participation. Client nodes execute the applet and report back results to the distributor, at which time they may request additional data for processing. These projects also do not include payment for work done by the client nodes, but literature on the POPCORN and distriblets projects [2, 5, 9] describes plans for micropayment mechanisms.

## 2. Types of Risks and Where They Occur

In this section, we identify a variety of risks that can occur in ADC. We note that the kinds of risks we are describing are well-known in the Internet community [6]. Our contribution is to examine how these risks affect anonymous distributed computations, and how the systems for ADC can be modified to avoid or ameliorate these risks.

Some of these risks can occur accidentally, by an unplanned malfunction of the network or one of the computers participating in the distributed computation, and some can occur deliberately, through the actions of a malicious user. In many cases, it is not necessary to distinguish between the accidental and deliberate cases, because the effect is the same.

One set of risks arises from the use of the Internet to communicate among the participants in the distributed computation. Data can be corrupted or lost during network transmission. Alternatively, since data on the Internet passes through computers under the administrative control of many different organizations, some organization or some individual with access at some organization may wish to delete or modify the data passing through their computers.

Another set of risks revolves around the anonymous nature of traffic on the Internet. Although each message on the Internet carries the address of the sender, it is relatively easy for senders to spoof their identity, so that each message they send does not carry the sender's correct address. Even if a message carries a true address, it may be difficult to know what organization controls that address. In the context of anonymous distributed computations, this identification problem means that neither the distributor of a computation nor the client in a computation can know with assurance with whom they are communicating.

Knowing the identity of the distributor can be crucial to assure clients that it is safe to install and run an application. Users might be willing to run a downloaded application on their computer because they have heard from others that they have downloaded and run the application without any harmful effects. They might have read about the application in a publication they consider reliable. But this assurance might be misplaced if they are mistaken about the identity of the distributor from which they are downloading the application. For example, the SETI@home computation discussed in Section 1 is distributed by the Web site http://setiathome.ssl.berkeley.edu/, and users connect to this site to download the SETI@home screensaver. A malicious individual could obtain a similar sounding URL and use that URL to distribute a harmful application

Knowing the identity of a client may be crucial as well. For example, a distributor may wish to limit the distribution of a computation to a restricted set of clients, either because the computation involves confidential data or because the distributors trust this restricted set of clients to execute the computation correctly. In such cases, it will be a problem for the distributor if it is not able to know the identity of the clients with which it is communicating.

Aside from the risks related to network transmission and distributor / client identification, there are additional risks related to the fact that in these systems the client and the distributor may be unknown to each other, and each may not know if the other is trustworthy.

As an example of a risk to the distributor, consider a system in which the distributor makes payments to clients for their participation in the distributed computation. The Popcorn system [9] includes an extensive system for payments to clients. The distriblets papers [2, 5] discuss the possibility of using a micropayment system for making small payments to clients. The risk to the distributor arises from the temptation for clients to provide spurious results in order to earn undeserved payments. For example, in the distriblet system, a client could replace the applet provided by the distributor with a client which returns a random number to the distributor instead of actually performing the required calculation.

A risk to the client arises if the distributor is untrustworthy. As discussed above, it's possible for the distributor to provide a program that will actually harm the client computer. But the distributor might provide a program that doesn't harm the client's computer, but performs a computation that the client considers unworthy. For example, the distributed computation might involve an illegal activity, like cracking an encryption scheme in order to commit an electronic theft. As another example, the distributor might provide a program that contacts a remote Web site repeatedly, taking part in a denial of service attack.

## 3. Dealing with Risks

### 3.1. Accidental Communication Problems

There is a chance that programs and data can be inadvertently corrupted *en route*. This can be easily handled by telecom protocols. For example, TCP includes packet checksums and automatic retransmission of corrupted packets. If this is not sufficient, additional checks, such as application-level error detection and correction codes, can easily be added.

Because Internet connectivity can be slow or intermittent, it is possible that a distributor will send out a request for computation and either never receive a response or receive it too late to be useful. Adding a timestamp to each request and response will enable the clients to decide whether or not to process the request, and the distributor to decide whether or not to accept the response. Some systems, such as Seti@Home, allow clients to participate if they know they will be disconnected from the Internet. In that case, the client retrieves and caches multiple requests, then saves the results and reports them later.

### 3.2. Deliberate Communication Problems

Deliberate interception and/or modification *en route* can be detected by encryption, e.g. by using IPSec [7]. But IPSec itself provides only a uniform protocol to support encryption and authentication over the Internet; administrative issues are equally important.

Modern encryption systems use two basic approaches: private key and public key methods.
- In a private key (symmetric) system, two parties that wish to communicate securely must share a secret key known only by the two of them.
- In contrast, in a public key (asymmetric) system each party has a matched pair of keys, public and private. Each party keeps its private key secret, but allows anyone to know the public key; this is safe because it is computationally infeasible to derive the private key from the public key. Someone wanting to send a secure message encrypts

it using the receiver's public key; since this message can only be decrypted using the matching private key, only the intended recipient will be able to read it.

ADCSs cannot use a private key system; since the parties don't know each other, the distributor would have to generate a separate shared secret for every one of the millions of clients, and distribute them securely. The only practical solution is to use asymmetric (public key) encryption. Combining IPSec with the Internet Key Exchange (IKE) protocol [8] allows keys to be generated and distributed automatically and securely.

IPSec also includes the option for authentication, separate from whether the message is encrypted. The sender computes a hash function on the message, using a key. The receiver can be sure that only the true sender could have generated this hash.
The result is that, once IKE negotiation is complete, it is guaranteed that whatever machine is at the other end of the connection will continue to be at the other end—no other machine can impersonate it. But, at the start, how does each machine know the identity of the other machine?

Both encryption and authentication depend on reliably knowing the public key for the other party, that is, the party it is claiming to be. The current solution to the problem of confirming the public key uses a digital certificate issued by a certification authority (CA). But this has risks too:

- Can the CA be trusted? Perhaps it is run by a criminal organization or a hostile government. Even if the CA is legitimate, some of its employees could be corrupt.
- Can the CA really guarantee that this entity is who it claims to be? Will the CA require some form of identification, or perform some stronger check, before issuing a certificate? A law enforcement agency issuing certificates for its own staff would presumably know who they are and could vouch for their trustworthiness; a commercial CA might not be as careful about its clients.
- Even if the identity of the entity is known, is it someone who can be trusted to be either non-malicious or competent? And even if the organization is safe, does this apply to all its members? This could be especially important at a university, which has the same computers shared by many people with differing skills and agendas.
- Finally, certificates expire or need to be revoked (e.g. because the CA's security has been compromised), but this information takes time to propagate through the network.

### 3.3. Malicious Client Code

The possibility of a downloaded program damaging a client machine is minimized or eliminated when using Java applets, because the Java Virtual Machine executes applets in a "sandbox", an environment with limited privileges. For example, applets cannot read or write files on the client machine without explicit permission from the user. Note that the details of these protections depend on the version of Java, and are likely to change as the language evolves [3]. In contrast, screen savers and ActiveX controls in Microsoft Windows do not have such protection. They execute with the same privileges as any other programs, which in practice means they have essentially unlimited access to all system resources.

Client programs running on Unix or similar systems would have whatever privileges the user who is running them possesses. Therefore, they should not be run by individual users. Rather, the programs should be run from a special account, analogous to the ones used by daemons, with only the privileges they need. Even when running with restricted privileges, a malicious client program can still incapacitate a computer or inconvenience its users. A Java applet could open multiple windows on the screen, send email with the client computer's return address, or consume so many system resources as to render the machine unusable.

A Java applet running in the sandbox has an additional limitation: it can only open a network connection back to the server from which it was loaded. This eliminates the risk of the applet being used to directly participate in a distributed attack (e.g. a denial-of-service attack from multiple locations), but greatly restricts the amount of parallelism the computations can achieve, because the distributor machine could act as a bottleneck.

Another approach would be to send the client code to clients in source form, so they could check it for maliciousness. Aside from the question of whether the clients have the time and expertise to do this checking, revealing the source code would make it almost impossible to guard against counterfeit client code.

### 3.4. Counterfeit Client Code

The Popcorn project discusses several approaches to overcoming the risk of having a client provide spurious answers. One approach is to send out each portion of the computation to several independent clients. If one of them is providing spurious answers, its results will not be the same as the results provided by the other clients. We note that this approach is expensive but generally applicable; although it is conceivable that several clients would conspire to defraud the distributor, the vast number of clients and the inability of a client to know which parts of the problem it will be assigned make this impractical. Another approach is to organize the computations so that it's easy for the distributor to check the answers after they have been returned by the clients. For example, if the distributed task were to factor a large integer into primes, it would be relatively easy to check whether the factorization returned as a result is correct or not (although not necessarily which factor is incorrect). This approach is less expensive than the preceding one, but it is not generally applicable to all computations. The question on both these approaches is whether the resources spent on checking exceed those gained by parallelism.

There are several approaches that could guard against a client substituting its own counterfeit client code, for whatever reason. The most promising is probably to have the distributor and client engage in some sort of challenge-response authentication scheme; only the true client code would be able to authenticate itself. It remains to be seen if this can be done. Since the object code of the client (whether in machine language or Java bytecodes) is visible, it could conceivably be decompiled and reverse engineered to form a convincing counterfeit. There is also the possibility that a third party could compromise the client machine, planting a "Trojan horse" which would later corrupt or replace the client code.

Any authentication scheme should include a *nonce* mechanism, ensuring that authentication of a particular piece of downloaded code expires in a short period of time. This reduces the window of opportunity for counterfeit code to successfully masquerade as the true client.

### 3.5. Portals

In several of the proposed anonymous distributed computation schemes, clients connect to a well-known central portal to participate in a computation. It would seem that such an approach would provide some additional protection to the client. However, the fact that the client is connecting through a well-known, and possibly trusted, portal doesn't necessarily mean that the distributor using that portal can be trusted. For example, in the current version of the distriblet system, anyone with a computation to perform may distribute it using the central server. It is possible to modify the system to require prior registration before a computation is distributed, but even if registration is required, that only guarantees that the individual distributing the computation can be identified, not that the computation is harmless.

What level of protection should be provided by using a central portal? There are two issues to consider: 1) what level of protection the client expects, and 2) what kinds of protection are technically feasible. With respect to point 1), the risk to users is certainly no greater than the risk of downloading software from a Web site dedicated to distributing shareware. Even if the administrators of the Web site examine the software they are offering for download, neither they nor the users can be certain that the software is completely harmless. With respect to point 2), the administrators of the portal site would find it difficult to examine a proposed distributed computation and know with certainty whether it is harmless, and even more difficult to determine whether its computation would be considered unethical by some users.

Even if the operators of a portal or distributor issue disclaimers, they must still exercise some sort of due diligence. Despite this, they may still be open to liability if their site has been used as an accomplice in nefarious activities.

## 4. Conclusion

Anonymous distributed computing systems share the risks of any distributed system, but present unique challenges. Some of these can be addressed with current technology, but many solutions await future research. The ultimate test of the seriousness of these risks is whether users are dissuaded from participating in anonymous distributed computations because of the risks.

## 5. Acknowledgements

We gratefully acknowledge the comments of Christof Parr and Richard Stanley from WPI, and of the INC2000 reviewers.

## References

1. A. Baratloo, M. Karaul, Z. Kadem, and P. Wyckoff. "Charlotte: Metacomputing on the Web", *Proceedings of the International Conference on Parallel and Distributed Systems*, Dijon, France. September, 1996.

2. James F. Carlson, David V. Esposito, Nathaniel J. Springer, David Finkel and Craig E. Wills, "Applet-Based Distributed Computing on the Web," *Proceedings of the Workshop on Distributed Computing on the Web* (June, 1999), pp. 69 – 76.

3. Eva Chen, "Poison Java," IEEE Spectrum (August 1999). pp. 38 – 43.

4. Distributed.net, "Distributed.net Node Zero", http://www.distributed.net/, 1999.

5. David Finkel, Craig E. Wills, Kevin Amorin, Adam Covati, and Michael Lee, "An Applet-Based Approach to Large-Scale Distributed Computing", to appear in *Proceedings of the International Network Conference 2000* (July, 2000)

6. Warwick Ford and Michael S. Baum, *Secure Electronic Commerce*, Prentice-Hall PTR, Upper Saddle River, New Jersey, 1997.

7. Network Working Group, "Security Architecture for the Internet Protocol", http://www.ietf.org/rfc/rfc2401.txt, 1998.

8. Network Working Group, "The Internet Key Exchange (IKE)", http://www.ietf.org/rfc/rfc2409.txt, 1998.

9. "The POPCORN Project", http://www.cs.huji.ac.il/~popcorn/index.html, 1999.

10. "SETI@home: Search for Extraterrestrial Intelligence at Home", http://setiathome.ssl.berkeley.edu/, 1999.

# A Distributed Access Control Architecture for Mobile Agents

Nick Antonopoulos, Kyriakos Koukoumpetsos and Khurshid Ahmad

Department of Computing, University of Surrey, Guildford, Surrey, GU2 7XH, UK
e-mail: N.Antonopoulos@eim.surrey.ac.uk

## Abstract

The mobile software agent paradigm provides a generic, customisable foundation for the development of high performance distributed applications. The provision of an efficient and general purpose access control mechanism is needed to support the development of a wide spectrum of applications. This is achievable if the design of the access control system is based on the principles of simplicity, programmability (customisation) and reusability. However existing mobile agent architectures either neglect this issue at all or offer centralised schemes that do not support adaptive on a per-agent basis access control and do not address the issues of security knowledge sharing and reusing. In this paper a simple, distributed access control architecture is presented based on the concept of distributed, active authorisation entities (lock cells) any combination of which can be referenced by an agent to provide input and/or output access control. Furthermore it is demonstrated how these lock cells can be used to implement security domains and how they can be combined to create composite lock cells.

## Keywords

Mobile agents, access control, architecture, security, authorisation.

## 1. Introduction

Traditional distributed computing has proved inadequate and inefficient if the resources that a computation frequently needs to utilise are spread across large scale heterogeneous networks such as the Internet [General Magic 1996]. This observation led to the creation of two new distributed computing paradigms: the distributed objects [Orfali *et al* 1997] and the mobile software agents [General Magic 1998, Peine *et al* 1997, Johansen *et al* 1995]. An entity in these paradigms can concurrently be involved in multiple computations either as client or server. Access control is of paramount importance for such systems in order to ensure that an entity possesses enough authorisation to invoke a specific operation on a specific target entity. Some important properties that an access control architecture should possess are the following:

1. Integration with the computational model. Any computation that roams across a network of servers poses serious security hazards to its recipient. Security in general must be treated of at least the same importance as the architecture of the computational model.
2. General. In order to maintain the property of generality of the distributed objects and mobile agents paradigms the access control architecture should also be general purpose such that it can represent the security requirements of a range of applications.
3. Customisable. Applications should be able to create and dynamically modify their own access control policies and mechanisms.
4. Simple. Complex architectures are less programmable and more difficult to manage.

5. Distributed. Centralised access control can not support customisation on a per entity basis since this would require every entity to possess administrative privileges for the management of the central access control architecture. This of course is not acceptable since malicious entities could use these privileges to modify the access control schemes applied to other entities.
6. Security knowledge sharing and reuse. Parts of the access control structure of an entity can be shared with other entities. In this way access policies can be applied to groups of entities rather than individuals (security domains). Furthermore existing access control knowledge can be used as a building block for creating more complex access control structures thus promoting efficiency through reusability.

Unfortunately the existing access control approaches do not possess most of the aforementioned properties. Security in general is either neglected at all [Johansen *et al* 1995] or it is based on complex centralised architectures [Gosling *et al* 1995] that contain hidden security holes [Dean *et al* 1996].

The predominant approach for inter-agent access control is based on the notion of Access Control Lists (ACL). In this approach each agent carries certain attributes assigned to it based on the principal (user) who owns the agent. Access to an individual agent is controlled by a single central ACL in every host. This mechanism, although simple, is inherently static and passive. An agent usually has to carry all the privileges of its principal throughout its distributed execution. The ACLs are static entities which can be customised only by an administrator. In CORBA for example the security administration interfaces are hidden from the application objects. Furthermore there is no concept of security knowledge sharing and reuse. Implementation of security domains on these systems require the introduction of further entities (security domain managers in CORBA) thus making the system more complex. In summary this access control mechanism suits static distributed applications whose access control requirements are known before their deployment and mainly remain constant throughout their lifetime. On the other hand the world of mobile agents is anything but static. The contents and functionality as well as the environment of execution of an agent can change dramatically during its lifetime. In this case it is imperative that the principal or indeed the agent itself should be able to update efficiently its access control schemes to support and safeguard its current functionality.

In this paper a distributed access control architecture for mobile agents is presented based on the abstract access control model described in [Antonopoulos *et al* 1999]. In section 2 an overview of the abstract model is given. In section 3 the main entities and mechanisms of the architecture are presented. Finally section 4 has the conclusions.

## 2. Overview of abstract model

The abstract model of the proposed access control architecture is shown in figure 1. The access control model is an integrated component of the Surrey Architecture for Mobile Agents (SAMA). A cell in the context of this system is a trusted agent wrapper encapsulating untrusted user-defined functionality. Users can create wrappers and then use them as containers of passive data entities and active program entities. Each cell advertises an interface via which other cells can use to access the contained user defined functionality through synchronous or asynchronous message passing. An important service each cell offers is a synchronisation store which supports the collaboration of cells into invoking a function of a target cell. Cells can provide partial invocation data (i.e. function name and arguments) and the target cell has the functionality of combining these inputs into a single complete function invocation. The provision of this form of synchronisation/collaboration is taken into account in the authentication mechanism of the concrete model.

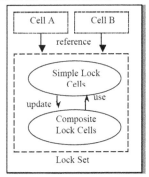

**Figure 1. The abstract access control model**

Cells are *locked* with a *lock expression*. Each cell maintains a *lock table*. This table assigns different authorisation criteria (lock expressions) to different users or groups of users. Messages are provided with a *key*. The purpose of the lock expression in a cell is to restrict the access to that cell only to those messages that possess a key that *fits* that lock expression. The locking mechanism is based upon the concepts of *lock* cells and *locked* cells. A cell is said to be *locked* if it references by name one or combination of lock cells. In its simplest form every lock is just an independent named registration centre maintaining a list of User Identifiers (UIDs) . The registration procedure and requirements that a user must follow and satisfy respectively in order for his UID to be included in the lock's list can differ dramatically between locks.

The successful registration of a user $x$ with a lock $l$ is equivalent to giving $x$ a personal key for $l$. The possession of a personal key for a lock $l$ by a user grants him the capability of being partly or fully authorised to access any cell that is locked by the single lock $l$ or a combination of locks that include $l$ respectively. The functionality of a lock cell resembles that of an Access Control List (ACL). The main difference being that a lock cell is an independent list of registered subjects that can be referenced by any object, in combination with other locks, to provide partial access control to that object. The lock expression is an arbitrary regular expression consisting of the logical AND, OR operators applied to locks. Composite lock cells can be created to represent lock expressions of arbitrary complexity. The aforementioned logical operators have the following context:

- The logical OR between two locks is equivalent to a composite lock whose registration list was produced from the concatenation of the lists of the first two locks. This definition means that a user $x$ is authorised to access any cell whose lock expression is $a+b$, where $a$, $b$ are locks, iff the user is registered with at least one of these two locks.
- The logical AND between two locks is equivalent to a composite lock whose list was produced from the intersection of the lists of the first two locks and a user $x$ is authorised

to access any cell whose lock expression is $a*b$, where $a$, $b$ are locks, iff the user is registered with both of these two locks.

## 3. The concrete access control model

The abstract model described in the previous section is based on two assumptions:
-   The system is deployed as a network of dedicated trusted servers.
-   There are safe interpreters for every language a user can use to encode his programs and insert them into the cells. The aim of these interpreters is to restrict an executing function of a cell from accessing directly the underlying operating system. Both assumptions are realistic and impose no serious constraints. Moreover the abstract model has several advantages over the existing access control models:

1.  Simplicity. The only entities of the model are the lock cells.
2.  Integration. The lock cells are $1^{st}$ level objects in the system. They are at the same level with the user defined computational agents (cells). A cell interacts with a lock cell the same way it interacts with the other cells.
3.  Dynamic customisation. A cell can create and manage its own access control policies by creating and interacting directly with the appropriate lock cell respectively.
4.  Distributed. The lock set in figure 1 is distributed since each lock cell is an independent software entity possibly located at a different host.
5.  Security knowledge sharing. The lock cells created by an agent can be used (referenced) by other agents to provide access control (security domains). The lock cells themselves are protected by referencing other lock cells.
6.  Security knowledge reuse. Existing access control policies (simple lock cells) can be combined to produce new, more complex policies (composite lock cells). Figure 2 shows the proposed concrete access control model which clarifies and extends the abstract model of figure 1:

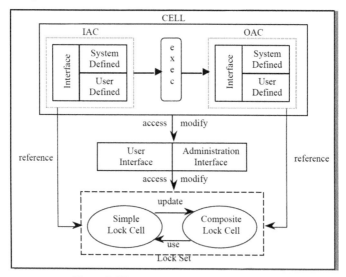

**Figure 2. The concrete access control model**

The access control architecture is divided in two layers : The access control functionality embedded within the cell and the set of simple and composite lock cells. As it can be observed from figure 2, cells can reference a combination of simple and composite lock cells for input and/or output access control. Furthermore the cells can access and manage the contents of the lock cells via a standard user and administrator interface that all lock cells implement. The simple lock cells are aware of the composite lock cells that depend on them so that they can update the contents of the appropriate composite lock cells when a change occurs in their contents (automatic consistency). As it was mentioned earlier, the composite lock cells need to be co-located with the simple lock cells they are based on. In this way the update traffic is localised and the period of inconsistency of a composite lock cell when a change occurs in one of its component simple lock cells is minimised. Below an analysis of these two layers is provided:

The access control related functionality of a cell has two aims: a) to provide and enforce input and output access control to its encapsulated user functionality and b) to participate in the authentication procedure of incoming and outgoing messages. Authentication is a necessary prerequisite for authorisation. Any access control scheme has to be based on a reliable, secure authentication mechanism.

The authentication mechanism of this system is based on the notion of *ownership graph*. Each message exchanged between cells is appended on its header its ownership graph in the form of a string. The purpose of the ownership graph is to describe the owners of the message and the relationship among them. There are two possible relationships between the principals of a message. The first relationship is collaboration. A collaboration relationship among $n$ principals indicates that these principals provided partial inputs which were combined to form a complete function invocation. The second relationship is nested invocation. Two principals $A$ and $B$ form such a relationship if a cell that belongs to $A$ invoked a function from a cell that belongs to $B$. Any message that the invoked function sends during its execution (further nesting of invocations) will be appended a ownership graph showing that this message is the result of principal $A$ invoking a function that belongs to principal $B$ which in turn requests the invocation of another function at another cell. This relationship is also represented in the composite delegation scheme in CORBA.

The collaboration relationship between two principals $A$ and $B$ is represented by the symbol ','. The nested invocation is represented with the symbol '/'. For example the string $(A,B,C)/D/E$ represents an ownership graph of a message that was produced as a result of principals $A$, $B$ and $C$ collaborating to invoke a function belonging to principal $D$ which in turn invoked a function of principal $E$ . Each cell is responsible in ensuring that every outgoing message contains the correct ownership graph. The user defined functions of the cell do not have access and as a result can not modify the ownership graph. The only entities of the cell that can read and modify the ownership graph are the Input Access Controller (IAC) and the Output Access Controller (OAC) respectively. There are two simple rules which dictate the updating of the ownership graph: a) The reply message a cell sends in response to a message with graph $G$ possesses the same graph $G$ as the request,  b) any message a cell sends while executing a function that was invoked by a message with graph $G$, will have a graph of the form $G/H$ where $H$ is the ownership graph of the cell itself.

The novelty of the described scheme lies in the fact that the ownership graph of a message is more informative that the simple list of principals utilised in existing systems. The fact that a new relationship (collaboration) is represented in the graph means that a cell can enforce more complex access control schemes where for example certain collaborations are allowed and others are rejected.

Furthermore more complex trust models can be implemented by accepting messages where untrusted principals provide partial input but rejecting others where the same untrusted principals participate in a simple nested invocation. The reason is that a simple graph of the form $(A,B)/C$ means that the results of the processing in $C$ are quaranteed to be returned to both $A$ and $B$ whereby a graph of the form $A/B/C$ indicates that the results of the processing will be returned to $A$ after being further processed in $B$. If we assume that principals $A$ and $C$ are trusted but principal $B$ is not then the target cell could accept the former graph since it quarantees the integrity of the results sent back to $A$. Instead the latter graph could be rejected because it is not quaranteed that either the results from $C$ will not be modified maliciously from $B$ before they are sent back to $A$ or $B$ will not consume the results and never send a reply to $A$.

From the above analysis it is clear that the ownership graph of a message must form the basis for the authorisation of messages in cells. For this purpose a cell contains two security related modules: the Input Access Controller (IAC) and the Output Access Controller (OAC). These modules decide according to proprietary privilege-based ACLs whether an incoming request is authorised to access the cell and whether an outgoing message is permitted to be sent respectively. The existence of the OAC is another novelty of the proposed architecture. Access control can now be source based instead of target based which is offered by existing approaches. The OAC allows the principal of a cell cut off any communication attempt with untrusted principals or cells. In the case where the "no trust" is mutual (bi-directional) between source principal and target principal, this scheme stops messages at their source and thus reduces redundant communication. The CORBA standard defines a client-based part in secure invocations. Its scheme though is centralised and oriented towards providing a required "quality of protection" which does not include the capability of rejecting the transmission of messages based on their destination. The IAC contains the tables of figure 3.

| Message type | Authorisation expression | Security info | Security value |
| --- | --- | --- | --- |

| Access path | Security value | Privileges |
| --- | --- | --- |

| Privileges | Operations |
| --- | --- |

**Figure 3. Data structure of the input access controller**

When a message arrives, its characteristics (i.e. ownership graph and other message attributes) are checked against the first table to determine what authorisation expression (lock expression) the message has to satisfy in order to be granted access to the cell. The IAC will utilise any pertinent security information caches and might contact the relevant lock cells directly to acquire security information that it has not in its cache. If the authorisation expression is satisfied then the message is assigned a security value (label). This label together with the access path the message followed to reach the agent determine its privileges. Finally it is checked as to whether the function this message requests to invoke is allowed based on its privileges. The IAC can also reference a lock cell that all incoming requests have to pass through in order to be authorised to access this cell while the IAC can still enforce further access control with its proprietary tables. The referenced lock cell acts in this way as an input security proxy of the cell. The IAC also implements a standard interface via which authorised principals can modify its tables and settings.

In a similar way when a executing function of the cell produces an outgoing message, then this message activates the OAC. The OAC decides whether the message according to its destination can : a) be allowed to be sent or b) be denied transmission or c) be forwarded to a nominated lock cell which acts as output security proxy for the cell. If the message is allowed to be sent then the OAC can specify any security information, pertinent to the specific target cell, to be added to the message (i.e. capabilities, access certificates that the target has provided to the source cell, lock cells to be contacted, etc.). The OAC also possesses a standard interface via which its contents can be customised.

The lock cells in general act as independent authorisation centres. They are classified into two categories: the Simple Lock Cells (SLC) and the Composite Lock Cells (CLC). All lock cells implement a standard interface that enables : a) specific principals or graphs of principals to register themselves by following a predefined registration procedure and b) specific cells to register pairs of ownership graph patterns and associated values to be used for proprietary access control. Each such pair has an owner field in order to distinguish between entries belonging to different cells/principals. There are two different types of simple lock cells:
a) Binary lock cells. These lock cells contain a list of ownership graph patterns. They act as binary security switches. When they are requested to authorise a message they first check whether the target cell has registered any entries in their list. If this is the case the message's ownership graph is matched against the sub-list of graphs that belong to the target cell. If a match is found then they send a notification that the message is authorised.
b) Layered lock cells. These lock cells contain a list of pairs of ownership graphs and values. The values belong to a range of security values the specific lock cell utilises. Different types of layered lock cells can be defined based on the range of security values they associate with the ownership graph patterns. Their functionality is similar to that of the binary lock cells with the difference that they also return the value associated with an ownership graph if a match is found. Clearly the layered lock cells act as labelling mechanisms for messages. The target cell of an invocation can utilise the label a predetermined layered lock cell assigned to the incoming message as an input for its own proprietary access control mechanism (IAC).

Both types of simple lock cells also include a data structure, similar to that the OAC maintains, based on which they can provide output access control. Furthermore the simple lock cells maintain a list of composite lock cells that are based on them so that they can notify them of any changes of their contents. The CLCs behave like simple lock cells when they are requested to authorise a message. Each CLC implements a lock expression. Their contents (input and output access control structures) are produced by combining the contents of their component simple lock cells such that each entry in their data structures satisfies the lock expression they implement. Three simple rules are applied to determine the contents of CLCs: a) one entry in a SLC $A$ matches an entry in SLC $B$ if their associated ownership graphs are identical, b) if an entry appears identical to two SLCs $A$ and $B$ then it will appear the same in both their intersection and union, c) if an entry has a different associated security value in $A$ and $B$ then this entry will appear in the intersection with the smallest of the two security values whereby in the union it will be associated with the highest value of the two.

Cells can create simple and composite lock cells by sending an appropriate request to the lock cell factory. The functionality of the lock cell factory is dual: It acts as a lock cell type repository. The type of a SLC is defined as an ordered list of security labels it can assign to the ownership graphs that will be registered in it. Secondly it ensures that a CLC will be created only if the types of the component SLC are identical. Figure 4 shows an object-oriented view of the presented access control architecture:

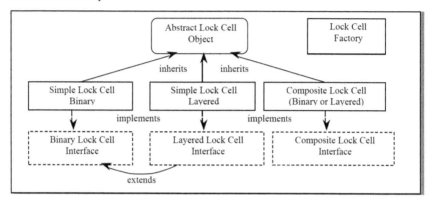

**Figure 4. An object-oriented model of the architecture**

## 4. Conclusions

In this paper the architecture of a distributed access control system for mobile agents was presented and analysed. The architecture is based on a natural abstract model which satisfies the principles of simplicity, customisation and security knowledge sharing and reuse. The agents can create and dynamically manage their own proprietary access control policy parts of which can become public and shared with other agents. Overall the presented architecture provides a simple, customisable base that mobile agents can use to program their security requirements as an individual or as a group.

## References

[1] General Magic, Inc. (1996), *Telescript Technology: Mobile Agents.* , http://www.genmagic.com/Telescript
[2] R.Orfali, D. Harkey, J. Edwards. (1997), *Instant CORBA.* John Wiley & Sons, Inc. , USA.
[3] General Magic, Inc. (1998), *"Odyssey Web Site".* http://www.genmagic.com/agents
[4] H. Peine, T. Stolpmann. (1997), *The architecture of the ARA platform for mobile agents.* Mobile Agents, Lecture Notes in Computer Science Series, vol. 1219, Springer, pp 50-61.
[5] D. Johansen, R.v. Renesse, F. B. Schneider. (1995), *An Introduction to the TACOMA Distributed System.* technical report 95-23, Department of Computer Science, University of Tromso, Norway.
[6] J. Gosling, H. McGilton. (1995), *The Java Language Environment.* Sun Microsystems, USA.
[7] D. Dean, E. W. Felten, D. S. Wallach. (1996), *Java Security: From HotJava to Netscape and Beyond.* IEEE Symposium on Security and Privacy, Oakland, USA.
[8] N. Antonopoulos, G. Aggelou, A. V. Shafarenko. (1999), *An Asynchronous Internet Computing Model and its Applications.* Conference on Practical Applications of Multi agents Systems (PAAM99), London, UK.

# Flexible Management of Shared Groupware Objects

Stephan Lukosch and Claus Unger

University of Hagen, Department for Computer Science, 58084 Hagen, Germany
{Stephan.Lukosch, Claus.Unger}@Fernuni-Hagen.de

## Abstract

Synchronous groupware brings together users, which are geographically distributed, but connected via a network. In this paper we describe an object manager, which simplifies synchronous groupware development. It offers a variety of services for controlling an application's shared data, including flexible object distribution, flexible object coupling, latecomer support and configurable concurrency control. After a brief description of the development platform and the object manager basic concepts we focus on its configurable services, e.g. consistency maintenance and object coupling. A description of the runtime architecture and directions for future work conclude the paper.

## Keywords

Groupware development, shared objects, consistency maintenance, and object coupling.

## 1. Introduction

Groupware systems are computer-based systems that support two or more users engaged in a common task, and that provide an interface to a shared environment (Ellis et al., 1991). In this paper we focus on the development of synchronous groupware, which allows users at different places to interact at the same time. Until now synchronous groupware encompasses a wide range of applications like collaborative whiteboards, text editors or Web browsers. All these applications have to share data and maintain data consistency.

When developing several groupware applications, e.g. a distance teaching environment (Lukosch et al., 1999), we noticed that shared data and maintaining data consistency are among the main obstacles for groupware development. In our opinion, groupware development should be almost as easy as the development of single-user applications. This idea lead to an *object manager* in coherence with *DreamTeam* (Roth and Unger, 1998).

DreamTeam is a platform for synchronous collaboration and offers a variety of services for application developers as well as for end-users. The environment consists of three parts: a *development environment*, a *runtime environment*, and a *simulation environment*. DreamTeam as well as the object manager are based upon a completely decentralised architecture, thus there is no central server holding session states. The decentralised architecture leads to more complex algorithms, but avoids performance bottlenecks and makes the system much more reliable. The object manager extends DreamTeam's development and runtime environment as it offers services for the developer, which are used to handle shared objects at runtime. It offers a variety of services for controlling the application's shared data. For the normal developer, the object manager abstracts away distribution characteristics and offers default mechanisms, while an expert developer may customise the default mechanisms to her special needs.

This paper is organised as follows: after a brief description of DreamTeam and the object manager's basic concepts we focus on the object manager's services. A description of how the object manager is embedded in the runtime architecture and directions for future work conclude the paper.

## 2. DreamTeam

As mentioned above DreamTeam mainly consists of three parts: a development environment, a runtime environment, and a simulation environment. The development environment offers a huge hierarchical class library with groupware specific solutions. These include, e.g., awareness widgets like distributed mouse pointers. It is entirely written in Java, thus runnable on many operating systems. We strictly paid attention to using platform independent language elements only, and tested the programs on *Solaris*, *Windows95*, *OS/2* and *Linux*.

The runtime environment provides an infrastructure with special groupware facilities, which allow to start sessions and shared applications. To interact with the system, a front-end is included in the runtime environment. The following figure shows a typical working environment.

**Figure 1: The DreamTeam working environment.**

In addition to the front-end, the following tasks have been started:
- The *Archive Manager* can be viewed as a small database for long-term data such as old user profiles or profiles of terminated sessions.
- The *Connection Manager* is active during a running session and handles the communication between the different sites of a running session.
- The *Log Manager* collects and stores relevant system messages.

- The *Rendezvous Manager* determines which users are online and want to join a collaborative session (Roth and Unger, 1999).
- The *Session Manager* handles session profiles, starts and stops sessions and enables joining and leaving sessions.
- The *Transfer Manager* provides data transport for slow data, e.g., for file transfer.

The simulation environment is called *DNS* (*DreamTeam Network Simulator*). DNS is able to simulate networks with limited bandwidths and network delays. Every communication channel can be configured separately. To detect performance problems, DNS provides report functions for network loads. Testing shared applications inside the simulation environment ensures stability for real usage and avoids performance problems which otherwise would be detected very late in the development cycle.

## 3. The Object Manager

The development of a single-user application mainly differs from groupware development with respect to controlling the application's data. An application's data must be shared to support interactions across distributed, collaborating users. As several users may modify the same data at the same time, it is up to the developer to maintain data consistency. Until now, applications based on DreamTeam had to use data sharing services provided by the DreamTeam environment. These services had to be called explicitly. The new object manager hides these services.

The first version of the object manager (Lukosch and Unger, 1999) handled shared objects by replacing them with *proxies* (Shapiro, 1986), as proxies provide a powerful way to hide data sharing services. Although this approach already simplified the handling of shared groupware objects, the class hierarchy was quite complex and the developer had to handle and define several different classes.

To simplify the handling even more, we now replace shared objects with what we call *substitutes*. This name stems from the substitution principle of object-oriented languages. Due to this principle substitutes offer the same interface as the shared object they are used for, and thus can easily be used as a placeholder. Using substitutes the developer has not to specify any additional classes. Substitutes are either generated automatically at runtime or by the developer from the command line. Inside a groupware application the developer uses the substitute in the same way as a local object. She does not have to care about an object's distribution, as the necessary mechanisms are hidden.

A substitute generalises a shared object and overwrites some of the shared object's methods to add additional functionality. To share data, a substitute distributes method calls and encodes the corresponding arguments. Moreover, a substitute stores additional object information, e.g. the used concurrency control scheme or the distribution mode.

Fig. 2 shows a class diagram for a replicated object class *SampleRObj* and a central object class *SampleCObj* in UML syntax. For each type of object, the developer must extend a basic shared object. The class SampleRObj extends the basic shared object class *ReplicatedObject* and thus is replicated. The class SampleCObj extends the basic shared object class

*CentralObject* and thus is central. Both basic shared object classes extend the class *SharedObject* containing features identical to both classes. One important feature of this class is its aggregation of the class *SharedObjectReference*, which is used to identify a shared object. The classes *SampleRObjSubstitute* and *SampleCObjSubstitute* both extend the corresponding developer-defined classes. The object manager uses these classes upon registration (see section 3.1) to replace the developer-defined classes. The developer can either start a substitute generator from the command line to create the corresponding substitute class for a shared object class or leave it to the object manager to create the necessary substitute class at runtime. Especially in the last case the developer does not really notice that she is using shared objects.

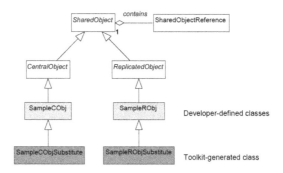

**Figure 2: Shared object class diagram.**

There are no limitations to the complexity of a shared object. A shared object can include references to other shared objects, which may be necessary in complex collaborative application like in (Anupam and Bajaj, 1994). In contrast to other approaches in object-oriented distributed programming (Guerraoui and Fayad, 1999) new distribution modes or techniques for handling shared data can easily be included in the toolkit. To include a new distribution mode, a new basic shared object class is simply added to the object manager's class library.

In the following, we describe the object manager's basic services (see section 3.1), its configurable concurrency control (see section 3.2) and its flexible object coupling (see section 3.3).

### 3.1. Basic Services

One of the object manager's basic services is object distribution. Since the discussion about the best distribution mode for groupware is still going on, our toolkit supports replicated as well as central objects. We favour the use of replicated objects, when high responsiveness is needed, e.g. in group editors. Central objects fit well, when the object itself contains a significant amount of data, e.g. a video, and only small parts of the object must be transmitted to users, e.g. single frames.

The developer defines a shared object's distribution mode by either extending a basic central object class or a replicated object class. To access the shared object at runtime, it must be registered in the object manager, which upon registration returns the corresponding substitute.

To register a shared object, the developer must provide the shared object's classname and a unique registration name. The object manager creates an instance of the shared object's substitute class and adds this instance to its object registry. After this, the object manager informs all other object managers about the newly registered object and returns the substitute. If the newly registered object is replicated, the object manager distributes a replica of the shared object. Otherwise only its reference is distributed.

To be informed whenever a new shared object is registered, a developer can bind a callback to the object manager. Thus the developer can dynamically create shared objects.

Another basic service is the transparent distribution of method calls. Due to the nature of central objects all method calls from a remote site must be mapped to the site maintaining the central object. In the case of a replicated object the developer must specify the methods which modify the shared object's content and therefore have to be distributed. This is the only point during the development of shared objects, where the developer has to be aware of a shared object's characteristics. To map a method call, several steps have to be executed. For the distribution of the method call its arguments have to be encoded. Possible shared object arguments are replaced with their references. After this, the method call is multicasted to other object managers, which execute the method. In case of a central object the result has to be transmitted. To establish object coupling or maintain consistency, further steps must be performed. In the following sections we describe these steps. The developer does not have to care about these mechanism, although she may configure them to her individual needs.

## 3.2. Consistency Maintenance

As described above, instead of distributing object versions themselves we distribute method calls on the shared object. If all methods, which modify the content of a shared object, are executed under distributed mutual exclusion, consistency is guaranteed.

Our concurrency control configuration bases on this idea. Usually, not all methods of a shared object modify all components of the object. To allow simultaneous method execution, if possible, our concurrency control scheme uses multiple locks. In our opinion this is more intuitive than the definition of transactions. When using transactions, a lock on all involved objects has to be obtained.

Let a shared object offer a set $M = \{m_i \mid i=1,...,n \wedge n \in I\!N\}$ of methods. The developer can group these methods into sets of mutually excluded methods, $EM_j \subseteq M$, which form the object's exclusive method set, $OEM = \{EM_j \mid j=1,...,k \wedge k \in I\!N\}$. All necessary locks are elements of a sequence $L = (l_j \mid j=1,...,k \wedge k \in I\!N)$. Each set of exclusive methods $EM_j$ is assigned a lock $l_j$ using the function $lm : OEM \rightarrow L$, $lm(EM_j) = l_j$. Whenever a method $m_i$ of a distributed object is called, all locks of the method's lock set $ML_i = \{l_j \mid m_i \in lm^{-1}(l_j)\}$ are requested. To avoid deadlocks, locks are requested according to the order defined by the sequence $L$. This approach originally stems from resource allocation in operating systems (Havender, 1968).

Consider a shared object that realises a text box in a multi-user diagram editor. Let this object offer a set of four methods, $M = \{m_1, m_2, m_3, m_4\}$. Method $m_1$ may modify box properties, method $m_2$ may modify text properties, $m_3$ may modify the common colour, and $m_4$ may modify the position in the diagram. Method $m_1$ and $m_2$ can be executed concurrently whereas $m_3$ and $m_4$ modify the properties of both, the box and the text. This leads to the following set $OEM = \{EM_1, EM_2\}$ with $EM_1 = \{m_1, m_3, m_4\}$ and $EM_2 = \{m_2, m_3, m_4\}$. The methods' lock sets are $ML_1 = \{l_1\}$, $ML_2 = \{l_2\}$, $ML_3 = \{l_1, l_2\}$, and $ML_4 = \{l_1, l_2\}$. Instead of locking the whole object our approach achieves a maximum of concurrency as independent properties can be manipulated concurrently.

Fig. 3 shows a deadlock-free example lock allocation graph. A directed edge from method $m_i$ to lock $l_j$ means that $m_i$ requested $l_j$. An edge in the opposite direction means that $m_i$ holds $l_j$. If $m_3$ held $l_2$ there would be a cycle in the allocation graph. Such a situation cannot happen because the locks are requested in sorted order, i.e. $m_3$ must hold $l_1$ before requesting $l_2$.

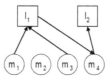

**Figure 3: Lock allocation graph.**

For each shared object, the developer can define individual sets $OEM$, thus compromising between consistency and time consumption. In this case it is her task to ensure that all conflicting methods are executed exclusive. If the developer does not care about individual synchronisation, she can choose from two predefined schemes:

- *Full synchronisation*: All methods are executed under mutual exclusion.
- *Null synchronisation*: All methods may be executed concurrently.

At the moment, two pessimistic locking mechanisms have been implemented, one for replicated objects and one for central objects. For replicated objects, we adopted Singhal's token-based heuristically-aided algorithm for mutual exclusion (Singhal, 1989) by extending it to situations where users may dynamically join or leave a running session. We chose Singhal's algorithm because it reduces user response times:

- a site holding the token may enter a critical section without requesting permission from other sites like in, e.g., message based algorithms.
- Singhal's algorithm only requests permission to enter a critical section from sites which are supposed to hold the token. Thus the number of exchanged messages to enter a critical section is reduced.

For central objects, the corresponding object manager has simply to ensure that locally no exclusive methods are executed in parallel. Here we implemented local semaphores as known from operating systems.

By using the programming technique *open implementation* (Kiczales et al., 1997) we added even more flexibility. Open implementation allows the developer to change a toolkit's implementation strategy. In our toolkit both realised kinds of locks extend the same superclass. By extending this superclass a developer can define her own locks and exchange the predefined ones. This may be useful if the application uses, e.g., *Mbone* instead of the default *TCP* (see section 4). Since the number of exchanged messages is less important in case of Mbone, a simpler algorithm may work more efficiently.

## 3.3. Object Coupling

The object manager offers a configurable object coupling service. This service allows a developer to track changes in a shared object. It is realised with a kind of extended callback mechanism.

Every object of a groupware application can become a listener of a shared object. The developer can register any object of a groupware application as a method listener in the object manager. Whenever a shared object's method is called, the listener is informed.

If the developer does not care about an individual object coupling, she may use a default mechanism: a method call event, which contains the method name, the method call arguments and the method call result is passed to the listener. The developer has to implement a special method, which usually is just a big conditional code block. After receiving a method call event, it must be unpacked and be applied accordingly. It is not easy to keep control on this code block and to maintain it.

To overcome this situation, the object manager offers an extended callback mechanism which frees the developer from unpacking the event information. This mechanism just passes the specified information to a developer-defined listener method. Thus the usual conditional code block is divided into separate methods and coupling can be maintained easier. Imagine, e.g., a collaborative sketch editor, where object coupling is being used to synchronise different user views. Whenever the replicated object that keeps the history of the user's actions changes, they are forwarded to the user interface. Such changes may, e.g., include adding of lines or removing parts of the sketch. Using the default coupling mechanism, the developer has to provide code that decides whether a line is added or a part of the sketch is removed. With the extended callback mechanism the developer may provide a coupling that executes different methods corresponding to the shared object's different method calls.

For this the developer has to define a *method mapping* between a shared object's method and a listener method. The listener method is called whenever the shared object's method is executed. Its parameters can be composed from the shared object's method parameters and the method call result, and may contain information about the site which called the method. Thus the method mapping consists of:
- a shared object's method name,
- a listener's method name,
- and the listener's method parameters.

This coupling mechanism supports a clear separation between shared data objects and listeners. Many architectural styles for groupware applications like *multi-user MVC*, which stems from (Krasner and Pope, 1988), *ALV* (Hill, 1992), or *PAC\** (Calvary et al., 1997) postulate such a separation of an application's data and its user interface as a prerequisite for an effective development and maintenance of groupware. The power of this separation results from the fact that quite different user interfaces can be generated from the same shared data. Using our coupling mechanism, this separation can easily be realised and maintained.

## 4. Runtime Architecture

The object manager extends DreamTeam. Fig. 4 shows the structure of DreamTeam's runtime environment with the arrows indicating a service use. At top level, the runtime environment can be divided into four parts:

1. The operating system and the included network services, as well as the Java virtual machine.
2. The runtime environment consists of the *Kernel Layer*, the *Manager Layer*, and the *Front-End*. These layers are embedded in runtime control and monitoring. Managers, including the object manager, fulfil special tasks (see section 2). Kernels offer low level services, e.g. for controlling persistent objects. The *Network Kernel Interface (NKI)* (Roth, 1999) can be used to establish network connections or to multicast messages. As default, all services the kernel offers are mapped to *TCP*. To use *Mbone*, the network kernel has to be exchanged. At the moment we are developing an adaptable kernel which maps its services to the best, actually available network.
3. Groupware applications which are connected with the runtime environment via the *Application Service Layer (ASL)*.
4. Possible framework extensions can be integrated into the framework via the *Framework Developer Interface (FDI)*. FDI allows to add managers to the manager layer without modifying the rest of the platform. For this the manager has to extend a basic manager class and the name of the manager has to be added to the FDI start-up script.

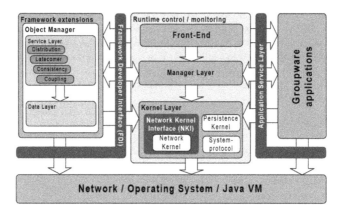

**Figure 4: DreamTeam's runtime environment's structure.**

The object manager is integrated into DreamTeam's runtime environment via the FDI and thus belongs to the manager layer. Groupware applications can access the object manager via the ASL. It is divided into two layers:

1. *Service layer*: This layer contains the object manager's services, including object distribution, object coupling, latecomer support and consistency maintenance. Some of these

services, e.g. the consistency or the coupling service, may be configured by the developer to adapt the special needs of different groupware applications.

2. *Data layer*: This layer can only be accessed via the service layer. It, e.g., contains the shared object registry.

## 5. Related work

Most of the existing groupware platforms differ with regard to shared objects' distribution modes or the application architecture. A well-known classification of groupware application architectures can be found in (Patterson, 1995). Patterson distinguishes three basic architectures:

1. *Centralised state architecture*: All input or output operations are directed to a central server, which also manages the shared data. The clients have only the task to display the shared data and to send requests to the central server. An example for this architecture is *Rendezvous* (Hill, 1992).

2. *Replicated state architecture*: The application itself and the shared data is replicated. As the shared data can be accessed locally user's response time is reduced, though more complex algorithms must be used, e.g. for consistency maintenance. *COAST* (Schuckmann et al.,1996), *DECAF* (Strom et al., 1998), or *GroupKit* (Roseman and Greenberg, 1996) rely on a replicated state architecture.

3. *Hybrid architecture*: The hybrid architecture is composed from the two previous ones. The shared data can either be maintained centrally or replicated. The most common approach is to replicate the application and to maintain shared data centrally. *Suite* (Dewan and Choudhary, 1992) uses this approach.

In our opinion no architecture fits well for every groupware application. Therefore our object manager offers two distribution modes for shared objects and the developer can choose the architecture, which fits for her application best. She can even combine the different approaches as it is possible to create applications using replicated as well as central objects. In the following we will describe some other groupware platforms, which also deal with a more flexible approach to groupware development.

*Clock* (Graham et al., 1996b) is a component-based groupware platform. Groupware applications are composed of components which are specified via Clock's own functional programming language. To facilitate the development of a groupware application, Clock provides the visual programming environment *ClockWorks* (Graham et al., 1996a) used to compose components and define their attributes, e.g. concurrency control algorithms or distribution mode.

In *Prospero* (Dourish, 1996), open implementation is used to build a flexible groupware framework. Prospero mainly aims at realising a flexible concurrency control scheme based on *consistency guarantees* and *promises*. Based upon promises about its future actions an application is granted a consistency guarantee. If the application does not hold its promise, the consistency guarantee may not hold as well. A developer may change the guarantee's implementation (Dourish, 1998).

In contrast to Prospero, *GEN* (O'Grady, 1996) focuses on flexible distribution strategies. As default, the GEN toolkit includes implementations for a replicated or centralised architecture.

GEN is no longer maintained. However, some results are incorporated into the most recent version of GroupKit (Roseman, 1998).

Our object manager goes a big step further by providing a flexible concurrency control scheme as well as flexible distribution methods. By using substitutes, it supports various kinds of shared objects, manipulation of the object's exclusive method set and developer-defined locks.

## 6. Future work

The development of the object manager is still going on. There are a lot of further fields of interest. A concept of dynamic distribution will allow the system to dynamically define and change the distribution mode of a shared object, e.g. depending on current network conditions. The latecomer support will provide latecomers with overviews about recent events. Other fields have not been touched yet, e.g. access control or asynchronous services like shared object persistence. Beside the two predefined pessimistic locking schemes, future versions will contain predefined optimistic locking schemes as well. They will, e.g., allow the direct execution of a method before the lock is granted, and thus provide an undo method in case the lock grant is denied. The interface for defining individual locking schemes will then be extended to support the definition of individual optimistic locking schemes.

## 7. Acknowledgement

We deeply appreciate in-depth discussions with our colleague Jörg Roth.

## 8. References

Anupam,V. and Bajaj, C.L. (1994), "Shastra: Multimedia Collaborative Design Environment", *IEEE Multimedia*, Vol. 1, No.2, pp. 39–49.

Calvary, G., Coutaz, J., and Nigay, L. (1997), "From Single-User Architectural Design to PAC: A Generic Software Architecture Model for CSCW", *Human Factors in Computing Systems: CHI'97 Conference Proceedings*, pp. 242–249.

Dewan, P. and Choudhary, R. (1992), "A High-Level and Flexible Framework for Implementing Multiuser Interfaces", *ACM Transactions on Information Systems*, Vol. 10, No. 4, pp. 345–380.

Dourish, P. (1996), "Consistency Guarantees: Exploiting Application Semantics for Consistency Management in Collaboration Toolkit", *Proceedings of the ACM 1996 Conference on Computer Supported Cooperative Work*, pp. 268–277.

Dourish, P. (1998), "Using Metalevel Techniques in a Flexible Toolkit for CSCW Applications", *ACM Transactions on Computer-Human Interaction*, Vol. 5, No. 2, pp. 109–155.

Ellis, C.A., Gibbs, S.J., and Rein, G.L. (1991), "Groupware some issues and experiences", *Communications of the ACM*, Vol. 34, No. 1, pp. 38–58.

Guerraoui, R. and Fayad, M.E. (1999), "OO Distributed Programming Is Not Distributed OO Programming", *Communications of the ACM*, Vol. 42, No. 4, pp. 101–104.

Graham, T.C.N., Morton, C.A., and Urnes, T. (1996a), "ClockWorks: Visual Programming of Component-Based Software Architectures", *Journal of Visual Languages and Computing*, pp. 175–196, July.

Graham, T.C.N., Urnes, T., and Nejabi, R. (1996b), "Efficient Distributed Implementation of Semi-Replicated Synchronous Groupware", *Proceedings of the 9th annual ACM symposium on User interface software and technology*, pp. 1–10.

Havender, J.W. (1968), "Avoiding deadlock in multitasking systems", *IBM Systems Journal*, Vol. 7, No. 2, pp. 74–84.

Hill, R.D. (1992), "The Abstraction-Link-View Paradigm: Using Constraints to connect User Interfaces to Applications", *Human Factors in Computing Systems: CHI'92 Conference Proceedings*, pp. 335–342.

Kiczales, G., Lamping, J., Lopes, C.V., Maeda, C., Mendhekar, A., and Murphy, G. (1997), "Open Implementation Design Guidelines", *Proceedings of the 1997 International Conference on Software Engineering*, pp. 481–490.

Krasner, G.E. and Pope, S.T. (1988), "A Cookbook for Using the Model-View-Controller User Interface Paradigm in Smalltalk-80", *Journal of Object-Oriented Programming*, Vol. 1, No. 3, pp. 26–49.

Lukosch, S., Roth, J., and Unger, C. (1999), "Marrying on-campus teaching to distance teaching", *Proceedings of the 19th world conference on open learning and distance education*.

Lukosch, S. and Unger, C. (1999), "Flexible Synchronisation of Shared Groupware Objects", *ACM GROUP'99 Workshop on Consistency Maintenance and Group Undo in Real-Time Group Editors*.

O'Grady, T. (1996), "Flexible Data Sharing in a Groupware Toolkit", Master's thesis, University of Calgary, Department of Computer Science, November.

Patterson, J.F. (1995), "A Taxonomy of Architectures for Synchronous Groupware Architectures", *ACM SIGOIS Bulletin Special Issue: Papers of the CSCW'94 Workshops*, Vol. 15, No. 3, pp. 27–29.

Roseman, M. and Greenberg, S. (1996), "Building Real-Time Groupware with GroupKit, A Groupware Toolkit", *ACM Transactions on Computer-Human Interaction*, Vol. 3, No. 1, pp. 66–106.

Roseman, M. (1998), GroupKit 5.0 Documentation. *http://www.cpsc.ucalgary.ca/projects/grouplab/groupkit/gk5doc/*, University of Calgary GroupLab, June.

Roth, J. (1999), "Network Kernel Interface", Internal Technical Reference, *http://dreamteam.fernuni-hagen.de/dreamteam/paper/nki.pdf*, University of Hagen, October.

Roth, J. and Unger, C. (1998), "DreamTeam - A Platform for Synchronous Collaborative Applications", *Groupware und organisatorische Innovation (D-CSCW'98)*, pp. 153–165.

Roth, J. and Unger, C. (1999), "Group Rendezvous in a Synchronous, Collaborative Environment", *11. ITG/VDE Fachtagung, Kommunikation in Verteilten Systemen (KiVS'99)*.

Strom, R., Banavar, G., Miller, K., Prakash, A., and Ward, M. (1998), "Concurrency Control and View Notification Algorithms for Collaborative Replicated Objects", *IEEE Transactions on Computers*, Vol. 47, No. 4, pp. 458–471.

Shapiro, M. (1986), "Structure and Encapsulation in Distributed Systems", *Proceedings of the 6th International Conference on Distributed Computer Systems*, pp. 198–204.

Singhal, M. (1989), "A Heuristically-Aided Algorithm for Mutual Exclusion in Distributed Systems", *IEEE Transactions on Computers*, Vol. 38, No. 5, pp. 651–662.

Schuckmann, C., Kirchner, L., Schümmer, J., and Haake, J.M. (1996), "Designing object-oriented synchronous groupware with COAST", *Proceedings of the ACM 1996 Conference on Computer Supported Cooperative Work*, pp. 30–38.

# Hierarchical Peripheral Distributed Directory Service for Enterprise Computing

Robert Löw[1], Udo Bleimann[1], Jeanne Stynes[2], Ingo Stengel[1], Aidan McDonald[2]

[1] Distributed Systems Lab – University of Applied Sciences Darmstadt, Germany
[2] Department of Mathematics and Computing, Cork Institute of Technology, Ireland
Email : robert@loew.com

## Abstract

It is increasingly difficult to handle the administration of employee information in big enterprises efficiently. Storing information locally and maintaining them locally facilitate local processing. However, access to such information tends to be required from all over the enterprise and a centralised approach would be more appropriate. Unfortunately this is a very expensive undertaking.
In this paper we discuss how locally trimmed information can be found and used in large enterprises. We also present the Hierarchical Distributed Directory Service, a mechanism for integrating enterprise-wide information.

## Keywords

Directory Service, LDAP

## Goal

Today different systems are used for the administration of employee information. We have the usually centralised Human Resource Management Systems, the different accounting systems used by varying operating systems (e.g. Windows NT, UNIX and mainframe accounts), the access mechanisms to different information systems (e.g. protected parts of Intranet servers), the special repositories (e.g. email server and workflow management systems), the single application accounts (e.g. document management systems, user helpdesk).
In the near future, Public Key Infrastructures (PKI) and certifying systems will also need to be administered. In fact, private branch exchange or physical access systems often manage their own data stocks.
The aim of this paper is to show how all kinds of employee information infrastructures can be integrated in a single service. All applications should be able to process this information using standardised methods.

## Requirements

The following requirements have been set for the system :
· integration of all information regarding employees,
· simple information management in the form of hierarchical structures that are adapted to the particular organisation,
· location transparency,

- flexible, extendable information structure,
- usage of existing standards,
- integration of methods already used to synchronise different information infrastructures (i.e. the Network Information Service [2] (NIS)).

## Employment of a Directory Service (DS)

Using existing directory services is a solution for many infrastructures that are waiting to be integrated.

In the Internet and Intranet area the Lightweight Directory Access Protocol (LDAP) has been enforced as a standard interface to directory services. Compared with ISO's X.500 standard, LDAP is easier to implement and to use. While traditionally administering their own user information, more and more systems will offer at least one of these two standardised interfaces.

## Central Directory Service

The administration of big data stocks is expensive if a Central Directory Service is employed. This is because data sets must be modified either at a central point or using a special application to ensure that every manager of a DS can only modify the information for which he is responsible.

Furthermore, access to the directory service can be performed over a long distance. This can, e.g., in the case of Virtual Private Networks (VPN), result in security problems and loss of performance. Caching information from the directory service on different locations of the enterprise has proven to be ineffective since accounting information tend to be short-lived (i.e. password changes can be claimed every x days).

## Peripheral Distributed Directory Service

The employment of many local directory services allows a better, easier and more competent management of smaller amounts of information. Data is more up-to-date as employees and software systems can independently modify information as required.

For example, to change their password, employees use the change password facility provided by the operating system; they may not be aware that the operating system automatically advises the directory service to change the password too.

The physical proximity of the directory service to systems that use the information of the DS prevents a loss of performance , a phenomenon common with big networking distances. Security is also enhanced since security- relevant data seldom pass the VPN.

At the moment, using the LDAP standard, the only way to replicate directories of the same structure is via the LDAP Duplication/Replication/Update Protocols (LDUP) [1]. Using this kind of replication the contents of a directory service can be assimilated by other directory services. Unfortunately, the method has the following crucial disadvantages :
- Two directory services matched using replication must have symmetric structures.
- All Information must be kept redundantly on different places. During replication the whole data must be transmitted through the network, which leads to a higher network load.

- Between modification and the next replication, information is not up to date throughout the network.
- A method must be found, which guarantees that during replication, modifications on existing data can only be made by authorised sites (e.g., after an employee moves from one place to another, which department is authorised to modify his data ? Will it be the administrator of the new department or the replication mechanism, which replicates the information from the new department to the old department ?).
- There is a danger of wiretapping since there are some points in the network (e.g. modem port of the router) where all security relevant enterprise information pass during the replication process.

## Meta Directory

A Meta Directory is a superior instance of a directory, which uses different data sources. There are different Meta Directory Models :
- The Replication Model, where all data from all sources will be read and replicated.
- The Online Model, where every request of a DUA is answered by reading the requested information from the data source.

Up to now Meta Directories, which use a Central Directory, have the same disadvantages concerning performance and security problems like the Central Directory Service.

The use of this Replication Model implies the same actuality problems like those of the Peripheral Distributed Directory Service.

## A Hierarchical Peripheral Distributed Directory Service

Assuming a Peripheral Directory Service exists, a system may nevertheless not know the appropriate local directory service to access. One solution is to use broadcasts. In this case, every system that requires information from nonlocal directory services has to implement the broadcast functionality.

The Hierarchical Distributed Directory Service (HDDS) aims to offer applications access to nonlocal directory services. It uses standard protocols exclusively.

A HDDS implementation consists of 1 to n peripheral, distributed, arboreal arranged directory services with a root directory service. A system using HDDS , also called a Directory User Agent (DUA), can address one and only one directory service. For example, in Figure 1, all systems of the computing department can directly access only the "ds.comp.dep.fhd.de" Directory Service.

Using existing standard interfaces of directory services, e.g., NIS [2], the DUA requests information about a certain employee via LDAP from the known Directory Service. If the requested information is available to the directory service, it will be forwarded to the DUA. Otherwise, the following steps, which form the technical innovation of the HDDS, occur :

a) The solicited directory service requests information using a special PlugIn. The request is send via LDAP to the next higher directory service in the hierarchy. The DNS name of the latter is obtained by omitting the sub-domain (prefix) of the original DS. For example, by dropping the sub-domain "comp" in the name "ds.comp.dep.fhd.de" of the DS of the computing department, one gets the name of the next higher DS, namely "ds.dep.fhd.de".
b) If the next higher directory service is unable to furnish the requested information step a) is repeated.
c) When the information is found, it is passed to the requesting node by a directory service, which may have received it from a directory server in the hierarchy.If the query reaches the root node, this node will reply with a pointer to the actual information, if the latter exists. Otherwise, a message that the required information is non-existent is returned to the requesting node. All requests concerning the directory service will be processed by the PlugIn used. The PlugIn of the directory service queried by the DUA, gets a reference.

This reference points to the name of a certain directory service, depending on the requested information, and can be queried using LDAP. Many directory services can be involved in the request process. At all times, directory services manage local information.

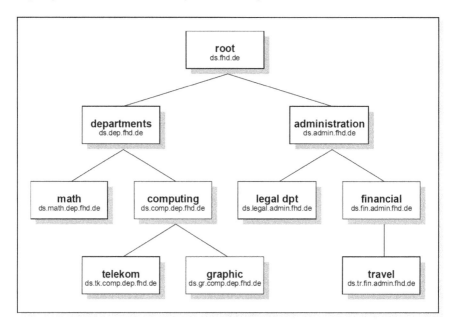

**Figure 1 : Hierarchical Distributed Directory Service (HDDS)**

For the HDDS to function properly, the following conditions have to be fulfilled :

1) The creation of new employee records in a directory service must be communicated to theroot of the HDDS, which holds an index of the whole HDDS. This index contains important

employee characteristics (e.g. UserID, Name, Title) and the name of the managing directory service.

2) Every directory service used by the HDDS must provide a special PlugIn. This allows the directory service to process queries on employees that are not managed by the local node. In this case the PlugIn passes the query to the next higher directory service.

3) The relocation of an employee to a different directory service necessitates his deletion from his initial (home) directory service and the creation of a new entry in the target directory service. Both processes must be communicated to the root node.

## PlugIn

The PlugIn must be installed on every host that uses directory services belonging to the HDDS. Its main function is to process nonlocal information requests generated from the local directory service as a result of the absence of local information.

The PlugIn is implemented by extending the API provided by the producer of the directory service used. Since the APIs of the directory services are not standardised a special PlugIn had to be implemented for each directory service.

Furthermore during the selection of the implementation of LDAP-compliant directory services, it has to be checked that the offered API allows an extension, which can solve our problem.

Since the requested information may not be located in the local data stock, the directory service used must allow the execution of programs files and must be able to pass requests originating from the DUA to the starting executable. The PlugIn must perform the following functions :

· It passes DUA and PlugIn requests to the next directory service in the HDDS hierarchy. If necessary, the request is forwarded to the next higher directory service.

· It accepts replies from directory services queried.

· It automatically reports new record generation and deletion in the database of the local directory service.

## Backup Concept

The weakest point of the HDDS is the root and this is therefore set up in a redundant way (i.e., there are at least two redundant root systems). This is made possible by the use of dynamic DNS. When a node fails while the search process is proceeding, the PlugIn bypasses the node that broke down by discarding a sub-domain from the name of the directory service used, e.g. if the "ds.comp.dep.fhd" node from Figure 1 is down, the PlugIn from the node "ds.gr.comp.dep.fhd.de" can access the next higher node "ds.dep.fhd.de" directly by discarding the "comp" sub-domain. If the required information lies within the failed node, the request will eventually reach the root node, which will have a reference to the directory service that is down and the search will remain unsuccessful. One solution lies in the redundant planning and usage of important directory services such as directory services located at the root node. If this is not done, DUAs may have no directory service to communicate with, since DUAs communicate with just one local directory service.

## Extensibility

Enterprises using the HDDS concept can easily integrate their Directory Services by creating a higher instance to serve as a new root node. The original root's Directory Service will require a configurable PlugIn to recognise the new higher instance (see Figure 2).

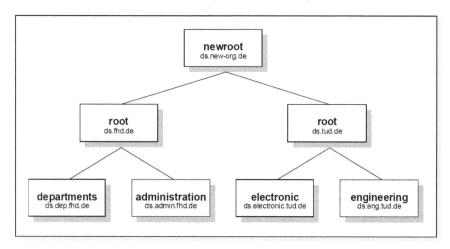

**Figure 2 : Extending the HDDS after the merging of two organisations**

If all the index information can be copied from the Directory Services of the original root nodes, no new functionality is demanded from the new root . Otherwise, the names of all the root nodes integrated into the new HDDS must be made known to the new root as the latter processes a query from a former root node by passing on the query to all the other former roots.

By using XML records the extensibility of the employee information stored in the database of the Directory Service is guaranteed. First of all, XML-compliant browsers are able to read and present the information records. Secondly, XML records contain structural information and information about the way these information are displayed. Thus information structures can be extended without any modifications to the relevant data structures.

### Administration

The administration of the HDDS is similar to the administration of a simple local Directory Service. The administrator has access to his local Directory Service only. For each record addition or deletion in the local database, the PlugIn automatically generates and sends messages to the root. Specific administrative tasks include setting up the HDDS tree, naming the nodes and installing the PlugIn in the HDDS.
To increase robustness, duplicate copies of the Directory Services should be maintained and the redundant nodes should use replication to guarantee that the same data stock is held.

### Security

As the main role of the HDDS is to provide employee information, the information requesting process is the weakest point in the system. This implies that both the links between distinct DUAs and the local Directory Service, and the links between Directory Services must be protected. The nodes and Directory Services involved can identify themselves using X.509 compliant certificates. For practical reasons we prefer the Secure Socket Layer Protocol (SSL) as a standard protocol between two endpoints. Therefore, we need to install a certificate on every Directory Service and on every DUA. These measures guarantee authentication and secure data transfer.

However, a big security breach still remains : whoever has administrative rights on the Directory Services and DUAs involved can access the complete information stored in the HDDS, e.g. passwords, private keys, certificates, etc. This problem can be resolved by the use of smartcards, which contains, among other information, a second "private key for encryption" (see Figure 3).

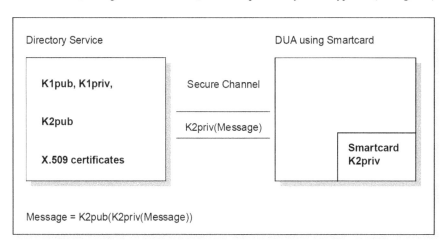

**Figure 3 : The Smartcard solution**

The Directory Service that manages the users' data uses a second public key to encrypt the messages encrypted with the second "private" key stored on the smartcard. Only if the correct key combinations have been used access to security relevant data like passwords will be allowed.

**Usage**

By means of the HDDS, it is possible for every employee to access, without big risks, data, settings, certificates, different keys, etc. from any workplace in the enterprise. For example, it is possible to set up Windows NT as a DUA. This will then receive accounting information from the HDDS, allowing users that are not known on the local system to log in.

Services with their own infrastructure can be integrated without problems, e.g. key management in a public key infrastructure, access to a central certificate pool needed to install local systems.

**Advantages using HDDS**

· Simplified administration since only the local view of the administrators need to be maintained, data volume is limited and assignment responsibility is simple, as in central systems.

227

- More up-to-date information compared with replication / synchronisation as there is no latency during information modification (important when accounting information, e.g. password, are modified).

- No need to match Directory Services (using replication / synchronisation).

- The use of open standards between the nodes of the HDDS as well as between a DUA and "its" Directory Service.

- Location transparency for the DUAs.

- Usually a local usage of the Directory Service. It has been proven that department-wide information are seldom needed. This results in less network load than in the central model using replication / synchronisation.

- Robustness since the information is distributed among different systems.

**Disadvantages using HDDS**

- The failure of the root will prevent a node from accessing HDDS nodes located on a different sub-tree in the hierarchy. A possible solution is to set up duplicate roots.

- Information can be attacked enterprise wide.

## Conclusion

The HDDS concept enables enterprises to combine the advantages of central Directory Services with the advantages of local Directory Services. When a breakdown occurs at a node, HDDS allows further access points all the way to the root. Contrast this with a Central Directory Service where no data access is possible after a breakdown.
A prototype is currently being implemented to evaluate the functionality of a HDDS in large financial enterprises.

## Bibliography

[1]    RFC2251 - LDAP v3
[2]    RFC2307 - An Approach for Using LDAP as a Network Information System
[3]    RFC2256 - X.500 User Schema for use with LDAPv3

# Management of Service Level Agreements using INSMware

M.H.Knahl and S.M.Furnell

Network Research Group, University of Plymouth, Plymouth, United Kingdom
e-mail: knahl@jack.see.plym.ac.uk

## Abstract

The paper presents a component-based approach to implement a new framework for Integrated Network and System Management and its application on management services to implement Service Level Agreements (SLAs). Applications are assembled from a set of pre-fabricated components rather than being developed from scratch and are being incorporated into new management domains. In this paper, we describe a project, componentware based Integrated Network and System Management (INSMware), which was built using only component-based techniques. We describe an approach that integrates the software component paradigm with network and systems management and its application upon SLAs. We focus upon the monitoring of SNMP-capable network elements. The requirements for new management services implementing SLAs are outlined and a prototypical implementation is presented.

## Keywords

Service Level Agreements, Network Management, System Management, Componentware, SNMP Networks

## 1. Introduction

The disciplines of Network and System Management encompass all actions taken to enable and guarantee the maintenance and operations of the resources - either hardware or software - in a network. This includes the communication network as well as the server and the end-systems in a network. ITU-T defined five management categories (namely Fault, Configuration, Performance, Accounting and Billing, Security Management) that define the different disciplines and requirements for the management of heterogeneous networking environments.

This paper presents research leading to a component-based framework for Integrated Network and System Management (INSMware) and its application upon the management of Service Level Agreements (SLAs). The transferability of INSMware to other management domains is realised because of a consistent component-based development approach to meet the requirements for integrated management services (Knahl et al. 1999). There are two versions of INSMware: one using the CORBA (OMG, 1998) component model and a Microsoft DCOM (Brown and Kindel, 1996) implementation. This allowed us to study both middleware architectures in detail.

The aims of INSMware are to hide the complexity of the heterogeneous network environment and underlying technologies and to provide a universal framework for the various management services. In addition, INSMware can be applied to several application domains within the INSM area. In this paper, we present the application of INSMware to the management of SLAs.

## 2. Integrated Management of Service Level Agreements

Limitations and restrictions of existing Network and System Management frameworks, such as distribution of the management services, adoption and integration of new services can be overcome by providing a component-based approach (Knahl et al. 1998; Knahl et al. 1999). Furthermore, the management must be configurable to enable the provisioning and management of Service Level Agreements.

### 2.1 Service Level Agreements

Service Level Agreements (SLAs) are formal negotiated agreements that help to identify expectations, clarify responsibilities and facilitate communication between a service provider and its customer (Karten, 1998). In a typical customer / provider relationship, a customer demands (and pays for) specified services and for a Quality of Service (QoS) that are defined in the SLAs. To enable (and prove) the fulfilment of those SLAs it is necessary for the provider to have management services that can monitor and control the service status.

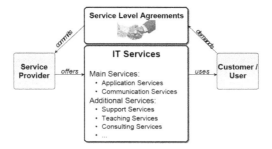

**Figure 1: Service Level Agreements**

In order to observe the quality of delivered services it is necessary to negotiate QoS parameters as well as modes for the measurement and evaluation of these parameters. QoS parameters must reflect the expectations of the customer and they are part of the SLAs between the customer and the provider. SLAs are for several purposes, e.g. if a service is not delivered with the specified quality the customer may get a discount. Therefore, the SLAs and QoS parameters have to be supervised by the management system of the provider. Further, the provider is obliged by the SLA to report the compliance with agreed QoS parameters. Customer Service Management (CSM) offers a management interface between customer and network provider which enables the customers to monitor and control their subscribed services (Langer et al. 1998).

Examples for SLAs customer/provider relationships could include:

- Network provider (e.g. Deutsche Telekom, a network operator who is acting as a service provider) and customer (e.g. PanDacom, a system integrator with branches all over Germany who is using the services offered by this or another service provider);
- System Integrator (e.g. PanDacom as a system integrator that is offering remote management services based upon QoS parameters to its customers) and customer with service contract.

One example for such QoS parameters is the response time which implies the connectivity or the availability of a certain service where these parameters have to be measured and valued from the customer point of view when the customer uses a specified service, which requires parts of the management system to be installed at the customers side (e.g. intelligent agents or management gateway that report to the provider's management framework). This allows the monitoring and measurement of the services from the customers side, e.g. from an end-system to monitor end to end-connectivity.

SLAs will always change in the course of time due to new requirements for services that demand modified or new QoS parameters. It must be possible to extend the management framework with additional functionality, e.g. for the configuration and monitoring of a new QoS parameter. It is, therefore, important that the architecture is flexible and that it enables fast and cheap integration of these new services. For large scale, distributed networks it is also essential that the management system scales well. Furthermore, the variety of the different hardware and software in existing and future networks requires a high-degree of platform independence for the management system.

## 2.2 Integrated Management Architecture

Distributed systems allow the partitioning of applications into logical and physical self-contained entities: distributed objects. These distributed objects represent a part of the system-global object model. The possibility to use distributed objects for the realisation of different applications makes them into so-called software components. A software component is a piece of software with one or more well-defined interfaces that is configurable, integrable, and immutable (Langer et al. 1998, Hofmann 2000). By configurable we mean being able to set parameters affecting the properties of a component without requiring its modification. The integration of software component means the connection of incoming and outgoing interfaces, i.e., interfaces being used in the client role and in the server role of a client/server component communication while immutability requires a component to be *physically immutable*. Such physically immutable forms of software are, for example, executable files or dynamic link libraries (DLLs).

The most important criterion of our component definition above is immutability since it allows a dissociation from object-oriented concepts such as Classes and Design Patterns. The functionalities of presented management framework consist of the processing, filtering, and analysis of management relevant data, the presentation in a Graphical User Interface (GUI) and user notifications at the occurrence of predefined states that represent important network states. The system allows that one or more users may be notified over varying communication channels.

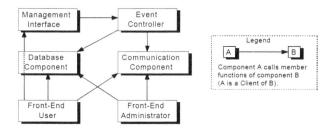

**Figure 2: INSMware Components and their Connectivity**

The design of the individual INSMware components (see Figure 2) is based on a domain specification which subdivides the entire application domain into subdomains. The data processing system requires a connection to a data source (physically existing system). This is realised by the Management Interface component which exists, similar to device drivers of an operating system, in several different forms and is configurable, as required, for different SLAs. The Management Interface component is installed at the customer side to monitor the specified SLA. The filtered service level data is then forwarded to the SLA provider's management framework using the services of the underlying middleware technologies. The Management Interface component interprets the received data, filters and analyses it, and notifies the event controller component when particular pre-defined exception states occur. Data storage is accomplished by a call to the database component and user notification is effected over the communication components. It must be emphasised that all information about the users that need to be notified (e.g., access to user, user's role regarding the monitored processes) are stored in the system. The communication component itself consists of a set of several components that again implement subdomains, e.g., sending of faxes, voice mails, e-mails. The user can visualise system states by using the front-end user component and can maintain the system by using the front-end administrator component.

### 2.3 Application Domains and Sub Projects

INSMware was originally conceived to monitor the various network elements and to provide management services in heterogeneous network environments. With INSMware, a timely user intervention in the running of the network processes is made possible when required (e.g. user notification when a network critical condition occurs).

INSMware was applied to the application domain of monitoring SLAs. SNMPv1 and SNMPv2 based managed objects at the customers side can be monitored and relevant management data is then forwarded to the management framework. Two of the components, namely the Management Interface component and the front-end user component, have to be modified to integrate SLA services (e.g. SNMP) into the management framework and the database structure has to be adapted to the service relevant information while the remaining four components can be reused with no modifications. The application domain implemented by the Management Interface component is actually very limited and a universal Management Interface component was developed which can be adapted to different systems by configuration (Amrhein, 1998). The graphical data representation supported by the front-end component to visualise the management information has to be adapted to the respective service domain and remain user-friendly and simple (Vierow, 1998). By generating source code responsible for inter-component communication, a tremendous reduction in the development time for front-end components was possible. Using a CORBA/ DCOM bridge, a platform-independent connection of partially generated front-end components is achieved.

## 3. INSMware

### 3.1 Customer scenario

The scenario provides an insight into a whole range of different Management and SLA requirements (see Figure 1). First of all, each provider must manage its own network. An integral part of this is network element management, which concerns the supervision of the availability, capacity utilisation and fault-free operation of the network elements. Added to this is the functioning of the network as a whole. At the access to a network, the providers aim to offer their customers services with a certain Quality of Service based on an SLA. The constant monitoring of service quality is a management task. The management of the customer / provider interface also includes procedures for fault-reporting and for service adaptation or service provisioning. It is essential that customers have access to specific management information (e.g. service quality, service availability) because this is the information they need if they themselves want to develop added value and other new services based on the network services they are already using. For customers, it is the service related information based on the customer SLA that is generally interesting rather than the 'raw' data from the component management of their providers.

In principle, SLAs should exist for all the services of a provider's service offering and used by customers. The SLA contains an exact description of what is offered in a service and defines which costs are applied when a customer uses the service. Since providers of networked systems (e.g. of an enterprise network) are just now slowly being accepted as IT service providers, a large number of services in the IT area are still being used without explicit SLAs. Furthermore, customers require these specifications for planning the use of the IT services in their own business processes (Corsten, 1997).

The current framework implements the Simple Network Management Protocol (SNMP) (Case et al. 1990) to monitor and control managed objects for the provisioning of the SLAs. SNMP is a set of network and system management standards that describe the asynchronous requests and responses for the exchange of management data between SNMP management objects (Stallings, 1998). Virtually all major vendors of end-systems, workstations and network devices such as routers and switches offer SNMP support. In addition, enhancements to the initial SNMP have been pursued in a number of directions (e.g. RMON, SNMPv2, SNMPv3).

The SNMP Manager is network management software that implements the SNMP protocol and is represented in our case by the Management Interface component. The SNMP Agent resides in a managed network element, such as a router or switch or in an end-system such as a PC or Unix Workstation. The agent stores management information in the Management Information Base (MIB) and processes SNMP requests from the SNMP Manager and responses from the agent itself. The proposed INSMware framework is based on a multi-lingual SNMP implementation (Levi et al. 1999). The multi-lingual implementation of the management interface supports the different SNMP versions and enables the seamless integration of the (typically mono-lingual) SNMP based managed objects. Besides that, additional protocols or access policies can be integrated into the Management Interface component.

## 3.2 Management Interface component

This section describes the Management Interface component for the management of SLAs. The Management Interface component can be installed at the customers side to collect and analyse the management information. It then forwards the required management data to the SLA provider's management framework where it is processed and the required management tasks are undertaken.

### 3.2.1 Architecture of Management Interface component

One advantage of component-oriented software is the relatively easy reuse of individual parts of the system to adapt the framework for different SLAs, e.g. Network Element Monitoring or Service Management (see Figure 3) . Hence, the SLA provider can reuse the existing systems to offer services to different customers. Modifications to the system to integrate new services and reuse existing components are required on the graphical user interface to represent the service states and the interface to the managed network (Management Interface component for the communication with the managed objects).

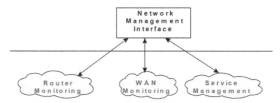

**Figure 3: Management Interface Application Domains**

To improve and optimise the reusability of the Management Interface component it is split into several smaller components. The filtering functionality analyses the data from the managed objects and decides whether a critical value has been exceeded or whether a critical event has occurred. This evaluation can proceed without further knowledge of the underlying technology (e.g. whether SNMPv1 or SNMPv2) of the managed objects because solely the protocol independent data stream (from the managed objects) has to be analysed. The SNMP component provides the initialisation and de-initialisation of a connection with a managed object. This is individual for every kind of managed object with different management protocols, e.g. differs the initialisation of a connection and the access to a SNMP managed object very much from the access to a file system and has, therefore, be abstracted. For each access technology, a specific component is developed that implements a specific defined interface and which can be used from the general Filter component. This specific component is responsible for the communication with the managed object and transforms/translates the received data into a format that can be used by the Filter component. Whilst developing different management domains it has been discovered that a few parts – particularly in the area of the interface implementation – are similar. For these similarities, source code can be reused. Beside that, the Management Interface offers a high degree of flexibility and provides good reuse for additional and future management domains.

### 3.2.2 Distribution of Management Interface

The INSMware Architecture allows the distribution of its components over the network. The separate components can also be used for the different tasks involved in SLA Management. The collection and filtering of SLA relevant data at the remote locations reduces the management related traffic over the network. The distribution of management procedures means the realisation of the Client/Server principle on the software level. The different software components of a distributed software system may act as a client or a server, or also as a client and a server if the application requires this.

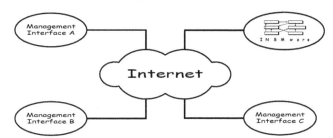

**Figure 4: Distribution of Management Interface via Internet**

The realisation of distributed software systems is made possible by the increase of low-cost bandwidth on Wide Area Networks (for example the Internet, a new generation of network-enabled desktop operating systems and middleware technologies, such as CORBA and DCOM, that enable the seamless distribution of software components). The possibility to access remote resources (e.g. via the Internet) enables software developers to distribute their software components, even over the boundaries of a corporate network (see Figure 4).

### 3.2.3 SNMP-Interface

The analysis and design stage of the SNMP-Interface was based on the layered model of the Management Interface. Dynamic access mechanisms have been implemented to read the configuration from an ODBC database. The prototypical implementation of the Management Interface component is written in C++. The SNMP functionalities have been implemented using two different SNMP frameworks based on C++: the SNMP interface of the Microsoft Foundation Classes (MFC) which only implements SNMPv1 and the SNMP++ framework from Hewlett Packard which offers support for SNMPv1 and SNMPv2c (Mellquist, 1997). Functionalities of the implementation include the Monitoring and collection of SNMP Traps and monitoring of SNMP managed objects using SNMP Get / GetNext. This makes it possible to actively monitor and control changes within the SNMP agents.

New SNMP functionalities such as SNMPv3 start to occur. These can be implemented into the SNMP++ framework and, therefore, with minor modifications into the INSMware framework (Katz, 1999). Figure 5 illustrates the layers of the Management Interface and the integration of the different SNMP frameworks into the Management Interface.

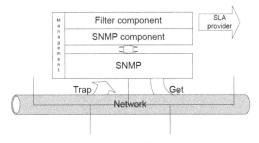

**Figure 5: Management Interface layers**

The INSMware management framework offers management services for the collection and monitoring of SNMP-Traps and offers services for SNMP Get and GetNext operations. This enables INSMware to act as an SNMP Manager. Traps, which are sent from SNMP managed objects such as routers or even from software in the network, are collected and further processed for the Filter component. The SNMP component then forwards the data to the Filter Layer for further analysis. The Filter component then analyses the data using the configuration parameters from the INSMware Framework. The filtering uses the source address as well as the Object ID (OID) of the trap, e.g. to discover a cold-start of a managed object.

The collected management data is compared against predefined values using different operators (e.g. <, >, =) to discover status or administrational changes such as change of System Administrator or critical network conditions such as high collisions on an Ethernet or the failure of a WAN connection. When the Management Interface discovers - due to an incoming Trap or a MIB value - that a critical event occurred it protocols the event and arranges the notification the related INSMware user on its GUI or forwards the notification to a manager via telephone or E-Mail. The protocolisation and messaging functions are provided by the Event Controller and the Communication Component.

The specification of the relevant data for the managed objects and events - for the configuration of the SNMP managed objects (e.g. IP-Address, SNMP Version and Community) and the related Get/GetNext and Trap events (e.g. OID, Value, Operator) - is fully implemented via the GUI and saved in the management database (implemented in Microsoft Access). The type of notification can be dependent on different parameters (e.g. dependent of day or time) and can be configured for each individual event that occurs. Furthermore, it is possible to set the intervals for the polling and controlling of events according to the requirements and to individually add/delete intervals according to specific management requirements.

### 3.3 Visualisation of Network infrastructures and service states

As previously mentioned, the second component of INSMware that has to be adapted for new services in the domain of Integrated Network and System Management is the user and administrator front end. Two different design approaches were initially considered: A pure graphical approach that uses overview maps to represent the network structure as known from commercial Network and Sytsem Management platforms such as HP OpenView (see Figure 6) and a more Microsoft Windows Explorer-like view, showing the network structure as a tree (see Figure 7). The first approach visualises the network structure very clearly, particularly for experienced users of management platforms such as HP OpenView. A lot of network management tools use such a map-based interface and for this reason they are well known for experienced users, but they are also very space consuming and become unclear for really large networks, e.g. if an internetworking map consists of 30 routers and 50 networks.

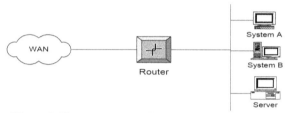

**Figure 6: Map representing Network Infrastrucuture**

The tree view is less space consuming and, for this reason, more suitable for large networks. A problem of this approach is that the network structure is not always hierarchical (e.g. cross links) and, therefore, the tree representation might not represent the logical and physical network connections as clearly as the established network maps.

To get the best of both worlds the implemented front end is a mixture of both approaches. The main user interface is shown in Figure 7. The network structure is represented by a tree on the left hand side. On the right side, four tabs show information about the node that is currently activated. If desired, the user can demand an overview map by pressing the "Network View" button which then shows a network map for the actual network or domain.

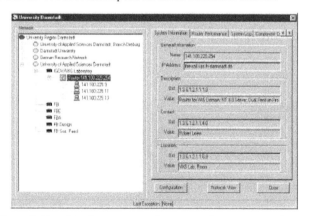

**Figure 7: User interface representing network strucures and states**

The tree view is configurable for every single user. Every user can name the nodes in his preferred way and it is also intended to make the part of the network that is shown by the tree determinable by the user. In order to enable such flexibility, all the data that is presented by the front-end is stored in the system database. This concerns the entire network structure – represented by the tree – as well as the user settings for the configuration.

The four tabs at the right hand side of the GUI provide quick access to the most important information of every network node. The "Information" tab displays the basic information like node name, description, location and contact person. The second tab visualises the performance of the network node. The network traffic, utilisation and error rates of the whole network or every single port in case of a router or a switch are presented. The "Log" tab displays an event log for every node. Restarts, port failures and breakdowns of the system will be registered with date and time. 'Component configuration' allows configuration of managed objects, e.g. to reset a network interface.

The information presented (except Component Configuration) provides the management data and are for monitoring and controlling the managed Service Level Agreements. The configuration facilities enable the user to configure the management services. The selection and monitoring configuration of specific MIB variables specifies the management services for specific managed objects. In addition, SNMP traps can be configured to monitor and configure events reports from the SNMP entities themselves. The user can define notification events by specifying threshold, notification channel (voice, fax, pager, email) and priority. All the configuration data – including the settings for the notification events – are stored in the system database.

## 4. Summary and Outlook

Our future INSMware research aims at the extension of INSMware Management Services to provide a unified, integrated management framework. INSMware's current shaping focuses on the management of hardware components. However, this represents only a reduced view of real world information systems, since there is a correlation between managed hardware components and software components operated on the basis of that hardware. Hence, future versions of INSMware will also integrate the management of software components and thus provide fully integrated management facilities.

Furthermore, the development of extended and new forms of user interaction, including the integration of Web-based management services and the integration of handheld devices such as the Palm Pilot to realise ubiquitous computing facilities will be considered. As no component models currently exist for such handheld systems and their operating systems, one task will be to develop appropriate integration mechanisms. The first prototype of the front-end component is realised as a Visual Basic program, but there are thoughts to produce a web-based front end in order to allow management and configuration from everywhere without installing client software. Another effort in this area will be the integration of speech input and output with INSMware, which is to facilitate system operation in scenarios in which no computing device is available. It also provides a more intuitive way of INSMware utilisation to the user.

## 5. References

Amrhein, M. (1998), *Wiederverwendung von Softwarekomponenten — dargestellt am Beispiel eines Überwachungssystems mit Sprachausgabe (Reuse of software components - described by way of example of a monitoring system with speech output).* Diploma Thesis, University of Applied Sciences Darmstadt/Germany.

Brown, N. and Kindel, C. (1996), *Distributed Component Object Model Protocol – DCOM/1.0*. Microsoft Corporation, Network Working Group.

Case, J. D. , Darwin, C., Fedor, M. , Schoffstall, M. L. (1990), *A Simple Network Management Protocol (SNMP)*. Request for comments (Standard) RFC 1157. Internet Engineering Task Force. May 1990.

Corsten, H. (1997), *Management von Geschäftsprozessen: Theoretische Ansätze – Praktische Besispiele*. W. Kohlhammer GmbH. Stuttgart, 1997.

Hofman, H.D. (2000), *Software Component Reuse by Adaptation*. PhD Thesis. Institute Of Technology, Cork, Ireland. March 2000.

Karten, N. (1998), "How to Establish Service Level Agreements". Karten Associates. Randolph, MA, USA, 1998.Katz, J. (1999), "SNMPv3 Support for SNMP++". *The Simple Times*. Volume 7, Number 1. March 1999.

Knahl, M. , Bleimann, U. , Furnell, S. M. , Sanders, P. W. (1998), "Integration of ATM management procedures into native integrated network and systems management architectures". *Proceedings of the International Network Conference 1998*, Plymouth, UK, July 1998, pp91-97.

Knahl, M. Hofmann, H. D. and Phippen, A. (1999), "A Distributed Component Framework for Integrated Network and System Management". *Information Management and Computer Security*, Vol. 7, No. 5, pp254-260.

Langer, M., Loidl, S. and Nerb, M. , (1998), "Customer Service Management : A More Transparent View to your subscribed services". *Proceedings of the 9th IFIP/IEEE International Workshop on Distributed Systems: Operations and Management (DSOM 98)*. Newark, USA. October 1998.

Frye, R. , Levi, D. , Routhier, S. , Wijnen, B. (2000). "Coexistence between Version 1, Version 2 and Version 3 of the Internet Standard Network Management Framework". Internet Engineering Task Force, SNMPv3 Working Group, RFC 2576. March 2000.

Mellquist, P.E. (1997), *SNMP++: An Object-Oriented Approach to Developing Network Management Applications*. Prentice Hall, 1997.

OMG. (1998), *The Common Object Request Broker: Architecture and Specification, Revision 2.2*. OMG Document 98-07-01, Object Management Group, Inc.

Stallings, W. (1998), "SNMP and SNMPv2 : The Infrastructure for Network Management". *IEEE Communications Magazine*. March 1998.

Vierow, T. (1998), *Entwicklung eines Generatorwerkzeuges zur Unterstuetzung der Gestaltung von graphischen Benutzeroberflaechen (Development of a generator tool for supporting the design of graphical user interfaces)*. Diploma Thesis, University of Applied Sciences Darmstadt/Germany.

# Reuse by Adaptation — a Step Towards Componentware

Holger D. Hofmann*, Jeanne Stynes†, Guenter Turetschek‡

*Asea Brown Boveri AG, Corporate Research Center, Heidelberg, Germany (former affiliation†)
† Department of Mathematics and Computing, Cork Institute of Technology
‡ Distributed Application Systems Lab, University of Applied Sciences, Darmstadt, Germany
e-mail: holger.hofmann@de.abb.com, jstynes@cit.ie

## Abstract

Software components are self-contained, immutable units of software. The immutability of software components leads to several obstacles in component reuse such as the existence of static caller relationships between software components, the lack of system configurability, and poor support of object-oriented reuse mechanisms such as inheritance. An approach to cope with these problems is presented which is based on delegation and adaptation of components to changing requirements — Component Adapters. A Component Adapter is a software component that acts as a surrogate for client components and that delegates client requests to implementations provided by server components. We discuss the design of the proposed approach and various applications which go beyond elementary component adaptation. We finally discuss the results of a performance test that is to show the feasibility and practicability of Component Adapters.

## Keywords

Software Components, Reuse, Adaptation, Distributed Systems

## 1. Introduction

In 1969 McIlroy envisioned an industry of reusable software components and introduced the concept of formal reuse though the *software factory* concept (McIlroy, 1976). Though using software components to build applications (componentware) is a well-known concept in computer science, there is no agreement about the formal definition of a software component (Sametinger, 1997).

We will base our discussion on the following definition given in (Hofmann, 1997) since it follows a hardware/software analogy and emphasises similarities between both domains: *A software component is pieces of software with one or more well-defined interfaces that are configurable, integrable, and not modifiable.* The most important point about this definition is the *immutability* of software components. Though it guarantees black-box reuse (Gamma et al, 1994), immutability can lead to static caller relationships between software components, a lack of system configurability, and poor support of object-oriented reuse mechanisms such as implementation inheritance (Sakkinen, 1992).

## 2. Reuse of Software Components

Generally, source code exists in a modifiable form and therefore does not meet our definition of a software component. As distributed objects (see (Hofmann, 1997), (Object Management Group, 1995)) meet our definition of software components, both terms can be used interchangeably. We will hereinafter discuss reuse aspects of software components being implemented as Common Object Request Broker Architecture components (CORBA, (Object Management Group, 1995)) or Distributed Component Object Model (DCOM, (Brown and Kindel, 1996)) components. These can, e.g., exist as executable files (EXEs) or dynamic link libraries (DLLs).

Software components can be regarded as a code packaging technique — a way for delivering software to consumers (see (Cox, 1986)). When instantiating a software component, it exposes one or more objects which themselves expose one or more interfaces. This is also the case for wrapped legacy software since the functionality of a software component is exposed via *interface objects* of the distribution infrastructure (see (Hofmann, 1998b)).

The interfaces of a software component can be *incoming* or *outgoing*. Incoming interfaces can be called by other components while outgoing interfaces call other components' interfaces (this is also called the *polarity* of interfaces). As software components are self-contained entities which are immutable, they only can be reused as a whole. The aspects of a software component that can be reused are its *interfaces*, its *behaviour*, and its *implementation*. We will now discuss the reuse of interfaces (syntactic specifications) and implementations (pragmatics). The reuse of behaviour (behavioural subtyping) does not play a significant role in real-life systems since behaviour cannot completely be specified using formal notations such as algebras or predicate logic ((Gruender and Geihs, 1996), (Gruender, 1998)). Therefore, it will hereinafter not be discussed.

## 2.1  Signature Reuse

Signature reuse represents a contract between components saying that the inheriting component at least has to implement the inherited signature. This contract is not very strict because an interface is an underspecification of a component's semantics. Therefore, a component inheriting an interface can have semantics completely different from the component providing the base interface. CORBA and DCOM both support interface inheritance.

Though a possible semantic incompatibility of different software components sharing interfaces with others can occur, interface inheritance can be used to support systems evolution (see (Hamilton and Radia, 1994)). Components implementing a problem domain similar to existing components can inherit their interfaces and thus be used polymorphically with these. This approach should be used very carefully since only complete interfaces can be inherited. If, e.g., a software component implements two domains such as persistent data storage and transaction management, a new component inheriting its interface cannot implement only one of these domains.

## 2.2  Implementation Reuse

*Implementation inheritance* and *delegation* can both be used to reuse existing implementations. In the case of software components, both mechanisms have to be applied at object level since software components are only accessible at run-time through the interfaces of the objects they expose. Aggregation is a special case of delegation since the component implementations being reused are physically contained in the component reusing their implementations.

*Implementation inheritance* is an often misunderstood object-oriented concept concerning distributed, object-oriented architectures such as CORBA and DCOM. CORBA and DCOM software components can be developed using programming languages that support implementation inheritance although the CORBA and DCOM object models do not support this object-oriented mechanism (see (Brown and Kindel, 1996), (Object Management Group, 1995)).

So when implementing software components based on CORBA or DCOM, inheritance relationships can only be applied at class level (static inheritance) and thus can only be defined between classes — not between objects being exposed by software components (dynamic inheritance). In ((Gruender and Geihs, 1996), (Gruender, 1998)), an approach for the realisation of distributed implementation inheritance is proposed which decouples a component's implementation («object engine») from its data and interface («object chassis»). The limitation of this approach is that object engines have to be subtypes of the object chassis. This prevents the use of, e.g., purchased components whose interfaces are not compatible with the chassis' interface. Another limitation of this concept is the necessity to define inheritance relationships at source code level. This prevents the integration of purchased software components with self-developed components. Furthermore, no management architecture is integrated with this approach which would enable the realisation of a system-wide object hierarchy resulting from inheritance relationships between distributed objects.

COM+, a future extension of the Microsoft Component Object Model (COM, a subset of DCOM), will support single implementation inheritance (Kirtland, 1998). Such as the previously described approach, COM+ implementation inheritance will only enable developers to derive components to be developed from existing components, not to derive existing components from existing components. *Delegation* uses the marshalling of requests to other objects which provide implementations for requested services. This means that, in contrast to implementation inheritance, implementations are reused through communication relationships, not through containment relationships. Neither CORBA nor DCOM do provide explicit support for delegation mechanisms at object level.

## 3.  Obstacles in Component Reuse

The driving force behind software components is reuse. Existing components can be used to build new components or even entire applications. Component reuse has a positive impact on productivity, software quality, and software costs.

### 3.1.1  Implementation Reuse

A component that reuses another component's implementation must access the latter via its interfaces in a client/server relationship. This restricts component reuse to the functionality exposed by the component's interfaces. The *reuse potential* of a software entity (Hofmann et al, 1999) depends on its *adaptability* and *modifiability*. The higher the reuse potential of a software entity is the higher is its ability to be reused. Figure 1 shows a taxonomy of reuse potentials covering five entities, namely software components, classes, objects, Design Patterns, and object-oriented applications.

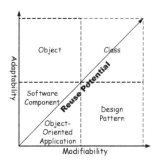

**Figure 1: Taxonomy of Reuse Potentials**

Classes exist in the form of modifiable source code and consequently have a very high reuse potential. They can also be adapted on the level of source code. Objects, on the other hand, exist only at run-time as instances of classes or copies of prototypes, and therefore, cannot be modified (black-box

241

reuse). However, an object's state and its relationships with other objects can be adapted at run-time. Design Patterns (Gamma et al, 1994) exist in graphical and/or textual format, and like classes, can be modified (white-box reuse). Because a Design Pattern is dedicated to a specific use, it has very limited adaptability.

Object-oriented applications, i.e., applications that have been developed using object-oriented techniques, also have limited adaptability. Moreover, they are not modifiable since they exist in an immutable physical shape (black-box reuse). It may come as a surprise to find software components at the lower left end of our taxonomy of reuse potentials. But a closer scrutiny reveals that software components share the same characteristics as object-oriented applications. They come in an immutable physical shape, having been implemented on distributed object-oriented architectures such as CORBA and DCOM. They provide, at most, limited support for inheritance, aggregation, and delegation, and are therefore not very adaptable either (black-box reuse). In fact, one may query the validity of describing CORBA and DCOM as *object-oriented* since neither supports implementation inheritance, a fundamental object-oriented concept.

Reuse mechanisms for software components should allow the realisation of implementation reuse by aggregation, delegation, and implementation inheritance. They should also allow the reuse of components that are not interface-compatible but are semantic-compatible. This extends the effectiveness of component reuse as component substitutability is not based on polymorphic substitutability at the interface level.

### 3.1.2  Systems Evolution

Another aspect of reuse to consider is systems evolution, i.e., parts of a component system are replaced by new parts while other parts are retained (Senivongse and Utting, 1996). In component-based systems, systems evolution can be classified into three cases: (i) new components act as clients to existing components, (ii) new components act as servers to existing components, and (iii) new components act as client and servers to existing components.

In case (i), the new components have to implement the existing components' incoming interfaces. In case (ii) the outgoing interfaces of existing components have to be implemented and case (iii) is a combination of (i) and (ii). All three cases are trivial to realise if the new components are self-developed. This is because the interfaces and semantics of existing components are readily available to the developers.

Integrating a component purchased from some component vendor is only possible if the component is interface-compatible with the existing components. This clearly restricts the number of software components that can be integrated with a set of existing components during systems evolution. Moreover, interface compatibility is a weak criterion since interfaces provide an underspecification of a component's semantics. Therefore reuse should be based on semantic compatibility.

### 3.1.3  Decoupling of Component Interfaces and Implementations

Due to the immutability of a software component, a component's implementations (its services) and its interfaces (its service representations) form an inseparable unit which represents the reuse granularity of a software component. Therefore the reusability of a software component's implementations highly depends on the reusability of its interfaces. This implies that software component integration requires the interface compatibility of software components in order to reuse their implementations. The problem with this is that even if a large set of software components would be available to the market, it would turn out to be a nearly insolvable problem to find software components providing suitable interfaces and suitable implementations.

### 3.1.4 Configuration of Software Components

Both the external (a component's interfaces) and internal (a component's behaviour) properties of a component may be affected when it is configured to suit a particular requirement. A component's interface can only be configured to the point where it still represents the component's functionality while the extent to which a component's behaviour can be configured is limited by restrictions in its implementation.

At the moment, component configuration is only employed in a restricted manner. Interfaces cannot be configured at will since there exists a correlation between a component's interfaces and its implementation. There would, for example, be no sense in providing a component that manages transactions with an interface of a component performing spell checking. But even when retaining the main aspects of a component's interfaces and only applying minor changes to it such as a change of parameter types, implementations must be available that are able to process those new parameter types. This leads us to the main problem of software component configuration: it requires a *prediction of design*. This means that every option to configure a component, be it internal or external, has to be foreseen by the developer.

### 3.1.5 Adaptation of Software Components

Adaptation represents a component-external mechanism, i.e., adaptation code is not realised inside the component itself, but comes from the outside. Adaptation is a mechanism that is not foreseen by a component's developer. This implies that it does not underlie the same constraints as component configuration, but also is more limited in its abilities.

The business logic a software component implements should be applicable to as many application domains as possible. But the more complex the functionality of a component is the less the component is going to be across different application domains.

There are times when a component whose functionality does not exactly match the required functionality is used. Perhaps due to development capacities or development costs, the required functionality could not be fully included when the component is constructed. Perhaps only parts of the functionality offered is required, for example, a componentware application may use the e-mail facility of a particular word processor but provide its own text editor. In both cases, adaptation is necessary to incorporate the component successfully in the componentware application. Note that components are only adapted when they cannot be configured to specific requirements (and components are not very configurable).

Unfortunately, neither CORBA nor DCOM provides any mechanisms for component adaptation so the set of components that can be integrated with other components is very limited. Any adaptation mechanism should be able to handle all types of interface and semantic incompatibilities.

### 3.1.6 Integration of Software Components

Software components are integrated, or «assembled», with a set of other components in order to build new components or applications.

We have already mentioned how component architectures such as CORBA and DCOM provide inadequate, and sometimes no, support for component reuse, configuration, and adaptation. This has to be compensated at the level of component integration, i.e., during component composition. Component composition is done using programming languages or scripts.

If a component does not provide sufficient options to be configured and no mechanisms for adaptation exist, the integration (adaptation) logic must be implemented at the level of the composition layer. This means that the code necessary for component adaptation is implemented by, for example, scripts.

Basing adaptation on component composition has the effect of transferring functionality to the level of the composition language, an action inconsistent with the component paradigm. Implementing the reuse of application parts as elements of a composition language raises the same problems as the reuse of object-oriented source code (see (Aksit and Bergmans, 1992)).

## 4. Component Adapters

To cope with the previously described problems in software component reuse, we propose the concept of Component Adapters ((Hofmann, 1998a), (Hofmann et al, 1999)).

### 4.1.1 Concept

A Component Adapter is a software component that represents a specific view of a software component to other software components, that acts as a surrogate, and maps requests of client components to appropriate implementations provided by server components (see Figure 2). The principle underlying this approach is *surrogate substitution*. Software components are accessed by using surrogates, i.e., computational entities representing the actual software components. The surrogates can be substituted by Component Adapters which delegate requests to the original surrogates or to surrogates of other software components. For instance, the connection of two software components $A$ and $B$ $(A \rightarrow B)$ is changed to $A \rightarrow B' \rightarrow B$, where $B'$ represents a Component Adapter for $B$. Surrogate substitution is transparent to client components.

We abstract the adaptation of a software component as the sum of the adaptations of the implementations it contains. Let $C_{org}$ be a component to be adapted that contains the implementations $I_j$, $\Delta I_j$ the adapting implementation, and operator $\oplus$ an operation to combine $I_j$ with $\Delta I_j$. Then the adapted component $C_{adapt}$ can be defined as

$$C_{adapt} = C_{org} \oplus \Delta I \text{ with } \Delta I = \{I_1 \oplus \Delta I_1, ..., I_n \oplus \Delta I_n\}.$$

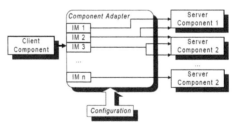

**Figure 2: Structure of a Component Adapter**

There are two applicable types of software component reuse: interface reuse and implementation reuse. Similarly, we distinguish between two different types of adaptation: interface adaptation and implementation adaptation. The former is used to make software components interface-compatible while the latter is used to establish implementation compatibility among a set of heterogeneous software components and to add behaviour to a set of existing software components.

### 4.1.2 Design

The design of a Component Adapter is based on a combination of the structural Design Patterns (Gamma et al, 1994) «adapter», «bridge», «decorator», «facade», and the behavioural Design Pattern «mediator» ((Hofmann, 1998a), (Hofmann et al, 1999)). For more information concerning the combination of Design Patterns, refer to (Zimmer, 1995).

The *adapter* Design Pattern realises the adaptation of interfaces, i.e., it establishes interface compatibility. This covers the conversion of signature names and signature types. Gamma et al. distinguish between «class adapters» and «object adapters». The former adapt class interfaces and inherit the required interface and the implementation to be adapted while the latter inherit the required interface and compose the required implementations. Since the software components to be adapted cannot take part in an inheritance relationship on a source code level, Component Adapters are used to realise the behaviour of object adaptation.

The *bridge* Design Pattern separates the inheritance hierarchies of interfaces from those of implementations and thus decouples an interface from its implementation. This separation is inherent in the Component Adapter approach since software components are self-contained and do not expose their internal inheritance hierarchy to clients. A Component Adapter may inherit the interfaces of the components to be adapted or simply aggregate these. Changes to implementations are not reflected in the interface and are therefore transparent to clients. The bridge Design Pattern also allows the sharing of implementations among multiple components.

By applying the *decorator* Design Pattern, functionality can be added to existing implementations without the necessity to modify these. «The decorator conforms to the interface of the component it decorates so that its presence is transparent to the component's clients» (Gamma et al, 1994). Component Adapters realise this behaviour by implementing specific functionality, or by sending requests to other components before performing the actual request that is sent to them.

The *facade* Design Pattern provides a high-level interface to subsystems. This is useful in cases where a particular interface required by a client component is not directly provided. In such a scenario, a Component Adapter provides a high-level interface to client components and implicitly calls the appropriate methods on the server side.

«A *mediator* is responsible for controlling and co-ordinating the interactions of a group of objects» (Gamma et al, 1994). It abstracts how components cooperate and centralises control. This would otherwise have to be realised by language elements of the used composition language. The former is inherent in the Component Adapter approach, as independently developed software components tend not to have any knowledge of each other. A centralisation of control is also desirable for component reuse. If the behaviour responsible for component adaptation is located in one place, it is easy to reuse.

### 4.1.3 Applications

Component Adapters allow the realisation of interface compatibility and implementation compatibility among a set of heterogeneous software components. Providing software component compatibility is the basis for integrating software components, but the application of different adaptation mechanisms to realise systems evolution remains a challenge in component-based software engineering.

All Component Adapter applications ((Hofmann, 1998a), (Hofmann et al, 1999)) have in common that they realise functionality that otherwise could not have been realised because of software component immutability. One or more Component Adapters interfere communication between client and server components and thus complement the components' functionalities. As this is done by *surrogate substitution*, the use of Component Adapters is transparent to software components concerned. A detailed discussion of Component Adapter applications would far go beyond the scope of this article. That is why we only introduce these informally. For a detailed discussion of Component Adapter applications refer to ((Hofmann, 1998a), (Hofmann et al, 1999)).

Example Component Adapter applications are: *inter-architecture bridging, decrease of client/server connection overhead* (bundling of client requests), *load balancing, component access restriction* (realisation of specific access constraints), *security* (authorisation and data encryption/decryption), *synchronisation of access* (solving the problem of concurrent components and inheritance anomaly), *dynamic inheritance* (state-based change of positions in an inheritance hierarchy), *inter-component communication analysis, intelligent, information-based binding mechanisms* (integration of sophisticated mechanisms for component binding), *agent-based configuration management* (integration of mobile code paradigms), *mediator functionality* (management of data transmission between mobile clients and stationary server components), *component monitoring* (component state management), and *customising*. Each of these application fields can be implemented separately or combined.

Without the use of Component Adapters, a modification of the software components concerned would be required, which strongly conflicts with the software component paradigm.

### 4.1.4 Performance

It is obvious that the addition of one or more software components to an inter-component communication involves a performance overhead. The question is how much overhead is introduced and how this overhead can be minimised.

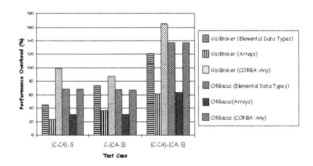

**Figure 3: VisiBroker and ORBacus Component Adapter Performance Overhead**

246

To show the feasibility and practicability of the proposed approach, we developed a Component Adapter performance test which measures relative communication overheads. This test is subdivided into three main test scenarios: (i) use on the client side, (ii) use on the server side, and (iii) use on both client and server side. For these scenarios optimised and non-optimised communication was considered. The former distinguishes between local and remote inter-component communication while the latter does not.

The implementation of the Component Adapter performance test was done under Microsoft Windows NT 4.0 with the Object Request Brokers (ORBs) VisiBroker for C++ 3.2 by Inprise (`http://www.inprise.com`) and ORBacus 3.1 for C++ by Object-Oriented Concepts, Inc. (`http://www.ooc.com`). Both ORBs are commercial products, but the latter can be used free of charge for education or non-commercial development.

Figure 4 shows the VisiBroker overhead for transferring an array of untyped data under CORBA using the *CORBA::Any* data type with each array containing 1024 bytes (1000 measured transmissions). It can be seen that, while for optimised communication, nearly no communication overhead can be measured, non-optimised communication can double response times.

Hence, the communication overhead introduced by Component Adapters when using optimised communication can be neglected. This means that the Component Adapter approach can be used nearly without any performance costs if the underlying communication architecture supports communication optimisation, i.e., it differentiates between local and remote inter-component communication.

But there may be communication architectures that do not support communication optimisation by default or only support this feature if software components have been especially developed to support it. In such a case, performance tests are to act as a decision factor of how Component Adapters should be used in a component system. Figure 3 shows the VisiBroker and ORBacus performance overhead introduced by Component Adapters when using non-optimised inter-component communication.

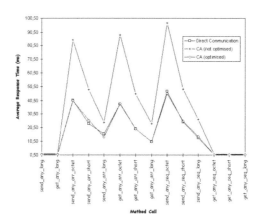

**Figure 4: VisiBroker Overhead for CORBA::Any Types**

It is grouped into the use of Component Adapters on the client side *(C-CA)-S*, the use on the server side *C-(CA-S)*, and the use on both client and server side *(C-CA)-(CA-S)*. As a detailed discussion of our test results would go far beyond the scope of this article, it should be only be pointed our here that the performance overhead introduced by Component Adapters highly depends on: the communication architecture used, and the parameter types to be transmitted (e.g., elemental data types vs. complex, structured data).

Thus, performance tests are to form the decision factor of how to apply the Component Adapter approach to component-based systems. The interfaces of the performance test's components should resemble those of the software components to be used with Component Adapters. Our performance tests have shown that Component Adapters involve a constant overhead to inter-component communication. The comparison of the results of our elemental test cases and our complex test case left us with the conclusion that elemental test cases implementing only parts of the component system to be adapted are sufficient to estimate the Component Adapter communication overhead for the whole system. This is also the case for a recursive application of our Component Adapter approach.

Component Adapters do not only negatively influence inter-component communication, but can also improve systems performance through a bundling of requests. We would like to illustrate this by a small example. In our VisiBroker performance test implementation, the sending of a *long* value (*send_long*) has a response time of 0.78 ms for direct client/server communication. The sending of an array of 1000 *long* values (*send_long_arr*) has a response time of 1.63 ms. This means that the sending of 1000 long values as an array is more than 400 times faster than sending these values separately. Component Adapters can implement communication optimisation features by bundling parameters, i.e., implementing sophisticated caching mechanisms. Note that this kind of communication optimisation requires empirical data on the frequency of specific method calls.

Our performance tests showed that our Component Adapter approach is feasible and that it is applicable to component-based systems using communication infrastructures such as CORBA or DCOM.

## 5. Conclusions and Outlook

Software components are self-contained units encapsulating specific functionality. Since they exist as immutable entities, they can only be reused as-a-whole. In order to exploit the inherent benefits of using software components to build componentware, mechanisms for component reuse have to be offered which enable different granularities of component reuse. Not only entire software components should be reused but also parts of a component implementing only parts of a specific service.

We have proposed an approach to cope with obstacles in reusing software components — Component Adapters. This approach adapts services exposed by components (server components) to service representations required by service requesters (client components).

Several questions arise in connection with the concept of Component Adapters: (i) Which alternatives could be used?, (ii) are Component Adapters performant enough to satisfy system and user requirements?, and (iii) what is about the maintainability of a set of Component Adapters being used in a distributed system?

(i) Since software components are immutable, they cannot be modified in order to adapt these to particular requirements. Thus, there is no alternative to adapting a component to specific requirements except implementing a new component from scratch.

(ii) The use of Component Adapters can add some communication overhead to a set of software components since — instead of one call to a server component — two or more calls have to be made. As there is no alternative to adapting components to particular requirements, on must consider carefully the expenses for developing a component from scratch against possible performance disadvantages when adapting an existing component to new requirements. Performance loss can partly be compensated by applying intelligent load balancing mechanisms and choosing suitable Component Adapter locations which enables clients to communicate locally with these.

(iii) The configuration of a Component Adapter represents parts of the configuration of a component-based application. As Component Adapters can be distributed over large networks or even over the Internet, we propose the use of a management architecture such as proposed in (Zimmermann, 1995) and discussed in (Hofmann, 1998a). Each configuration of a Component Adapter is managed by a local management component. The configuration information spread over the local management components is managed and synchronised by a global management component.

Our current work aims at the following goals: integration of Component Adapters with development tools and development of direct Component Adapter support for middleware architectures.

# 6. References

Aksit, M. and Bergmans, L. (1992), *Obstacles in Object-Oriented Software Development*. Proceedings of the ACM Conference on Object-Oriented Programming: Systems, Languages, and Applications (OOPSLA) 1992, pp. 341-358, Vancouver/Canada.

Brown, N. and Kindel, C. (1996), *Distributed Component Object Model Protocol — DCOM 1.0*. Microsoft Corporation, Network Working Group, http://www.microsoft.com

Cox, B.J. (1986) *Object-oriented programming — An evolutionary approach*, Addison-Wesley.

Gamma, E., Helm, R., Johnson, R., and Vlissides, J. (1994), *Design Patterns — Elements of Reusable Object-Oriented Software*. Addison-Wesley.

Gruender, H. and Geihs, K. (1996), *Reuse and Inheritance in Distributed Object Systems*. Proceedings of International Workshop on Trends in Distributed Systems (TreDS'96), Aachen/Germany.

Gruender, H. (1998), *Zur Anwendung des Objektmodells in verteilten Systemen* (Towards the application of the object model in distributed systems). PhD Thesis, Johann Wolfgang Goethe University, Frankfurt/Germany, Shaker, Aachen/Germany.

Hamilton, G. and Radia, S. (1994), *Using Interface Inheritance to Address Problems in System Software Evolution*. ACM SIGPLAN Notices 29(8), pp. 119-128.

Hofmann, H.D. (1997), *Componentware — Integration of Software Components in Distributed Computing Environments*. M.Sc. Thesis, Cork Institute of Technology/Ireland.

Hofmann, H.D. (1998a), *Implementation Reuse and Inheritance in Distributed Component Systems*. Proceedings of Twenty-Second Annual International Computer Software and Applications Conference (COMPSAC'98), Vienna/Austria.

Hofmann, H.D. (1998b), *Component-Oriented Software Development*. Proceedings of International Network Conference (INC'98), Plymouth/UK.

Hofmann, H.D., Stynes, J., and Turetschek, G. (1999), *The Component Adapter Approach*. Science and Computing Research Colloquium, 26th to 28th May, Institute of Technology, Letterkenny, Ireland.

Kirtland, M. (1998), *Das Programmiermodell von COM+* (The COM+ Programming Model). Microsoft Systems Journal, (2), pp. 32-40, Unterschleissheim/Germany.

McIlroy, M.D. (1976), *Mass-produced software components*. In J.M. Buxton, P, Naur, and B. Randell (editors), *Software Engineering Concepts and Techniques*, pp. 88-98, 1968 NATO Conference on Software Engineering.

Object Management Group, Inc. (1995), *The Common Object Request Broker: Architecture and Specification. Revision 2.0*, Object Management Group, Inc., **http://www.omg.org**.

Sakkinen, M. (1992). *Inheritance and Other Main Principles of C++ and Other Object-oriented Languages*. PhD thesis, University of Jyvaeskylae/Finland.

Sametinger, J. (1997), *Software Engineering with Reusable Components*. Springer.

Senivongse, T. and Utting, I.A. (1996), A model for evolution of services in distributed systems. In: Schill, A.; Mittasch, C.; Spaniol, O.; Popien, C. (edts.), Distributed Platforms, pp. 373-385, Chapman and Hall.

Zimmer, W. (1995), *Relationships between Design Patterns*. Proceedings of PLoP '94 — Pattern Languages of Programs, Addison-Wesley.

Zimmermann, M. (1995), *Konstruktion und Management verteilter Anwendungen* (Construction and Management of Distributed Applications), PhD thesis, Deutscher Universitaetsverlag, Wiesbaden.

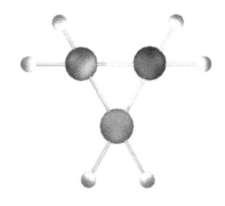

# Chapter 5

## Security and Privacy

# Enhancing Operating System Authentication Techniques

P.S. Dowland and S.M. Furnell

Network Research Group, University of Plymouth, Plymouth, United Kingdom
e-mail: pdowland@plymouth.ac.uk

## Abstract

The need for enhanced user authentication has been evident for some time; but has not been addressed at the operating system level to any degree. Whilst all mainstream operating systems offer some level of user identification and authentication, this is generally based on the username/password combination. Although a number of extensions to operating system security have been proposed (with some reaching implementation) none, as yet, have been integrated into the core operating system kernel. Although there are examples that extend the operating system security model with additional measures (e.g. plug-in fingerprint scanners), these merely extend the operating system security rather than replace it with a more secure version.

This paper will consider the need to improve operating system security focussing upon the enhancement of user identification and authentication. In particular, the security weaknesses of the Microsoft Windows NT environment will be considered, leading to a discussion of supervision techniques that may be integrated within the NT security model. Finally, the conceptual integration of an Intrusion Monitoring System (IMS) architecture is considered.

## Keywords

User authentication, user supervision, security, intrusion monitoring, Windows NT.

## Introduction

The most commonly used form of operating system user authentication is the username/password pair. In most systems, the allocation of passwords (and sometimes usernames) is entirely at the discretion of the users and, as such, is the cause of many security loopholes. The weaknesses of passwords as the primary form of user authentication have been documented in previous works (Jobusch and Oldehoeft, 1989; Cherry et al, 1992) and will not be covered in detail here. However, typical weaknesses include passwords being easily guessed, shared among users, the use of dictionary words (which are more vulnerable to attack) and being written down near PCs. Even when passwords are more selectively chosen, they are still vulnerable to brute force attack, especially with the fast processors and distributed password cracking software now freely available (Savill, 1999).

It is clear that the 'out of the box' configuration for an operating system is inadequate for most systems. For example, most UNIX installations leave many security 'back-doors' into the system wide open by default (e.g. default password settings that administrators *should* change, but often do not), which provide an easy target for hackers (Stoll, 1989). Similarly, a standard installation of Microsoft Windows NT requires many steps before it can be considered secure (Microsoft, 1999a). Relying on passwords in their common form is inadequate and, therefore, some form of advanced user identification is desirable. Ideally, this should also be combined with some form of user monitoring; thus ensuring that a user's session cannot be hijacked. Hijacking occurs where a users' active session is taken over by another user (intruder). This can occur on a number of levels; firstly an intruder can simply resume a session by waiting for the user to leave their desk and then taking advantage of an unprotected computer. Alternatively, an intruder may connect a device (computer) to the target computers' network connection and masquerades as the target computer. Whilst hijacked sessions are most likely to occur in a corporate networked environment, there are still risks to SME's and individuals – this is especially true with the trend towards e-commerce and the increased confidence in purchasing on-line (NOP, 1999). An intruder may be able to capture a credit-card purchase and then either modify or replay that same exchange of data to their advantage. Enhancing user authentication is, therefore, of value to both the commercial and private sectors.

Another problem, which is often overlooked during the selection of appropriate security systems, is that of internal misuse of computer systems. Most systems rely on the username/password pair to identify and authenticate a user. Once this authentication has been given, the user is often free to access the system without further checks or monitoring. Whilst most systems offer the ability to selectively exclude users and/or groups from specific shared resources, this is not usually the default setting. For example, under Windows NT, shares are, by default, accessible to all users and an administrator must specifically set access rights to ensure a shared resource is protected from internal misuse. A similar issue relates to private use of computing resources. Although this is not usually considered to be a security risk, it can represent a loss to a business either through physical resource usage or loss of computer processing time. Often the biggest loss to a company is that of lost employee time; not just through the time lost by the employee concerned but also in the time taken to investigate the problem and prevent further misuse (Audit Commission, 1998).

## Operating system security weaknesses

With operating systems such as Microsoft's Windows NT4 comprising several million lines of code, it is, perhaps, no surprise that security weaknesses should occur. However, it is often surprising to see the scope and frequency with which such fundamental flaws are found. Using Microsoft Windows NT4 as an example, the Microsoft Product Security Notification Service issues several warnings each week, each identifying a potential security problem with the operating system or its sub-components (Microsoft, 1999b). Of course, Microsoft Windows NT is not the only operating system to suffer with such security problems – the many flavours of Unix also generate hundreds of security patches each year (see http://www.faqs.org/faqs/computer-security/most-common-qs/index.html). However, the wider distribution of Windows means that the consequences of security vulnerabilities are potentially more wide reaching. A further drawback with a "popular" operating system is that as its popularity increases, it becomes a greater target to hackers partly due to the increased usage (and, therefore, potential targets) but also because of the greater availability of information relating to security weaknesses. This has been particularly prevalent with the appearance of "script-kiddies" (young inexperienced hackers), who frequently use the many resources (called "filez") which are available from hacking sites on the Internet. A noticeable side effect of this is the use of alternative operating systems where security is of prime concern. For example, the US Army has switched to a MacOS-based web server platform, following a hacking incident when the server was running Windows NT (Donoghue, 1999). This is not to say that MacOS is any more secure than Windows NT, just less widely targeted.

Despite the frequency of these vulnerabilities, the only standard form of security provided by these operating systems for authentication purposes is the password.

## Enhancing Windows NT security

Windows NT security can be considered on two levels, local machine and domain or remote login (Figure 1).

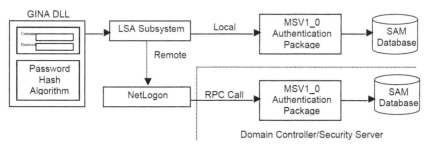

**Figure 1 Local/remote user authentication**

When a local user presses the "Control-Alt-Del" combination to initiate a login they are prompted to enter their username/password pair. The NT hash algorithm is then applied to the password and is passed on to the Local Security Authority (LSA) which calls the MSV1_0 authentication package. This hash is finally compared with the hash stored in the local Security Account Manager (SAM) database by the authentication package. Once a users' password is authenticated, an access token is issued that is valid for that users' session.

When a user wishes to be authenticated across a network (to log-in to a domain controller or for access to a remote machine), the password hash must be transferred across the network. When the user is prompted for their username/password they are also required to enter a valid domain. When the authentication package identifies that the account is not held locally, a call is made to the NetLogon service which sets-up a secure Remote Procedure Call (RPC) session to the domain controller to authenticate the login. The domain controller then issues a 16-bit challenge (the nonce). This challenge is then encrypted together with the password hash and is returned to the domain controller for authentication. Finally, the domain controller returns an access token which is valid for that users' session.

One of the main problems of the above technique is that once the challenge (nonce) has been intercepted and with knowledge of the encryption algorithm it is possible to determine the password hash. Given a known hash, it is feasible (with today's technology) to guess (using a dictionary and/or brute-force attack) the original password.

To achieve a more comprehensive approach under Windows NT would require a replacement GINA Graphical Identification aNd Authentication DLL (core user login system library e.g. username/password prompt). The GINA DLL provides an interface through which a user can provide his/her identification. This typically takes the form of the traditional username/password, but can be replaced with any form of identification (e.g. fingerprint scanner, iris scanner etc.).

There are a number of "add-on" software/hardware packages that can be used to enhance Windows NT security. One of the most common packages currently available is the fingerprint scanner. This is a small device that connects to the PC and provides a cost-effective way of authenticating a login attempt. These devices typically provide an additional security module that integrates into the NT security model. Similar devices are also available to capture handprint geometry, facial patterns and there are devices appearing that are capable of iris scanning. Although these packages allow the enhancement of NT security by removing the need for the user to remember a password, they are not completely integrated into the operating system and only provide a replacement for the username/password prompt. There is also a significant cost overhead to be considered (for example, a fingerprint based authentication system would require the purchase of sufficient scanners for all the PC's in an organisation). Many of these solutions also depend on additional hardware that is dedicated to the task of providing enhanced authentication and, therefore, provides no additional benefit to the organisation concerned (i.e. no purpose other than security).

Even if these techniques were integrated into the NT security model, there are still gaps which leave significant security weaknesses. For example, even with a fingerprint scanner, once the user has logged-in using their finger, there is no guarantee that the same user will sit down and continue with the session. Similarly, if a user leaves their workstation, there is no means of checking if the user who continues the session is the same that started it. (Although all versions of Windows allow the configuration of a screensaver with password protection, this is not set by default. It should also be noted that the computer is unprotected from the time the user leaves their desk to the point at which the screensaver is activated, unless they explicitly lock the terminal). Due to these risks, some form of ongoing user supervision is required to ensure that the current user is the same as the user who activated the session. The remainder of this paper considers the adoption of an Intrusion Monitoring System (IMS) and the technical aspects involved in integrating into the Windows NT security model.

## Description of an IMS

Following previous research work, a proposed IMS architecture is shown in figure 2. The specific functionality of this architecture has been described in a previous paper and will not be described in detail here (Furnell et al, 1997). At the basic level, the approach involves an IMS host monitoring activity occurring on a series of client systems. The client/server relationship of the IMS architecture shown fits neatly into the Windows NT security model architecture and the proposed IMS integration is described later in this paper. Further research work is necessary to fully integrate the IMS architecture into the Windows NT security model and will be the subject of a later paper.

The **Anomaly Detector** analyses the data gathered by the IMS client for signs of suspected intrusion. This data can be compared against both the user's behaviour profile and the generic intrusion rules (i.e. attack signatures).

The **Profile Refiner** allows the automatic modification of a user's profile in response to a valid session profile. This recognises the fact that a user's behaviour pattern may change over time (e.g. in a scenario where typing style has been profiled, their typing skill may improve) and allows a user's profile to evolve. Due to the nature of the data and the difficulty in recognising gradual behavioural pattern changes, it is likely that this would be implemented using some form of neural network (Furnell, 1994).

The **Recorder** stores a temporary record of system and user activity during a session (session profile) which can be used by the Profile Refiner to update the user profile, providing the session was not considered anomalous.

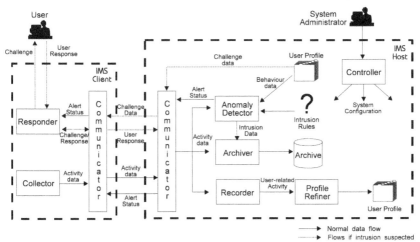

**Figure 2 Proposed IMS Architecture**

The **Archiver** provides an audit log, storing all security relevant events. This could also be extended to monitor *all* events if an organisation requires a more detailed log of user activity (e.g. to monitor user performance).

The **Collector** provides an interface between the IMS client and the applications running on the client computer. The collector is responsible for gathering information relevant to the user and his/her system activities. Under Windows NT the collector would be implemented as a mediator, collecting information gathered by low-level system functions that intercept system messages (e.g. keystrokes, mouse movements etc.) and forwarding this information on to the communicator.

The **Responder** provides user interface between the IMS software suite and the end-user. Its main task is that of monitoring the signals send from the server to the client and taking appropriate action where necessary. Possible actions include; issuing a user authentication challenge, suspending a session, limiting a user's actions or cancelling a process.

The **Communicator** provides the interface between the client and server IMS software. The communicator is responsible for ensuring a consistent, reliable and secure exchange of data between the client and server. Where an IMS system is implemented in a heterogeneous environment, the communicator is also responsible for data translation to provide consistent data formatting between different client platforms.

The **Controller** provides a management interface to the IMS server software allowing an administrator to configure the IMS system-operating parameters. The controller also allows an administrator to configure client-monitoring characteristics on a global, group, machine or individual user basis.

An Intrusion Monitoring System incorporates identification and authentication of users, monitoring of users for unusual behaviour or characteristics, together with the ability to modify the profile of a user to reflect changing patterns of use/behaviour. An IMS can rely on many physiological characteristics of the user (e.g fingerprint, voice etc.) and can also monitor behavioural traits such as keystroke patterns, mouse dynamics and application/resource usage. However, it should be noted that the majority of commercially available IMS systems rely on traditional methods of user authentication

A strong potential candidate for a monitoring characteristic is that of keystroke analysis. This is a particularly attractive characteristic, as it requires no additional hardware (cost) or proprietary drivers (development time). By monitoring a user's typing profile it is possible to determine, with some accuracy, the identity of the current user. The use of a users' typing pattern as an authentication characteristic has been described in a number of papers (Furnell et al, 1996; Brown and Rogers, 1993) and has shown to be a strong distinguishing factor in certain contexts with overall False Acceptance Rate (FAR) figures as low as 4.2% being observed.

Although keystroke analysis is a good characteristic upon which to base user authentication, there are limitations. One of the major drawbacks of this characteristic is the very fact that users have a broad range of typing patterns. An inexperienced typist will use a keyboard in a slow deliberate manner, having a slow typing rate and most probably a high error rate. A trained touch-typist will type quickly with a low error rate. However, most inexperienced typists will type equally slowly and most touch-typists will type equally quickly. It is quite possible that the inter-keystroke time will be such that two typists may be indistinguishable in normal working environments.

Keystroke analysis may also be inappropriate depending on the environment in which it is used. For example, if a user is typing in numeric data for a prolonged period, it may be impossible to achieve a statistically valid sample of keystroke data upon which to base the authentication judgement. Similarly, if a user were drawing with a mouse, there would be no keystrokes to analyse.

From this, we can see that a composite approach is needed, where several appropriate authentication and monitoring techniques are applied. For example, a user may be initially authenticated by their fingerprint, after which their typing profile and application usage can be monitored. Similarly, if that user then starts to draw using the mouse, data can be recorded to determine if the dynamic movement of the mouse is consistent with the users' profile. This technique can also be applied where users *hotdesk*. If a user moves to a desk with an additional security-relevant device (e.g. a camera for faceprint recognition), the additional measures can be detected during an audit and then utilised for that user depending upon the settings in their profile.

## Integrating an IMS into the Windows NT security model

If we consider the concept of an IMS, the username/password pair could be used to identify the user with a partial degree of certainty, whilst the continuously evaluated characteristics would allow the user to be monitored throughout the session. Using the previous example of keystroke analysis, a users' typing pattern can be monitored throughout the active session and compared with a historical profile. Deviation from this profile can be flagged and a threshold set beyond which further authentication of the user would be required (Furnell, 1995). This trust level can also determine the frequency of monitoring and, where further authentication is considered necessary, the degree of certainty needed (and, hence, the form of authentication to request).

To achieve an Intrusion Monitoring System (IMS) under Windows NT would require a replacement GINA DLL and an additional piece of software to provide the required continuous monitoring together with a remote security server. A security server (or some form of centralised system) would be used to store, maintain and update the user profiles. This server would (in an ideal system) process all authentication requests together with local system audits and updates to profiles. This role is slightly different to that of a network server, which, usually, only authenticates requests for access at the beginning of a session. Instead, the security server would be responsible for ongoing authentication of a user throughout a session.

A user login would be performed locally (or remotely via a domain controller) and once the user's credentials are confirmed the monitoring program would be loaded to provide continuous user authentication (Figure 3). To prevent tampering, the IMS system would store user profiles remotely on a security server. The profiles would be encrypted and downloaded at login to the local computer (although for higher security the profiles could be maintained on the server, with authentication requests being handled by the server). To also offer security for the hardware (to ensure monitoring hardware had not been removed) a local machine audit can also be initiated, together with checks for dependent entries in configuration files or registry keys. An IMS system would also allow updating of the user profiles, to take into consideration changing user behaviour (e.g. keystroke patterns, application usage etc.) or appearance (e.g. facial recognition).

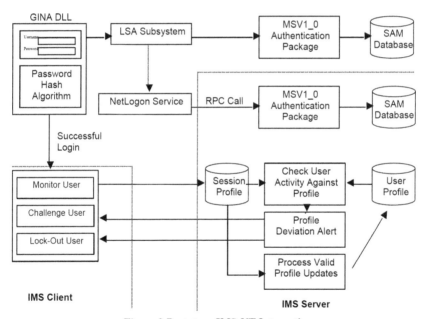

**Figure 3 Prototype IMS-NT Integration**

To reduce network traffic, it is envisaged that the user authentication would be performed on the local computer with only warnings or profile updates being fed back to the security server. Under certain scenarios it may be necessary to lock local computers if contact is lost with the security server to ensure an intruder had not removed a computer. However, it should be noted that this creates a weak point and appropriate measures will be needed to prevent a single server stopping the entire network, this could take the form of a backup server (in a similar fashion to a secondary DNS server in an Internet context). Alternatively, the range of facilities available to the user can be restricted until the user can be re-authenticated. Another possible weak-point is the profile update process. It is important that the profile update is only performed once a user authentication confidence level is exceeded and it is established that the computer concerned has not been tampered with. In the event that a users' authentication threshold has been uncertain and/or the computer may have been tampered with, any proposed changes to the user profile should be discarded.

One of the most important factors in the implementation of continuous user monitoring is ensuring the transparency of the monitoring process. A system that requires users to continuously re-authenticate themselves will not be successful. Therefore, an IMS should allow background monitoring of an authenticated user, only interrupting the user in the event that further authentication is necessary (e.g. in the form of a challenge-response question).

Clearly an IMS system can provide enhanced user authentication. However, there is no single system configuration that will meet all the needs of all the users. Instead configuration of the security server and client monitoring software is dependent on the level of security required by the organisation and amount of inconvenience that is tolerable to the users (the classic False Acceptance Rate versus False Rejection Rate dichotomy) (Cope, 1990).

## Conclusions

As the need for enhanced user authentication grows, operating systems will be extended to provide the necessary services. Windows NT already allows the use of a replacement GINA DLL, which allows OEM security vendors to supplement the Windows NT username/password login with additional/replacement authentication techniques. Alternative login techniques (e.g. fingerprint identification) allow the system confidence in user validity to be increased, but further security is needed to ensure the continued confidence in the user once past the initial login process. A process of continuous user authentication and monitoring, as described in the paper, is therefore desirable.

## References

Audit Commission (1998), *Ghost in the Machine – An Analysis of IT Fraud and Abuse*, Audit Commission Publications, UK, ISBN 1-86240-056-3.

Brown, M. and Rogers, S. J. (1993), "User identification via keystroke characteristics of typed names using neural networks", *International Journal of Man-Machine Studies*, p999-1014.

Cherry, A., Henderson, M.W., Nickless, W.K., Olson, R. and Rackow, G. (1992), "Pass or fail: a new test for password legitimacy", Argonne National Laboratory, Mathematics and Computer Science Division, Paper Ref.: MCS-P328-1092,
http://www-proto.mcs.anl.gov/division/publications/abstracts/abstracts92.htm

Cope, J.B. (1990), "Biometric systems of access control", *Electrotechnology*, p71-74, April/May 1990.

Donoghue, A. (1999), "US Army scraps NT for MacOS", *Computing*, p14, 7th October 1999.

Fausett, L. (1994), *Fundamentals of Neural Networks: Architectures, Algorithms and Applications*, Prentice-Hall International, New Jersey, USA, ISBN 0-13-042250-9.

Furnell, S.M. (1995), *Data security in European healthcare information systems*, PhD Thesis, University of Plymouth, UK.

Furnell, S.M., Morrissey, J.P., Sanders, P.W. and Stockel, C.T. (1996), "Applications of keystroke analysis for improved login security and continuous user authentication", *Proceedings of IFIP Sec '96*, Island of Samos, Greece, 21-24 May 1996, pp283-294.

Furnell, S.M., Illingworth, H.M., Katsikas, S.K., Reynolds, P.L. and Sanders, P.W. (1997), "A comprehensive authentication and supervision architecture for networked multimedia systems", *Proceedings of IFIP CMS '97*, Athens, Greece, 22-23 September 1997, pp227-238.

Jobusch, D.L. and Oldehoeft, A.E. (1989), "A survey of password mechanisms: Weaknesses and potential improvements. Part 1", *Computers & Security*, p587-603.

Microsoft Corporation Web Site (1999a),
http://www.microsoft.com/security/issues/deployingc2.asp

Microsoft Corporation Web Site (1999b),
http://www.microsoft.com/security/services/bulletin.asp

NOP Research Group (1999), "E-Commerce in Britain to reach £9.5 billion by 2000",
http://www.nopres.co.uk/survey/internet/internet_item8.htm

Savill, J. (1999), *NT FAQ Web Site*,
http://www.ntfaq.com/ntfaq/security21.html#security21

Stoll, C. (1989), *The Cuckoo's Egg*, Doubleday, New York.

# User authentication for keypad-based devices using keystroke analysis

T.Ord[†] and S.M.Furnell[‡]

[†] Spinnaker International Ltd., Spinnaker House, Budshead Road, Crownhill, Plymouth, United Kingdom
[‡] Network Research Group, School of Electronic, Communication & Electrical Engineering, University of Plymouth, Plymouth, United Kingdom
email: sfurnell@plymouth.ac.uk

## Abstract

The use of a Personal Identification Number (PIN) is a common means of ensuring user authentication on numeric keypad devices. However, like passwords and other forms of authentication based upon secret knowledge, PINs have the potential weakness that they may become known to other people.

This paper describes a potential approach for strengthening PIN-based authentication, by incorporating a biometric measurement of the user's typing style when keying in their number. Such keystroke analysis techniques have previously been used in a full keyboard context, but the keypad scenario is considered to represent a more complex problem.

An experimental study is described in which a neural network approach was used to classify and discriminate between 14 test subjects. The main results, using a 6-digit PIN, yielded a False Acceptance Rate (FAR) of 9.9%, with an accompanying False Rejection Rate (FRR) of 30%. Further experiments were able to significantly reduce the error, but at the expense of a longer PIN. The paper also considers potential application areas, in view of the results observed.

## Keywords

Security, Authentication, Biometrics

## 1. Introduction

The accurate authentication of users represents an important issue in a variety of information technology systems, including computers/networks, Automated Teller Machine (ATM) systems and mobile phones. There are various techniques and technologies that can be used to achieve this, the most common being the use of passwords or Personal Identification Numbers (PINs). However, these share the weakness that they are based upon a foundation of secret knowledge. If this information is ever shared or discovered, the system becomes vulnerable to attack (Jobusch and Oldehoeft, 1989). This paper examines the use of keystroke analysis, which recognises that a person's typing pattern on a keyboard or keypad may exhibit unique characteristics. Keystroke analysis is based upon utilising these characteristics to differentiate one user from another. The pattern in keystroke analysis is formed from the different inter-keystroke latencies.

Keystroke analysis is an example of a biometric. Biometric-based authentication systems aim to verify a user's claimed identity by measuring physiological or behavioural characteristics (i.e. something that the user *is* as opposed to something that they *have* or *know*). There are numerous other biometric techniques, including fingerprints analysis, facial recognition, retinal scanning, iris scanning, vascular patterns, voice dynamics and signature dynamics (Miller, 1994). The first five of these are based on physiological characteristics, whilst the last two, along with keystroke analysis, are based upon behavioural measures. The advantage of keystroke analysis over other biometrics is its low cost (the technique can be implemented entirely in software) and the fact that it can be transparent to the user when they type in their PIN code.

As with other biometric-based systems, the effectiveness of keystroke analysis can be judged on the basis of two types of error:

-   False Acceptance Rate (FAR): The extent to which the authentication system will falsely judge an impostor to be the legitimate user. Sometimes referred to as Impostor Pass Rate.

-   False Rejection Rate (FRR): The extent to which legitimate users will be incorrectly judged to be impostors and, therefore, denied access by the authentication system. Sometimes referred to as False Alarm Rate.

These errors have a mutually exclusive relationship, such that the decrease of one will generally result in the increase of the other. The level of error must be controlled in the authentication system by the use of a threshold to determine the point at which users will be accepted and rejected. Selecting an appropriate threshold is, therefore, very important: too lax a setting will result in a high level of false acceptance, whereas too strict a threshold will cause legitimate users to be falsely rejected on a frequent basis.

The idea of using keyboard characteristics for authentication is not unique, and there have been a number of previous papers published on this topic, the main results of which are summarised in table 1 below.

| Authors | %FAR | % FRR |
|---|---|---|
| Gaines et al. (1980) | 0% | 4% |
| Legget & Williams (1988) | 5% | 5.5% |
| Joyce & Gupta (1990) | 0.25% | 16.67% |
| Bleha et al. (1990) | 2.8% | 8.1% |

**Table 1: Summary of previous keystroke analysis studies**

In these previous experiments, the full keyboard has been utilised in examining user's typing patterns. In this study, however, a numerical keypad approach has been taken. This provides a more complex problem than the previous experiments in that only one finger is normally used to enter codes on a numerical keypad, as opposed to the two hands when typing on a full keyboard. When typing with two hands, more information about the user can be obtained, as not only is there a pattern from the typing of each individual hand, but also in the interaction of the two hands (Gentner, 1983). Gentner states that one-finger digraphs have lower variability, which makes the classification of users more difficult than with two finger or two hand digraphs (because the 'signatures' are closer together).

The paper presents an experimental study of keystroke analysis in a numeric keypad context, in order to obtain a practical measure of its effectiveness. It is considered that the successful implementation of such an approach would have value in contexts where traditional secret knowledge PINs are currently the only form of protection.

## 2. Methods and Procedure

In order to examine the inter-keystroke times of users entering numerical codes, a data acquisition system had to be designed. The inter-keystroke times were required to be measured in milliseconds and stored together with the code of the keys that were pressed. The keypad on a standard PC AT-101 keyboard was used for this purpose, with appropriate modifications to the PC timer and key action interrupt routines to enable the required information to be collected at the appropriate resolution. In order to make the PC keyboard layout correspond more closely to that found on ATM machines and telephony devices, the arrangement of the numeric keys was reversed (i.e. so that the keys 1,2,3 appear at the top of the keypad rather than the bottom).

The experiments were conducted within the Research Department of Spinnaker International, Plymouth. The data acquisition system was operating for 6 months, from 0900 to 1730 each day. Co-operation was encouraged by making the system serve as a fire register, which the test subjects were required to use whenever entering and leaving the building. The participants were all experienced with using PC's and, therefore, had basic typing skills, but none were touch typists. In fact, as was expected, all the participants only used one finger to type in the numerical password. All users were asked to type in the same numerical code, 288970, which was selected as it was a number that they were already familiar with. The ASCII code of every key pressed and the corresponding inter-keystroke latency were stored to a text file as the users typed in the code.

A total of 50 samples were collected for each user, which were then used as inputs to a neural network to assess the effectiveness of the authentication technique. The first 30 samples were used as reference data for training the neural network, while the last 20 were used for testing purposes. As the data collection system was running for a total of 6 months and from 0900 to 1730, any effects from the uncorrelated sources of noise from the state of the user or from the equipment itself, is expected to be averaged out. These sources of noise could include minor illnesses, the time of day the entry is made, stress, and tiredness. The analysis stage of the experiments took place in non-real time. Any latency less than 40 milliseconds and greater than 1 second were not used. This was because a latency of less than 40ms could arise if a user hit two keys together, and it was assumed that latencies over 1 second arose from the user being distracted from an external source (and, hence, not part of their natural rhythm).

The neural network was constructed on a simulation package called NeuroSolutions. The neural network used was a Multi-Layer Perceptron (MLP) with the Back-Propagation Learning Rule (Bishop, 1995). The training of the network can be split into three sub-stages: the feed-forward of the reference samples through the network, the back-propagation of the error, and then the weight update. The MLP, when used with the Back-propagation learning rule, is an example of supervised learning (Looney, 1997). Each feature vector (in this case represented by a typing sample) is fed into the system, along with its known class identifier as the desired output vector (0 or 1 in this case), and the network learns to map the input feature vector into the desired class identifier. For each user, the network is trained on recognising that user's 30 reference samples, whilst at the same time recognising that the other 13 users' samples (390 in total) are not from the same user. To facilitate this the desired output for the target user is set to '1', whilst the desired output for the other 13 impostors is set at '0'. This process is repeated for each user acting as a target and the other 13 users as impostors.

One complete training iteration is referred to as an epoch (i.e. when all training samples have been presented to the network once). Batch learning was applied in this experiment, where after each epoch all the weights for each sample were stored, and the weights updated with the average weight update. The appropriate number of epochs for training the network for each user was found to be 5000 by Cross Validation. On average there was no advantage in increasing the number of epochs. Cross Validation shows if the network is being over-trained, which results in the network being unable recognise the general case of that pattern, only the specific patterns it was trained with.

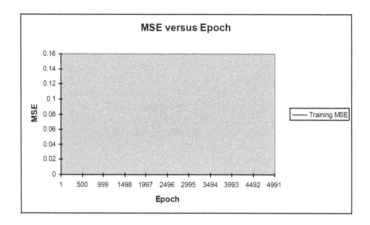

**Figure 1: Example of the Neural Network learning curve**

Figure 1 illustrates how the Mean Square Error at the output of the Neural Network is reduced as the number of iterations of presenting the set of training patterns into the Multi-Layer Perceptron Network increases. This is essentially the learning curve of the neural network. As the curve does not reach 0, it has not learned the tasks of separating each user class exactly. As such, the error of this classifier is greater than 0. This was expected, as there are certain limitations to this classification, which are caused by the data itself. The features may be inadequate to distinguish the different user classes no matter how well a discriminant function can separate the classes.

The network was trained for each user, resulting in each user having their own sets of weights. The network topology, epochs, and all other variables were the same for each user. This method was chosen so as to minimise the potential hardware and software that would be involved in a practical implementation. One neural network could be used, with a particular users' weights loaded when identified, which could then be used to authenticate that user.

For these experiments, the maximum acceptable FRR was set at 30% as it is considered to be the highest level that could be tolerated by users. Currently, PIN-based authentication systems, such as ATM's and mobile phones, typically permit the user three attempts to enter the code correctly. As such, a window of opportunity would still exist for them to recover from a false rejection. The probability of a valid user being denied access after three attempts is therefore 2.7%. Given the mutually exclusive relationship between the FAR and FRR that was described earlier, the advantage of allowing a relatively high FRR is that it enables a corresponding reduction of the FAR – which is considered to be the more important measure from the security perspective. The goal of these experiments was, therefore, to determine the FAR that could be achieved with a FRR of 30%.

## 3. Results

This section of the report details the actual results obtained from the neural network experiment. Following this, additional experiments were undertaken to further analyse and improve the results.

| User | 1 | 2 | 3 | 4 | 5 | 6 | 7 | 8 | 9 | 10 | 11 | 12 | 13 | 14 | Average |
|------|-----|-----|------|------|-----|-----|-----|------|-----|-----|-----|-----|-----|-----|---------|
| 1 | | 0 | 83 | 15 | 0 | 0 | 0 | 85 | 15 | 0 | 0 | 0 | 5 | 0 | 15.6 |
| 2 | 0 | | 5 | 10 | 0 | 0 | 0 | 5 | 0 | 30 | 0 | 0 | 0 | 0 | 3.8 |
| 3 | 20 | 5 | | 55 | 0 | 5 | 5 | 15 | 0 | 0 | 0 | 0 | 0 | 15 | 9.2 |
| 4 | 10 | 5 | 36 | | 0 | 5 | 5 | 15 | 0 | 0 | 10 | 5 | 0 | 30 | 9.3 |
| 5 | 0 | 5 | 21 | 0 | | 5 | 0 | 0 | 0 | 0 | 0 | 0 | 0 | 0 | 2.4 |
| 6 | 0 | 0 | 13 | 0 | 20 | | 0 | 20 | 0 | 0 | 0 | 0 | 0 | 0 | 4.1 |
| 7 | 0 | 0 | 90 | 25 | 10 | 0 | | 0 | 0 | 0 | 0 | 0 | 0 | 55 | 13.8 |
| 8 | 25 | 0 | 55 | 35 | 0 | 0 | 5 | | 5 | 0 | 0 | 15 | 0 | 0 | 10.8 |
| 9 | 20 | 0 | 88 | 0 | 0 | 0 | 5 | 75 | | 0 | 40 | 0 | 0 | 0 | 17.5 |
| 10 | 20 | 20 | 10 | 45 | 0 | 0 | 0 | 20 | 0 | | 5 | 0 | 0 | 0 | 9.2 |
| 11 | 0 | 0 | 86 | 10 | 0 | 0 | 0 | 10 | 30 | 0 | | 15 | 0 | 0 | 11.6 |
| 12 | 0 | 0 | 36 | 5 | 0 | 0 | 20 | 90 | 5 | 0 | 0 | | 0 | 5 | 12.4 |
| 13 | 0 | 0 | 43 | 5 | 10 | 0 | 25 | 10 | 0 | 0 | 0 | 0 | | 25 | 8.3 |
| 14 | 0 | 0 | 78 | 20 | 0 | 0 | 45 | 10 | 0 | 0 | 0 | 0 | 0 | | 11 |
| Average | 7.3 | 2.7 | 49.5 | 17.3 | 3.1 | 1.2 | 8.5 | 25.8 | 4.2 | 2.3 | 4.2 | 2.7 | 0.4 | 10 | 9.9 |

**Table 2: Neural Network Results**

Table 2 presents the overall FAR results observed for the comparison of user reference profiles against test samples (with the FRR of 30%). Each column indicates the false acceptance rate that was observed against the profile of a particular user by other user's test samples. The rows indicate the level of false acceptance achieved by each user when their samples were used to represent impostor cases (e.g. User 4 was able to pass as User 6 in 5% of cases). The bottom row gives the average FAR against each user, for an FRR of 30%. The final column gives the average impostor performance of each user (e.g. User 9 appears to be the most likely candidate to be able to masquerade as another user, with 17.5% chance of false acceptance). The average FAR of the classifier was determined as 9.9%.

Figure 2 illustrates the overall classification performance in graphical terms. Most significantly, it shows the average percentage FAR that was observed against each user's reference profile. These are the results used to measure the overall authentication performance of the classifier, indicating what percentage of impostors would be allowed access to a user's protected resources when that user themselves were rejected 30% of the time. The dashed line indicates the average percentage of each user's test samples that were falsely accepted by the other user's references (i.e. how much each user contributed to the overall FAR that was observed).

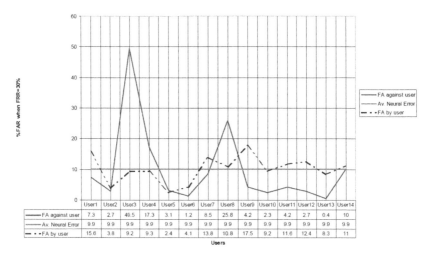

| | User1 | User2 | User3 | User4 | User5 | User6 | User7 | User8 | User9 | User10 | User11 | User12 | User13 | User14 |
|---|---|---|---|---|---|---|---|---|---|---|---|---|---|---|
| FA against user | 7.3 | 2.7 | 49.5 | 17.3 | 3.1 | 1.2 | 8.5 | 25.8 | 4.2 | 2.3 | 4.2 | 2.7 | 0.4 | 10 |
| Av. Neural Error | 9.9 | 9.9 | 9.9 | 9.9 | 9.9 | 9.9 | 9.9 | 9.9 | 9.9 | 9.9 | 9.9 | 9.9 | 9.9 | 9.9 |
| FA by user | 15.6 | 3.8 | 9.2 | 9.3 | 2.4 | 4.1 | 13.8 | 10.8 | 17.5 | 9.2 | 11.6 | 12.4 | 8.3 | 11 |

**Figure 2: Overall False Acceptance (FA) results with a 30% FRR**

The overall FAR of 9.9% was considered to be high (particularly in view of the accompanying high FRR). However, as indicated in table 2 and figure 2, this overall result was adversely affected by a minority of cases in which particular users scored extremely high levels of false acceptance (thus distorting the overall average obtained). As such, additional experiments were conducted in an attempt to further investigate and improve the results.

In the full study conducted by the authors, the neural network classifier was one of three classification techniques evaluated (the others being the Minimum Distance and Mahalanobis Distance classifiers). Across the three sets of results, the worst overall False Acceptance Rate observed was that of User 3's samples against User 4's reference (55%). As such, this was selected as the target for further investigation (note: it can be seen from table 2 that when considering only the results of the neural network approach, the comparison of User 3 against User 4 was *not* the worst case result). Further training of the network with the existing samples and additional layers did not yield any worthwhile improvement, so it was decided that the experiment should be repeated with longer signatures.

The data acquisition stage was repeated, but only using Users 3 and 4. It was decided that a 10 inter-keystroke latency signature should be tested, and the code chosen for both users to type was 01752237101. This was Spinnaker International's fax number with the area code. It was important to use a code that both users could remember easily. If this were not the case, additional error sources would have been added to the problem. Both users entered the same number of samples as before, i.e. 50. The first 30 were used as reference samples to train the network, and the next 20 as test samples.

The results showed that, for a threshold of between 0.073 and 0.098, the FAR and FRR were both 0, thus giving perfect classification. As illustrated in figure 3, only one of User 4's samples was less than 0.95, but as it was greater than all of User 3's output values, the threshold could be set between the highest User 3 output and the lowest User 4 output, to give the no error.

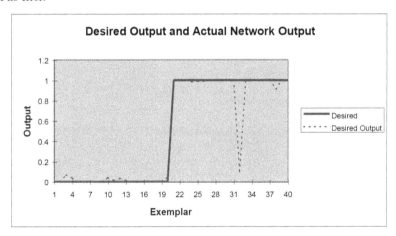

**Figure 3: Output of network with longer samples**

These results indicate that even the most difficult classification tasks can be alleviated by increasing the length of the feature vectors. A longer feature vector provides more information and thus it was expected that the results would improve. However, increasing the length of the input code has practical implications for the end user (i.e. limiting their ability to easily remember it). As such, it would not represent a solution in all contexts.

The full results of the study, which also included the investigation of the Minimum Distance and Mahalanobis Distance classifiers, can be found in Ord (1999). These other classifiers were found to produce inferior results to the neural network approach reported in this paper.

## 4. Practical applications

The techniques used in this study can be implemented in any application that involves user authentication with a numeric keypad. The most common application that involves the user authenticating themselves via a numerical keypad is in ATM systems. The authentication in this case is currently provided by the user's knowledge of their PIN code. If an impostor obtains this code, that user's resources can be accessed. The incorporation of keystroke analysis would add an extra layer of security, in that knowledge of the PIN would not guarantee access – the typing style of the impostor would also be required to be similar. Other biometric technologies are already being considered in an ATM context, an example being an iris recognition system that has been under trial in the UK by the ATM manufacturer NCR (NCR, 1999).

Another potential market for products using these techniques, is a Universal Personal Telecommunications (UPT) terminal. UPT aims to deliver a personal mobility, allowing a user to receive telecommunication services on any terminal in any network, by identifying users by a unique personal number. Additional transparent security could be provided by this system, as apart from a terminal transmitting the UPT number to a Central Control System, the inter-keystroke times could be transmitted as well. The latencies would be measured at the terminal, and the Central Control System would calculate whether the identified user was an impostor or valid user. It would then withhold any service rights if the system decided that the user was an impostor. These techniques can also be applied to terminal mobility scenarios, such as mobile handsets, for PIN-based user authentication and other security numbers (Furnell et al. 1996).

A major concern in practice would be the robustness of the authentication technique. In an application such as ATMs, the potential users could be in various states of mind or body, i.e. they could be intoxicated, ill, or have an injured hand. This could seriously effect the performance of the classifiers, as users could deviate from their 'normal' inter-keystroke signature. Any biometric used in an ATM or UPT application has to take these factors into account. Hence, authentication techniques that rely on a user's actions, such as these, cannot perform to the same accuracy in these circumstances as physiology-based biometrics. Physiological characteristics, such as the iris, do not change whatever the state the user is in. However, two major advantages that keystroke-analysis based authentication techniques have are that they are transparent to the user and require no additional equipment, making them cheaper to implement. The one major limitation of iris and retinal recognition systems is that they rely upon the co-operation of the user and many users have reservations about staring into a device which is going to scan their eyes.

The results observed suggest that the approach is currently not accurate enough for use with large-scale systems such as ATMs and UPT. To give an example of the error rates that would be considered acceptable in these contexts, error for iris scan ATM biometrics are in the order of 0.00076% for when the FRR equals the FAR (Biometric Consulting Group 1998). A more appropriate application could include keypad-based access control for secure systems or areas within an organisation.

## 5. Conclusions

The use of biometrics in commercial environments is rapidly increasing as the technology required decreases in cost. The low cost and transparency of the keystroke analysis biometric has made it possible for it to compete with the other more expensive alternatives. This study investigated the possibility of its use in conjunction with codes typed on a numeric keypad.

The overall results were an FAR of 9.9% with an FRR of 30%. This result was higher than observed in the previous studies summarised earlier in the paper. However, these previous results were based on a simpler problem, as a full keyboard was used in all for data collection. The code used for the main experiments in this study was only 6 digits long, dramatically shorter than in these previous experiments. Consequently, a decrease in the performance was expected. The use of an 11-digit code (i.e. with 10 measurable latencies), proved that the results of the neural network classifier could be significantly improved (with the worst error component being reduced from 60% to 0%). However, it must be acknowledged that, in a practical context, a PIN code of 11 digits would represent too long a string for most users to easily remember.

Additional experimentation is required with longer numerical codes and for an increased number of users, to test the viability of keystroke analysis for large-scale biometrics such as in ATM's and UPT services. This study demonstrated that the Multi-Layer Perceptron Classifier has potential in this application, and further development in this area could improve these results further.

## 6. References

Biometric Consulting Group. 1998. Web Page: http://biometric-consulting.com/bio.htm.

Bishop, C.M. 1995. *Neural Networks for Pattern Recognition*. Oxford University Press.

Bleha, S., Slivinsky, C. and Hussien, B. 1990. "Computer-Access Security Systems Using Keystroke Dynamics", Transactions on Pattern analysis and Machine Intelligence", vol 12., no. 12.

Furnell, S.M., Green, M., Hope, S., Morrissey, J.P and Reynolds, P.L. 1996. "Non-Intrusive Security Arrangements to support Terminal and Personal Mobility", in *Proceedings of EUROMEDIA 96* (London, UK, 19-21 December 1996): 167-171.

Gaines, R., Lisowski, W., Press, S. and Shapiro, N. 1980. "Authentication by keystroke timing", Rand Report R-256-NSF. Rand Corporation.

Gentner, D.R. 1983. "Keystroke timing in transcription typing". in W. E. Cooper (Ed.), *Cognitive aspects of skilled typewriting*. New York: Springer-Verlag: 95-120.

Jobusch, D.L. and Oldehoeft, A.E. 1989. "A Survey of Password Mechanisms : Part 1", *Computers & Security*, Vol. 8, No. 7: 587-604.

Joyce, R. and Gupta, G. 1990. "Identity Authentication Based on Keystroke Latencies", Communications of the ACM, Volume 33, February 1990.

Legget, J. and Williams, G. 1988. "Verifying identity via keystroke characteristics", International Journal of Man-Machine Studies, 28.

Looney, C. 1997. *Pattern Recognition using Neural Network*, Oxford University Press.

Miller, B. 1994. "Vital signs of identity", IEEE Spectrum, February 1994.

NCR. 1999. "NCR announces iris recognition trials with Nationwide Building Society". http://www3.ncr.com/product/financial/press/sensnat.htm

Ord, T. 1999. *User Authentication using Keystroke Analysis with a Numerical Keypad approach*. MS.c. Thesis. University of Plymouth, Plymouth, United Kingdom.

# Deception and the Information Security function

Dr William Hutchinson[1] and Dr Matthew Warren[2]

[1]School of Management Information Systems, Edith Cowan University, Churchlands, Western Australia, Australia.

[2]School of Computing & Mathematics, Deakin University, Geelong, Victoria, Australia.

E-mail Contact: mwarren@deakin.edu.au

## Abstract

With the proliferation of electronic information systems in the last two decades, the integrity of the stored data and its uses have become an essential component of effective organisational functioning. This digitised format, used in input, output, processing, storage, and communication, has given those wishing to deceive new opportunities. This paper examines the nature of deception, and its potential in the information age.

## Keywords
Deception, Information Security.

## 1. Introduction

Caelli et al (1994) specify that the three main functions of information security is to ensure that data remains confidential, has integrity and is available. The aim of a deceiver is to attack the integrity of the data in an effort to gain some benefit. The digital medium is ripe for exploitation. Its major advantage over other media is the ability to easily manipulate the bits that constitute its messages. It is also one of its major disadvantages. For instance, Roberts and Webber (1999) trace the history of photographic manipulation and clearly show the ease with which images can be changed to give a totally different perspective. In the digital realm, this is sold as one of the major advantages of computerised imagery. Photographic images, which were always slanted versions of reality, cannot even be taken to be that in today's digitised world. See figure 1 as an example. These photographs were manipulated in the by a relatively novice person. It took about two hours to produce these. The ease of manipulation allows any component of the image can be changed to reflect whatever is required. Barry (1997) demonstrates the power of visual imagery and how subtle changes can disproportionately change the meaning of an image. This is just as appropriate auditory messages or with simpler, conventional text messages.

Contemporary organisations with their reliance on information technology are vulnerable to deception. Of course, this technology also provides an opportunity. Each person or group can become a deceiver as well as being a victim of deception. Any management regime needs to be fully aware of the potential for deception, and its potential impacts on organisation decision making and operations.

## 2. Data, Information, and Knowledge

Boisot (1998) has an interesting slant on the relationships between data, inforamtion, and knowledge. It is this model that is used in this paper. In it, data is associated with a *thing*, and discriminates between different states of the thing it describes. However, knowledge is an attribute of an *agent*. Knowledge is a set of perceptions about data activated by an event. Information is this set of data filtered by the agent. It establishes a link between the agent and the data. This perspective has profound implications for those wishing to deceive. Changing data can determine the information perceived by the agent as it changes the attributes of the *thing* being considered. Altering the agent's perception of the situation will alter the information derived by changing the *set of data* used to derive the information. In information technology terms, it means manipulation of data (as it is input, stored, output, or communicated), or the alteration the context in which the data are interpreted.

**Figure 1: Which image is a real reflection of past events, or are either of them?**
**(Image 1 Is False)**

# 3. The Nature of Deception

Deception has been used since the dawn of time to gain advantage. The purpose of deception is to create an illusion, which somehow benefits the perpetrator. By its nature, a deception should not be discovered to be successful. Deception is the deliberate manipulation of data or a situation to produce a desired *reality*. Thus, decisions and behaviours of the target are changed to the benefit of the attacker.

Bowyer (1982) classifies deception into two main types:
- Level 1: Hiding the real;
- Level 2: Showing the false (although this type of deception always involves Hiding).

These fundamental types are further divided into six categories of deception

### Hiding
- **Masking**, blending in, e.g. camouflage.
- **Repackaging**, something is given a new 'wrapping'.
- **Dazzling**, confounding the target, e.g. codes.

### Showing
- **Mimicking**, a replica of reality which has one of more characteristics of reality.
- **Inventing**, creating a new reality.
- **Decoying**, misdirecting the attacker.

# 4. Frameworks for the tactics of deception

There are a number of ways to develop tactics for deception. Two frameworks will be examined in this paper: using organisational functionality, and using the processing cycle from data collection to interpretation.

## 4.1 Organisational functionality

Beer's (1984, 1985) Viable System Model (VSM) provides a integrated functional model of information flows within an organisation. The VSM is basically an ideal model of the functional necessities for a viable system and the interactions required between each of the functions. The VSM specifies five main functional areas:

- Policy making;
- Intelligence and planning;
- Control (and audit);
- Coordination;
- Operations.

The operational, coordinating, and controlling functions are there to ensure the efficient and effective running of the system. Information regarding the operational performance of the system is synthesised and fed into the controlling function, which then sends it to the intelligence and planning function. This is all internal information. The intelligence and planning function takes this and information from the external environment, analyses it, and offers the policy making function some alternative scenarios. The policy making function then makes decisions, and passes it thought the intelligence and planning function to be interpreted and presented to the controlling function to enforce the policies on the operational units. Beer's model does not include information flow form the intelligence and planning function into the environment, but this is important to most organisations as a means of manipulating its environment. Figure 2 summarises the data flows into and from the intelligence function. This paper interprets the intelligence function as that which analyses information to make decisions and hence, real world changes. It is a fundamental management function.

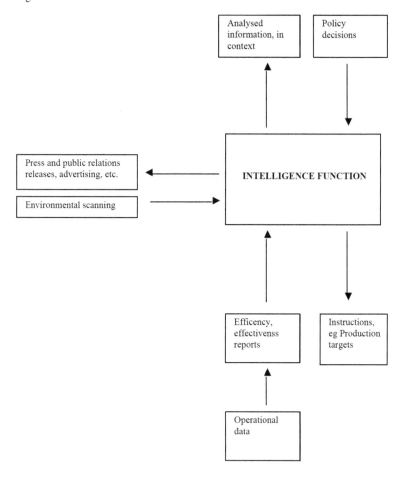

**Figure 2: Information flows and the Intelligence function in an organisation**

It is the assumption of this paper that the information/knowledge management function in an organisation is responsible for all information whether internal or external in nature, and whether it is flowing around the organisation internally, or to or from the external environment. It does not assume that this is all done by a single entity within the system. When viewed from this perspective the opportunities for manipulation of data, and its misinterpretation are manifold. The information/knowledge manager has to ensure the integrity of internal systems, data flowing from the organisation, and that flowing into the organisation. If this, all encompassing, nature is accepted, there appears to be a need to integrate such functions as security, public relations, advertising, and information systems. This will ensure a system, which coordinates, secures, distributes, and uses information, in whatever form, effectively.

Any deceiver will need to determine the level (data or knowledge) before any tactic and desired outcome is finalised. For instance, changing data will alter the information derived, as will changing the context of the problem at hand. The tactic of the deceiver will need to fit the outcome required.

Figure 2 illustrates the magnitude of the information manager's problem, and the numerous avenues that an attacker wishing to deceive has. This figure describes the raw internal, operational data (internal data) being used in collated form to produce management reports (internal information). This information is fed into the intelligence function, as is environmental scanning data (external data) to provide the raw material to be analysed providing intelligence (the intelligence product not the function). This intelligence is provided to the policy making function, and policies are fed back into the system. Using these policies, instructions are then sent to the operational functions for action.

Deception can occur at any of these stages by 'attacking' data by addition, deletion, or amendment. This can occur by targeting internal or external data. Another way to classify an intelligence system is given by Richelson (1993, p.3). The tasks within an intelligence system's cycle are to collect, process, analyse and produce, and disseminate information. Thus, deception techniques can be used at any stage of the cycle. These tactics are similar to the above, and involve data or context manipulation.

## 4.2 Processing cycle

Tactics can also be developed using the processing cycle for information. The classic, if mechanistic, communication model developed by Claude Shannon (see Jones, 1979; Severin and Tankard, 1992) can be the basis of a framework. The transmission of a signal from source, through a transmitter, across a medium affected by noise, to a receiver, and hence, its destination exposes the basic potential elements to be attacked. Of course, each stage can have a message storage function. Manipulation of the data can occur at each stage. Input, output, and storage devices can be compromised. The signal being communicated across the transport medium can be changed, or noise created to alter the receipt of the message. This is the stuff of classic computer security practice with its concern with protecting the integrity of the data. This process based model is very useful for both the protective and attacking tactics concerning data. Another deeper model is required to protect the knowledge/information nexus.

Severin and Tankard (1992) describe a number of models developed in the years following Shannon's work. All of these models stress elements such as perception, message encoding, and the nature of the message's language. In other words, it is not just the raw data that needs to have integrity, it is the implied *meaning* of the message as well. This meaning can be manipulated by changing, deleting, or altering words, pictures, sounds, or other stimuli. Deception in the context of information technology is related to the topic of information warfare (or, information operations). Denning (1999) examines the elements in information systems, which are vulnerable to attack, and hence, targets for deceivers. She lists five classes of resources involved in information warfare. They are:

- containers, eg computer and human memories;
- transporters, eg humans, telecommunication systems;
- sensors, eg scanners, cameras, microphones, human senses;
- recorders, eg disk writers, printers, human processes;
- processors, eg microprocessors, humans, software.

Each of these elements, or groupings of them, can be the focus of an attack. Thus, the range of targets can vary from public opinion to a microwave link.

Each combination of attack factors such as, the information and communication medium, the type of attacker, tactic, and the determination of the attacker (opportunistic/long term) make protection against every factor difficult. Whichever framework chosen to develop strategies and tactics for deception, the methods tend to be based on the same criteria: attack the data and/or the environment in which the data is interpreted.

## 5. Deception and modern organisations

Organisations and the people in them have always been prone to deception. The modern electronic organisation has both people and machines, which are vulnerable to false input. The increasing dangers of electronic attack by 'hackers' are well documented (for example, Denning, 1999; Schwartau, 1996). These dangers are increasing as attacks come not from individual hackers, but more organised competitors, criminal gangs, and foreign states (as the concept of economic warfare grows). You can now get more information about organisations or people with computers than by using any other means (Fialka, 1997), this is a strength and weakness of the Information Society. Table 1 lists some of the possibilities for deception. Of course, deception can be a two way activity: an organisation may perpetrate deception as well as being a victim of it. The deception can occur at any stage of the information flows with a system (see Figure 2).

| TYPE OF DECEPTION | EXAMPLES |
| --- | --- |
| Masking | Stenography (Denning, 1999): hiding a message in other data. |
| Repackaging | Computer virus hiding in an existing program such as Trojan Horses. |
| Dazzling. | Encryption, codes. Sending false messages to make believe something a being carried out when it is not. |
| Mimicking | Web page looking like target's. |
| Inventing | Propaganda, public relations, advertising. |
| Decoying | Sending information so target directs effort to an activity beneficial to the attacker, e.g. by sending false market opportunities. |

**Table 1: Examples of types of deception**

To avoid the likelihood of deception, the security function has responsibilities are in five areas:

- To ensure the integrity of data collected, both internal and external;
- The secure storage of the data;
- The secure transmission of data;
- The effective collation of data into information;
- The correct analysis of information to provide knowledge, i.e. the correct reading of the context of the information provided;
- The correct dissemination of the knowledge internally, and externally.

This is based upon the CIA aspect of computer security, that of confidentiality, integrity and availability of data.

Deception can occur anywhere in the process of: data/knowledge to information. Deception at a lower level necessarily affects the higher. In the contemporary, organisational environment with virtual worlds created by computerised systems, which increasingly determine the decisions taken, attitudes, beliefs, and actions, the need to be vigilant in guarding the human virtual world (the mind) is imperative. The techniques for attacking computerised systems are well known (see Waltz, 1998 for a comprehensive review), and so will not be repeated in detail in this paper. But common attack methods would include the use of password sniffing and cracking software, spoofing attacks, denial of service attacks and direct attacks such as hacking.

# 6. Conclusion

It is interesting that in a recent survey of Australian IT managers (Hutchinson and Warren, 1999), 66% did not think there was any threat from competitors attacking their systems in any way. This perception does not bode well for the detection of acts of deception. Data integrity is an extremely important component of information management, but it must not just concentrate on internal processes of access and amendment rights. Strategies to cope with deliberate and organised attacks of a subtle nature need to be developed.

On the other hand, organisations need to reflect on the benefits of using deception themselves. Whist the word 'deception' is not often used in the context of advertising, or public relations because of its negative nature, this is really what these functions are. Advertising is not just informative, it is designed to change perceptions.

Deception techniques can be used to influence clients, the public, government agencies, and competitors. It can be used by criminals to commit fraud. It is the information management function's responsibility not only to ensure the integrity of information and data, but also to guarantee that information is collected and used to the best advantage of the organisation. In this Information Age, the pervasive nature of digitised data provides ample opportunities for deceivers to apply their skills.

## 7. References

Barry, A.M.S. (1997). *Visual Intelligence*, State University of New York Press.
Beer, S. (1984). The Viable System Model: its provenance, development, methodology and pathology. In, Espejo R, Harnden R.(eds.), *The Viable System Model,* John Wiley & Sons, Chichester. pp.211-270.
Beer, S. (1985). *Diagnosing the System for Organisations.* Wiley, Chichester.
Boisot, M.H. (1998) *Knowledge Assets.* Oxford University Press, Oxford.
Bowyer, J.B. (1982). *Cheating,* St.Martin's Press, New York.
Caelli,W., Longley, D., Shain, M. (1994) *Information Security Handbook,* MacMillan Press, London.
Denning, D.E. (1999). *Information Warfare and Security,* Addison Wesley, Reading: Mass.
Fialka, J. (1997). *War by other means: Economic Espionage in America,* W.W.Norton & Company Inc, New York: London.
Hutchinson,W., Warren, M. (1999). The attitude and practice of Australian Information Technology managers toward Cyber-Vigilantism, *InfoWarCon99,* Washington, USA, September, 1999.
Jones, D.S. (1979) *Elementary information theory,* Clarendon Press ; New York.
Rapaport, R. (1997). PR finds a new cool tool, *Forbes,* Oct 6, 1997, p.101-108.
Richelson, J.T. (1995). *The U.S. Intelligence Community – third edition.* Westview Press, Boulder.
Roberts, P., Webber, J. (1999). Visual Truth in the Digital Age: Towards a protocol for Image Ethics, *Australian Computer Journal,* **31**:3; 78-82
Rothkopf, D.J. (1999). The Disinformation Age, *Foreign Policy,* **114**, 82-96.
Schwartau, W. (1996). *Information Warfare – second edition.* Thunder's Mouth Press, New York.
Severin, W.J., Tankard, J.W. (1992) *Communication Theories: Origins, Methods, and Uses in the Mass Media – Third Edition.* Longmans Publishing Publishing Group, New York.
Ulfelder, S (1997). Lies, damn lies and the Internet, *Computerworld,* **31**:28, 75-77.
Waltz, E. (1998). *Information Warfare – Principles and Operations.* Artech House, Norwood.
Winkler, I. (1997). *Corporate Espionage,* Prima Publishing, USA.

# Intranet Security from the Organizational Point of View
# - The Re-emerging Insider Threat

Jorma Kajava

University of Oulu, Department of Information Processing Science, Linnanmaa,
FIN-90014 Oulu University, Box 3000, FINLAND
E-mail: jorma.kajava@ oulu.fi

## Abstract

This paper discusses the three dimensions of information security: confidentiality, integrity and availability. The key to understanding Intranet security involves recognizing the crucial differences between Intranets and the Internet and the various co-operation possibilities that virtual networks offer. The specific security threats of Intranets can be found in communications, software, data and operations security. When protection technologies and tools against criminals outside organizations have improved, the new emerging threat is insiders. In this paper, we shall put forward some ideas concerning protection against such threats.

## Keywords

Information Security, Intranets, Insider Threats

## 1. Introduction

The use of Intranets as internal information transmission channels within organizations serves to emphasize the importance of their secure realization. Information security threats between Intranets and other networks and information systems are rather similar. The technology used in Intranets and the way that technology is used comprises a new threat source. Information security solutions in Intranets are based both on experiences gained from the Internet and on new solutions designed particularly for Intranets. Special areas of interest within Intranet security are communications, software, data and operations security. By researching these four areas, we hope to find usage differences in information security solutions between Intranets and the Internet.

## 2. Intranets versus the Internet

Intranets have been defined as internal communication systems of organizations based on the standards of the Internet and World Wide Web (WWW) (Telleen, 1996). Intranets are based on Internet technology, i.e., technologies that all together generate the Internet (Hinrichs, 1997). For example, Internet routers and their communications connections constitute a part of this technology. Intranets could also be defined as the use of Internet technology in organizational networks (Levitt, 1996). In yet another sense, Intranets could be viewed as private networks based on WWW servers (Pal, 1996).

By combining all these definitions, Intranets could be regarded as internal information systems owned by single organizations employing Internet technology. And like the Internet, Intranets may also be global. Communications between the various sites of an organization are transmitted via its computer network or via the Internet.

As a conclusion, we offer the following definition:

*An Intranet is an internal computer system based on Internet technology and owned by a single organization. Outsiders have strongly restricted access to the Intranet. The communication networks of the Intranet are based on local networks at the different sites of the organization and the interconnecting networks between them. Communication between the remote sites of the organization is carried out via the Internet, the network of the organization or a hired network supplied by a network operator. The user interface consists of WWW browsers, enabling the transmission of text, voice and image files.*

Although this definition does not include a reference to the technical background of Intranets, a measure of technical knowledge is necessary for understanding and detecting threats posed by the technology.

What makes Intranets particularly attractive targets for external and internal attacks is the internal information of the organization. The use of Intranets as internal information systems emphasizes the importance of threats against Intranets from within organizations. It goes without saying that the connection to other networks outside an organization must be designed very carefully during the Intranet construction process. However, the same careful design and construction work is necessary even when implementing connections to other networks within the organization. A potential attacker working inside the organization should not find it any easier to gain access to confidential information. Most networks are protected against external attacks, while failing to address insider attacks adequately. Such internal attacks tend to be underestimated, although can be extremely harmful to the organization.

The main idea of Intranets is the same as that of the Internet, i.e., to facilitate the flow of information. Intranets enable users to keep in touch with physically remote sites of their organizations by using the Internet or other communication networks, which simplifies the transmission of information between the different sites. When using the Internet, the information security threats posed by the Internet to the organization must be borne in mind at all times. For example, the Internet service could be shut down for a while constituting a severe threat for the availability of information.

## 3. Intranets and organizational personnel

The way an organizational Intranet is used has great effect on how the personnel perceives the system. Thus, the following arrangements in the personnel policy must be carefully considered:

- How to organize the technical maintenance of the Intranet
- How to produce information from systems
- How to publish information on the Intranet
- How to use the Intranet.

As far as the ease of use in information maintenance is concerned, the optimum situation would include that all information producers on the Intranet would transfer their documents to the right place in the system and delete them when they become obsolete. This would enable maintenance personnel to concentrate their efforts on the technical administration of the Intranet. However, the free presentation of documents on Intranets is not a good option from the point of view of information security. Lack of content control could result in the publication of incorrect information either intentionally or unintentionally. This, in turn, could have an adverse effect on the organization, for example, in making decisions concerning the development of new products.

The lines of responsibility for the logical design of the system must be defined. Those in charge should make administrative decisions concerning the Intranet and make plans for dividing the activities of the Intranet to accommodate different user groups.

Intranet users comprise the fourth group of people involved. Users do not produce new materials, they only use the information produced by others.

## 4. Information Security Threats in Intranets

The use of Intranets as internal information channels emphasizes the importance of information security. The assets held on internal Intranets may increase the interest of potential misusers. The protection of Intranets and the data and information transmitted via them is an extremely important consideration. Various threats endanger the confidentiality, integrity and availability of information.

There are several ways of classifying information security threats. In this research, we use the following classification: threats based on technology (WWW technology, software, software code under process, telecommunications and viruses), threats based on human activities and natural phenomena.

### 4.1 Threats based on human activities

Hacking comprises the most serious threat for the modern society in the next millennium. All other types of harm may be derived to hacking. Thus, hackers may be behind virus attacks, software piracy, theft, information misuse and sabotage.

Hackers exploit human illiteracy and weaknesses in computer systems to gain access to these systems. Hackers may study the system they attack, damage it or steal information held on it (Simonds, 1996) causing harm to the owner of the system. Even if a hacker does not cause any damage, there will be expenses for the owners as they have to study whether any damage has occurred or not.

Using the Internet as a part of an Intranet poses a serious threat, because the Internet is inherently nonsecure. As a result, users must be very careful particularly in encrypting their communications. Imitation (spoofing), reply (rapid fire), alteration of message contents (superzapping), prevention of service availability and active and passive wiretapping are among the most malicious threats. Wiretapping, for example, could lead to a situation where strategic knowledge regarding an organization gets in the hands of outsiders, if communication encryption is not implemented by means of strong encryption methods.

Hacker tools, although developed for the Internet, are also usable on Intranets. They can be software or hardware based or a combination of both. Their authorized use includes finding and correcting information security weaknesses on Intranets. However, they also anable insiders to hack such communication systems and access information which they are not authorized to access. Hacker tools can be divided into six categories:

- Tools for finding attack objects (searching telephone numbers and network addresses)
- Password tools (stealing and opening passwords)
- Communication tools (following, disturbing and misleading communications)
- Security hole tools (searching and "defining" security holes)
- Damage and teasing tools (viruses, worms and chain letters)
- Other tools (based on well-known information security holes of systems and combination tools) (Miettinen, 1995).

Threats caused by people, employees in particular, can be much more serious on Intranets than on the Internet. Personnel invariably constitutes the most severe information security threat. Intranets have made it easier for employees to access information, but they have also made it easier to misuse this information.

Dishonesty among personnel is always an information security threat. After all, it is easier for corporate personnel to gain access to sensitive information than outsiders. Authorized users may be tempted to misuse vital information. Even unauthorized members of staff may access sensitive information, if, for example, they know the weaknesses of the system.

Also carelessness and negligence among personnel may result in sensitive information landing in the hands of unauthorized persons. Papers left lying on a table are easy to read and copy. Printing a document into a wrong address may also have an undesirable outcome.

A low level of knowledge concerning security among personnel is a clear vulnerability. This is partly a result of the current employment situation in which it might in some cases be a problem finding educated personnel to recruit. Shortcomings in training and education combined with the use of uneducated personnel in the realization and maintenance of Intranets may seriously undermine the security of the information held on Intranets.

The use of outsiders in the construction and maintenance of Intranets could also be detrimental to information confidentiality. Therefore, security concerns are of utmost importance in designing outsourcing and in drawing outsourcing contracts.

## 5. Protection Methods

In an attempt to provide protection against Intranet security threats a number of governments have adopted the model of the Canadian Mounted Police (1981) based on eight security levels. The most important levels in Intranets are those of communications, software, data and operations security. These are the areas in which Intranet security solutions differ most from their Internet counterparts.

### 5.1 Communications protection

Communications security is very important, particularly when the Internet is employed as a communication channel between the different sites of an organization. The same solutions are applicable for isolating Intranets from external networks than in protecting internal networks. Intranets may be protected against external hacking and other information security threats by firewall hardware. Firewalls are used to control traffic in communication networks (Siyan and Hare, 1995), and they do it by examining the communication passing through them and by imposing certain restrictions on it. Such communications as fail to follow the restrictions are filtered out. Firewalls use one or more of the following basic technologies:

- Router-and-server-based packet filtering
- Server-based communications filtering
- Server-based communication transmission for every single application software (Bernstein et al, 1996).

The various parts of an Intranet can be isolated with firewalls thus increasing information security against internal misuse. Such firewalls also prevent external intruders from moving on the Intranet.

An organization's network addresses can be encrypted for outsiders using address translation. In address translation, all data packages have an identical network address when they leave the network of the organization. Address conversion disables outsiders from making decisions based on real network addresses and the number of addresses within the organization (Bernstein et al, 1996).

Encryption precludes external parties from examining the contents of messages in networks and information in systems. Encryption is realized by means of encryption methods based on encrypting algorithms. The most common methods are DES, IDEA and RSA. One popular method on the Internet is SSL, which is used in WWW contacts. In Intranet communications, encryption works with application software that uses some encryption algorithm. It is of paramount importance that the encryption software fulfils the requirements of the organization and is applicable to the intended application area. The strength of the encryption is particularly important, if the organization uses the Internet as a communication channel.

Another method of protecting communication on the Internet is known as tunnelling. In this method, the data area of a communication packet contains another communication packet in its entirety. To enhance the degree of protection, a tunnelling communication contact may also be encrypted.

### 5.2 Software protection

Development is faster within software security than in any other area of Intranet security. The application software used on Intranets constitutes the most salient difference between Intranets and the Internet. In practice, Internet software security equals browser and server software security and security of software for producing WWW applications. Also Intranet software security is based on application programmes in browsers. This fact has far-reaching consequences, because many Intranet applications are tailor-made for one single organization.

It is essential to establish the trustworthiness of CGI scripts in Intranet applications. If possible, scripts readily available on the Internet should not be used at all. Erroneous software code may unintentionally open a trap door for intruders. The following considerations should be attended to in Intranet applications involving CGI operations:

- CGI scripts must be compiled, not interpreted
- The application software must always check the correctness of user inputs, before allowing the inputs to operate
- The minimum requirement involves that the right formulation and length of content of every input is controlled
- No assumptions should be made with compiled scripts. (Pabrai & Gurbani 1996).

All critical Intranet applications must require user identification. Together with password controls, user identification provides protection against unauthorized use of applications. From the organizational point of view, the right to use critical applications could be enhanced by one-time passwords.

Audit trails record exceptional incidents and other security relevant events in the use of Intranet applications. Audit trails should be produced and stored for an agreed period of time to assist in eventual investigations and to monitor access control by recording, for example, all dates and times for logon and logoff.

Virus protection is an important aspect of Intranet security. Intranets make it easy to transfer documents and files between the different sites of organizations. Moreover, e-mail attachments can also be used as a vehicle for transferring computer viruses and infecting new computer systems and networks.

### 5.3 Data protection

Appropriate data protection decreases the probability of internal information security threats. Personnel should have guidelines concerning all materials that can be published on a corporate Intranet. A simple, yet effective way of providing a security classification on an Intranet is to divide all corporate data into data that can be published and data that cannot be published on the Intranet. When publishing confidential data on the Intranet, the limitations of user rights are an essential consideration. There must also be clear guidelines about the deletion of data on the Intranet. In addition, all data published on the Intranet must be backed up using appropriate back-up media. Finally, user rights for every Intranet directory and file must also be defined carefully.

### 5.4 Operations protection

Intranet operations security consists of activities which advance security without influencing practices. Thus, security threats posed by corporate personnel should be prevented in a simple and efficient manner without compromising the efficiency of the system as perceived by the users. The right to use the different parts of an Intranet and the right to access each data directory must be defined for every employee in accordance with to his/her tasks (Code of Practice, 1993). Remote access must also be carefully regulated to ensure security.

The design and implementation of effective user rights management is in many ways a demanding process, but a successful solution significantly decreases information security threats posed by corporate personnel.

## 6. Conclusion

Intranets have gained in popularity during the past few years. Unfortunately, also the number of security problems has increased. From the organizational point of view, these problems call for particular Intranet solutions. Intranets started out as private communication channels, but their use has been extended to include DSS, CSCW, expert systems, database maintenance tools, private phone catalogues and user guidelines.

Intranet security solutions are similar to those of the Internet. However, as the usage area of Intranets differs from that of the Internet, it is important to re-examine well-known security threats on the Internet and try to find ways of protecting Intranets against these threats. Intranets make organizations more vulnerable to internal threats.

In 1995, Internet security came under discussion. Owing to poor security, a lot of organizations started seeking better security solutions for their private networks. One measure that is widely used today is firewalls. Efficient as they might be, firewalls are no panacea. As a result, Internet security remains relatively poor, although there are a number of successful software and hardware protection solutions in use. At the same time, also protocols have improved their security-related definions. Consequently, if we exclude "professional" criminals, amateur criminals find it exceedingly hard to gain access to organizational networks.

It is a sad fact that the difference between good and bad escapes a lot of people. During the mainframe period 20 years ago, insiders posed the worst threat to organizations. And today, barring professional criminals, insiders have regained their positions as the most common threat to organizations.

So, after all those years, we are back in square one. The question is, what can be done to remedy the situation. In my view, we need more education and training inside organizations, and we need information security awareness programmes. In addition, novel network solutions enable us to understand the importance of the non-technical implications of information security.

After every developmental stage in information and communication, people seem to return to their old ways. Perhaps we should not talk so much about the intelligence of the human race, if people are incapable of learning the basic rules of society.

## 7. References

Bernstein, T., Bhimani, A. B., Schults, E. and Siegel, C. A. (1996), Internet security for business. John Wiley & Sons Inc.

Code of Practice, (1993), A Code of Practice for Information Security Management. Department of Trade and Industry. GBIS. PD 0003, England.

Cortese, A. (1996), Here comes the Intranet. Business Week. February 26, 1996.

Hinrichs, R. J. (1997), Intranets: What´s The Bottom Line? Prentice Hall.

Levitt, L. (1996), Intranets: Internet Technologies Deployed Behind the Firewall for Corporate Productivity. http://www.process.com/Intranets/wp2.htp

Miettinen, J. E. (1995), Internet Hackers Basic Tools. HETKY. Helsinki..

Pal, A., Ring, K. and Downes, V. (1996), Intranets for Business Applications; User and Supplier Opportunities. Ovum Ltd.

Remes, T. (1997), Intranet Information Security Threats and the Protection against them. University of Oulu, Department of Information Processing Science, Oulu.

Royal Canadian Mounted Police  (1981), Security in the EDP Environment. Security Information Publication, Second Edition. Gendarmere Royale du Canada. Canada, October.

Siyan, S. and  Hare, C. (1995), Internet Firewalls and Network Security. Indianapolis, USA: New Riders Publishing.

Telleen, S. T. (1996), The Intranet Architecture: Managing information in the new paradigm. Sunnyvale, California. Amdahl corporation.  http://www.amdahl.com/doc.products/bsg/intra/infra.html

# A System for Self-Revocation of Digital Certificates

O. Cánovas[1], A. F. Gómez[2], and G. Martínez[2]

[1]Dept. Ingeniería y Tecnología de Computadores
[2]Dept. Informática, Inteligencia Artificial y Electrónica
University of Murcia, Murcia, Spain
e-mail: {ocanovas,skarmeta,gremar}@dif.um.es

## Abstract

Nowadays, it is common the idea that a certificate is a digitally signed statement binding the identity of the key-holder to a public key. Digital certificates provide, among other services, a method for authentication of subjects not previously known each other, and revocation is an essential feature of an authentication service. Revocation is necessary because valid information changes with time, due to a compromise of an entity private key or to another reason. When a compromise is discovered, quick mechanisms for revocation of certificates are required to prevent unauthorized use of resources. This paper presents a distributed system for self-revocation of X.509 certificates, an approach which increases the availability of revocation mechanisms.

## Keywords

Revocation, PGP, X.509, Servlets, Trusted Directory

## 1. Introduction

Public key cryptography is widely recognized as being a fundamental technology on which several essential security services can be built, such as authentication, integrity, non-repudiation and confidentiality. But in order to give users the necessary level of assurance (or trust) much work still needs to be done to specify and implement the security policies, procedures and infrastructures that underlie the use of the technology.

Crucial to the operation of a global public key cryptosystem on the Internet is a practical and reliable method of publishing the public keys, called a Public Key Infrastructure (PKI). As it is known, there are two basic operations common to all PKIs: certification and validation. How these two operations are implemented is the basic defining characteristic of all PKIs.

Traditionally, most of research efforts have been focused on certification, since this is the fundamental function of all PKIs. It is the way by which public key values, and information belonging to these values, are published. However, mechanisms for revocation are also needed, because it is possible that the information contained in a certificate becomes unexpectedly invalid. The most troubling scenario involves the compromise of a private key, so without an effective revocation capability, a security solution based on PKIs is at risk of general system compromise.

However, it seems that there is not a standard solution for revocation mechanisms. One revocation technique is the issuance of Certificate Revocation Lists (Hosley et al, 1998), but as it is explained in different papers in the literature (Rivest, 1998), it is possible to eliminate them in favour of other mechanisms. Even, if we assumed the use of CRLs or another technique in order to notify revocations, there would be another question related to the current proposals for revocation mechanisms: availability. Nowadays, it seems that the main X.509-based solutions, like Netscape Certificate Management System, are centralized systems including privileged agents and elements that manage revocations. If registration authorities also are used, there will be more elements able to deal with revocations when the information contained in a certificate becomes unexpectedly invalid. However, a question emerges from the analysis of these solutions: What is the real availability of the revocation system? Is it 24 hours, seven days a week? It seems that the answer is NO. These systems have privileged agents able to request and issue revocations using authorized certificates. The reliability of revocations is determined by the availability of these privileged agents.

Who should be allowed to declare a key as compromised or lost, and on what basis? In current systems based on the X.509 standard, staff responsible for registration or certification authorities (privileged users) perform this task (if it was specified in the certification policy). In key-centric PGP (Callas et al, 1998), key holders are responsible for notifying their correspondents of a key compromise: a form of self-revocation. We think that the key pair owner should be able (think for a while in an analogous case: compromise of a credit card) to unilaterally revoke the certificate when his private key has been compromised.

The solution presented in this paper is based on PGP self-revocations, but oriented to X.509 infrastructures. We consider that the key owner should be able to self-revoke his certificate without paying attention to questions like business hours. Our service is divided into two phases: first, users store their self-revocation requests securely, using a client authenticated connection, based on SSL (Alan et al, 1996); then, when a certificate must be revoked, users can issue his request entering a login and password determined during the first phase. This service is part of an innovative PKI designed by our research group in order to establish a high-security infrastructure for e-commerce applications.

## 2. A Self-Revocation model

The design described in this paper is focused on revocation of people certificates. The main idea is to provide people a mechanism to revoke digital certificates in a user friendly, non-attendant, and simple way.

This model is one part of an innovative infrastructure that is being developed. In order to provide a global vision, and to understand some components and processes of the model, it is necessary to make a brief description of some of the main elements belonging to this infrastructure. Our PKI main objective is to establish a high-security infrastructure for e-commerce applications. It is determined by previous designs constituting the current PKI of our University (Cánovas et al, 1999), but adding some elements in order to increase the security capabilities, such as a trusted directory (Myers, 1998), validity control based on re-issued certificates, a custom implementation of PKCS#11 standard (RSA, 1997), and so on.

Our self-revocation system is similar to make one's will. In a first phase, one user establishes his will (a self-revocation request) and the system saves it in a safe place. Later, the user could change his will (a self-revocation request modification). Then, when the user identity is "dead" (compromise of his private key), an authorized person (in our case, the user himself) can publish user's will (issuance of revocation).

Furthermore, as the World Wide Web is one of the most widely used services of the Internet, we have developed this model based on web technology. Web browsers, such as Netscape, provide a very familiar interface to users, and will contribute toward fulfilling the goals of ease of use and accessibility of the self-revocation system. Thus, a set of HTML forms and servlets constitute the system core, in addition to other elements like our cryptographic module implementing PKCS#11 standard.

Our proposal can be implemented safely using these elements since they provide all the security services needed. Specifically, this implementation assures robust authentication from client to servlets and viceversa, confidentiality to exchanged information, access control and information integrity.

## 3. Main components

This scenario is based on two kinds of elements: servlets and HTML pages. As we explained above, WWW represents a user-friendly platform for this service, and some technologies such as SSL, secure web servers (like Apache) and cryptographic standards (PKCS#11) provide a secure framework in order to achieve basic security capabilities.

Figure 1 shows the collaboration scheme of the overall scenario. In this illustration we can appreciate how the communication is performed, what kind of element is involved, what is the information exchanged by the processes, types of authentication used, and concerned databases.

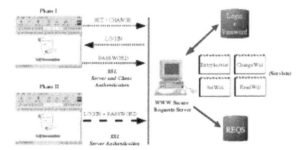

**Figure 1. Self-revocations scenario**

### 3.1 HTML Pages

First, we are going to make a brief description of the HTML pages involved in the scenario. Data entered in these HTML forms is submitted via SSL using the *HTTP post* method. The user must perform this connection using the digital certificate that finally could be revoked by this service.

**Main page**

From this page it is possible to access both first and second phase. There are two buttons, one for each option.

**Page to set the password**

The user can establish, in this page, the password protecting his self-revocation request. Furthermore, this page gives to the user the login related to his request, which is composed by information contained in his digital certificate.

**Page to change the password**

The user is able to change his previously entered password, or even to destroy his current self-revocation request. In order to do this, the user must enter the last password (and login) protecting his request.

**Page to issue the request**

This page throws the revocation of the user digital certificate. In order to accomplish it, the user has to enter the right login and password pair. This information is submitted via HTTPS, but using only a server side authentication (previously explained cases use both types, client and server authentication), since, most probably, the user could not use his private key to establish any secure communication.

**3.2 Servlets**

The function of these servlets is the management of self-revocation requests. There are different servlets for each operation, but the most important ones are:

- *EntryServlet*. Its function is to verify the current state of a user request, in order to return a suitable HTML page to the user (a page to set the password, or to change it).
- *SetWill*. This servlet creates an entry for the user in the self-revocation requests database, and sets the password protecting his request.
- *ChangeWill*. This servlet changes the password protecting a request, or even deletes such request.
- *ReadWill*. The function of this servlet is to activate the process that makes effective the revocation of the digital certificate.

# 4. Operations in details

If a user wants to self-revoke his digital certificate, he must use this system twice. In a first stage, when his digital certificate is still valid, the user sets the password protecting his self-revocation request. Previously, it is performed a SSL authentication for both communicating elements. At the second stage, when the digital identity of the user has been compromised, he must enter his login and password in order to revoke his digital certificate. Now, this communication cannot be done using client authentication (only SSL server authentication), since the user identity is not trustworthy if his private key has been compromised. If SSL were not used, the system would be reduced to an interchange of plain text, without authentication or confidentiality. The system stages are explained below in detail.

### 4.1 The access point to the system

The access point to the system is an HTML page which presents two links for both phases. On the one hand, if it is the first time the user logs in the service, or if he wants to change the password protecting his request, he must then enter in the first phase. On the other hand, if a situation like a private key compromise happened, the user must enter in the second phase. This page is only accessible via the HTTPS protocol, in order to provide confidentiality, integrity and server authentication.

### 4.2 First phase

The first phase has two main pages. One is for the first password establishment, and the other one allows to change the previous password or even to delete the request. From the first page, the servlet *EntryServlet* returns to the client an HTML page annunciating the login (built using information contained in the user digital certificate) univocally related to the digital certificate presented to the system. This page also contains an input field to enter the password. When the user submits the information, the *SetWill* servlet creates a new entry for the user in the self-revocation requests database. This entry contains the login and a hash, MD5 digest (Rivest, 1992), of the password entered by the user.

From the second page, when a first password was established, *EntryServlet* returns to the client an HTML page with three input boxes: the first for the login, and the second for the current password protecting the request. In the third box the user can introduce the new password, if he wants to change the previous one. On the other hand, if the user was to delete his current request, he has to select this option using a checkbox field. When the user submits the information, the *ChangeWill* servlet checks if the password (its digest) matches with the one stored in the database. It also verifies, with information contained in the user digital certificate, if the user presents the same certificate than the time before.

Both cases require an SSL connection, with client and server authentication. Some servlets obtain information from client certificates, in order to manage the database. Moreover, *ChangeWill* and *SetWill* check if a SSL communication, with full authentication, has been performed between the client browser and the web server. In our system, built upon *Apache + JServ* for servlets running, it is performed analyzing some web server attributes, such as *SSL_PROTOCOL* or *SSL_CLIENT_S_DN*.

### 4.3. Second Phase

This phase enables users to revoke one of their digital certificates. Obviously, it is necessary that the user had created his self-revocation request. Only those certificates used in the first phase will have the chance to be self-revoked.

From the HTML page corresponding to the second phase, it is possible to throw the revocation process. The user has to enter the right login and password pair. This information is submitted via HTTPS, but using only a server side authentication as we commented in a previous section. This data is received by *ReadWill* servlet, and is compared to the one contained in the database. If the current password digest is equal than the digest stored in the database, the involved request is supplied to the revocation subsystem. This subsystem is a set of autonomous processes which propagate all the events related to revocations, and delete the related digital certificates from repositories like the Trusted Directory.

## 5. Conclusions

The need for fast and efficient revocations is not yet clearly understood by many organizations, but will become crucial since public key systems are increasingly used to protect valuable assets, and attackers learn to profit from compromised keys. In order to avoid this kind of situation, it is necessary to design and develop schemes that increase the availability of revocation mechanisms. This distributed system for self-revocations of certificates increases availability, since it solves common problems derived from centralized schemes, like revocations based on key elements not continuously available. It is an additional mechanism to issue and publish revocations, which should not be seen as an isolated scenario for revocations. This is an additional mechanism to the traditional revocation systems (based on RA or CA), which are also required.

The solution is simple, easy to use, and complete (despite it is not supported by common certification systems). As we explained previously, there are three elements that manage the system trust. First, the web browser must verify the web server identity. To do this task, it is necessary to trust on some of the certification authorities included between the web server digital certificate and the root CA. Then, the web server must (in the first phase) identify every client connecting to the service. In order to do it, it checks if certificates presented by users belong to any recognized CA. Finally, servlets are responsible for verifying login and password pairs, assuring the SSL utilization, and avoiding possible forgery mechanisms.

This requires each user to have a World Wide Web browser supporting forms and SSL v.3.0, such as Netscape Navigator. The reasons to choice a web-based user interface are: familiarity to users, functionality (most of the web browsers provide security capabilities), and availability (most of the web browsers are widely available and platform independent).

Nowadays, several control access systems are based on passwords protecting resources. This situation leads to users having to remember many passwords (at most one for each resource they access) and, normally, passwords have to be communicated securely to each user. In the current Internet this means to use an out-of-band (non-Internet) medium. If the password is ever changed, each user must again be securely contacted. However, our system provides a secure method for password establishment, using SSL protocol in order to assure confidentiality, integrity, and authentication. Inside our PKI, each user has to remember only this password, since the other services are certification-based.

We will continue developing our proposal of a PKI suitable for e-commerce applications, based on the idea of positive sentences. Self-revocations service is only one scenario of six proposed. Currently, we are developing a service for multicast notification of events such as revocations, certificate renewals, etc.

## 6. Acknowledgements

This work has been partially supported by TEL-1FD97-1426 FEDER project (PISCIS), and AP98 22993030 MEC grant.

## 7. References

Alan A. O., Freier P., Kocher P. C. (1996) *The SSL Protocol Version 3.0*, Internet Draft.

Callas J., Donnerhacke L., Finney H., Thayer R. (1998) RFC 2440, *OpenPGP Message Format*.

Cánovas O., Gómez A.F., Martínez G. et al. (1999) "Providing security to university environment communications", *Proceedings of TERENA-NORDUnet Networking Conference*.

Hosley R., Ford, W., Solo D. (1998) *Internet Public Key Infrastructure, Part I: X.509 Certificate and CRL Profile*, Internet Draft, draft-ietf-pkix-ipki-part1-04.

Myers M. (1998) *"Revocation: Options and Challenges"*. *Lecture Notes, Financial Cryptography*.

Rivest. R. (1992) RFC 1321, *The MD5 Message-Digest Algorithm*.

Rivest R.L. (1998) "Can we eliminate Certificate Revocation Lists?". *Lecture Notes, Financial Cryptography*.

RSA Laboratories. (1997) *PKCS#11: Cryptographic Token Interface Standard*. Version 2.0.

Self-Revocations Home Page. URL: http://ants.dif.um.es/circus/pki. October 1999.

# ISDN Channel Security Demonstration Board

R. Ingruber, H. Leitold, W. Mayerwieser, U. Payer,

K.C. Posch, R. Posch, J. Wolkerstorfer

Institute for Applied Information Processing and Communications (IAIK)

Graz University of Technology

e-mail: Udo.Payer@iaik.at

## Abstract

Plain old telephone services (POTS) get more and more replaced by technologies, that are capable to integrate voice, data, and video communication services. Due to the digital signalling and communication schemes used, the integrated services digital network (ISDN) represents a better embedding for such communication services, resulting in a better quality of services offered to the users, or to transmit confidential information if necessary or desired. This makes confidential communication a challenging basic condition.

This paper presents a Security Demonstration Board, to show ISDN channel encryption —based on a special encryption chip that was developed to satisfy ATM requests as well as other requirements— supporting different proprietary data interfaces. The prior purpose of the presented Security Demonstration Board was to satisfy ISDN requirements. But during developing an ISDN Channel Security Module, we recognized the great variety of possibilities to use this basic approach at any speed (starting at 0 up to 155Mbps) and for any thinkable service (e.g. ISDN, xDSL, etc.).
Confidential transmission, like voice facsimile and binary data can be transmitted by using standard hardware and software components to link LANs or single workstations by using secure channels or to provide confidential communication channels to make use of standard communication devices —such as telephone, answering machines, fax, etc.— in a secure manner.

This scheme aims to point out the common use of encryption hardware in the application areas of any digital service, based on B-ISDN security specification.
The presented Security Demonstration Board —by the means of ISDN channel encryption— is focused towards independence of both, the hardware of the end user device, and the application utilizing different transport services. Therefore, the data stream is intercepted, and encrypted by a high-speed data encryption standard (DES/TripleDES) encryption hardware, addressed by using well-defined and standardized interfaces. Beyond this, simple integration of any parallel or serial interfaces —by using programmable hardware devices (FPGAs)— can instantly support different services.

## Keywords

ISDN, ATM, Security Module

# 1. Introduction

This paper will show the simple way of adapting the Presentation Board, to support channel security based on different services, by the means of ISDN channel security. The reference model —depicted below— visualizes the embedding of an ISDN Channel Security Module in a conventional ISDN Network Terminator (NT) based on ISDN reference points [9]. As shown in the figure below, the ISDN Channel Security Module can be considered as an additional hardware component, inserted between ISDN reference points S and U.

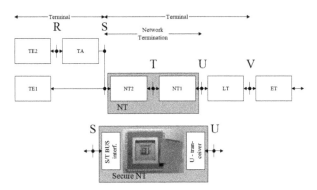

Figure 1: Embedding of Secure NT into the ISDN Reference Point Model

For want of obligatory standards in the field of confidential communication in ISDN networks, the ATM Forum Specification Version 1.0 [3] was the basis of this ISDN Channel Security Module.

Call establishment, security negotiation as well as call release phases are the main functionalities of an ISDN Channel Security Module. These functions are implemented on the Security Demonstration Board and can be subdivided into several phases. In the course of a confidential and secure communication, several states of this communication protocol are passed through, under the control of a finite state machine. This state machine can be described by six basic states, listed in the figure below.

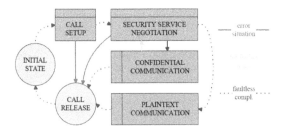

Figure 2: Secure NT State Diagram

In a sense of definition and notation of meanings, this paper will give a global overview of the ISDN Channel Security Module, based on this finite state machine. Phases of relevance will be specified in a more detailed way in the following section.

## 2. Hardware Prototype

In connection with specifying the interfaces of the ISDN Channel Security Module, to get access of B- and D-channel information, and to verify the functional correctness of the whole arrangement, a hardware prototype was developed. Based on test results on this hardware prototype, the following schematic assembly of an ISDN Channel Security test board can be depicted by figure 3.

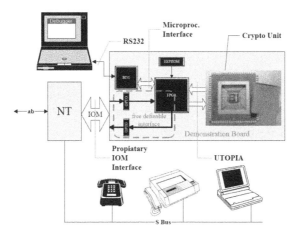

Figure 3: Installation of the Channel Security Module Demonstration Board into ISDN environments (SecNT)

It's easy to find out the proprietary IOM interface [10] between the S/T-bus and the U-transiver, which forms the basis of B- and D-channel data access and is intercepted for encryption purpose. B-channel data can be received on the Rx IOM-interface, changed by the encryption unit and sent by the Tx IOM-interface in the case of downstream data transfer. The same reflections can be done for the upstream in the same manner. A more detailed description is given in the following sections.

### 2.1. IOM-Interception and Arrangement of Security Module Components

On condition that B1- and B2-channels are threaded in a separate way, we have to distinguish between three data flows, corresponding to three basic phases (Call Setup Phase, Security Service Negotiation Phase, and Confidential Communication Phase). A result of the common consideration is the basic structure of the ISDN Channel Security module, depicting the upstream and downstream direction of B1- B2- and D-channel data flows.

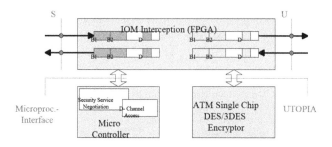

**Figure 4: IOM Interception Module and its interfaces**

## 2.2. Synergy with other Projects

Based on an ATM encryption chip, we would think that bandwidth and capacity is sufficient to meet the requirements to encrypt data of an ISDN Basic Rate Interface (BRI) with two 64 kBit/s B-channels and one D-channel for the upstream and downstream simultaneously.

In the sense of synergy between the ISDN Channel Security Module and a current ACTS-project "Secure Communication in ATM Networks (SCAN)" and based on strong interactions between the ISDN Channel Security Specification and the ATM Forum Security Specification 1.0 we are endeavored to profit from a resulting ATM DES/TripleDES encryption chip.

This high-speed ATM encryption unit (HADES) is based on a standardized interface - the Universal Test and Operations Physical Interface for ATM (UTOPIA) [1][2]. This interface is designed to schedule incoming and outgoing data on byte level with a clock rate of 25 MHz. The UTOPIA interfaces for up- and downstream are completely independent and do not influence each other. The main objective of these crypto chip was, to support Data Encryption Standard (DES) [8]/Triple DES [5], featuring Electronic Code Book (ECB) and Cipher Block Chaining (CBC) as operational modes [7]. This Very Large Scaled Integrated (VLSI) circuit is to be specifically designed for ATM requirements, which is mainly the high bandwidth (155Mbps). Moreover the key agility —required to switch rapidly between the session keys, that are negotiated uniquely for each virtual circuit (VC)— forms a basic requirement for the encryption unit. Therefore, this encryption unit is called key-agile [6] high-speed ATM DES/TripleDES (HADES). Thus, this unit excellently meets the requirements of a two channel ISDN encryption as well.

The loading of a whole 8 byte DES-block must be finished in less than 320ns. Thus, the whole time of loading, encrypting (decrypting) and unloading the DES-block is by far shorter than the arrival time of a single byte via IOM interface. Based on this circumstance, a simple DES-block buffer on the receiving- and transmitting interface of the IOM interception element is more than sufficient. Conflicts between upstream and downstream are excluded by a common control machine for both directions (ARBITER).

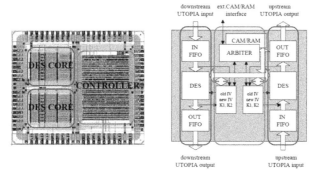

downstream UTOPIA input   ext.CAM/RAM interface   upstream UTOPIA output

**Figure 5: High Speed ATM DES/3DES Encryption Unit (HADES)**

Additional delay caused by the ISDN Channel Security Module is most of the time a result of incoming an outgoing DES-block buffer and less a result of delay by data encryption. To receive a single DES-block, consisting of 8 octets, received during 8 IOM frames with a duration of 125µs, results in a DES-block time of 1ms. Subsequent storage in the outgoing buffer increases the time of delay to 2ms by paying attention, that encryption time can be neglected. This delay is symmetric since up- and downstream is under common control and less than 25ms (500ms with Echo Cancellation) requested by ITU-T G.164.

The way how to load the corresponding key or key pair, as well as the alternating loading of B1- and B2-channel DES-blocks will be described in a further description. ISDN Cannel Security control states are enumerated as follows:

## 2.3. Initial State

In principle, all B-channels are treated in the same way, and are completely independent of each other - this means that all B-channels of a BRI (B1+B2) can be considered as independent connection and are capable to handle different services, based on different security levels or plaintext communication. Thus, the principle approach is independent of party access nature. The dependence on the number of simultaneously established B-channels is only limited by the control unit, which has to handle all B-channel information as well as to store the corresponding states.

In this document, a transmission on the local subscriber loop, starting at the local subscribers and ending at the central office is called "upstream" and called "downstream" in the reverse direction.

The initial state of a B-channel is characterized by a closed connection and the key pool of the encryption unit doesn't contain a valid session key for none of all B-channels. During this state, the access control unit is tracing the D-channel and is searching for active or passive connect-requests. In the case of a detected request for connect, the encryption unit is changing to the Call Setup State. The B-channel allocation to the corresponding logical connection must be done during this Call Setup State.

### 2.4. Call Setup State

During the Call Setup Phase, the ISDN Channel Security Module has to fulfill two major tasks:

- o **ISDN Call Establishment:** is dealing with the establishment of ISDN connections according to ITU-T Standards (Q.931, etc.).
- o **Security Support Services:** are services to provide communication channels, which are of important use to identify secure connections, negotiation of relevant parameters as well as servicing relevant parameter to maintain secure channels.

Only after a successful termination of a Call Setup State, the finite state machine is allowed to switch over to the Security Service Negotiation State.

### 2.5. Security Services Negotiation State

Once again, the ATM Forum Security Specification 1.0 [3] forms the base for Secure Service Negotiation in connection with the ISDN Secure Channel Module.

Even though the ATM and ISDN characteristics are fundamentally different, the basic principle and interactions in ATM Secure Service Negotiation and its interaction with ISDN Channel Security should be commented now. Security Service Negotiation is based on models of ATM communication channels, which are used to transmit secure information via a negotiation protocols in the case of ATM. Methods of ATM Forum Security Specification 1.0, used in this context, should be summarized here:

- o **Initial Security Services Negotiation:** The negotiation of security service parameter agrees with the ATM Forum Security Specification 1.0 in connection with local exchange offices as well as in connection with terminal equipments in a transparent way, by temporary interrupting the user plane, shortly after establishing a connection.

- o **Embedding of Support Services:** As a layer 2 transport protocol to exchange security services negotiation parameter, a functional reduced HDLC protocol is used.

- o **Security Services Re-negotiation:** Security Services Re-negotiation was not planed for the presented prototype but the idea was noted for further studies.

Based on reflections above, a consolidated specification of Security Service Negotiation and its subdivision in several sectors is given in the following:

- o **Authentication:** Since the chosen Diffie Hellman Key Exchange method is not resistant to Man-in-the-Middle-Attacks, authentication of communication partners is required. So an agent-authentication via Multiple Subscriber Number (MSN) was realized. Thus, the fast prototype is based on Digital Signaling System 7 (DSS-7). Even though not implemented, authentication based on public key methods, specified in ATM Forum Security Specification 1.0 should be the base for further developments. Thus, possible future extensions stays in consistency with present developments with regard to the possibility to include smart cards in the authentication concept.
- o **Channel Identification:** Before establishing a confidential connection, the ISDN Channel Security Module has to identify the communication partner, and has to decide whether plaintext communication or confidential communication has to be selected.

- ○ **Key Exchange:** The exchange of session keys follows in accordance to a process, specified in ATM Forum Specification 1.0. This standard represents a three way-message exchange protocol, as well as an alternative two-way method. Relating to the specified possibilities, certificates, respectively Certificate Revocation Lists (CRL) have to be exchanged. Three-way message exchange protocols have to be preferred, even though this method is not implemented in the fast prototype.
- ○ **Key Management:** Even though Key Management is not a real part of Security Service Negotiation, the Key Management is an integral component of ISDN Channel Security Module and implies the certification infrastructure based on ITU-T X.509.
- ○ **Synchronization:** If Security Services Negotiation phase is finished, the connection is changed into the state of a secure, confidential communication. For that purpose, the ISDN Channel Security Modules on both ends of transmission have to be synchronized.

## 2.6. Confidential Communication State

After successfully terminating the Security Service Negotiation State, confidential transmission of sensitive data can be done during the Confidential Communication State, possibly interrupted by a re-negotiation mechanism:

- ○ **Confidential Communication:** Irrespective of the used terminal equipment (telephone, fax, data, etc.) the ISDN Channel Security Module offers a transparent secure channel. Thus, it is not possible to decide from outside, whether this transparent channel is used for communication between commonly used ISDN devices or is used for confidential communication between two ISDN Channel Security Modules from endpoint-to-endpoint.
- ○ **Security Service Re-negotiation:** As a thinkable, future extension, this mechanism is under discussion to allow a re-negotiation of security characteristics, based on an already established ISDN connection.

## 2.7. Plaintext Communication State

The alternative to confidential communication is plaintext communication. The ISDN Channel Security Module has to decide, if it is possible to establish a secure channel, and whether the second party possesses the same security module, and is interested in confidential communication. Emergency calls are recognized, and SecNT is forced to switch to plaintext communication. This is urgently needed to meet lifeline requirements.

## 2.8. Call Release State

Starting a channel disconnection, the ISDN Channel Security Module or rather the state entry of the corresponding B-channel is changing to Initial State. As a result of active or passive disconnect, we have to distinguish between two events:

- ○ **Regular Channel Disconnection:** In this case, the request for disconnect was caused by the terminal equipment (TE) or respectively signaled by the local exchange office. All Q.931 signaling messages are passed-through unchanged to satisfy the disconnect request.

o **Disconnect by ISDN Channel Security Module:** In the case of malfunction, like a unsuccessful user authentication or caused by a timeout, the ISDN Channel Security Module forces an active disconnect, as a result of the Initial Security Services Negotiation.

## 3. Conclusion

This paper has discussed a project targeting confidential communication in ISDN networks, and has been carried out in cooperation with Telekom Austria. The presented approach of secure ISDN communication is making use of a special ATM encryption chip and is adapting ATM specifications to ISDN requirements. Confidential communication —by using any type of terminal equipment— should be enabled to be done. Intercepting the serial IOM interface, as well as assemble DES encryption blocks with a length of 8 octets, sent to the encryption unit in ATM like cells, was discussed in this paper. The main advantage of the resulting ISDN encryption hardware is the independence from the hardware being used. There are no differences between any types of services, since encryption occurs completely transparent in a network terminator, directly connected to the local loop. This concept doesn't impose limitations in the number of B-channels. Support of primary rate interfaces (PRI 30B+D) may also be thinkable as well as the basic rate Interface (BRI 2B+D), as it was realized by the ISDN Channel Encryption prototype.

## 4. References

[1]     ATM Forum, Utopia Level 1, Version 2.01, af-phy-017.000, The ATM Forum, Technical Committee, (1994).

[2]     ATM Forum, Utopia Level 2, Version 1, af-phy-039.000, The ATM Forum, Technical Committee, (1995).

[3]     ATM Forum, ATM Security Specification Version 1.0, ATM-SEC-01.0100, The ATM Forum, Security Working Group, (1999).

[4]     American National Standard for Data Encryption Algorithm (DEA), ANSI 3.92, American National Standards Institute, (1981).

[5]     W. Tuchman, Hellman Presents no Shortcut Solutions to DES, IEEE Spectrum, vol. 17, no.7, (1979).

[6]     T. D. Tarman, Algorithm-Agile Encryption in ATM Networks, IEEE Computer, September (1998), vol. 31, no. 9, pp. 57-64.

[7]     ANSI, American National Standard for Information Systems-Data Encryption Algorithm-Modes of Operation, ANSI 3.106, American National Standards Institute, (1983).

[8]     ANSI, American National Standard for Data Encryption Algorithm (DEA), ANSI 3.92, American National Standards Institute, (1981).

[9]     ITU-T, B-ISDN Protocol Reference Model and its Application, Recommendation I.321, International Telecommunication Union, Telecommunication Standardization Sector, (1991).

[10]    SIEMENS, IC´s for Communications ISDN Subscriber Access Controller ISAC-R PEB 2085, SIEMENS, Users Manual, (1989).

[11]    Otmar Feger, Die 8051 Mikrocontroller Familie, Markt und Technik Verlag, Users Manual, (1990).

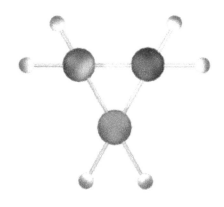

# Chapter 6

## Social and Cultural issues

# MOOsburg:
# Supplementing a real community with a virtual community

John M. Carroll, Mary Beth Rosson, Philip L. Isenhour,
Christina Van Metre, Wendy A. Schaefer, Craig H. Ganoe
Center for Human-Computer Interaction and Department of Computer Science
Virginia Tech, Blacksburg, VA 2406 1-O 106, USA

**Abstract:**
MOOsburg is a community-oriented multi-user domain. It was created to enrich the Blacksburg Electronic Village (BEV) by providing real-time, situated, interaction, and a place-based information model for community information. We are experimenting with an implementation fundamentally different from classic MOOs, supporting distributed system development and management, and a direct manipulation approach to navigation. To guide the development of MOOsburg, we are focusing on a set of community-oriented applications, including a virtual science fair.

**Keywords:** Multi-user domain (MUD), MUD Object-Oriented (MOO), community computing

## 1. Vision

MUDs (Multi-User Domains) and MOOs (MUDs Object-Oriented) offer an interesting combination of synchronous and asynchronous communication mechanisms. Users in a MOO can chat with one another, but the database that underlies the MOO is persistent: users can create, modify and manipulate objects, changing the state of the MOO for subsequent users. For example, users can leave messages posted on bulletin board objects. MOOs are fundamentally spatial-the content is organized into "rooms," and users navigate the information structure with directional commands (for example, "go north"). This evokes an experience of immersion and co-presence with other participants (Benford et al. 1996). Although these environments have been used chiefly for fantasy-oriented entertainment and informal social activity (Curtis, 1992), they have also been used for professional meetings (Glusman & Prilusky, 1996) and as learning environments (Haynes & Holmevik, 1998), and as navigational tools (Diebeger, 1996; Kies et al. 1996).

MOOsburg is a community-oriented MOO. It models the geography of the town of Blacksburg, Virginia, and its intended users are the residents of the town and its surrounding area. Thus, MOOsburg is not merely spatial; it is place-based. It is not fantasy or recreation oriented, it is community-oriented. The project goal is to enhance community development by supporting better access to local information and to new kinds of collaborative activities. Thus, MOOsburg supports construction and end-user programming activities that enrich the community's options for cooperation, commitment, and concerted action (Kies et al. 1996).

MOOsburg developed in the context of the Blacksburg Electronic Village (BEV; http://www.bev.net), an advanced community network in southwest Virginia (Carroll & Rosson, 1996). More than 90 percent of the population, over 30,000 people, have network access in Blacksburg. Public-access kiosks are available at the public library and in some business establishments. All 20 county public schools have high-speed network access, and a variety of network-based projects are underway (Koenemann et al., 1999). Over 150 community groups and more than 400 local businesses maintain Web sites (>75%). There are many unique community-oriented initiatives, such as a senior citizen's online nostalgia archive . The Town of Blacksburg makes extensive use of the BEV, providing on-line forms for surveys, house check requests, and e-mail to town officials, as well as on-line town chats and electronic dissemination of schedules and other documents.

Our vision of MOOsburg is that it can help to integrate the BEV, to make it a more a coherent environment or system. Many people visiting the BEV wonder "where" it is, since it is the union of otherwise unrelated community-oriented software and information. We also hoped to make the BEV more interactive. The core of the BEV is a distributed hypertext of community information: Lots of reading material. We wanted to emphasize collective local action in support of shared goals as a central aspect of the BEV.

## 2. Infrastructure

The goal of the MOOsburg architecture design has been to preserve the most useful aspects of traditional MOOs while extending both the client-side user interface and server-side components to take advantage of emerging Internet technologies. As with traditional textbased MOOs, the MOOsburg software architecture provides access to a central database of user-created, manipulable objects. Some of these objects represent *places* such as rooms and buildings, while others represent characters and items that populate the MOO spaces. Also as in traditional MOOs, end-user authoring of objects in the database is a basic feature of the environment.

MOOsburg preserves other fundamental concepts found in traditional MOOs. In particular, support for synchronous text-based communication between users visiting the same place is provided. There is also a seamless integration of synchronous and asynchronous collaborative activities: a user can see the effects of other users' actions in real time, and can also see the preserved effects of past actions.

However, the MOOsburg architecture reflects two significant departures from traditional MOOs. The first is *the* use of *Java object replication,* instead of streams of text, for communication between client and server. The second is support for well-defined *hierarchies* of places within the MOOsburg environment.

### 2.1 Client-server communication

Traditional MOOs rely exclusively on text for user interaction. MOO client software has been written to hide arcane textual commands and provide more graphical user interfaces for displaying MOO output, and interacting with the MOO (http://www.du.org/iava/CupOmud/). However, the underlying commitment to text limits the flexibility and sophistication of these enhancements. Perhaps the most significant issue with the text-based interaction of traditional MOOs is the use of a single "stream" for all input and output. Users move from place to place, communicate with each other, and manipulate objects in the MOO by entering commands at the appropriate place. Similarly, output describing the content and inhabitants of the current location, incoming communication from other users, and system-generated messages describing other users' actions all appear in the same (often quickly-scrolling) stream of text. Expert MOO users adapt to this style of interaction, but novice users can quickly become overwhelmed.

MOOsburg employs a very different approach, relying on Java object replication to provide each user with a lightweight, replicated, Java object for each interesting entity (place, person, or thing) encountered in the environment. A generic object replication package called CORK

(Content Object Replication Kit; Isenhour et al., 1999) ensures that, where permissions allow, changes made to any replicated object by any user are reflected in all other object replicas. A master replica of each object also exists on the MOOsburg server, and is saved periodically to non-volatile storage. Where appropriate, distinct user interface components can be provided for interacting directly with each of these replicated objects.

With this flexible object replication scheme, MOOsburg can support a variety of graphical navigation tools. The architecture makes a clean distinction between the semantics of where a user is, what objects are there, and so on, and how the place and its contents are presented and manipulated. Thus, the client-side software retrieves lightweight objects describing the user's current location as well as nearby locations in the environment. Navigation widgets then provide a user interface for viewing this information and allow the user to move from place to place. Object replication ensures that changes made by any user are reflected in all nearby users' views and navigation tools.

In our current prototype, the default navigation widget is a simple, 2-dimensional map. When the user enters the system the map shows a view of all of Blacksburg. Buildings and other locations for which content has been built are marked on the map. Users can move to a place by clicking on the map. They can also use the map to specify the locations of new places that they wish to construct. Advanced users can implement additional mechanisms for visualizing and navigating through the spatial database; these enhancements can be added to the MOOsburg client and made available to all users. Support for this kind of user-defined extension is described in more detail below.

MOOsburg's use of object replication also enables enhanced awareness of people and objects at each location. A user in a traditional MOO can request a textual description of the other inhabitants of any place that they enter, and they received automatic textual updates as people or objects enter or exit. In MOOsburg, lists of co-located people and objects are always displayed and automatically updated. Further, the information about inhabitants and activity at a given location can be used as a basis for even more useful visualization and navigation widgets. For example, a map widget could examine the contents of each location being rendered and then provide visualizations of the number of people or objects present, or of movement into and out of each location.

## 2.2 Spatial database

A second novel feature of MOOsburg is its spatial database. Traditional MOOs support construction of a *directed graph* of rooms, with very few restrictions. Containment structures, such as rooms within a building, can be defined by convention, but are not enforced by the MOO software. A room's position in the space is determined solely by the rooms that it is adjacent to (see Haynes & Holmevik, 1998, for more information on room construction in a traditional MOO.) Except again by convention, there is no concept of absolute location, and only a crude concept of distance. This ambiguity allows structures to be created within a MOO that could not exist in the physical world. While potentially interesting, the ability to create "impossible" structures generally limits the types of graphical navigation tools that can be added to a traditional MOO to those that translate mouse actions into textual MOO commands. For example, an earlier version of MOOsburg, based on a traditional MOO architecture, included a compass widget which used JavaScript to generate and send commands like "go north". However, since MOO structures often cannot be mapped onto a Cartesian coordinate system, it is typically not possible to reliably render a map of a space in a traditional MOO.

MOOsburg solves this issue by supporting more structured hierarchies of locations and by allowing assignment of Cartesian coordinates to each location. In our model, a place that contains other places is a *space; any* location that a user can navigate to is a *landmark.* A user either navigates "to" a landmark (i.e., position herself next to it), or-if the landmark is itself a space with a substructure-the user can go "into" the landmark. Streets and buildings are typical spaces; street corners and rooms are typical landmarks within these spaces. A room in a building that contains its own subspace (e.g., a gym with a spatial array of science fair exhibits) acts as both a landmark within the building, and a space containing the science exhibits. This model ensures that a map can be rendered for each space, showing the space's substructure and the location of landmarks within it. The maps provide a way to visualize the space and a means for navigating from landmark to landmark and into or out of subspaces.

As with rooms in a traditional MOO, landmarks in MOOsburg can be occupied by characters and objects. Where permissions allow, characters can create, destroy, and move objects from landmark to landmark. Characters and objects have actions (or "verbs" in traditional MOO terminology) that can be invoked on them. In MOOsburg's graphical interface, these actions are accessed by selecting items from pop-up menus rather than by entering textual commands.

A fundamental component of MOOs is support for end-user authoring. Like a traditional MOO, MOOsburg supports several levels of authoring. The simplest form is manipulation of existing objects. A landmark can hold shared whiteboards, shared notebooks, or other editable objects that users can modify. Since these objects typically use data replicated with CORK, they support both synchronous and asynchronous collaboration: Changes made to a notebook or whiteboard are visible in real time to others currently viewing or editing the object, and are preserved for users who access the object at a later time.

Users can also create new spaces, landmarks, and instances of existing object types. For example, a user could add a library room to a building and put notebook objects in it. By default, newly-created landmarks contain an object that supports text chat within the room and a toolbox object that allows the instantiation of other objects for use in the room. Users can also populate landmarks with objects brought from other rooms.

Finally, more advanced users can implement new kinds of objects. For example, a book object might be created to present online reference materials. The mechanism for building and deploying user-defined objects resembles the mechanism used to publish and access Java applets: Developers write an implementation of a new kind of MOO object and make it available on the Web. When other MOO users create or use an instance of this object in the MOO, the code that defines the object's behavior is automatically downloaded as needed. This mechanism supports a wide range of extensions to MOOsburg such as multi-player games, ballot boxes, and enhanced navigation tools.

## 3. User Interface

The current user interface to MOOsburg was motivated by two major concerns. First, we wanted a GUI interface that would be familiar and engaging to a community audience familiar with modem windowing environments, and in particular, with Web browsers as a user interface for navigating and interacting with large information spaces. Second, we wanted to address specific problems that had appeared in our early prototypes of a Webbased MOO.

The earlier prototypes reflected a sometimes awkward combination of a traditional MOO and a graphical user interface to MOO locations, objects, and characters. For example, the "chat" was simply a standard MOO teletype log. This means that everything that happened in terms of location and object interaction was reflected in that text window, and then repeated (sometimes) in the graphical user interface. The result was both redundancy and inconsistency in whether and how information was available in the graphical view of the MOO. There were multiple ways to navigate, either through conventional text commands (e.g., "go north"), by pressing a Java-script widget labeled north, or by following links out of the Web page representing the current location. It was also very easy to "leave" the MOO environment without even realizing it, because a location in the MOO could have links to arbitrary Web pages. If a user did this, they were forced to use standard Web browsing interaction (e.g., the "Back" button) to return to the MOO, then pick up again with the MOOspecific commands.

## 3.1 Layout

The prime goal of the MOOsburg user interface is to ensure users' *awareness* of location, other participants, and opportunities for action. A secondary goal is to promote consistency throughout the environment, so that users feel they are moving around and interacting within a coherent space. These two goals motivated the standard view exemplified in figure 1.

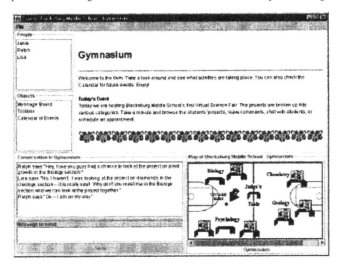

**Figure 1: A MOOsburg screen, visiting the Virtual Science Fair.**

This view has live basic components: a visual representation of the user's current location (upper right); a scrollable map showing where the user is currently located along with other navigation options (lower right); a list of other participants currently at the same location (upper left); a list of objects with which the user can interact in this location (middle left); and a chat window for communicating with other participants at this location (lower left).

In addition to a consistent overall layout, the visual representation of each landmark includes a visual "signature" that identifies it as part of the MOOsburg database (Mullet & Sano, 1995): the title of the landmark at the top, followed by a bold horizontal line and the room description. The material displayed in this frame is generated and rendered with HTML, so anything that a landmark designer can create as part of a standard Web page can be included in this depiction.

The map available at each location in the MOO provides a single and direct mechanism for navigation. Users no longer have to know reserved words or room names. They also no longer need to navigate from room to room to get to a destination. The map always available in the bottom right of the interface informs the user of his or her current location, and displays other locations to which he or she can navigate.

Landmarks are indicated as spots on the map. A filled spot means that the user can only go "to" the spot; an open circle means that the user, can also go "into" that location (i.e., that there is a substructure and a new map defined for it). To support browsing and feedthrough, we display a location's name at the bottom of the map when the user positions the mouse over a spot. A single click on a spot will bring the user to that location; the map is updated with an arrow showing "You are here", and the standard MOOsburg depiction of that landmark is shown in the location description frame (e.g., typically containing information that one would find on a "Welcome page" of a Web site). If the landmark also contains a subspace (i.e., is shown as an open circle), a double click will take the user directly into the subspace, and the map will be replaced with the new map, with the user positioned at a predefined entry point (the default landmark) in the new space.

The People list indicates who else is co-positioned at the current landmark, encouraging informal interaction among visitors. Group chat takes place in the frame at the bottom left of the screen and is similar to standard Internet-based chat tools. Text is typed into the "Message to send" input field and sent explicitly with the "Send" button, or implicitly by pressing "Enter" on the keyboard. This eliminates the need for the "Say" command used in conventional MOOs, minimizing the typing needed for informal conversation.

By default, messages sent at a landmark will be seen by anyone else also located there. However, one-to-one chat can be initiated by selecting a user's name from the People list and double clicking. Again, this is a simplification to standard MOO functionality, wherein private chatting was accomplished through the special "Whisper" command. This point-andclick technique for initiating one-to-one chat increases the feeling of a direct link among users, as well as simplifying the request itself.

### 3.2 Object Interaction and Sharing

As with the chat tool, interactive objects "stored" at a landmark are accessed through a pointand- click interface. The user can open objects in the Object list by choosing an appropriate verb from the object's popup menu. An important design decision was to open any such object (whether a whiteboard, a slide projector, a notebook, etc.) in a separate window. This means that users can open and interact with multiple objects at the same time. Although this increases the complexity of window management by the user, it supports multi-threaded activities, for example simultaneous interaction with a whiteboard (for informal drawing) and a notebook (for editing and archiving text). The decision of whether to automatically close an object when a user leaves the landmark is left to the designer of the object. Again, here we have opted for flexibility, allowing for scenarios in which users want to compare and contrast objects associated with different locations. An important specific consequence of opening objects in separate windows is that there is now a clear distinction between what is "in MOOsburg" versus what is "on the Web". Any URLs stored at a MOOsburg location are opened in a secondary window, a simple Web browser. Recall that these objects are also automatically shared, so Web navigation can be shared, whiteboards used for synchronous communication, and so on. Objects in MOOsburg can be "picked up" and "moved" from one landmark to another, much as in traditional MOOs. The only significant difference is that these interactions are supported by our general point-and-click interface.

### 3.3 Map-based Navigation.

A signature feature of traditional MOOs is compass-based navigation: go north. This "maze metaphor" for space is appropriate when the overarching task for users is exploration, but it is not consistent with more goal-directed tasks, such as "going to the Middle School for a virtual Parent-Teacher meeting".

The maps available in MOOsburg correspond to the hierarchy of locations. At the top level is a street map of the town of Blacksburg. The map indicates landmarks at this highest level-for example buildings or parks-that the user can visit. Subsequent levels are defined by the subspaces created for landmarks. For example if a building is given a substructure, it is presented as a floorplan; if the building has multiple floors, stair widgets provide access to different floors.

We are currently experimenting with fish-eye maps that will facilitate easy viewing and navigation of a large geographic space (Furnas, 1986). Fisheye views employ a focus+context technique that allows users to see" the details needed for local interactions and yet provide a view of the overall structure. For MOOsburg, the goal is to display a user's current location as the focus, with the rest of the town as context. One way to do this is to enlarge the focus location in the center of the map and render the other locations smaller and smaller as you move further away from the focus. In this way, users have a sense of what is nearby them as well as a notion of where they are located in town.

]We have experimented with different mathematical mappings that provide this focus+context map view. Using an arc tan function has produced the smoothest and most understandable view, although we found that a zoom function is a desirable feature. We are also exploring a zoomable flat map. In this technique, all locations have the same size and the context is obtained by zooming out.

## 4. Application Development

We are coordinating the development of the MOOsburg infrastructure with development of specific applications and activities within MOOsburg. In some cases, these example activities are merely imported; for example, a Web-forum for community history developed with local senior citizens is an object in the Senior's Center (Carroll et al., 1999). More ambitiously, we are trying to integrate existing community systems in the MOO, and to develop new applications and activities that exploit the MOO infrastructure and help us to develop appropriate authoring and integration support.

### 4.1 The Virtual Science Fair

The flagship application for MOOsburg development has been a virtual science fair, conceived as an integration of an existing school-based collaboration system - the Virtual School (Koenemann et al., 1999) - with MOOsburg. Science fairs typically exhibit projects that students have developed outside of class, over a period of weeks or months. The exhibition usually occurs at the school during a single evening toward the end of the school year. We believe that this traditional activity could be enhanced if the projects could involve community members more actively, and if the exhibition of the projects could be carried out over a longer period of time, and more conveniently accessed by community members. In our virtual science fair concept, students use the Virtual School to collaborate with one another and with community members over significant periods of time to carry out projects, which they exhibit to the community using MOOsburg. The exhibit can itself become an extended collaborative activity, since the virtual science fair is not constrained to be a onetime event.

### 4.2 Authoring and Integration

A crucial enabler for the ongoing development of MOOsburg is the support of authoring by end-users. Community groups need to be able to create and manage their own meeting places and projects. This both empowers them with respect to utilizing technology to achieve their own goals, and makes MOOsburg more feasible: It is difficult to imagine how any community could fund central management for a community MOO. But this in turn requires us to develop support for authoring activities and for integrating independent development efforts.

MOOsburg currently supports only a modicum of end-user programming (e.g., a form tool for creating rooms). We are building on these early experiments to provide similar tools for creating other objects (e.g., a slide show, a bulletin board in a classroom, a comment on a student project). Some of this is taking place through group projects under development for a graduate course in computer-supported cooperative work at Virginia Tech. Six MOOsburg activities are being prototyped: an event publicity system, a software engineering room, a Virginia Tech Off-Campus Housing office and fair, advertisement and connectivity for adhoc sports activities, and a children's collaborative story writing at the public library.

These student projects represent a small sample of the diverse software applications that MOOsburg can support. The event publicity system and software engineering room are developing general, reusable objects that can be made available to all MOOsburg users. The Virginia Tech Off-Campus Housing office and fair, along with the children's collaborative story writing at the Blacksburg Public Library, provide virtual counterparts to current reallife activities that take place in the Blacksburg community. Allowing community members to plan local ad-hoc sports activities or hold a real-time, auction online are new types of virtual : support for collaborative activities in Blacksburg.

We are very interested in the enhancements to the MOOsburg infrastructure that will enable MOO users with diverse needs, like the student groups, to contribute to the system. In this sense, the student projects are an important source of requirements for end-user authoring support. Some of the key areas we are now exploring include distributed software development and installation; simplified programming of collaboration features; security requirements; and increased options for multi-user awareness.

## 5. Plans

Our strategy for the near future is to coordinate further development of infrastructure, user interface, and new applications for MOOsburg. We want to develop general tools and techniques that can be useful in a variety of specific contexts. For example, many users of MOOsburg will want to conduct moderated real-time discussions with whiteboard and forum tools for organizing interactions and preserving results. We need especially to support the development and integration of individual MOO-sites by end-users.

Our principal focus in user interface development is on the interactive map. We need to automate the acquisition of map data in order to be able to map larger regions (for example, all of Montgomery County, as opposed to merely downtown Blacksburg). We need to improve map navigation; we plan to experiment with displaying the names of distant landmarks on the horizons of the currently-focal mapped region in order to mitigate the downsides of spatial distortion near the margins.

Our application development work is focussed chiefly on the goal of conducting a virtual science fair activity in spring of 2000. We are also planning further activities with other community groups, including the League of Women Voters, a local natural history museum, and the Town of Blacksburg. For example, we want to help coordinate water quality monitoring stations along the New River, and support public discussions with local political candidates. We also need to develop techniques and perhaps further tools support for assessing the usability, usefulness, and civic impact of MOOsburg software and activities.

Community computing seeks to enhance participation in community life at a time in history when traditional communities appear to be eroding (Putnam, 1996). It investigates and facilitates the development of local *social capital* -the trust, social interactions, and norms of mutual reciprocity throughout a community . For example, we have hypothesized that educational activities can be more meaningful for children, more valued by their parents, and thereby more effective if those activities are grounded in local people, issues, and events (Carroll & Rosson, 1999).

The MOOsburg project is attempting to bring new technological approaches and applications to community computing. This is not to impugn the pervasive and exciting vision of what McLuhan ( 1964) anticipated as the "global village." We all participate in a global village of international collaboration, electronic commerce, telework, and so forth, mediated by the Internet. But we live in physical communities, next door to someone, down the street from someone else. We believe that a critical complementary element, one often missing in contemporary visions of information technology and society, is an appreciation of the importance of local commitment, initiative, and cooperation. We believe that environments like MOOsburg may allow networking technology to play a more constructive role in supporting people where they live.

## Acknowledgements

Thanks to Jonathan Kies, Brian Amento, Michael Mellott, and Craig Struble for implementing the original MOOsburg software and activities, and investigating the use of MOOsburg, in 1995. Thanks in particular to Craig Struble for continuing to design and develop MOOsburg during 1996- 1998. Thanks also to Cara Struble for developing the original concept and implementation for map-based orientation and navigation in Fall 1998. Thanks finally to Dan Dunlap and Dennis Neale, members of the current MOOsburg team, for suggestions.

The MOOsburg project is supported by the Hitachi Foundation and the Office of Naval Research. The Virtual School project was supported by the National Science Foundation .

## References

Benford, S., Brown, C., Reynard, G., & Greenhalgh, C. (1996). Shared spaces: Transportation, artificiality, and spatiality. Proceedings of CSCW'96 (pp. 77-86). New York: ACM.

Carroll, J.M. & Rosson, M.B. (1996). Developing the Blacksburg Electronic Village. Communications of the ACM, 39( 12), 69-74.

Carroll, J.M. & Rosson, M.B. (1999). The neighborhood school in the global village. IEEE Technology and Society, 17(4), 4-9, 44.

Carroll, J.M., Rosson, M.B., VanMetre, C.A., Kengeri, R., & Darshani, M. (1999). Blacksburg Nostalgia: A Community History Archive. *Proceedings of Interact '99*. Amsterdam: IOS Press/IFIP, pp. 637-647.

Curtis, P. (1992). Mudding: Social phenomena in text-based virtual realities. Proceedings of the 1992 Conference on the Directions and Implications of Advanced Computing Berkeley, CA.

Dieberger, A. (1996). Browsing the WWW by interacting with a textual virtual environment. *Proceedings of Hypertext'96*. New York: ACM, pp. 170-179.

Furnas, G.W. (1986). Generalized fisheye views. *Proceedings of CHI'86*. New York: ACM, pp. 16-23.

Glusman, G. & Prilusky, J. (1996). Real-time, Online Conferencing for Biologists. *Conference on Bioinformatics and Structure* (Jerusalem, November 17-21).

Haynes, C. & Holmevik, J. R. (Eds.) (1998). *High Wired: On the Design, Use, and Theory of Educational MOOs*. University of Michigan Press, Ann Arbor.

Isenhour, P., Rosson, M.B. & Carroll, J.M. (1999), submitted. Supporting asynchronous collaboration and late joining in Java groupware. *Interacting with Computers*

Kies, J.K., Amento, B.S., Mellott, M.E. & Struble, C.A. (1996). *MOOsburg: Experiences with a community-based MOO*. Technical Report, Center for Human-Computer Interaction, Virginia Tech, Blacksburg, VA.

Koenemann, J., Carroll, J.M., Shaffer, C.A., Rosson, M.B. & Abrams, M. (1999). Designing collaborative applications for classroom use: The LiNC Project. In A. Druin, (Ed.), *The design of children's technology*. San Francisco: Morgan-Kaufman% pp. 99- 123.

McLuhan, M. (1964). *Understanding media: The extensions of man*. New York: McGraw-Hill.

Mullet, K. & Sano, D. 1995. *Designing visual interfaces*. Englewood Cliffs, NJ: Prentice Hall.

Putnam, R.D. (1996). The strange disappearance of civic America. *The American Prospect*, 24, Winter.

316

# EVoice using an Interactive Voice Response System for Developing Countries

Palaniappan A., Vivek Rajendran & Narayanan Srinivasan

Sri Venkateswara College of Engineering
Pennalur, Sriperumbudur 602 105,India.
Phone: 91-44-642 1239,Fax: 91-44-642 2029
E-mail: pal@bitsmart.com or ammuns@yahoo.com

## Abstract

This paper discusses a new perspective of voice based email - EVoice aimed at developing countries. While computers and associated peripherals like high-speed modems are relatively scarce, pay booths with telephone have become wide spread especially in rural areas. Hence we propose a system that caters to such a population allowing them to access email through a telephone line. A cost-effective telephone to voice integration hardware, combined with Integrated Voice Response System (IVRS) and optimal voice compression is proposed. In our system voice data is compressed and sent as an attachment to a destination email address. Any incoming message (voice or text) is played back to the user. Wide spread internet-portability issues are discussed. The paper stresses on service provider independent hybrid voice email, fostering Internet communication in developing countries.

## Keywords

Internet communication, Email and Telephone.

## 1. Introduction

In recent years, the Internet Protocol (IP) has come to play a key role in new multimedia and advanced communication applications in the telephone industry. As the demand for packet based data traffic grows exponentially, it is likely to eclipse the conventional circuit-switched voice on the communication networks throughout the world and eventually emerge as the "in-sway" method of providing telecommunications by the next decade. Voice/data traffic crossover is foreseen in the next few years, driven in particular by IP based applications on both public Internet and private Intranets.

In the third world nations the availability of different service providers with high-end server networks for voice mail though likely, is prohibitive. Many companies are offering either online or offline services based on voice transport mechanisms. Online services include real time telephony using Internet as backbone. Offline services include voice mail and Web based voice mail. Current voice mail services use voice data both upstream and downstream. Web based voice mail requires users to log in to a website to check their voice mails i.e., the voice data resides in the server.

These systems do have some limitations. For example, individual service providers implement voice mail using proprietary standards. This requires customers at both ends to be part of the private vendor network. In addition, voice mail cannot reach places where the same service providers' server does not exist. Web based voice mail requires users to log on to the net. Since different service providers setup their own high end server networks through out the world for voice mail, compatibility with the global net community is limited (i.e. not portable to email). Voice data both to and from a user increases network overload.

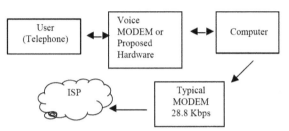

**Figure 1. General block diagram of the proposed system**

In developing countries the major deterrent for progress in Internet communication is cost. The lower the "quantifiable" cost the more rapid the rate of development. We propose a system that is economically viable, effective and easily accessible. The system aims at purveying to the areas where computers and associated peripherals like high-speed modems are relatively exiguous. The system is designed with the aim of providing email receive and voice mail sending facility to the rural populace through a Public Switched Telephone Network (PSTN) telephone line.

The key factor is to exploit the capabilities of many small-scale DeskTop Publishing (DTP) operators' system resources without affecting the main stream of work. The potential DTP operators in the locale can cater to the rural population, alleviating the necessity of long distance calls to a dedicated high-end server of the big service providers. This system operated by many small-scale entrepreneurs effectively lets the end user communicate to any Internet user at large, without the use of computer at their premises. The proposed system is similar in spirit to architectures' [Huitema C., *et al*, 1999] proposed for Internet telephony that works with just a telephone owned by a PSTN subscriber.

Voluminous data resulting in traffic is cited as a major detriment with regard to the Internet. The proposed system uses the GSM (Global System of Mobile Communication) [Jutta Degener, www] standard of speech compression to efficiently compress the voice data obtained from the user. The voice data is uploaded after compression, which makes the process of communication more efficient. Our system consists of a minimal hardware circuit proposed as a cheap alternative to a voice modem and allows communication between the user (telephone) and a computer. An end user calls our local service provider from their telephone or a pay-booth to check e-mail or send voice mail. The system is guided by a computer synthesized IVRS, which makes it adaptable to individual responses rather than fixed pre-recorded responses. Voice data is obtained from the user and is compressed using the GSM codec. The compressed voice data is sent to the destination e-mail address. For a

318

user who wants to receive e-mail can hear the message through the telephone. If the e-mail data is in text format, it is converted to speech using Whistler [Microsoft, www], a text-to-speech synthesis system. In the next section we will discuss the proposed hardware and section 3 discusses the software for communication.

## 2. Hardware

A voice modem is sufficient for the purpose of communication between the telephone and the computer. But high-end modems might be expensive in our environments, especially rural areas. Further a service provider (DTP operator in our case) may wish to handle many telephone lines corresponding to the growth in traffic as well as income. Additional line capability can be brought forward using this design which couples with a sound card to provide total voice handling features. A low cost alternative hardware is suggested here in case of non-availability of voice modem or for multi-line telephone handling capabilities. Parallel port design is preferred here, as the serial ports normally would be occupied by the other devices (e.g. mouse & modem).

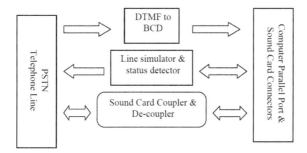

**Figure 2. Block diagram of the proposed hardware**

The proposed hardware circuit (see Figure 2 for a block diagram description) can be attached to the parallel port of a computer and linked with sound card, speaker, and mike connections. An incoming call is checked for Caller ID in case of availability or through time lapse since first ring. The BCD (Binary Coded Decimal) data is fed to the computer through parallel port operated in bi-directional mode [*IEEE Std.1284.*, 1994]. Once the software processes a particular "call", the on/off hook simulator can attend the call. Further the sound cards (speaker / mike connections) are linked to the telephone line via a coupling stage. In the case of a call transferred to the operator, the piezo buzzer beeps indicating call to the operator or other calls, there by eliminating the need for dedicated lines for operation of the device.

To stick to economy rather than performance the design involves the use of four simple blocks to achieve telephone handling. They are
- DTMF (Dual Tone Multi-Frequency) detector
- On/off hook detector
- Off/on hook simulator
- Sound card I/O Coupler / De-coupler

319

- **DTMF detector**:

This block uses a DTMF-BCD decoder Mitel 8870 for the conversion; incoming DTMF from the line is AC coupled via a step down transformer, as initial line ring is around 90V RMS (typical).

- **On/off Hook Simulator**:

This block places a load of $330\Omega$ and an LED in series with the line to drop line voltage and close the local loop. Selective loading is achieved by two transistor stages.

- **On/off Hook Detector**:

The detector detects line voltage drop below 20V and fires an optical isolator to indicate on/off hook condition.

- **Audio Coupler / De-coupler**:

Playback of email message by text-to-speech synthesis and recording of wave files is achieved by using the sound card speaker out and mike in connections to be coupled or de-coupled using a simple double throw relay or better optimized with an analog multiplexer. The use of sound card DSP hardware avoids the necessity for constructing separate speech processing hardware and results in the reduction of the total cost. If the call is not to the system, the buzzer beeps and the call is manually answered hence avoiding dedicating the line.

## 2. Software

Fully functional software was developed using VC++, VBASIC & C++ Builder. The voice communication between the user and our IVRS is achieved through our simple hardware circuit, and handled by the software running as a background process. The voice recorded from the user is compressed using the GSM [Michel Mouly and Marie-Bernadette Pautet, 1992] encoder algorithms and converted into RIFF wave#49 (Resource Interchange File Format) for sending as an attachment with e-mail. Microsoft Text to Speech synthesis system – Whistler, implemented in SAPI (Speech Application Program Interface) version 4, was used for the email to voice conversion for playback on telephone. Net connectivity and uploading were done using standard winsock controls.

A general software algorithm for the IVRS is as follows: When the user makes a call to the system, the telephone exchange issues a DTMF signal carrying caller ID. The software checks caller ID or waits for some pre-specified time. It simulates off hook condition and acquires user access key. It validates the key from the database and a non-member call is transferred to manual operation. On receiving a proper member access key it retrieves the user's mail box, carries out the required interactive email playback / recording. On completion of the task the software resets the system.

The destination party email address is keyed to system through the telephone Dual Tone Multi-Frequency (DTMF) mode -1(abc) 2(cde) etc. (optionally the customer can also specify the common email address and give key macros for them). The user speaks into the receiver and the speech is recorded as a 16-bit PCM wave file. The data from the user is actually sent under the RIFF (Resource Interchange File Format) wav#49 format to the destination email address. To achieve this the 16 bit PCM wave file is encoded to GSM format, which is then converted to a RIFF wav#49 format file. RIFF wav#49 allows the receiver to hear to the voice attachment using Windows Media player, avoiding the use of separate decoding software. GSM Codec allows a compression of 10:1 from the original PCM file.

The wave to .GSM file conversion was achieved with the GSM encoder/decoder algorithms (DLL implementation of the algorithm, available at the University Of Berlin website) [Jutta Degener, www; Guido Giorgetti, www]. GSM was preferred to the wave format and the comparisons between GSM and wave formats are shown in Table I.

| Audio Format | 16-bit PCM | GSM 06.10 |
|---|---|---|
| File Extension | .wav or .aiff | .gsm |
| Data rate | 128 Kbps | 13.2 Kbps |
| File size per minute | 960 K | 96 K |
| Compression factor | 1:1 | 10:1 |
| Relative compression speed | N/A | 0.75 |
| Higher sample rates | Yes | No |

**Table I: Comparison of PCM wave files with GSM files**

In the GSM standard proposed by European Telecommunication Standards Institute (ETSI) [ETS 300 961,1998; Moe Rahnema, 1993], a speech signal from the PSTN is converted from 8-bit µ law to 13 bit PCM. The average bit rate for encoded speech is 13Kbps (Sampling frequency = 8KHz). The Codec in GSM is the Regular Pulse Excitation with Long Term Prediction (RTE-LTP) – linear predictive coder. The simplified block diagrams of the RTE-LTP encoder is shown in Figure 3. In GSM, short-term analysis is followed by long-term analysis and finally RPE encoding. The compression is achieved in the encoding of reflection coefficients obtained from RPE encoding. After preprocessing of 160 speech samples, the coefficients of the short-time analysis filter are obtained by Linear Predictive Coding (LPC) analysis. Short-term residual samples are obtained by filtering with the coefficients obtained by LPC. The short-term residual samples (total of 160) are divided into blocks of 40 each. The parameters of the long-term analysis filter are calculated based on the current block and the past 3 blocks. Estimates of the short-term residual values are subtracted from the short-term residual signal to obtain a block of 40 long-term residual samples. These long-term residual samples are fed to regular pulse excitation analysis, which leads to compression of the speech data. RPE analysis results in representation of the long-term residual samples with 4 candidate subsequences of 13 pulses each. After identification of the subsequence selected based on RPE grid position, Adaptive Pulse Code Modulation (APCM) is used to encode the RPE pulses.

The decoding process follows the inverse path i.e.; RPE decoding followed by long-term synthesis and finally short-term synthesis. The GSM file obtained by RPE-LTP encoder is converted to the RIFF-WAVE#49 format for sending voice to the destination address.

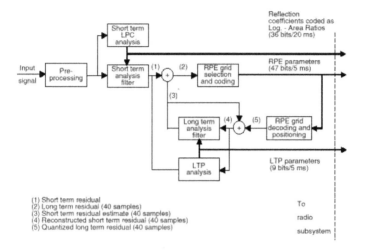

**Fig 3 Simplified Block diagram of the RTE-LTP encoder (from ETS 300 961 – GSM 6.0 Version 5.1.1)**

Regarding reception of messages, any person can send an email to the end user by specifying the name of the end user in the subject header & email address of the service providers (DTP operator).

Example:

> To: firststep@vsnl.com
> Subject: userGanesh
> Compressed Voice data sent as standard MIME attachment
> Normal Email as Usual

On retrieving this email, our software sorts it and places it in the user mailbox. During the next mail check by the user, the user can hear the content of the e-mail. If the e-mail is in the form of a .GSM file or RIFF wav#49, the software can play it back for the user. If the e-mail is a text document, the text is converted into voice for playback to the user using Microsoft Text-to-Speech synthesis system – WHISTLER [Huang X., *et al*, 1996,1998], implemented using Speech API version 4. Whistler's front end consists of a text analysis component based on Lernout and Hauspie's commercial TTS system [Van Coile B., 1993]. The Whistler prosody model that generates prosody parameters using context-dependent units follows the text analysis component. While some of the traditional Text-to-Speech system use rule-based generation, Whistler uses data driven modeling techniques for the generation of Prosody parameters. Prosody generation is followed by unit concatenation followed by the speech output. The basic unit for synthesis in Whistler is called a Senone, which is a context-dependent sub phonetic unit. They are organized in the form of decision trees. Segmentation of units from speech is done using Hidden Markov Model (HMM) training. The use of such stochastic based learning techniques allows Whistler to provide a fairly good quality speech.

## 4. Conclusion

The proposed system provides a cheap and viable alternative for voice communication over Internet for developing countries like India. It also offers a fair amount of decentralization in its workings. The whole scheme encourages divided profits among many small-scale service providers. The scheme offers minimal hardware overload. Ability to send voice mail to any Internet user and receive email from any Internet user without the use of computer at the customer premises makes the system well suited for typical rural areas in developing countries. Further since the user is receiving text email, one way network overload is drastically reduced. Uploading the email to the local ISP is done during the night when line conditions are expected to be good. Increase in revenue or traffic may lead to more frequent email checks by the service provider. Charging a minimal amount for the outgoing mails will result in good profitability even with as little as 50 users calling on a day. Further improvements might involve translation of English email to local language script and adapting text to speech conversion for those local languages. Better voice coders can be implemented for more optimal data compression and less network overload.

## 5. References

*ETS* 300 961, (1998), *Digital cellular telecommunications system (Phase 2+); Full rate speech; Transcoding.* (GSM 06.10 version 5.1.1).

Guido Giorgetti, C++ Builder DLLs, - *http://www2.sienanet.it/users/guido/*

Huang, X., Acero, A., Hon, H., Ju, Y., Liu, J., Meredith, S., & Plumpe M., (1998), "Recent improvements on Microsoft's trainable text-to-speech system – Whistler". *IEEE International Conference on Acoustics, Speech, and Signal Processing.*

Huang, X., Acero, A., Adcock, J., Hon, H., Goldsmith, J., Liu, J., and Plumpe, M., (1996), "Whistler, A Trainable Text-to-Speech System". *International Conference on Spoken Language Processing,* Philadelphia.

Huitema, C., Cameron, J., Mouchtaris, P., and Smyk, D., (1999), "An Architecture for Residential Internet Telephony Service", *IEEE Network May,* pp 50-56.

*IEEE* Std.1284., (1994), "Standard Signaling Method for a Bi-directional Parallel Peripheral Interface for Personal Computers".

Jutta Degener, "GSM 06.10 lossy speech compression", http*://kbs.cs.tu-berlin.de/~jutta/toast.html*

Michel Mouly and Marie-Bernadette Pautet, (1992), *The GSM System for Mobile Communications,* Published by the authors.

Microsoft's Research's Speech Technology Group web page (Speech API 4.0): *http://www.research. microsoft.com/research/srg/*.

Moe Rahnema, (1993), Overview of the GSM system and protocol architecture, *IEEE Communications Magazine,* April, pp. 92-100.

Van Coile, B., (1993), "On the development of Pronunciation Rules for Text-to-Speech Synthesis", *Proceedings of Eurospeech Conference*, Berlin, pp 1455-1458.

# Information Warfare- Prevention and Recovery

Karanjeet Singh Kahlon[1]  Hardeep Singh[2] Gurvinder Singh[3]
Reader                 Reader          Lecturer

Department Of Computer Science & Engineering
Guru Nanak Dev University, Amritsar, Panjab
India
e-mail: k_kahlon@yahoo.com
Kskahlon@gndu.ernet.in

## Abstract

The need for defending against potential information Warfare is becoming important due to increased threat by hackers. Information system is a vital organ to most of the organisations and any attack on them, which could damage, can be devastating. There is a possibility of illegal use of the functions and services that must be in place to carry out needed, legitimate functions. These attacks can be either prevented or rejected but there is need for recovery after the attack has accrued. The objective of this paper is to focus on defending and repairing damage to the information maintained within a system.

## Keywords

Information warfare, Prevention, Forward Recovery, Backward Recovery

## 1. Introduction

Sophisticated hackers and crackers work diligently to find security loopholes and use these loopholes to break into systems. Besides attack from outsiders over the network, there remains the possibility of an invasion of one's system by insider turned foe. Any such malicious attack against an organisation's information base through electronic means is termed information warfare. Preventive measures are necessary to protect information system against attacks, however it is not possible to avert all the attacks at the outset. Attacks that succeed somewhat are unavoidable, and a comprehensive support for identifying and responding to attack is required. Information system must be able to consider the whole process of attack, response and recovery. This requires that information system must consist of multiple phases out of which prevention is one. The goal of information system is to keep available as many of the critical systems element as possible in the face of attack. It is undesirable to use recovery techniques that require halting system operations for repair, for denial of service may be the attackers objective at a critical time. Repair work in event of attack must proceed along with other applications that are not part of the attack.

## 2. Information Defence cycle

Attack and defence are continuous processes in an information system, and defensive approaches must consider the entire process. The attacker observes the system and gathers data from any available sources to determine the system's vulnerabilities He finds the most critical functions or data to target – this information is used to plan the means of attack and the resulting plan is carried out. The attacker then gathers further information from any new vantage point established, assesses the impact of the attack on the system so far, and plans further actions. As part of this cycle, an attacker may also attempt to anticipate the responses that will be made by defenders. Attacker either act to counter them or even take actions specifically designed to instigate a defensive response that would have side effects damaging to the system's operational function. The defender must also attempt to anticipate and block possible means of attack. Detect those that occur, and respond in a way that limits damage, maintains system availability for its critical functions, and allows recovery of full operating capabilities to proceed [6]. The defender's cycle of activities can be divided into phases. These phases correspond loosely to a typical protect-detect-react cycle, which is shown below in the figure.

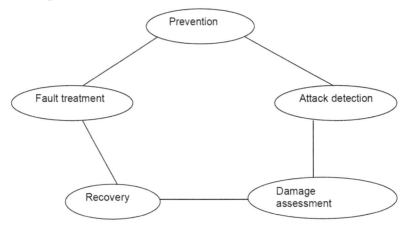

## 2.1 Prevention

The defender puts protective measures into place.

## 2.2 Attack detection

The defender observes symptoms of a problem and determines that an attack may have taken place or may be in progress. The defender gathers further information to diagnose whether the symptoms are due to unusual but legitimate system activity or to an attack, and if there is an attack, what type [6]. The defender can gather information by changing monitoring thresholds, deploying additional sensors, or using specialised analytical tools.

## 2.3 Damage assessment and containment

The defender examines the system to determine the extent of any damage the attack may have caused, including failed functions and corrupted data. The defender takes immediate action to try to eliminate the attacker's access to the system and to isolate or contain the problem to prevent further spread [6].

## 2.4 Recovery

The defender may reconfigure to allow operation to continue in a degraded mode while on non-critical services to maximise the ability to continue critical services, for example. The defender then recovers corrupted or lost data and repairs or reinstalls failed system functions to re-establish a normal level of operation.

## 2.5 Fault treatment

Fault treatment relates closely both to reaction specifically to the prevention phase when a system is first developed and put into place, and when new releases or other significant changes occur. During times when the system is operating in a steady state, the fault treatment and prevention phases can be viewed as taking place simultaneously. To the extent possible, the weaknesses exploited in the attack are identified, and steps are taken to prevent a recurrence.

## 3. Types of recovery

Three recovery models are available to formalise recovery methods

1) Hot Start
2) Warm Start
3) Cold Start

The Hot Start is primarily forward error recovery method, and is appropriate for attacks in which the system can or must respond transparently to the user. Suppose, an attacker introduces a corrupt binary executable at a particular site and uses that executable to launch availability, trust, or integrity attack. The attack can be handled with a Hot Start model if two conditions hold. First, the attack must be detected early enough that damage is confined to the executable. Second, a hot standby of the executable- an uncorrupted standby, preferably at a different location – must be available to take over. The hot standby effects a recovery transparent to the user, even though the system is in a degraded state. It is still necessary to identify the path by which the adversary introduced the corrupt binary, disable that path, and restore the proper binary from a back-up store.

Sometimes it is not possible to hide the effects of an attack from the users, and in these cases a Warm Start model is desirable. Damage can be confined such that key services are available, trustworthy, and reliable. Nonetheless, the users are aware of the attack because the system is visibly degraded. The exact level of service depends on the extent of the attack. Some functionality may be missing, untrustworthy, and/or based on incorrect information. Key mechanisms for managing Warm Start are checkpoints for quick recovery and audit trails for intercepting the attacker.

A Warm Start response to an availability attack results in non-transparent but automated recovery from confined damage. A Warm Start response to a trust attack means that some system operations but not others can be trusted while the response to the attack is under way. A Warm Start response to an integrity attack means that some system functionality but not all is enabled.

The Cold Start model is appropriate for the most severe attacks. The chief difference from the Warm Start is that the attacker succeeds in halting the delivery of system services. The goal of the Cold Start recovery is to bring the system back up as quickly as possible to a usable, trustworthy, and consistent state. Policies and algorithms are required to support efficient Cold Start.

## 4. Recovery methods

Recovery method is a research area studied extensively by researchers in the fault tolerance and database areas. In the fault tolerance area, two types of errors are considered: errors that are anticipated and those that are unanticipated [2]. Depending upon the extent of prediction and assessment of damage errors are categorised as anticipated or unanticipated. To recover from anticipated errors, forward recovery methods are used. Since the errors have been foreseen, either contingency update instructions can be specified or a means of deriving an acceptably correct value can be formulated. Forward recovery methods have two limitations. First, these methods are usually very system specific. Second, the success of these methods depends on how accurately damage from faults can be predicated and assessed. To recover from unanticipated errors, backward recovery is considered to be the only viable approach. This requires that the entire state be replaced by a prior state that is consistent. Clearly, this approach is less than optimal because it requires that the system be temporarily halted.

Database Management Systems provide a rich set of recovery facilities [1]; however, they mostly rely on backward recovery methods to restore the database to a consistent state. There are several limitations to be backward recovery methods used in DBMS, especially in the face to malicious attacks. First, if a transaction is aborted, the transaction isolation property supports recovery, in a sense, by ensuring that it can be backed out [1] without affecting other transactions. The isolation property does not help, however, in the case of malicious transactions, because they appear to the DBMS to be ordinary transactions and complete normally. Undo/redo logs support recovery when the system fails with a number of uncompleted transactions in progress, but such recovery methods do not apply when transactions complete successfully but create bad data. Now, suppose that some time after a malicious has been committed, the bad data it created is discovered through some means (perhaps a user has noticed it). Meanwhile, other transactions may have read the bad data, based their computations on it, and unwittingly then written bad data of their own to other items. The only general mechanism available to remove the effects of one or more prior, successfully committed transactions is backward recovery, which rolls the database back to a previously established checkpoint. However, the use of this mechanism poses a dilemma, because the penalty for doing so is that all other, valid work that has been accomplished since the checkpoint was taken is also lost.

### 4.1 Redundancy

The most fundamental technique for recovery is redundancy. This means that either an information element is stored redundantly somewhere in the system or it can reconstruct from some other elements stored in the system. Such redundancy might take the form of backups at geographically distributed locations, alternative algorithms, compensation methods for unrecoverable objects, and audit trails for tracking system access and usage.

Redundancy can be useful for all three types of recovery. For an example of Hot Start recovery, suppose an attack has been detected that has damaged an executable. A hot standby of the executable- an uncorrupted standby, possibly at a different locations- can take over. Derived data attributes evaluation rules attached to them; evaluation rules describe how the values of these attributes are to be derived from other values. These other values do not have to be in the system; they could come from the outside. Recovery logs provide an example of Cold Start.

## 4.2 Backward recovery

In the case of errors for which no corrective compensating action can be determined, backward error recovery must be done. Backward recovery uses database mechanisms such as the undo/redo log to erase recent transactions and restore the database to a prior state [1].

Backward recovery methods can be used to achieve not only Cold Start, but Hot Start and Warm Start as well. Suppose we have determined a collection of transactions to be malicious (these transactions may be all generated at a particular site or executed by a single suspicious user). If we can identify the extent of damage caused by these malicious transactions, we can take immediate steps to confine the damage (see the following discussion). We use the log to undo the changes by the malicious transactions, and redo the changes by the normal transactions. This would require augmenting the database log to capture the date elements read by transactions; exactly how this is to be accomplished is to be investigated.

## 4.3 Forward Recovery

In some cases, detected errors can be corrected through forward error recovery. These are cases in which either the particular type of error has been foreseen and contingency update instructions specified or a means of deriving an acceptably correct value is known. If the semantics of the application support forward recovery, compensating transactions can anticipate error scenarios. For items that are replaced periodically through normal processing, the error may be corrected merely by waiting until the next replacement occurs.

## 4.4 Static partitioning of information elements

Designing the database and its applications so that transactions can touch data only in a single region limits the extent to which damage can spread and allows applications that use other partitions to proceed normally while one is under repair. Since this may be impractical for many databases, a more flexible alternative is to define boundaries of regions, identify triggers or propagated updates that cross those boundaries, and limit the bandwidth or conditions under which data may flow across.

## 4.5 Dynamic partitioning of information elements

The goal in dynamic partitioning is to use recovery methods to identify information elements that can be taken out of use, repaired, and reintegrated for use dynamically. This technique is essential for Hot Start.

## 4.6 Versioning

In a concept borrowed from concurrent engineering, it is possible that maintaining trees of versions, in which versions are inter-transaction checkpoints, would allow more graceful restoration of a consistent state. If the current Database State were found to be unsound, a different branch could be followed. This type of versioning would be tied closely to states of the database applications. Further exploration is needed to determine whether it offers advantages in an information warfare context.

### 4.7 Countermeasure transactions

Countermeasure transactions are transactions specifically designed to detect and/or repair damage. An attack might be detected by a large variety of means. Some are internal to the database, such as integrity constraint violation detection via the firing of an action rule in an active database. Others are external to the database, such as an alert officer noticing that an abnormally high number of aircraft are scheduled to refuel at a particular tanker. Also, damage might be repaired by a drastic action such as reset of the entire database to a prior state or a simple approach such as merely waiting for good data to overwrite bad data. Many of these countermeasures can be modelled as transactions on the information system. The benefit of doing so is that the power of the transaction model can be used to implement fault tolerance across the system as a whole.

## 5. Conclusion

In this paper the phases of activity with which information warfare defenders must be concerned are discussed. While much work in detection and reaction focuses on catching illegal entry into the system, concentrating on the operating system and networking levels, here focus is on defending and repairing damage to the information maintained within the system. This focus responds to the need to defend against subtle corruption of information intended to degrade a system's ability to perform its mission in a manner unknown to its users and operators. It also responds to the need for defence against attacks by real and apparent insiders.

## References

1. Gracia-molina H, Salem k sagas, *Proceeding of the ACM SIGMOD International Conference on management of data*, 1987, pp 249-259.
2. Gray J, Reuter, *A Transaction processing: Concepts and Techniques*. Morgan Kaufmann, San Mateo, CA, 1993.
3. Lee P.A., Anderson T, *Fault Tolerance: Principles and Practice*, 2nd edition-1990.
4. Mukherjee B, Heberlein L.T, Levitt K.N, *Network intrusion detection. IEEE Networks*, vol. 18,1994,pp 26-41.
5. Forrest S., Hofmeyr S.A, *A Computer Immunology. Communication of ACM*, vol. 40,1997,pp 88-96
6. Goan, T. *a new integrated approach to intrusion prevention, Detection, and response.* Tech. Rep. SHAI, San Mateo, California, 1998.

# An Information Warfare Risk Analysis Model
# (A Conceptual Model)

Dr Matthew Warren[1] and Dr William Hutchinson[2]

[1]School of Computing & Mathematics, Deakin University, Geelong, Victoria, Australia.
[2]School of Management Information Systems, Edith Cowan University, Churchlands, Western Australia, Australia.

E-mail Contact: mwarren@deakin.edu.au

## Abstract

As we move towards the development of an information society we are faced with a situation where new threats and risks could undermine its very existence. Information warfare is a term used to describe the systematic attack of the information infrastructure whether it be for economic or military purposes.

The paper describes a conceptual system that is being designed to determine the risks associated with the new threat of information warfare. It is intended that this new computer system would be used by organisations to help them to protect their most sensitive organisational information.

## Keywords

Information Warfare, Computer Security, Security Risks.

## 1. Introduction

Since the end of the cold war and the increased development of global networks new threats and vulnerabilities have developed. Many governments are concerned about the fact that their national information infrastructure (NII) is completely dependant upon computerised networks, whether military or commercial. This means that an enemy, many thousands of miles away, can remotely attack and damage a country's NII via electronic means. Countries such as the USA have taken the threat so seriously that they have set up a presidential commission (Presidents Commission on Critical Infrastructure Protection, 2000) to determine the risks and vulnerabilities that the US NII could face. All developed countries are now heavily reliant upon their national and in some cases regional NIIs.

Australia is no exception and is vulnerable to information warfare attacks. There are many exposed critical nodes in key elements of the NII that can be exploited by aggressors (Cobb, 1997). Due to the isolated spread of the population even small scale attacks could have a dramatic effect.

At the moment, extensive research is being undertaken by military and intelligence organisations on how to protect the countries military NII, but unfortunately no research is being undertaken on how to protect the economic aspect of the NII. Many companies are unaware of information warfare and struggle just trying to implement standard computer security countermeasures. Therefore a model is being developed to try to help organisations determine the impact that information warfare could have upon them and their organisations.

The new risk analysis model will have unique features including the fact that the threats and vulnerability of the NII will be considered. The NII can be defined in the most simple terms as comprising those components that make up the national network within and over which information is stored, processed and transported (Defence Signals Directorate, 1997). Without the NII, there would be no electronic commerce, hence any damage to the NII would have a direct impact upon these services. The term Information Warfare (Denning, 1999) is used to describe attacks upon the NII. The research will focus upon the attacks aimed at the economical aspect of the NII especially Electronic Commerce. Attacks types might include hacking, spoof attacks, denial of service attacks etc. and the research will focus upon the impact of these attacks and determine future security risks posed by Cyber Terrorists, Hacker Groups and attacks by fellow organisations.

## 2. Risk Analysis and Information Warfare

The aim of traditional computer security risk analysis is to eliminate or reduce risks and vulnerabilities that affect the overall operation of organizational computer systems. Risk analysis not only looks at hardware and software, but also covers other areas such as physical security, human security, and business and disaster protection. In practice, there are major problems with the use of risk analysis; the time taken to carry out a review, the cost of hiring consultants and/or training staff. To overcome these negative aspects, baseline security standards were developed. Baseline security standards offer an alternative to conventional risk methods as they represent the minimally acceptable security countermeasures that an organization should have implemented. These countermeasures are applied in a generic manner, e.g. every organization should have the same baseline security countermeasures.

The advantages of using baseline methods include (Warren, 1997):

- it is cheap to use;
- it is simple to use;
- no training is required to use the method;
- it is quicker then undertaking a full security review.

The disadvantages of using baseline methods include (Warren, 1997):

- the generic nature of baseline security methods mean they may not solve all of the organizational security requirements;
- the fact that they have been designed for use within a general environment mean that they may not be suited for all environments, i.e. healthcare or small businesses;
- there is no suggestion about how the security countermeasures may be implemented;
- they do not contain cost /benefit details.

The problem with Information Warfare is that risks and threats are aimed at a countries NII, therefore conventional computer security risks analysis approaches cannot deal with the complexity of the problem. New approaches will have to be developed in order to deal with the new risks.

## 3. An Overview of the Information Warfare Risk Analysis Model Approach

As stated before the Information Warfare Risk Analysis Model (IWRAM) is a system that is being designed to be used by business organisations to help them protect against future risks to their computerised systems.

The system that is being developed is based upon a risk analysis model (see figure 1). The model is broken down into the following stages:

Stage 1: Attack Methods
The user will be able to determine the appropriate attack method(s) which could be used against a particular organisation such as denial of service attacks, virus attacks, hacking, etc.

The attack can be focussed upon a number of different aspects - attacks could be focused upon the machine - eg trying to crash the machine through denial of service attacks or trying to corrupt data by introducing computer viruses.

Stage 2: The Organisation
After the attack methods have been selected in stage 1, the appropriate organisational computer system should be selected, e.g. financial systems or decision support systems. This aspect is further complicated by the globalisation of organisations and their dependence on technology to connect their global operation. The user will then have to answer questions about the system, such as the importance of the data, how easy would it be to replace lost data, what business function does the data support, etc.

Stage 3: The Impact
This stage will determine the internal (the impact to the actual organisation) and external (the impact to customers/competitors/country) impacts. It will demonstrate the impact that different attack methods could have upon an organisation, illustrating the different impacts. This stage helps to show the importance of the information contained on the organisation's computer systems and how they relate to core business functions. The impact itself could be of various types - physical destruction of data, loss of business through lack of availability of system access, etc.

Stage 4: Outcomes and countermeasures
This stage shows the impact of stage 3 and suggests appropriate countermeasures in order to protect the organisation's data and systems, e.g. recovery plans, mail filters, increased internet security, etc. Stage 4 is concerned with reducing the impact that an attack could have upon an organisation. There is further complication in this stage by the fact that various countermeasures may have to be implemented at various levels to fulfil a particular security requirement - e.g. Intrusion Detection will have to be implemented at the server level, virus protection at the machine level.

Stage 5 - Offensive Countermeasures

This part of the model is concerned with suggesting offensive countermeasures which organisation may use. This stage of the method is optional. Most organisations have only defensive computer security countermeasures implemented. In the USA a new security approached called "Strike Back" or "cyber vigilantism" (Hutchinson and Warren, 1999) has been developed. This is based on the use of offensive computer security features. The aim of this approach is for an organisation to determine they are being attacked and then automatically attack the attacker with the aim of stopping the unauthorised access attempt. This approach is not concerned with harming the attacker but stopping an attack when it takes place before an organisation loses data or has data damaged. This part of the model is the most radical since it can be defined as being unethical or illegal to carry out such attacks. But in the new millennium - new security paradigms may be more widely accepted to reduce security risks. The conceptual model for IWRAM is shown within Figure 1.

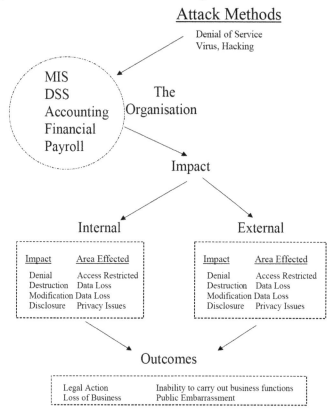

**Figure 1. The IWRAM Model**

The IWRAM risk analysis model is different from conventional risk analysis models in the fact that it is event driven. This relates to actual physical events taking place and also temporal issues related to those events. This new approach will result in a system that is more adaptable to organisational needs; this will help to make it more proactive rather than reactive. The model also shows the impact of different IW attacks; this will help organisations plan their risk management strategies to cover all hypothetical occurrences.

## 4. System Design

It is important to develop a system that encapsulates the methodology. Therefore at the moment the following areas are being looked at:

Environmental Analysis

Environmental analysis is concerned with determining the need for, and value of, knowledge within the organisations. Particular importance will be placed upon analysing the cultural environment of the organisations, e.g. staff interaction, management methods, etc.

User Analysis

User analysis is concerned with analysing the way in which organisations carry out their primary functions and determine their attitudes toward security issues. Another area that will be examined is how organisations perceive the importance of their data. This will help them to become more aware of which data they hold has the greatest strategic value. This, in turn would help to persuade them to enhance their existing security, particularly for the data of most strategic value.

Security Knowledge

The security knowledge for the system will be acquired from a number of sources, including:

- relevant Information Warfare literature (Schwartau, 1996);
- relevant Information Warfare reports, e.g. the report of the President's Commission on Critical Infrastructure Protection (Presidents Commission on Critical Infrastructure Protection, 1997);
- results obtained from Information Warfare questionnaires sent to major Australian businesses;
- interviews with security and related experts;
- existing international/national security standards (Australian Standards Institute 1996).

The knowledge reflected within the system will contain the latest opinions and facts relating to information warfare, but, as a matter of course, this information will be reviewed on a regular basis to ensure its current applicability.

The aim of the research is to produce a system which will give organisations an understanding of the impact caused by information warfare. Another important feature of the system will be that it suggests appropriate countermeasures.

Another consideration is the user aspect of the system design, especially issues such as the use of the system. Therefore the next stage will be to select an appropriate language to implement the system. Because of the usability and graphical user interface issues it is likely that the system will be developed using Visual Basic.

## 5. Conclusion

The seriousness with which the issue of Information Warfare is taken can be illustrated by recent activities by national governments especially the USA. In the United States, for example, concern over IT related threats has led to the establishment of the National Infrastructure Protection Centre (NIPC). This is a US$64 million facility, employing some 500 staff across the country, with representatives taken from existing agencies such as the Secret Service, the CIA, NASA, the National Security Agency, the Department of Defense and several others. The role of NIPC is to "detect, deter, assess, warn of, respond to, and investigate computer intrusions and unlawful acts" that threaten or target US critical infrastructures such as telecommunications, energy, banking and finance, water systems, government operations and emergency services (NIPC, 2000).

The paper has attempted to show the importance of developing the IWRAM model and system and how it can help to protect a countries NII. Once the full system has been developed it will provide a useful security tool which organisations can use to determine the impact that information warfare would have upon them. The event driven risk analysis model is also a major departure from traditional risk analysis models and should help to make the system more flexible in its approach.

The system should also help raise awareness of the new Information Warfare threat within the business sector and make businesses consider more closely their position within the NII and take appropriate action to secure that position.

The next major step within this project will be the physical implementation of the IWRAM model, this will form the basis for future investigations and development of the new computerised system.

## 6. Acknowledgments

This project is funded by the Australian research council under the small ARC grant scheme.

## 7. References

Australian Standards Institute (1996), *AS/NZS Standard 4444: Information Security Management*, Australian Standards Institute, Australia.

Cobb, A (1997), *Working Paper No.310 - Australia's vulnerability to information attack*, Strategic & Defence Studies Centre, Australian National University, Australia.

Defence Signals Directorate (1997). The National Information Infrastructure: Threats and Vulnerabilities, Government Publications, Australia.

Denning, D (1999), Information Warfare, ACM Press, USA.

Hutchinson, W and Warren, M.J (1999). Attacking the Attackers: Attitudes of Australian IT Managers to retaliation against Hackers, ACIS (Australasian Conference on Information Systems) 99, Wellington, New Zealand.

NIPC. (2000). Mission Statement, National Infrastructure Protection Centre. [On-line]. http://www.nipc.gov

Presidents Commission on Critical Infrastructure Protection (2000). USA. [On-line]. http://www.pccip.gov)

Presidents Commission on Critical Infrastructure Protection (1997), *Critical Foundations – Protecting Americas Infrastructure*, US Government Publications, USA.

Schwartau, W (1996), *Information Warfare* (2nd Edition), Thunder's Mouth Press, USA, ISBN 1-56025-132-8.

Warren M.J, (1997) "A new hybrid approach for Risk Analysis", *IFIP WG11.1 - Information Security Management Conference*, Copenhagen, Denmark, pp. 123 – 130.

# Networked Learning and the Delivery of Distance Education: Telematics at the University of Plymouth

S. Wheeler

Faculty of Arts and Education, University of Plymouth, United Kingdom
e-mail: swheeler@plymouth.ac.uk

## Abstract

The integration of life-long learning into the work place will become a familiar feature of life in the next decade. It is more than likely that distance education delivery will be the prime strategy many universities will employ in partnership with industry to deliver it. This paper outlines some of the network solutions currently being employed by the University of Plymouth to extend its operations to deliver distance learning opportunities to businesses and part-time learners in the South West of England. The paper discusses the current climate of change in universities and industry partnerships, defines telematic technologies, outlines the current network infrastructure at the University of Plymouth, and examines some of the human factors and pedagogical theories associated with flexible working and learning at a distance from the parent institute.

## Keywords

Distance Education, Telematics, Human Factors, Network Infrastructures

## Introduction

Distance education is expected to become an increasingly important strategy for many universities in the early part of this new century. The reasons for this are manifold, but primarily, universities must survive in an increasingly competitive world, and attempt to extend their boundaries beyond the traditional classroom. Student intake numbers are falling in many industrialised nations, forcing universities to examine new markets. In the UK, the University for Industry has been established to promote higher education and professional development in the workplace.

Many businesses are unwilling to release their employees on a long-term bases, so part-time study, preferably in a work-based environment, is becoming *de rigeur*. This is for four reasons: Firstly, students need to physically attend an institute to participate in courses; secondly, courses are not normally customised to the specific needs of a business or individual; thirdly, students cannot mix and match courses from several providers easily to provide customised learning routes; finally, the influx of professionals return to work after an absence require up-skilling or re-skilling in their chosen area of expertise. The integration of simultaneous working and learning has the potential to negate the unproductive down-time business managers wish to avoid (Granow, 1999).

The concept of life-long learning is here to stay, and this author predicts that distance education delivery will become the prime strategy many universities will employ in partnership with industry.

This paper outlines some of the network solutions currently being employed by the University of Plymouth to extend its operations to deliver distance learning opportunities to businesses and part-time learners in the South West of England. The paper discusses the current climate of change in universities, defines telematic technologies, outlines the current network infrastructure at the University of Plymouth, and examines some of the human factors associated with flexible working and learning at a distance from the parent institute.

## Changes in University Life

There are many factors that create the need for universities to modify delivery of learning and increase development of distance education strategies. The economic pressures being exerted on higher education are unprecedented. Demographic factors ensure that student enrolment numbers are falling in many industrialised nations. In order to compete, universities must exploit the new markets of mature, part-time student populations. Further, an increase in the number of subject options requires a rethinking of the role of the academic in teaching.

Universities in the current climate must contend with the following factors:

- Fewer academic staff
- Larger class sizes
- Greater diversity among students (ethnic, economic and social backgrounds)
- More subjects

Although by no means exhaustive, these factors have the potential to lessen the opportunities for small class teaching. This has fuelled the argument that quality contact time between learner and teacher is becoming non-existent and learning is suffering as a result (Martin, 1999: 8). This is an endemic problem, requiring radical solutions. One possible answer to the problem may be to instigate wide scale distance learning.

## Distance Learning and Telematics

Distance learning encompasses any set of learning activities that take place at a distance from the originator of the learning materials.

Teachers are relying increasingly upon telematic solutions to connect with remote students. Telematics can best be defined as the convergent action of computers and telecommunications (networks and telephony). Telematics embraces a number of technologies, all of which are currently employed to deliver distance learning materials to remote students. These include videoconferencing (ISDN and ATM), web based technologies, digital satellite and cable services and a combination of the essential features of these solutions.

## The University of Plymouth

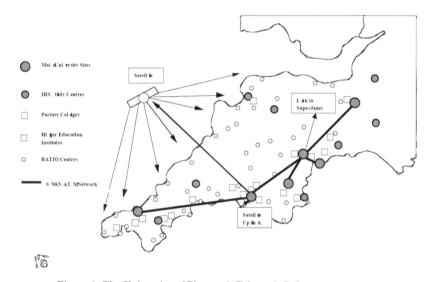

**Figure 1: The University of Plymouth Telematic Infrastructure**

The University of Plymouth is a regional university, located within the South West peninsula of England and distributed across almost 200 kilometres of predominately rural area. It has a growing number of 'outreach' learning centres known as RATIO centres and other distributed teaching sites, many of which are situated in very remote areas that are relatively inaccessible (Figure 1). Travelling between sites is often problematic due to the poor travel infrastructure and other factors such as the seasonal tourist influx that creates congestion on narrow country roads during the summer months. Dispersed student populations and increasing staff travel and subsistence costs encouraged the university to seek alternative methods of learning delivery. Distributed modes of education, and in particular, distance learning methodologies were the obvious choice, as they addressed many of the problems identified. Over a period of time the university began to rationalise its approach.

## Rationalisation Process

The first stage in the process of rationalisation was to identify the range of methods, modes and media currently available for the development, delivery and support of distance learning activities. To do this, the 'Martini' model of education ('anytime anyplace') was re-developed and applied.

S Y N C H R O N O U S

| | Same Time Same Place | Same Time Different Place | |
|---|---|---|---|
| | Chalkboard | Educational Television | |
| | Overhead Projector | Video Conferencing | |
| | Slide Projector | Audio Conferencing | |
| | Video & Audio Tape | Computer Mediated Comm. | |
| L | Classroom Technologies | Satellite Seminars/Keynotes | R |
| O | | | E |
| C | | | M |
| A | Resource Based Learning | Internet and WWW | O |
| L | Multimedia      CD-ROM | Electronic Mail | T |
| | Computer Aided Learning | Video Streaming | E |
| | Text            Simulations | Video On Demand (VOD) | |
| | Video & Audio Tape | Virtual Learning Labs. | |
| | Different Time Same Place | Different Time Different Place | |

A S Y N C H R O N O U S

**Figure 2: 'Any Time Any Place' Model of Education**

This model has been variously presented by Johansen (1991), Looms (1993) and Pohjonen (1995). The model was recently contextualised by Vanbuel (1998) and the most recent iteration, with modifications by the author is presented in Figure 2.

To be applied effectively, a model of this nature requires some qualification. The first quadrant in Figure 2 (synchronous/local) can be referred to as a traditional, or 'real time encounter' mode, as it is based upon face to face personal contact between the teacher and learner. This is still the most prevalent model for the delivery of education and training in most countries. The second quadrant (synchronous/remote) can be referred to as the simultaneously distributed learning model. In this model the teacher and learner are present in the same time frame, but separated by geographical distance. Quadrant three (asynchronous/local) can be referred to as the independent study model, and is exemplified in many higher education institutes as self-directed study or resource based learning. The final quadrant, (asynchronous/remote) is the most independent of time and geography, where learner and teacher are separated by both geographical and temporal distance. This quadrant features the most extensive technological support, and is also heavily reliant upon highly motivated students for its success rate. A distinction can therefore be made about geographical and temporal differentials, and appropriate technology solutions applied to create connections between tutor and student and between student and student.

The fourth model is characterised by the need to recognise that although distance may be bridged by technology, there is also a psychological gap, sometimes referred to as 'transactional distance' (Moore, 1991) or instructional gap (Willis, 1993) which can only be bridged by the sensitive social and pedagogical skills of professional teachers. If it is not effectively bridged, this differential may result in mismatches between what the course author desires to communicate and the students' interpretations (Marsden, 1996), and between the intentions of tutors and the expectations of students (Moore, 1973). Ultimately this will result in undesirable consequences such as confusion, frustration, demotivation and increased student attrition rates.

Recent studies by the authors have identified something of the nature of this gap, revealing that several discrete forms of learning support are expected by both remote and local students. These include social support, technical help, feedback and direct instruction. Also indicated in the study is the notion that remote students expect and receive a great deal more of this learning support than local students. Never the less they still receive less than they expect, indicating that remote students expect distance learning to be both a qualitatively different, and potentially problematic experience (Wheeler et al, 1999).

## Psychological Dimensions

Learning at a distance can be both complex and problematic. The perceptual gulf between teacher and learner in itself is potentially the most important factor contributing to success or failure. Some students who are self motivated have been known to succeed where others have failed and dropped out of courses. The psychological distance between learner and teacher, referred to in the literature as 'transactional distance' (Moore, 1973) is thought to be responsible for misunderstandings and mismatches between intentions and expectations. In a learning dialogue between teacher and learner, an element of trust and collaboration must be engendered. When learner does not meet teacher on a personal basis, the student may develop a feeling of remoteness or detachment from the learning process resulting in a 'perceptual gulf' (Moore, 1991). Without ownership of the material and the process, the student is in danger of becoming disillusioned and demotivated. Lack of access to expert tutorial help compounds the problem still further. In short, the twin requirements of telepresence and learner support are required if the distance learner is to develop as a learner and achieve subject expertise.

Moore (1991) has argued that structure in a course delivery limits dialogue. Conversely, a great deal of dialogue throughout a course causes structure to diminish. Transactional distance theory predicts that the greater the dialogue, the less is the perceived psychological distance between teacher and learner. Dialogue breeds student autonomy and enables students to gain independence in the learning process (Saba and Shearer, 1994). Without dialogue, the learner may feel isolated and quality learning outcomes may be hampered. It is important then, that good communicative infrastructures are built into distance course provision to enable effective telepresence and promotion of dialogue.

## Evaluation of Systems

Synchronous communication systems, enabling dialogue at a distance in real time, are the highest level of telematic learning support possible. Specifically, digital video conferencing with associated graphical user interface (GUI) environments such as whiteboard, text messaging and application sharing can provide excellent collaborative learning and tutorial facilities. Videoconference however, is arguably a poor medium for lecture delivery, as the visual information is limited by bandwidth, and the structure of a didactic presentation normally inhibits dialogue. This author considers satellite television is a better medium for delivery of keynote lectures and demonstrations. Experiences of delivering courses using satellite to rural businesses, for example, have indicated more favourable results than the use of videoconference. The RATIO project used extensive satellite transmissions for distributed lectures, whilst videoconference equipment was used for one-to-one interaction and small group work. Although in previous years costs of satellite transmission have been prohibitive, with recent developments in video compression techniques and price reductions in receivers and dishes, costs have tumbled, making live digital transmissions via satellite an attainable goal. Terrestrial transmission via cable and line-of-sight technologies are viable alternatives, providing easy access and workable bandwidths in most industrialised areas.

Integration of features must be undertaken with care. Cognitive overload for example may result if learners are bombarded with sounds, images and text for long periods of time. Cognitive overload occurs when the attentional span of the average human mind is exceeded and the quality and extent of learning decreases as a result (Sweller 1988; Tuovinen, 1999).

Web based delivery has been shown to be effective in promoting student autonomy as it is non-linear in nature and thus encourages students to spend time in areas of a topic that are of interest, and less time on familiar areas (Brown, 1997). Hypertext links create multiple pathways and layers for a student to explore, ensuring that individual students create meaning for themselves in unique ways. University of Plymouth web projects such as PILL and MTUTOR makes extensive use of this feature. This application must also be treated with caution however, as learners can get carried away, begin to digress in their searching, or become 'lost' and miss the purpose of a particular learning exercise.

Generally speaking, telematic technologies have several roles in connecting students and their teachers and with each other at a distance. These include:

- the promotion of 'telepresence'
- the facilitation of collaborative group working
- provision of access to a wide range of flexible learning experiences through multiple media
- a means of providing general learning support for the remote student.

The next section of this paper focuses in particular on recognised patterns of communication during the learning process.

## Patterns of communication in teaching and learning

There are many aspects of traditional teaching and learning that can be duplicated and also enhanced through the use of telematic methods. Patterns of communication between teacher and student, and between student and student are of course put under tension when participants are separated by geographical and temporal distance.

According to Collis (1996) there are four patterns of communication apparent within the learning environment. These are:

- Telling - traditionally, instruction has been achieved by lecture and printed text, this delivery method is essentially didactic, and on-way in nature. In telematic delivery, instructive activities can be achieved via a range of technologies, including web delivery and satellite television. In its purest form, 'telling' need not be synchronous to be effective - students can access information at a time that suits them, without the lecturer necessarily being there at the same time.

- Asking - traditionally achieved during question and answer sessions, seminars and discussion groups, this can be referred to as discursive or Socratic in nature. If 'asking' is primarily viewed by the teacher as a synchronous activity, technologies such as computer mediated communication (CMC) or video conference must be used to achieve real time dialogue. If however, time is to be given for students to reflect more on their answers, other, asynchronous forms of communication, such as electronic mail could be used.

- Responding - also achieved in traditional settings through question and answer, discussion and seminar sessions, this is different to asking in that it is essentially teacher initiated. Again, due to it's synchronous nature 'responding' should ideally be synchronous, as prompt answers can motivate and challenge students to advance in their studies and can focus the energy of groups (Mason, 1999). Electronic mail is a viable asynchronous option as it can be rich in expression and as Dooley has suggested an increase in the use of e-mail is often due to an increase in the cognitive demands of work and study (Dooley, 1996).

- Discussing - facilitating group work through collaboration - is the final pattern of communication commonly observed in many forms of education. Within four walls this is easily achieved. When the group is distributed geographically, this can be problematic. Synchronous and asynchronous formats are equally relevant, depending on the desired learning outcomes. If for example, a group has been tasked to achieve a consensus on a chosen issue, asynchronous computer mediated communication may be the most appropriate technology, giving students room to think and reflect on their contributions over a period of time. If on the other hand there are visual or audio aspects of the task, a synchronous tool such as videoconferencing or audiographics may be a more viable alternative.

## Technology Supported Learning

The technology employed to support distance learning is underpinned by the philosophy that students work and learn within an environment that must be quality assured. Continual evaluation is therefore required. Furthermore, it is assumed that the student is central to the learning process, and that the teacher must therefore play a supporting role. The student thus spends a great deal of time interacting with the learning materials and comes to the teacher when specialist input is required. Figure 3 represents these ideals.

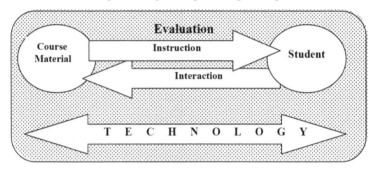

Figure 3: Technology Supported Learning Model

However, this model becomes hopelessly inadequate when the ideals of telepresence and group collaboration are attempted. A revised model incorporating these ideals may be seen in Figure 4.

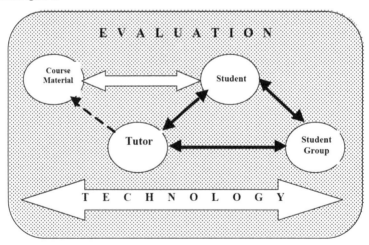

Figure 4: Technology Supported Learning and Communications Model

346

## Analysing Availability and Requirement

In order to see the whole picture of telematic learning delivery, and to be able to plan effectively for it, an integrated systems approach should be adopted. Many learning technologies are now multi-functional and can provide excellent flexible learning opportunities for students regardless of time, place and learning space. Telematic technologies are set to provide the vital foundations for a pervasive culture of any-time, any-place lifelong learning. One particularly interesting integrated approach to multi-media comes in the form of web based multi-casting. This approach utilises the Internet and provides teachers with the opportunity to transmit live audio and video lectures over the world wide web. Learners access the appropriate web server at a pre-arranged time and participate in a live lecture. At the same time, images of slide presentations or other graphical materials are injected into the data stream and reach the learner in a synchronised format. Finally, two-way text box messaging is available, providing a useful, if not totally interactive and flexible learning environment. Figure 5 shows a screen capture of one vendor's web based multi-casting system in action.

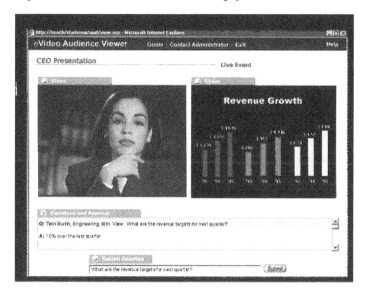

**Figure 5: Learner screen of PictureTel's StarCast ™ web based multi-casting system**

The University of Plymouth has developed a similar version of the webcasting system, incorporating a Module Authoring Tool (MAT) to aid teachers in the creation of tutorial material and lecture notes (Furnell *et al*, 1998).

347

## Conclusions

When embarking upon widespread delivery of education at a distance, it is vital that distance educators and planners select the correct network applications. This may only be effectively achieved by careful consideration of a number of factors, including the pedagogical, technological and psychological. It is also equally important that as they build pedagogical and technological infrastructures, they also plan for the future. Those who fail to future proof their activities can expect to fail in the long term. Effective planning can only be achieved by an intimate knowledge of the systems currently available and how they can be applied either singly or in an integrated manner to meet the learning needs of students. This can be either in isolation or as integrated systems in order to provide the best possible distributed learning environments.

The author plans to extend this work further to incorporate other important parameters such as interactivity, information richness and user perception and expectation. These are generally considered to be psychological dimensions and will thus be explored using appropriate evaluative methodologies. The results of these studies will be reported in future publications.

## References

Brown, A. (1997) Designing for learning: What are the essential features of an effective online course? *Australian Journal of Educational Technology*. 13 (2) 115-26.

Collis, B. (1996) *Tele-learning in a digital world: the future of distance learning*. London: International Thomson Computer Press.

Dooley, B. (1996) At work away from work. *The Psychologist*, 9 (4) 155-8.

Furnell, S. M., Evans, M., Phippen, A. D., and Ali Abu Regheffi, M. N. (1998) On-line Distance Education: Expectations, Requirements and Barriers. *Virtual University Journal*. 2 (2). http://www.fae.plym.ac.uk/tele/odl-1.html

Granow, R., (1999) Virtual University of Applied Science. *Paper presented at the On-Line Educa Conference, Berlin, Germany*. 25-26 November, 1999.

Johansen, R. (1991) GroupWare: Future directions and wild cards. In *ITCA Teleconferencing Yearbook 1991*. Washington D.C.: ITCA.

Looms, O. P. (1993) Technology supported learning (Distance learning*). Danish Ministry of Education Report*. No. 1253. Ringsted: Malchov.

Martin, E. (1999) *Changing Academic Work: Developing the Learning University*. Milton Keynes: Open University Press.

Marsden, R. (1996) Time, space and distance education. *Distance Education*, 17 (2), 222-246.

Mason, R. (1999) *The Globalisation of Education.* Milton Keynes: Open University Press.

Moore, M. G. (1973) Towards a theory of independent learning and teaching. *Journal of Higher Education.* 44 (9) 661-79.

Moore, M. G. (1991) Editorial: Distance education theory. *The American Journal of Distance Education.* 5 (3) 1-6.

Pohjonen, J. (1997) New learning environments as a strategic choice. *European Journal of Education.* 32 (4).

Saba F and Shearer R (1994) Verifying key theoretical concepts in a dynamic model of distance education. *The American Journal of Distance Education.* 8 (1), 36-56.

Sweller, J. (1988) Cognitive load during problem solving: effects on learning. *Cognitive Science*, 12, 257-85.

Tuovinen, J. E. (1999) Research framework and implications for online multimedia education practice based on cognition research. *Paper presented at the ComNEd Conference. Hameenlinna, Finland.* June 1999. 334-45.

Vanbuel, M. (1998) Choosing and using the appropriate technology platform. *Paper presented at the OnLine Educa Conference, Berlin, Germany.* 2-4 December, 1998.

Wheeler, S. (1997) Distance learning and convergent technologies: Videoconferencing. *Journal of Information Technology in Nursing.* British Computer Society. 9 (1) 19-22.

Wheeler, S., Vranch, A. T. & Reid, F. I. M., (1999a) Bridging the psychological gap in distance learning through telematics. *Poster presented at the World Open Learning Conference, Vienna, Austria.* June, 1999.

Wheeler, S., (1999b) Streaming through the Net: Combining video streaming and web casting for interactive learning environments. *Paper presented at the OnLine Educa Conference, Berlin, Germany.* November, 1999. http://www.fae.plym.ac.uk/tele/tele.html

Willis, B (1993) *Distance education: A practical guide.* Englewood Cliffs, NJ: Educational Technology Publications.

# Global Education in the Cyber Age:
# An Australian Example

Ms. Shona Warren, Dr. Matthew Warren and Dr. Jo Coldwell

School of Computing & Mathematics, Deakin University, Geelong,
Victoria, Australia, 3216.
E-mail Contact: mwarren@deakin.edu.au

## Abstract

Computer-mediated communication is becoming an ever-increasing way of facilitating education to students who are unable to attend a traditional on-campus university.

Research has shown that the communication medium used directly effects the positively of the experience to all parties involved. Deakin University, Australia is a prime example of where communication practices are important. The paper highlights the leading role that Deakin offers within the Distance Education Market within Australia, Asia, New Zealand and North America. This leading role that Deakin has allows for them to be at the leading edge of developing and using technology for distance education. This unique position also allows Deakin to have a full understanding of the advantages and limitations of these technologies. This paper will look at the problems associated with distance communication and how practices can be improved within the education sector.

## Keywords:

Computer Based Education, Distance Education.

## 1. Introduction

Within education a large amount of electronic communication is used. Especially in off campus teaching, electronic forms of communication have become the norm. The population of today's learners is defined as being over 25 years old, with a job and/or family responsibilities (Perkins and Schwartz, 1995). This vast student market requires a flexible program that can accommodate, for instance, job-related travel, and presents learning in a fixed location, at a fixed time.

The solution to this problem may lie in Asynchronous Learning Networks. Asynchronous learning is a relatively new yet continually growing field. This medium is based on having several benefits:
- constant access and availability to teaching materials;
- promotes interaction between students and between staff and students;
- fast feedback.

Using Web-based technology, these asynchronous learning networks allow students to learn from any geographic location, that has access to telephone communication. Unfortunately, very few empirical studies have addressed issues such as purpose of access, format and content of material and their effect on performance, timing of material availability, and impact on attendance. In this paper, we will focus upon the problems on performance and understanding of students learning through electronic forms of communication.

Although current electronic communication technologies make collaboration between dispersed groups more convenient, they reduce the set of modalities by which group members can communicate. Many channels through which face to face groups communicate auditory, nonverbal and paraverbal, are greatly reduced or eliminated.

Communication media affects group functioning and productivity in a large part by the degree with which they transmit social context cues (Straus and McGrath, 1994). However these cues are not required by a large majority of tasks that may be undertaken e.g. collaborative tasks such as idea generation tasks need little or no co-ordination and no consensus is required. Social context cues should have little impact on group performance, in fact it may even increase the amount of novel and diverse ideas produced by the group due in part to the removal of fear of evaluation by others.

The Internet allows for educational materials to be sent anywhere in the world. This data can take the form of distance learning material or just exam time tables. The Internet is a cost effective method for universities to compete in the global educational market (Bailey and Cotlar,1994). It is also the case that universities can compete for niche markets within the global educational sector, such as the following based Internet courses:

- University of Aberystwyth - Diploma of Healthcare Telematics (University of Aberystwyth, 2000);
- University of Wisconsin - Disaster Management Diploma (University of Wisconsin, 2000).

Research at the University of Technology (UOT), Sydney (Freeman, 1997) has been based upon using the World Wide Web (WWW) to teach finance modules. They interviewed a random selection of students who used the WWW system and found the following results:

| *Positive Comments* | *Negative Comments* |
|---|---|
| 80% - improved access to information | 60% - access to a Internet PC |
| 72% - reinforced learning | 44% - network problems |
| 56% - opportunity to use new technology | |
| 48% - improve staff interaction | |

**Table 1: Student Assessment of Internet trials at UOT, Sydney, Australia**

The study found that the students were enthusiastic about using the new technologies, that it helped to reinforce the conventional lectures and improved access to information. The studies found that the biggest problem was students getting access to Internet PC's and a slow access rate. To overcome the problems, more computers were provided, a new file server was bought and they redesigned existing web pages to speed up loading times. The system also allowed improved contact between the students and staff via the use of the E-mail, this can be reassuring to students to know that they can contact staff with questions.

## 2. E-mail as a communication tool

E-mail communication in off campus teaching has been widespread over the last five to ten years especially within Australia. It has become an extremely effective and efficient method both for students to contact lecturers, tutors and administrators, as well as benefiting lecturers, by cutting out a large amount of paperwork and inconvenience. However most people will know how difficult it is to converse via E-mail and also how difficult it can be to express yourself through the 'typed word'. There is no doubt that electronic forms of communication can be less effective than face-to-face communication, but studies have also shown benefits:

- asychnronsity;
- directness;
- overcoming geographical boundaries;
- fosters better relationships.

E-mail could improve students' involvement in University life, and decrease the frustration of contacting a lecturer by telephone, to find they never answer. It also allows students to have 'direct' access to a lecturer, something which could actually be more difficult if the student were based on campus. This can be a "window on the organisation" (March and Guje, 1984), which allows for the rapid sharing of expertise across an organisation, in this case within education. There is also the perception that those people that were once less accessible, can now be directly contacted, thus increasing the level of satisfaction, motivation and commitment. In this case perhaps this would be so of students. This increases the students feeling of 'belonging' and bridges the geographical divides between them and their place of study. E-mail has also been shown to foster relationships within universities, a large amount of undergraduate E-mail was found to contain a degree of social content (McCormick and McCormick, 1992).

The downside of relying upon E-mail within off campus study may mean that those computer illiterate users may well be alienated. Also computer-mediated communication has frequently been observed to be more uninhibited and disorganized than face-to-face communication. Also regarding education there are other issues that have to be addressed, it was found that academic dishonesty increased during a semester as students became more proficient at using E-mail (McCormick and McCormick, 1992).

It can be seen that there are several effects of using E-mail, both positive and negative, on human communication. It's the view that the positive and negative effects of E-mail could possibly serve to cancel each other out, leaving a powerful but neutral tool. The effects on which are dependent on the user. This view is supported by learning experts (McCormick and McCormick, 1992) finding that E-mail is used equally for patently neutral purposes, pro-social and anti-social purposes.

## 3. Deakin University Case Study

Deakin University has become the primary provider of off campus courses to undergraduate and post graduates students within Australia. In 1999 Deakin University had 4,490 students enrolled in off-campus mode.

These students do not physically attend lectures and historically have received study guides to work from. The development of Technology has dramatically altered the way in which materials and courses are offered to off-campus students.

The off-campus students face a number of problems, these include:

- a feeling of isolation;
- difficulty in contacting lecturer;
- difficulty in gaining access to the same teaching materials as on-campus students.

The use of new technology has overcome many of the problems described. The most commonly used technologies used are as follows.

### 3.1 E-mail

This represents the simplest Internet technology that is used by off campus students. This is used to allow students contact lecturers, exchange information. E-mail also allows students to form self-help groups via the use of mailing lists.

The advantage of this medium is that all students have access to E-mail since Internet access is a pre-condition of acceptance to Deakin. The advantage of E-mail is that it allows student to directly contact lecturers and help to reduce the feel of isolation – that is a common problem for many off campus students. However as mentioned earlier, the lack of social context cues can also create problems.

### 3.2 Information Repositories

The university, also makes use of Web-based Information Repositories such as the Web-CT system. This system is used as a central location for lecturer notes, course news, etc. A screen shot of Web-CT is shown in figure 1.

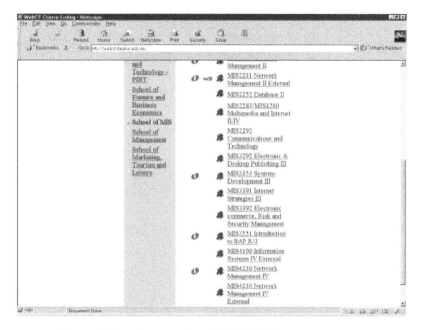

**Figure 1: Example screenshot of the Web-CT system**

Systems such as Web-CT are being widely adopted by Deakin University for a number of reasons:

- ensures off campus and on-campus students have access to the same materials as on-campus students;
- help to ensure that there is no difference between on-campus and off campus students;
- the Web-CT system is web-based which allows easy access for all students.

### 3.3 Group Discussion Tools

There are certain academic subjects that require an element of discussion as an important part of the academic unit. This requirement is outside the ability of standards information repository system such as Web-CT. Therefore what is required is the use of a more dedicated system that allow students to post messages and allow those messages to be structured in a orderly manner.

The system that is commonly used by Deakin University is called Firstclass (as shown by figure 2). The system is not web-based, and students are required to download a dedicated browser to connect to the Deakin firstclass server.

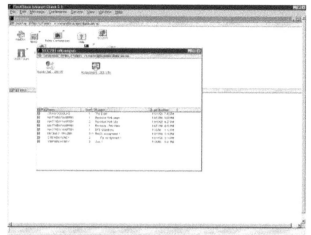

**Figure 2: Example screenshot of the FirstClass system**

The advantages of this system, is that it allows:

- off-campus students to take part in discussions;
- reduces any distinction between on and off campus students;
- allows students to directly interact with each other, whether they are on or off campus students.

### 3.4 Web-Cam

Deakin is also involved in trying to develop teaching new technologies that can be used to assist students and staff. One of these new developments has been the use of web-based cameras. At the moment pilot students have been undertaken to connect student and staff in remote campuses (as shown by figure 3). It is intended to expand the use of Web-cams in the future.

The advantage of this approach is:

- allows direct contact between staff and students;
- makes it cost effective to directly contact overseas students, an important issue in the global education markets;
- equipment required for video-technology is relatively inexpensive.

However, disadvantages of video technology can be (O'Conaill et al, 1993):

- overlapping speech between student and lecturer;
- interruptions in the sessions due to the technology;
- issue of standards, due to variety of systems available.

Figure 3: Web-Cam Example

## 4. The Next Step

These web based technologies seem to be proving successful within the Department of Computing and Mathematics at Deakin University, however it must be noted that they may not be suitable for all undergraduate courses. A subject such as Chemistry which relies on a large practical element, would be difficult to teach via the Internet, but it should be noted that this is a subject that would be hard to teach in an off campus mode, regardless of whether it is via the Internet or traditional distance learning methods.

The aim of this paper has been a discussion about the some of the issues related to using new technologies within education. The next part of the project will be conducting a survey of off-campus students to determine their feelings about the use of these new teaching technologies and whether those problems described in previous research have any bearing on the teaching technologies of today. Their feedback will allow for new strategies to be developed in order to utilise the current technologies in the most effective manner possible.

Another important part of developing strategies for global education is to be aware of new educational mediums and how these can be used within education.

## 5. Conclusion

We are beginning to see the new technologies have their impact upon the educational sector, we are unable to determine what the true impact will be upon the University of tomorrow.

Technology is now being used to give Universities competitive advantages over their rivals, In the future much more emphasis will be placed on teaching technologies as University fight for their share of the global university market.

Deakin University is trying to develop new teaching technologies in order to be a major player in tomorrow's global education market.

## 6. References

Perkins, D. N. &; Schwartz, J. L. (1995). *Software goes to school: Teaching for understanding with new technologies*. (pp. 255-270). New York, NY, USA: Oxford University Press.

Bailey E. & Cotlar M. (1994). "Teaching via the Internet", *Communication Education* 43 (2), 184-193.

University of Aberystwyth - Healthcare Informatics Site (http://www.uhi.ac.uk/).

University of Wisconsin- Disaster Management Center Internet Site (http://epdwww.engr.wisc.edu/dmc).

Freeman, M. A (1997) "*Flexibility in Access, Interaction and Assessment - The Case for Web-Based Conferencing and Teaching Programs*", Online Education Asia: International Conference on Technology Supported Learning, Singapore.

March, J. G. & Guje, S., (1984), "Gossip, Information and Decision-Making," In L. Sproull & P.D. Larkey (Eds.), *Advances in Information Processing in Organisations*, JAI Press, Greenwich, CT, 95-108.

McCormick, N.B. & McCormick, J. W. (1992), Computer friends and foes: Content of undergraduates' electronic mail. *Computers in Human Behaviour*, 8, 379-405.

O'Conaill, B., Whittaker, S., &Wilbur, S., (1993), Conversations over video conferences: An Evaluation of the spoken aspects of video-mediated communication, *Human-Computer Interaction*, 10, 401-444.

Straus, S. & McGrath, J., (1994), Does the medium matter? The interaction of task type and technology on group performance and member reactions. Journal of Applied Psychology, Vol 79(1), pp87-97.

# Course-Master: An Interactive Learning and Teaching Environment Over the World Wide Web

Shicheng Tian

School of Computing and Management Sciences, Sheffield Hallam University,
Sheffield, United Kingdom, S1 1WB
Email: S.Tian@shu.ac.uk

## Abstract

This paper is about the issue of using the World Wide Web (Web) for education. It contains an introduction, a brief survey and a discussion of the main issues related in this area, a design and a preliminary implementation of a prototype, the experience gained and future work. The prototype is for facilitating the teaching of a unit. A few conclusions are drawn at the end of the paper. Experience from the trial of the system shows that the Web is a cost-effective technology, to facilitate the development of educational applications across the Internet.

## Keywords

CBE, Web, CGI, Visual Basic, JavaScript

## 1. Introduction

The Web provides a distributed multimedia hypertext system that can be used in teaching, research and administration. Using the Web, we can: *retrieve* multimedia documents from around the world, *publish* documents globally, *run* programs on remote servers and *download* and *run* programs on local machines. With several million-host computers linked to the Internet, and estimates of many times that number of actual users, there are a huge number of potential Web page authors, who are adding new information to the vast information reservoir that already exists.

Many institutions have developed campus wide information systems using the Web. Students can access resources from around the world to assist them in their learning and take advantage of various distance learning courses which are now available on the Web (many of them are free!). Conferences, including reports, video, slide images, etc, can be published on the Web, allowing greater and more rapid dissemination. Clearly, the Web is an important tool for many applications, including education, and is expected to be so for some years to come.

In this paper, experience from the author is discussed on using the Web for facilitating teaching and learning. Apart from supporting normal web-site features (e.g. publishing lecture slides, providing reference information, etc.), this prototype Web site also supports the so called within-the-current-context features (e.g. after a lecture is selected, while keeping the main browser window display the slides of this lecture, in other small, pop-up windows, a student can make comments on the selected lecture, read the comments previously made on this lecture, view the self-asked questions for this lecture, etc.). Besides, students can communicate freely with each other or with the tutors using the built-in communication facilities: *feedback* and *email*. In order to be aware of who is using the system, an authentication procedure has been designed to ask students to submit their access *ids* and *passwords* when logging on to the system. After getting into the system, students can change their *passwords* at any time. In the following, discussions are given on some innovative computer based education (CBE) initiatives using the Internet and the Web, the main issues related to the use of the Web for education, a preliminary design and an implementation of a Web-oriented educational prototype, the experience gained, future work and a few conclusions.

## 2. Internet-and-Web-Oriented CBE Applications

The Internet can be used to facilitate teaching and learning. In these kind of applications, for example, students could submit their assignments over the network to a server machine where acknowledgements of receiving the work would be sent back to the students, and the assignments would be assessed by the computer, according to predefined standards.

The BOSS system (Joy and Luck 1998) is one of such kind of application. With the support of the system, it is possible to have student-programming assignments submitted, compiled and tested automatically. Although fully automatic marking is not supported yet by the system, it does support the process of marking, and enables marking tasks to be divided among several individuals while maintaining rigour and consistency. The developer of the system finds out that not only can this system alleviate the pressure of increasing workload due to having more and more students, it can improve the learning experience available to students (in providing them with facilities for immediate and effective feedback, for example), and also enable other administrative tasks to be automated, as part of a coherent approach to a full course management.

Some Web pages are purely written in HTML, others, however, begin to incorporate some form of interactivity. Normally, to make web pages interactive, script languages are used to implement small routines that are inserted into these pages. These routines carry out specific functionality, such as checking if the data that is entered to a text field is valid, etc. In order for the Web browsers to successfully present the Web pages that contain those routines, corresponding script language interpreters need to be incorporated into these browsers. Usually, these interpreters are called *plug-ins*.

Several script languages and Internet-oriented languages have been used to embed interactivity into Web pages (Hall 1998), including Java and JavaScript. Among them, Java is the most powerful tool to make Web pages interactive. This is because it is a proper object-oriented language, platform free and has more functionality than its competitors. Actually, *programming the Web with Java* remains the hottest topic in recent years in both the academic world and the computer industry. Java applets embedded into Web pages can be run on all kinds of computer systems, so long as machine-dependent Java virtual machines have been installed.

The Computer Assisted Teaching & Learning (CASTLE) project (Pownall and Mobbs 1998) is a good example of using the emerging Web technology for CBE. This system contains a MCQ bank, a Common Gateway Interface (CGI) marking program and a number of utility tools. The system provides teachers and students with an easy to use tool set for the delivery of on-line assessments. Using the provided tool set requires no prior knowledge of any CGI scripting and HTML. The only requirement to create an on-line test is the ability to use a Web browser. In this way, this system is platform independent. The assessment documents are in standard HTML. Therefore, the tests may contain any multimedia files, which can be delivered over the Web, from audio, images, or animated GIF files to links to other Web resources. According to the developer of this system, Java is going to be used to replace the current CGI approach, in order to take full advantage of the newly emerging, Web-oriented, object-oriented language, to further improve the functionality of the system.

Apart from using traditional approaches (e.g. CDs, videodiscs, single-machine packages), there is a trend now in using the Internet and especially the emerging Web technology to facilitate CBE applications. In the next section, discussions are given on the main issues related to using the Web for facilitating teaching and learning. These issues will lead to a design and a preliminary implementation of a Web-oriented CBE prototype.

## 3. Using the Web for Education: Six Basic Issues

Basically, CBE contains five components: *teachers* possessing the knowledge and being able to teach, *students* willing to learn, the *knowledge* itself, the means to *evaluate* the learning outcomes of the learners, and the enabling *technology*. The first four components are identified in (Pownall and Mobbs 1998). A careful reviewing of a face-to-face conventional educational context, however, will lead to adding an additional component to the list: the *communications* between teachers and students during the whole process of the teaching and learning activity. Indeed, teachers do have many communications with students, regardless whether on course work, projects, assignments, etc. It would be hard to imagine achieving any fruitful academic result without these vital communications. Hence, this factor ought to be considered when we try to use the computer technology to facilitate CBE. Therefore, the following six components should be considered for designing CBE systems: *teachers*, *students*, *knowledge*, *evaluations*, *communications* and the *enabling technology*.

*Evaluations* means conducting assessments to check if the learning outcomes have been achieved. Broadly speaking, assessments can be broken down into two kinds: formative assessments and summative assessments. The former refers to testings that can help students with their learning; it is a way of pinpointing weak points across a whole class or within individual students and a good way to aid student learning, while the latter refers to the end-of-course assessments whose procedures are more rigorous and the student is given a grade which contributes to his or her final degree on a particular course.

The most popular way of using network-oriented computer technology for education is to conduct formative assessments, e.g. MCQ tests. In this case, predefined MCQ tests are presented to students from local machines or over computer networks and the answers from the students are sent back to the computers, where assessing processes are carried out automatically, based on a predefined marking scheme. Although technology is predominantly used in formative assessments, effort from the CBE community is being made to use it for summative assessments as well. Some difficulties are to be overcome before we can fully take advantage of the technology, especially computer technology. For computer-supported summative assessments, these difficulties include insufficient security support, non-robust network connectivity (Kennedy 1998).

The following diagram shows the relationships between the six components mentioned above.

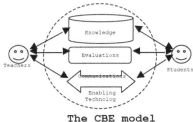

**The CBE model**

## 4. A Preliminary Design and an Implementation of a Web-Oriented Educational Prototype

Based on the model derived from the analyses in the previous section, a prototype design and a preliminary implementation are discussed in this section. Experience gained from using this prototype for teaching and learning is given at the next section.

### The Design

*Knowledge.* This is related to individual teaching tasks. For the author, it includes the following subjects: Network Systems, Java Programming Languages, JavaScript, Visual Basic and Distributed Object Management. The *knowledge* is stored in HTML files that can be viewed by students with a Web browser. These files can be constructed with Web authoring tools (e.g. the Microsoft Front Page) or any other text editors (e.g. the popular Notepad for PCs).

*Evaluations.* MCQ tests are designed to check if students achieve the required learning outcomes. Each test is constructed as an HTML page that contains a form within which a set of *MCQs* is designed. A student answers each question by selecting one of the several options. During an on-line session, he or she can make as many attempts as possible to answer one question, and immediate feedback is possible, if this is desired. After submitting a test page, the answers are assessed automatically by the prototype system, according to a predefined marking scheme. The answers and their marks are saved by the system for later reference and record-keeping purposes.

*Communications.* It is necessary to provide channels for teachers and students to communicate with each other, to facilitate their co-operation during a computerised teaching and learning process. Examining face-to-face teaching and learning processes shows that there are several kinds of communications going on between teachers and students. They include one-to-one communications, one-to-many communications and group communications.

Available communication means or dedicated innovative information software should be exploited or developed to provide support to the various communication needs identified above. These may include using the available electronic mail and computer conferencing facilities, and using or reengineering some groupware systems that are communication-centred and publicly available. From the author's experience, for example, only a limited amount of effort needs to be made to incorporate a discussing forum into the prototype, through reusing a suitable public-domain groupware.

*Enabling Technology.* It is closely related to all of the three components discussed above. HTML is used for storing the *knowledge*; HTML and assessment software is used for *evaluating* the expected learning outcomes; email, computer conferencing and groupware technology are used for *communications*. Apart from utilising the above technology resources, an overall communication framework needs to be designed. This includes using the Internet and the Web as a vehicle to pass and store information and course-related knowledge, and designing a middleware program. This program is responsible for co-ordination between teachers and students, automatically assessing student tests, enabling and controlling the email, computer conferencing facilities and the embedded groupware system.

*Teachers* and *Students.* They are the users who use the system. First, they need to be convinced that the system is effective, easy to use and helpful for their teaching and learning activities, compared with conventional approaches. Then, they should be given trials through which they learn how to use the system. It is important to encourage them to contribute comments on the system. Their feedback should be evaluated carefully, to modify the system and tailor its functionality, as well as the user interface, to the need of the users. User feedback should be collected regularly during the process of implementing the system and after it has been implemented, in order to continually modify the system to suit users' requirements.

**The Preliminary Implementation**

The prototype consists of two parts: the client and the server. For the client side, a Web browser is used by a student to access the *knowledge* stored at the server side. On the server side, a Web server is installed that hosts a CGI middleware program written in Visual Basic (VB), with Microsoft Access database accessing capabilities. The data from the users, is used to update a user database at the server side. The following are the main components of this prototype:

Client Side User Interface

The interface consists of four parts; the first part provides course-work related facilities, the second part provides teaching material updating facilities, the third part provides communication facilities and the fourth part provides house-keeping facilities. Only lecturer-users are able to access all these facilities; in contrast, student-users will be denied access to the updating facilities; in fact, such facilities disappear from the interface when student-users log on to the system. A menu bar has been designed and implemented. It consists of a number of menus. Each menu of the menu bar represents an individual facility.

The first part of the interface contains three menus/facilities: *unit*, *lecture* and *tutorial*. Teaching materials are organised under different unit titles. Selecting the *unit* menu will make a small window appear. This small window has a menu bar that allows a user to *create*, *delete* or *rename* a unit title, or *select* a particular unit in order to view its teaching materials. Only the *select* facility is available when a student-user logs on to the system. The *lecture* and *tutorial* menus allow a user to view lecture slides and tutorial notes from the currently selected unit. The user can also make a comment on the currently selected lecture or tutorial. After doing so, a tiny microscope icon will be displayed adjacent to the selected lecture/tutorial hyperlink. Multiple comments can be made on each individual lecture/tutorial by individual users. Clicking on the top of the small microscope icon adjacent to one lecture/tutorial hyperlink allows a user to view the comments and other useful information:

e.g. the author(s) of the comment(s), submit times, etc. Adjacent to the hyperlink of each lecture, under the *lecture* menu window, is another tiny question-mark icon. Clicking on top of this icon will make a small window appear, which shows the self-asked questions from this lecture. Around 10 such questions have been designed for each lecture, for students to attempt to facilitate obtaining a better understanding of the just-taught lecture.

Unlike student-users, lecturer-users can use the second part of the interface (*add*, *rename* and *delete*) to update teaching materials. This includes adding, renaming or deleting lecture slides or tutorial notes.

The third part of the interface consists of two menus: *feedback* and *email*. Using these two menus, students can send their generic comments on their course-work to the lecturers and send e-mail messages to their classmates, to discuss things of interest around the taught subjects. Comments and e-mail messages are accompanied with sender's names, to facilitate communications among lecturers and students.

The final part of the interface contains: *home*, *password*, *information* and *logout*. Clicking on *home* will always return the user to the front page the system. The *password* menu is used to allow a user to change his/her password, provided the user has submitted the same password which had been used during the authentication procedure at the beginning of this session. The *information* menu provides information about units, assignments, references, etc. Using the *logout* menu, a user can log out from the system explicitly. Otherwise, he/she could be logged out automatically after a predefined period of time. Currently, a 30-minute time-out has been set up for trial purposes.

Server Side Functionality

Three parts are composed with the server side: a HTTP Web server, the required CGI program and a backend Microsoft Access user database.

The Web server, currently in-use is WebSite-1.0 from the publisher O'Reilly. The CGI program is implemented with VB 6.0 that supports database-accessing primitives. In addition, VB 6.0 is easier for students to both learn and use in comparison to other programming languages, C++, for example. Microsoft Access database management system has been used to host all of the course related data and information: including the teaching materials, user feedback, messages, comments, references, etc. Updating the database is accomplished through issuing Structured Query Language (SQL) queries from within the CGI program. A user can query, modify, or delete available records from the database.

The diagram below shows the architecture of this prototype, which can be accessed over the Web with the following URL: *http://shicheng.cms.shu.ac.uk/coursework/html/login.html*, logging on as *guest* and using *guest* as the password.

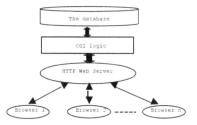

The Architecture of the Web-oriented CBE Prototype

## 5. The Experience

Our experience in utilising this learning and teaching environment is discussed below, around the six basic issues concerning CBE and the feedback of questionnaires from students, regarding using this prototype system to facilitate their learning process. The six issues on CBE has been described previously.

*Enabling technology:* from our view, the enabling technology now is mature enough to provide essential support for the basic needs of education over the network, especially over the Web. We can use off-the-shelf educational packages or use the latest technologies to develop preferable systems ourselves, to facilitate teaching and learning. The phrase - *technology looking for applications* - could be used to better describe the situation in this area (i.e. the development of technology is ahead of the demand of using the technology to implement innovative educational systems).

*Communications:* Two facilities - *feedback* and *email* - have been designed and implemented in addressing this important issue. To our surprise, however, few students have so far utilised them since the beginning of the trial during the first semester of the 99-00 academic year. Our early investigation reveals that there could be two reasons for this happening; students are used to using the university default e-mail system (FirstClass) for communications; and unless absolutely necessary, students always access this Web prototype purely for accessing the teaching materials and other course-work related information. The cold response to the communication facilities suggests that integrating the communication component into a CBE system may depend on the individual application scenario. In the case of a distance learning situation, for example, such integration could be necessary and welcomed. We are planning to try this prototype system with a group of distance learning students, who are currently registered with the department, and find out the response from them, especially on the integrated communication facilities.

*Evaluations:* Experience in conducting MCQ tests over the Web using another similar prototype causes our concerns as to in what way to conduct the tests so that the final objective - strengthening students' learning outcome - would be reached. Although the advantage of doing so is apparent (e.g. the ease of attempting such tests over the Web, the prompt replies from the server, efficient computerised marking processes, etc.), problems do exist which need further investigations, namely *credibility, fairness, reliability*, etc. For the problem of *credibility*: We found it very hard to have students attempt Web-oriented MCQ tests individually; cheating may lead a high similarity in some of the submitted answers, either answered correctly or wrongly. The problem of *fairness* is related to the problem of *credibility*; a strong student may get a mark lower than that of a weak student who has cheated. The problem of *reliability* is about the machines on which students attempt the MCQ tests; the machines should be robust and reliable. Unfortunately, the fact is some machines may crash down during an on-going test. Based on the above experience, we are planing to take a different approach to conducting MCQ tests over the Web. One test of about-10 questions will be designed for each lecture; we will *encourage* students to *discuss* with their classmates about the answers, when attempting such a test over the Web. Students will be told that no credit will be given towards their effort of attempting those tests, yet will be informed, however, that a final credit, formal, paper-form MCQ test will be given. The questions of this test will be selected randomly from the whole set of questions which they are encouraged to attempt over the Web, during the period of running the course. We expect a better learning outcome to be reached, after the new approach will have been conducted.

*Knowledge:* Thanks to the innovative features of Microsoft PowerPoint, the slides of each lecture are packaged into a series of associated html files (i.e. the first page pointing to the second one which in turn points to the third one and so on), makes it easy to view them. Besides, a small pop-up window has been designed. It floats on top of the main browser window all the time, displaying the list of lecture titles of the currently selected unit. Selecting another lecture title from this small pop-up window results in the main browser window jumping to the first page of the lecture slides of that lecture. This helps to achieve the so called *within-the-current-context* browsing effect. Our experience shows that students feel it is convenient to have the small window float on the top of the screen all the time and control the changing over of slides between different lectures. This small window can be minimised to an icon and moved to one of the corners of the screen, or closed. The design of the self-asked questions of each lecture and the ease of accessing them has been proved to be useful (see Appendix). Attempting those questions helps students to obtain a better understanding of the taught lectures.

*Teachers* and *Students:* They are the users of the CBE systems. Therefore, starting from the beginning of the development of such a system, this component of *teachers and students* needs to be considered. Teachers are mainly involved in providing teaching materials and marking submitted assignments, while students use the system to facilitate their learning process. Our preliminary experiences are, designing the CBE systems: *a)* according to different teaching and learning senior, and *b)* taking into consideration students' responses in using the developed system. For *a)*, for the case of this paper, the communication facility of this Web-oriented CBE system may not be necessary, while such a facility is likely to be welcomed for distance learning situations; for *b)*, as discussed in the *Evaluations* paragraph, the current approach of conducting MCQ tests ought to be changed accordingly.

This prototype system has been used to facilitate the delivery of a second-year Higher National Diploma (HND) unit. Twenty-one out of the twenty-eight students of the class have filled and returned the questionnaire (see the Appendix; the other seven students were absent from the class that day). Each question has five optional answers: Strongly Agree - *SA*, Agree - *A*, Neutral - *N*, Disagree - *DA* and Strongly Disagree - *SD*. In the table (see the Appendix), each row shows students' responses to a particular question. For example, the row for *Q1* shows that six students strongly agree, twelve students agree, two student response with a neutral answer and one student disagrees with this question. The total number of students (*NS*) who have submitted the questionnaires is twenty one. The average score (*AS*) in the table could be used as an indicator to show student's generic response to this prototype system. For example, the last figures of the SA and the A columns are 6.5 and 9.9; this could be interpreted that around 16 (6.5 + 9.9 = 16.4), out of the 21 students, have basically satisfied with the functionality of the developed teaching and learning environment. In contrast, the last figures of N, DA and SD are 3.5, 0.7 and 0.5. This shows that the system needs further improvements to bring its performance to the expectations of the students; along this line, further investigations are worth being conducted to find out what exactly the students' complaints are.

## 6. Future Work

From our work with this prototype, we think the following issues need attention, in order to best use the Web technology for developing innovative CBE applications.

*Using the communication facilities for distance learning.* As discussed in the previous section, the response to the communication facilities of this prototype is not positive. This may be due to the facts that the users using the system are full-time on-campus students (i.e. they meet and contact with each other face-to-face daily) and that they use the university default e-mail system as their communication tool. We are planning to try the system for a distance learning group of around-20 students and find out what the effectiveness will be for such students. These students have virtually no face-to-face contacts with each other, except from communicating via e-mail and talking over telephone occasionally. We think the importance of integrating communication facility into CBE systems is related closely to the applications of such systems; in case of distance learning, such a facility is likely necessary and of importance. We expect a positive result from the trial of this system for the distance learning students mentioned above, and will modify our system, especially relating the communication facility, to facilitate teaching and learning processes in the situation of distance learning.

*Integrating MCQs.* For time constraints, we have not physically implemented the MCQ facility into the current prototype system. We are going to implement this facility in our system and plan to conduct trials during the next semester.

*Evaluating other middleware alternatives apart from the CGI approach.* Apart from the popular CGI implementation, various other approaches to implementing the server side logic are to be investigated to achieve better efficiencies. Other alternative approaches include Microsoft Active Server Page (ASP), Servlets, Java client-server model and Common Object Request Broker Architecture (CORBA).

## 7. Conclusions

The work been done leads me to make the following conclusions:

*Exploiting the potential of the Web technology to facilitate the development of innovative CBE applications.* Several factors (Coffman and Odlyzko 1998) below support the above claim: *a)* accessing networked computers (i.e. computers connected to the Web) is becoming easy; *b)* tens of millions of Web servers are accessible, providing a vast information reservoir, and the number of servers keeps growing exponentially; *c)* the two main Web browsers (Netscape and Internet Explorer) are free and support various hardware platforms; *d)* Web-oriented programming languages/tools are becoming mature and widely available: e.g. HTML, Java, JavaScript, etc. All these factors offer us great opportunities to develop innovative CBE applications over the Web. These Web-oriented CBE applications promise that users are able to access the applications from anywhere around the world, where networked computers and public domain Web browsers are available, no matter what kind of machines the users work on and what kind of operating systems are running on those machines.

*It may not be appropriate to conduct credit, individual MCQ tests using network-oriented computer technology* (e.g. over the Web). From our experience, there are three main reasons for this claim: *a)* a poor reliability of the machines in the labs: some of the machines in the labs are down from time to time; *b)* when a machine is down, to fix the problem can be quite troublesome. On one hand, quite often, the help from departmental computer-support colleagues is neither prompt nor helpful, it may take a long delay to have the problem fixed, sometimes the problem would never get fixed. On the other hand, the tutor could not fix the problem on his or her own; then, the above situation leads us to a dilemma: we have to ask students to attempt credit MCQ tests with unreliable machines! *c)* it is difficult to prevent students from looking-over-each-others'-shoulder during a lab-based MCQ test unless dedicated testing areas have been arranged, where dividing boards are erected between computers. As described previously, however, it may be appropriate to conduct *uncredit* MCQ tests using the *network-oriented computer technology,* compensated with a *credit*, end-of-unit, paper-form MCQ test.

*Providing better Web graphic user interfaces* (GUIs). Better GUIs are needed for Web oriented CBE applications, to facilitate users' accessing the applications over the Web. To compensate the limitations of HTML and to design comprehensive GUIs, various browser plug-ins and Web-oriented programming languages should be investigated and used, including Shockwave, Java, JavaScript, etc. Among them, Java is a competitive candidate, because it is platform independent and its current version (Java 1.2) has adequate GUI support.

## 8. References

Coffman, K and Odlyzko, A. *The Size and Growth Rate of the Internet.* Fist Monday (http://www.firstmonday.dk/issues/issue3_10/coffman/index.html, peer-reviewed journal of the Internet), Vol. 3 No. 10, October 1998.

Hall, M. *Core Web Programming.* Prentice Hall 1998, ISBN: 013625666X.

Joy, M. and Luck, M. *The BOSS System for On-line Submission and Assessment.* CTI Workshop on Computer Assisted Assessment, University of Huddersfield, U.K., 7th, July 1998.

Kennedy, N. *WebMat - Experiences of Assessing LMU Students over the Web.* CTI Workshop on Computer Assisted Assessment, University of Huddersfield, U.K., 7th, July 1998.

Pownall, H. and Mobbs, R. *Integrating Computer Assisted Assessment & The CASTLE Project.* CTI Workshop on Computer Assisted Assessment, University of Huddersfield, U.K., 7th, July 1998.

**APPENDIX** - A questionnaire and its feedback from students, regarding the unit's Web site

*Q1. The Web site of this unit is useful:*
*Q2. The Web site of this unit is easy to access:*
*Q3. The password control mechanism of this unit's Web site is necessary:*
*Q4. The presentation of the lecture slides and tutorial notes of this unit's Web site is good:*
*Q5. The links to the self-asked questions of this unit's Web site are useful:*
*Q6. The communication facility (e.g. feedback, email, comment) of this unit's Web site is useful:*

*Students' feedback*

|     | SA  | A   | N   | DA  | SD  | NS  |
| --- | --- | --- | --- | --- | --- | --- |
| Q1  | 6   | 12  | 2   | 1   | 0   | 21  |
| Q2  | 5   | 8   | 6   | 1   | 1   | 21  |
| Q3  | 3   | 9   | 6   | 2   | 1   | 21  |
| Q4  | 11  | 7   | 2   | 0   | 1   | 21  |
| Q5  | 6   | 11  | 4   | 0   | 0   | 21  |
| Q6  | 8   | 12  | 1   | 0   | 0   | 21  |
| AS  | 6.5 | 9.9 | 3.5 | 0.7 | 0.5 |     |

# Author Index

www.ingramcontent.com/pod-product-compliance
Lightning Source LLC
Chambersburg PA
CBHW051044050326
40690CB00006B/593